GUARDIANS OF THE DRAGON PATH

Ancient Temples of the Pyrenees
The Way of the Stars Camino
A Magdalena Meridian

ANI WILLIAMS

Praise for
GUARDIANS OF THE DRAGON PATH

"A ground-breaking, exceptional book, Ani Williams brings a new dimension to all serious discussions about Mary Magdalene's life after the crucifixion and beyond. Richly researched and well-written, a masterwork of the legends, history, and spirituality which flourished in the Pyrenees and Catalonia."

—KATHLEEN McGOWAN,
New York Times bestselling author of *The Magdalene Line* series

"This volume is filled with astonishing new discoveries and will be my new go-to reference work on the secrets of Mary Magdalene's legacy! Williams follows her dreams to reveal a six-pointed star and a Great Cross defined by Magdalene and Templar churches, mysteriously aligned with the ancient Way of the Stars. Packed with jaw-dropping revelations. A life's work of the highest alchemical gold! What are you waiting for?"

—GRETCHEN CORNWALL,
speaker, author of *The Secret Dossier of a Knight Templar of the Sangreal, The Stars of the Magdalene,* and TV Personality

"A fascinating tour de force. Beware, Reader! This book challenges much of what we think we know about Mary Magdalene, the Grail, the Camino de Santiago, dragons—and so much more."

—ELYN AVIVA, PhD,
author of *Following the Milky Way,* co-author of
Where Heaven and Earth Unite and *Powerful Places Guidebooks*

"The breadth and depth of your book is awe-inspiring—a compilation of ancient wisdom, Christian lore, and European history. It's an amazing tour-de-force, reflecting years of careful study and devoted attention to detail. Your music adds an even greater dimension of appeal. Congratulations on creating this classic!"

—MARGARET STARBIRD,
author of *The Woman with the Alabaster Jar*

"A stunning new book by Ani Williams! Guardians of the Dragon Path *truly advances our knowledge of the lost world of Pyrenean myth, divine femininity, and places of ancient power for the very first time. Williams reveals patterns engineered by ancient surveyors of a magical landscape that is finally being understood. A valuable addition to every ancient mysteries bookshelf."*

—ANDREW COLLINS,
author of *The First Female Pharaoh, The Cygnus Key,* and *Origins of the Gods*

"Deeply spellbinding, evocative, and packed with geomantic information! Ani Williams reveals the celestial imprint upon the Pyrenean landscape, a design known and used by the ancient ancestors. An extraordinary book!"

—NICHOLAS R. MANN,
author of *Avebury Cosmos, The Secret Geometry of Washington D.C.,*
and *Sedona: Sacred Earth*

"An enticing mix of scholarly research and Gnostic mysticism. I'm hooked! Loving your ideas and words, the discoveries, and your emphasis on the positive, Empowered Feminine."

—BROOKE MEDICINE EAGLE,
feminine empowerment teacher, wise woman,
author of *Buffalo Woman Comes Singing* and *The Last Ghost Dance*

Guardians of the Dragon Path: Ancient Temples of the Pyrenees, The Way of the Stars Camino, A Magdalena Meridian
By Ani Williams

Published by Flower of Life Press
Hadlyme, CT 06439
Astara J. Ashley, *publisher*

To contact the publisher, visit floweroflifepress.com

Cover design by Tudor Sebastian Vlaicu

Interior design by Kirsten Livingston

Library of Congress Control Number: Available upon request.

ISBN-13: 979-8-9893441-2-3

In honor of the legacy of

my great-grandmother Harriet Williams Myers, and

her brothers Henry Smith Williams and Edward Huntington Williams,

who between them, wrote countless books

on ancient history, natural science, and medicine—

For their love of nature, poetry, and art,

without which we would not be truly alive.

Contents

Acknowledgments

In deep gratitude to my late friend Henry Lincoln, who believed in the early chapters and inspired my love of finding ancient sites and patterns in the landscape; to dear friends Gerda and her late husband Tobi Dobler for their loving welcome to Languedoc, France, and opening new understandings of the Knights Templar guardianship of Marie Madeleine; to Kaj Liliendal and Sus Krassel for fascinating conversations and introducing me to the ancient Greek city of Empuries in Catalonia; to Patrice Chaplin and Gerard Serrat, who opened the doors to Girona, "City of Secrets"; Juan Saez, friend and intrepid trekker through all kinds of weather to megalithic sites, and sharing his vast knowledge and sensitivity; Dani Valdés for his friendship, inspiring photography, and guidance to the megalithic route of Roca del Valleès; to Elyn Aviva and Gary White for their friendship and always suggesting the right museums for the next discoveries, and to Elyn for her finely tuned final edits; Luiz Pontuel for his love of Magdalena and her sites along the Way of the Stars; Sofia Rupp Hernandes for her friendship and guiding our quest up the mountain of Mary, Mare de Déus; to the magical late Robert Brydon for hints of the mysteries over late night brandy; to Lynn Picknett and Clive Prince for their knowledge of history and stealth in editorial expertise; to Astara J. Ashley and her team at Flower of Life Press for their patient support in birthing my first book; to Tudor Sebastian Vlaicu for his artistic gifts in the cover design and extensive site maps; to his father Paul Vlaicu and his family at Le Poulpiquet for filming the magical sites for the "Song Map"; Carlos Martin la Moneda for his generosity in sharing his extensive knowledge of the stages of the Camino de Santiago; to Andrew Collins for intelligent dialogue and generous contributions which fit perfectly with what was needed; to Angelique Peigne for her generous help with the nitty gritty lists, maps, and ideas; Barthelemy Izoard for his music recording magic; Alan Pearson for his guardianship of the Celtic ruins, sacred springs, and mentioning my Catalan Magdalena discoveries to his astrophysicist friend which produced more discoveries; to my forever friend Rosemarie Brown, who always believed in the wild adventures I was up to; to Kathleen McGowen for her support and enthusiasm for the chapter previews; and last, but certainly not least, my daughter Summer Rose Sizelove for keeping the magic alive, and for her brilliant feedback during long distance readings of the manuscript. And thank you to all my unnamed guardians, dragons, and guides in the invisible realms for showing me the way.

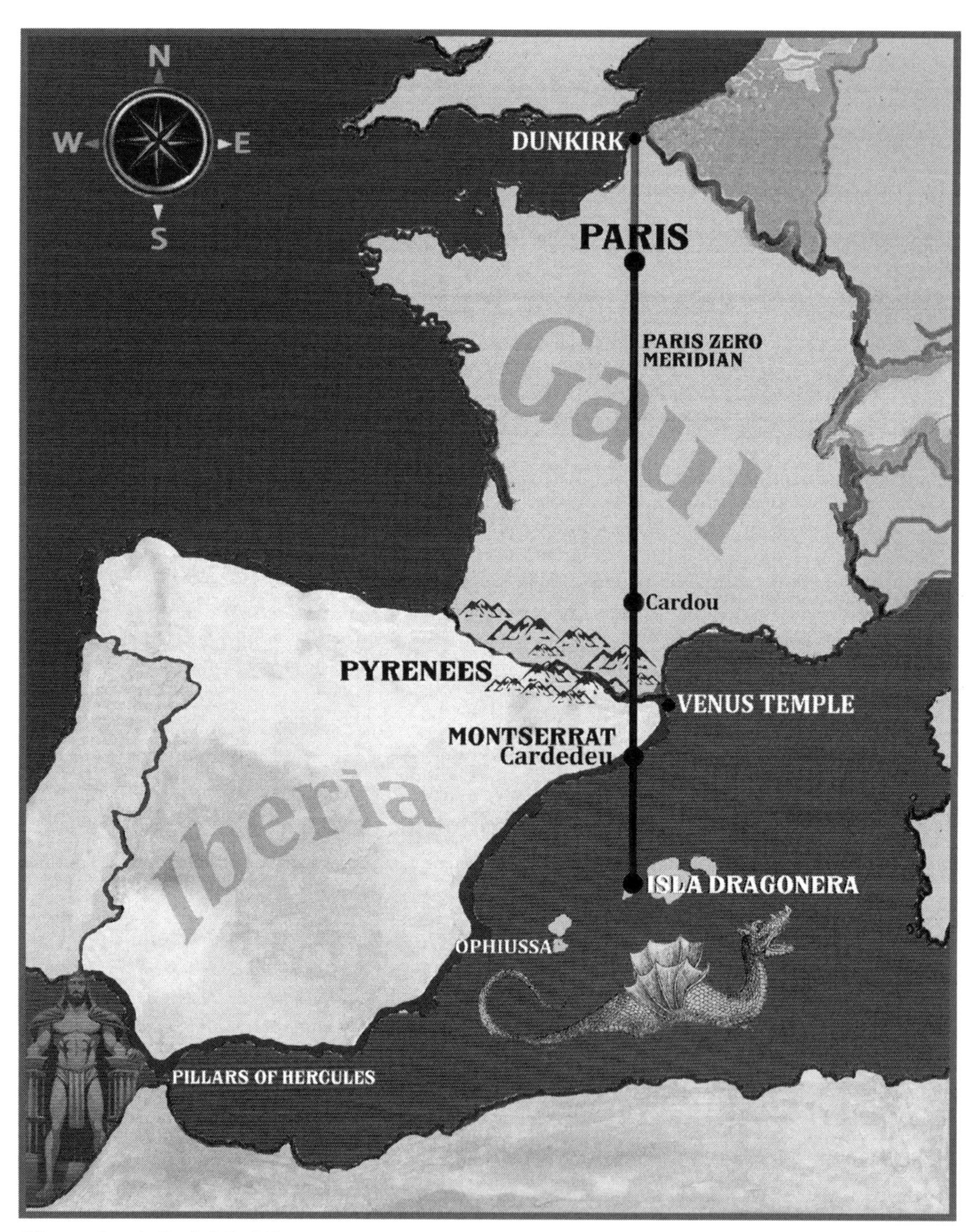

Illustration 1: Paris Meridian

INTRODUCTION

AWAKEN THE DRAGONS

"Benzozia [Mother Dragon] still sleeps fitfully beneath the earth, and sometimes fire escapes her jaws again, emerging from the cracks in the peaks of the mountains. Thus, not only are the Basque people born from a primordial dragon's fire, but the very Pyrenees themselves lie on top of Benzozia's [sleeping] ...body!"

MARTIN LOCKER, ARCHEOLOGIST[1]

BENZOZIA IS ONE OF THE MANY DRAGONS IN PYRENEAN LEGENDS, AND ACCORDING to Basque tradition she created this great mountain range from her rolling movements within the belly of the Earth. The Pyrenees reach from the Mediterranean to the Basque region and form the natural border between France and Spain, or as they were named in the past, Gaul and Iberia. The myths of dragons are especially strong on the southern side of the Pyrenees, with some being creator gods and goddesses, in charge of the elements and weather, guardians of the peaks, valleys, and multitudes of ancient megalithic sites across this region. The dragons have been long forgotten, yet humanity is beginning to remember, and as humans awaken, so too all of nature will arise and release the veils of separation, and the unseen guardians will once again be known.

My quest began as a journey across the Pyrenees to the base of the Dragon Path at Isla Dragonera, Majorca, a tiny island marking the southernmost point of the Paris Zero Meridian. As you may have guessed, Isla Dragonera means "Island of the Female Dragon" or, more exactly, tiny dragons known as lizards. Dragonera is not only home to thousands of little dragons, but the profile of the island looks very much like a great dragoness bathing in the salty waters of *Aphrodite's Pond,* more commonly known as the Mediterranean. Greek mythology says that this great goddess was born out of the brine and foam of the salty waves and her sirens can sometimes still be heard singing from the depths of the turquoise waters. Majorcan locals say that the name Dragonera is a reference to one of the island's caves where an underground river of fresh water roars and rumbles, which is the great dragoness mumbling in her sleep.

I had begun to investigate the numerous ancient sites located along the southern section of the Paris Meridian between the Pyrenees and Isla Dragonera. The meridian runs from Dunkirk on the North Sea at the northernmost point of France and continues southward, crossing the Pyrenees to Majorca, ending at the female dragon's lair. The number of ancient sites located on this north-south axis indicated its use long before it was measured and called the Paris Zero Meridian. I could imagine this alignment running from sea to sea as the spine of a great dragon, a receptacle and carrier of celestial and terrestrial currents. Science has shown that the magnetic field of the Earth is weakest at the poles, allowing particles from the Sun and other stars to enter our atmosphere. And most of these electrically charged particles enter at the North Pole.[2]

In my mind's eye, I could see paths of vibrant cosmic energy traveling across the Earth's meridians, creating magnetic rivers or Dragon Paths. Ancient people were more "in tune" with the natural rhythms of the Earth and stars, and temple builders would have used these subtle currents to guide the placement of their monuments along these meridians. French Egyptologist R. A. Schwaller de Lubicz wrote that celestial light is received in the magnetic North Pole of the Earth, which attracts the particles of the Sun, and this light continues to the South Pole. Science has shown this to be true and that the magnetic waves continue to encircle the Earth and form a donut shape.[3]

Retired English geological engineer Rory Duff has discovered unusually powerful terrestrial currents in the last several years, which he calls "Emperor Dragon Lines." Many of these *mega meridians* flow from the north toward the south, similar to what I was sensing. Duff states that these unique rivers of energy are the largest terrestrial currents that he has discovered during his thirty years of research and that the most numerous of these lines flow across Spain! He believes that these dragon currents are interacting not only with the iron and nickel at the Earth's core but also with the light particles from the stars. In 2017, a new Emperor Dragon meridian appeared that flows between the Earth's two poles, which Duff says may relate to a Hopi prophecy of a return of twin brothers who guard the North and South Poles, named Polangahoya and Pganghoya, respectively. Duff adds that these Emperor Dragon lines resonate at extremely low frequencies (infrasound), and the source is most likely galaxies beyond our own.[4]

Was this interaction between the Earth and stars occurring along the Paris Meridian and the other alignment paths in the region? During nearly two decades of traveling to research the Pyrenean region between France and Catalonia, I began to suspect this is indeed occurring. (Catalonia is the northeastern corner of Spain bordered by the Mediterranean and the Pyrenees and includes Majorca and the other Balearic Islands.) There were too many megalithic[5] sites constructed along these ancient meridian paths in the region to be totally random. The Pyrenean Basque people say that it was the giants who built the dolmens across these lands and that they worked with the elements, dragons, and subtle energy, something that we modern humans often classify as fantasy.

Many of these monuments were constructed nearly six thousand years ago to mirror the heavens and receive and *fix* this celestial energy on the Earth. The high quartz content of Pyrenean stone in these megalithic structures serves to amplify and transmit both cosmic and terrestrial energy. The orientation with celestial markers in Catalonia's stone chambers indicates that these sites were functioning as receptacles and guardians of light and time, and we will discover an extraordinary example of an acoustical interaction between the Sun, the Earth, and an ancient stone monument in Catalonia. Additionally, the incoming stellar energy carried a musical tone that I heard in the stones that was later verified by a polar scientist. Hence, the idea of singing stones and ringing stars is not only the stuff of fairytales and fiction but a part of the fields of science called archeoacoustics and archeoastronomy.

My long quest across the Pyrenees included a search for some of the sixty-four churches, monasteries, and hermitages dedicated to Maria Magdalena in Catalonia.[6] It is extraordinary to find such a concentration of her sites in one small corner of a country, revealing how important this woman was and continues to be for Catalan people. I will use the Catalan and Spanish spelling of her name, as that is how she is known in this land that adores her. An unusual number of her sanctuaries and even mountain ranges dedicated to Santa Magdalena are located along the Paris Meridian, too many to call it chance or coincidence. Was this attraction to the meridian related to the celestial rivers that flow across these paths, perhaps? The answer seemed to be yes and related to an ancient grid established in the Pyrenees region eons in the past.

In addition to the numerous Magdalena sites located on the north-south axis of the Paris Meridian, I discovered an equal number of her sanctuaries aligned on an east-west lying axis running along the southern flanks of the Pyrenees. This path begins at the Mediterranean, where the Pyrenees range meets the sea and follows the eastern section of an ancient pilgrimage route called "Way of the Stars," which later became known as the *Camino de Compostela,* meaning "Way of the Field of Stars."

Ultimately, I would discover that these two Magdalena paths running north-south and east-west formed the two axes of a great equal-armed landscape cross spanning the Pyrenees. (See illustration 2, The Great Cross.) In addition to the Santa Magdalena sites located on the two axes, there are groups of megalithic dolmens (stones shaped like small houses) and menhirs (standing stones) constructed between 3500 and 3000 BCE or earlier, marking the end of all four arms of this cross. Based on the numerous ancient sites located along the north-south axis, it became obvious that this Dragon Path existed long before the Paris Meridian was measured beginning in the 17th century. To some, this might sound strange, but I will clarify these findings in the chapters of this book. As one friend would often remark, "Truth is stranger than fiction!" Did this enchantment of the Pyrenean landscape and the extraordinary adoration of Maria Magdalena indicate her ancient presence in this land? Strong French and Spanish traditions, as well as historical references indicate this was indeed the case.

The journey was consuming, captivating much of my time in poring over historical documents in several languages and speaking with archeologists and museum curators. An equal amount of time was dedicated to exploring each site numerous times, and it became an obsession, with my journey often guided by clues and information received in dreams and intuitive hunches. At many of the locations, I heard songs in the sanctuaries, in the stones, and ringing from the stars. The journey became what I call a *Camino de Canciones,* a "Path of Songs," and the music honoring the sites and their

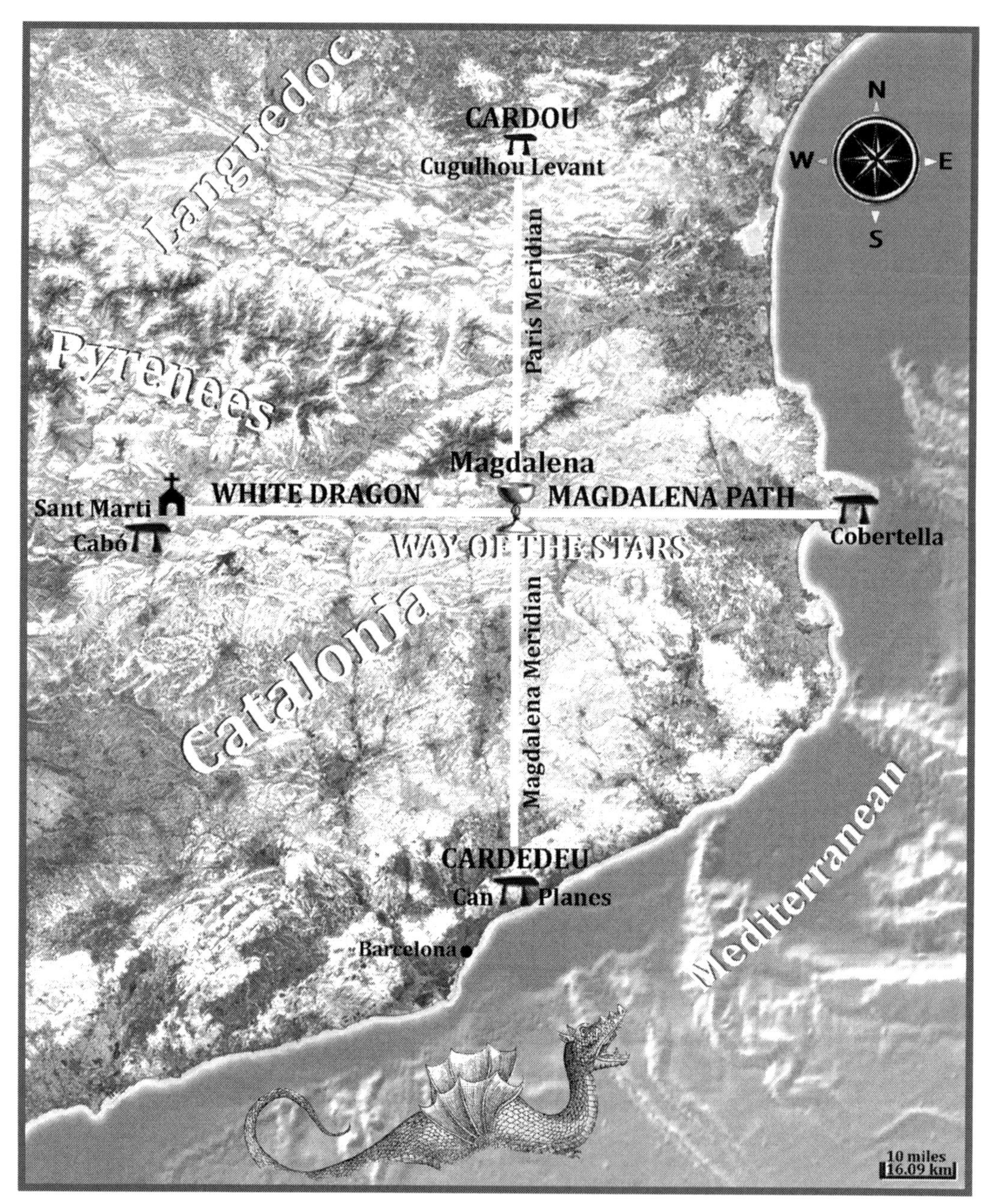

Illustration 2: The Great Cross

guardians was all recorded on numerous albums and music videos that will be referenced throughout the journeys to each site. Additionally, a special album, *Guardians of the Dragon Path*, has been created to include these songs and additional new recordings inspired by the discoveries.

The Dragon Path crossing the Pyrenees coincided with the old legends and my own encounters with the dragon guardians of these mountains. Some Pyrenean people believe these dragons control the fierce thunderstorms that crash down the peaks and echo through the valleys. They say that great dragons are still sleeping in the extensive caves and tunnels beneath the mountains, like the dragoness Benzozia in the opening quotation. Or like the Basque goddess Mari, who lives underground in the western Pyrenees with her dragon consort Sugaar, the great storm god, and together they bring fertility to the region. These lovers are known to meet every Friday or Venus' Day (Friday is named for Venus in the French *Vendredi* and Spanish *Viernes*), said to be the night of witches, and we can add, "the night of wizards and weather magic."

Catalan people honor the dragons in various annual festivals and parades, who they call *Drac* (the Catalan word meaning "dragon"). These dragons can be seen in nearly every town during Saint Jordi's (Saint George's) Day, celebrated in April with the focus more on the dragon as embodying wisdom and education than the Christian "let's all slay the dragon" story. In all of Catalonia, people give the gift of a book or a rose on Jordi's day, and the libraries traditionally stay open, a continuation of the ancient relationship between the dragon or serpent and the transmission of wisdom.

Dragons are the forgotten guardians of Earth, and their pathways form the ancient pilgrimage routes that eventually became Christianized, and sadly the dragons were not only forgotten but demonized. The dragon is guardian of the *axis mundi* (world axis), illustrated as the serpent wound around the meridian pole, or world tree, and this is illustrated in the elegant Apprentice Pillar in Rosslyn Chapel with its eight dragon-serpents wound around the base of the spiral column. They are the wise ones associated with the invisible elemental king- and queendoms who watch over this land from the Pyrenees to Dragonera and beyond. We will meet several of these guardians, including a fire-breathing dragon, an *egregore*, the "Watcher" on the Paris Meridian in the Pyrenees.

Nearly every ancient tradition considered dragons and serpents as powerful, creative deities worthy of respect. Dragons are the traditional guardians of treasure, the jewel or pearl of great price, often symbolizing secret knowledge, and their myths date back at least 5000 years. In the tombs of Egyptian pharaohs, images of serpents were often placed over the entrance for protection. Fire-spitting cobras form the Uraeus crowning the heads of Egypt's kings and queens, denoting protection, power, and initiation. And dragons and cobras were seen by many cultures to be creator gods who used sound to manifest the many dimensions of this world. (This will be explored further on in the book). Spiritual traditions such as the early Christian Gnostics believed that the serpent and dragon symbolized wisdom, medicine, and immortality. The late 19th century esoteric author Helena Petrovna Blavatsky writes in *The Secret Doctrine*:

> *"... the 'Serpent' and 'Dragon' were the names given to the 'Wise Ones,' the initiated adepts of olden times ... the Serpent has ever been... rejuvenation, of IMMORTALITY and TIME."*[7]

It was only during the 3rd and 4th centuries of this era that prominent Church Fathers interpreted these guardians of wisdom to be evil and an anathema to Christianity. One example is the 4th century CE Bishop Epiphanius of Cyprus, who wrote his diatribes against the Gnostics and their dragons. And ever since, there has been a long-accepted separation between organized religion and the ancient wisdom and healing traditions represented by the serpent and dragon. This view included all women being seen as fallen, seduced like Eve by the apple-bearing serpent of wisdom in the Tree of Knowledge.

It is important to say here that I am not criticizing religions in general and the important purpose they serve. My references to the "Church" and early "Church Fathers" normally refer to those leaders throughout history who sought to deny the feminine half of the human race and those who formed the inquisitions against the Cathars, Gnostics, and others who believed in freedom and the right to believe as they choose.

However, the wisdom traditions of the dragon and serpent continued to be depicted in Christian iconography in the great cathedrals and churches across medieval Europe, yet they were given a very different interpretation by the Church. In many churches of southern France, we can find the Virgin Mary standing on the Moon with the serpent coiled under her feet, often with the snake biting the apple from Eve's Edenic tree of knowledge, thus linking Mary with Eve. Certainly, this is indicating the wisdom traditions of Maria-Sophia, Sophia being the Greek word for wisdom, symbolized by the snake. We find eight fire-breathing dragons guarding the Black Madonna in the octagonal chapel of Saint Michael at Montserrat, Catalonia, her blackness symbolizing timeless wisdom, confirmed by the dragons at her feet. According to Blavatsky, Mary, "Queen of Heaven," portrayed with the Moon and serpent, links her with the ancient pagan dragon traditions.[8] One of Egypt's earliest guardians of life was the cobra goddess Wadjet, whose name meant "green one," and she was called "Great of Magic," often linked in this capacity with Isis.

Mary with fire-breathing serpent, Sainte-Radegonde, France

Serpents and dragons as emissaries of the wisdom traditions continued to survive in Christian iconography. A green snake, sometimes illustrated as a winged dragon, can often be seen rising out of the chalice of Saint John the Evangelist. One example is in a stained-glass window at the great Cathedral in Troyes, France, where the first medieval Grail legends were written, and there are many other examples throughout Europe's churches. The painting of Saint John in the Vic Episcopal Museum shows his chalice with a golden-winged dragon, which appears to be his ally rather than a devil. This is a perfect example of the Gnostic healing, wisdom, and resurrection teachings displayed in plain sight in one of Catalonia's churches of Sant Joan (Saint John). This serpent chalice symbology is a remnant of early Christianity's Gnostic and Eastern mystery traditions and was incorporated into the medieval Grail stories of resurrection and rebirth. Of course, the explanation from the Church of Rome claims that the serpent is an evil representative of the devil who is being trampled under Mary's foot, expelled from the "poisoned" chalice, and exiled from the garden. Philip Gardner and Gary Osborn, authors of *The Serpent Grail,* seem to agree with the earlier traditions:

Retable by Joan Gasco, 1529, Sant Joan de Faregues, Vic Episcopal Museum (V.E.M.)

> *"... both the Holy Grail and the Elixir of Life were originally linked to the serpent and the snake... [symbolizing] resurrection, rebirth, immortality ... enlightenment and wisdom."* [9]

Yet, the ancient wisdom traditions continued, despite the widespread repression, by going underground, still visible in symbolic art, music, and poetry, and heard in the songs of the medieval troubadours. (The word troubadour derives from *trobar*, the Occitan word meaning "to find," and *d'or*, "of gold," hence "the musicians who find the gold.") These traditions survived in the Gothic cathedrals that were designed using the ancient Hermetic principles of harmony and Golden Mean ratios. These temples create such perfect acoustics that when music and chant are performed, those listening often enter altered states of consciousness. These expansive acoustical properties were conducive to the constant rounds of perpetual choirs, according to the *Dance of the Dragon* by British authors Paul Broadhurst and the late Hamish Miller.[10] This tradition of perpetual choirs, the constant rounds of chant performed within these cathedrals, would have caused a field of beneficial waves of sound, an enchantment, to permeate the surrounding region.

Similar harmonic principles have been used by the Chinese for thousands of years in the science of Feng Shui, literally meaning "Wind-Water." This system works with the natural dragon currents of subtle energy moving across the Earth and the influence of the heavens in the harmonious placement of landscapes and buildings so that energy flows in life-enhancing balance. The Sun, Moon, planets, and even distant stars and constellations were used to map the arrangement of sites as a mirror of heaven on Earth. The late British author John Michell spoke of the musical aspect of this science of placement:

> *"In China until recently, as long ago in Britain, every building, every stone and wood, was placed in the landscape in accordance with a magic system by which the laws of mathematics and music were expressed in the geometry of the earth's surface ..."*[11]

Michell continues to speak of the Feng Shui tradition of dragon currents as paths for the gods and cosmic energy that move across the Earth:

> *"... [Dragon lines] are not only mythological paths down which the gods representing the various heavenly bodies pass at regular seasons, but have some further quality known to native magicians. American Indians, particularly the Hopi of the Southwest, appear to use them as cables of mental communication. In China they are known as Lung-mei, the paths of the dragon, and run between astronomical mounds and high mountains."*[12]

Dragons have long been honored around the world as protectors and guardians of the fertility of the Earth and its inhabitants. Many indigenous cultures believe that dragons and serpents are the guardians of their sanctuaries, springs, and waterways and oversee the well-being of the people and the land. The medicine men of the Hopi, Zuni, and other Pueblo tribes of the American Southwest still actively communicate with the dragon guardians of the water sources that are crucial for their survival. These deities are seen as either green serpents or dragons, varying according to medicine men of the different clans and villages. (Dragons and serpents are often interchangeable in ancient tradition and in the wisdom traditions.)

When the Neolithic people of Iberia built their stone temples across the base of the southern slopes of the Pyrenees, the sites were often aligned to the constellation Draco the Dragon. Circa 3500–2500 BCE, the pole star marking the Earth's northern axis was Alpha Draconis (Thuban) in Draco. This great dragon in the sky would have guided not only the orientation of their temples, but the pole star marking north would also have guided their navigation over land and sea. (see illustration 10: Dolmen Creu d'en Cobertella aligned with constellation Draco, page 249.) There are many other examples of sites created during this same period, including the Great Pyramid of Cheops at Egypt's Giza Plateau, featuring a north-facing shaft aligned to this same pole star, allowing the light of Draco the dragon to inseminate the dark interior of the King's Chamber.

I should mention that shortly before I arrived in France in 2006 and began this quest, I received a strange protection medallion as a gift. Several things stood out when first saw the piece: One side of the amulet featured the 5th-century Saint Benedict with a serpent in a chalice. The opposite side displayed an equal-armed cross with coded letters decorating the arms. (The medallion is displayed on the cover and throughout the book.) I quickly looked up the meaning of the letters *N D S M D*, which are abbreviations for *Non Draco Sit Mihi Dux*, a Latin phrase meaning "Let not the Dragon be my Guide."

As my friend helped to attach the chain holding the medallion around my neck, I decided then and there to delete the Latin *non*, "not," and affirmed that the dragon in the Grail would be my guide. And what I did not know at the time is that the pattern of the Celtic Cross on the medallion would soon be revealed in ancient alignments in the Pyrenean landscape: The vertical axis of the cross aligned with the Paris Zero Meridian and the horizontal axis with the ancient Camino de Compostela pilgrimage route, the Way of the Stars. I would discover so many medieval Maria Magdalena sites located along both alignments that it became obvious a master plan existed here since antiquity, and these quests of discovery will be revealed in the coming chapters.

Part I
Journey to Dragonera

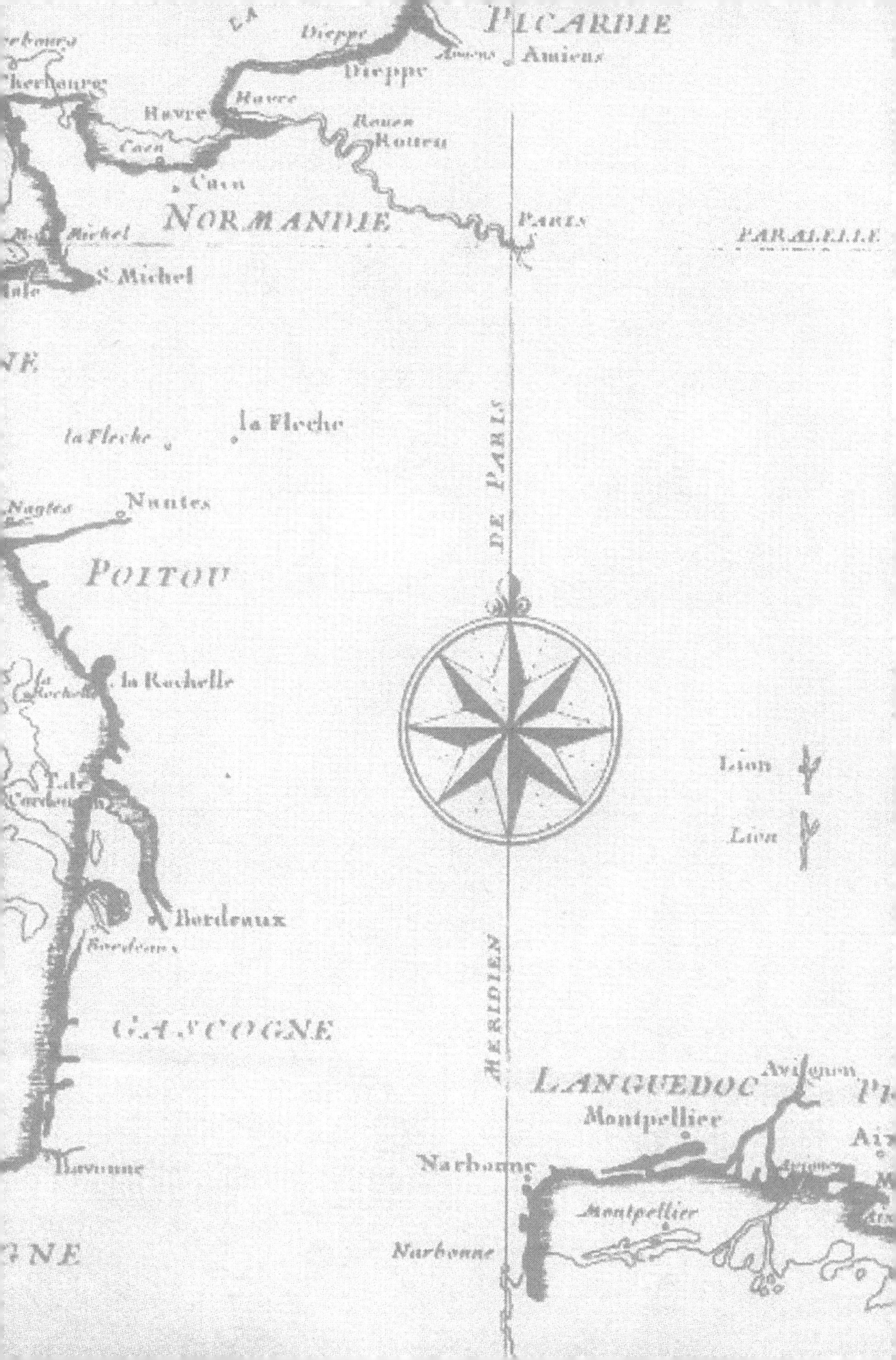

PICARDIE
Dieppe
Amiens
Amiens
Dieppe
Cherbourg
Havre
Havre
Rouen
Rouen
Caen
Caen
NORMANDIE
PARIS
PARALELLE
S. Michel
S. Michel
la Fleche
la Fleche
Nantes
Nantes
POITOU
DE PARIS
la Rochelle
la Rochelle
Lion
Lion
Bordeaux
Bordeaux
MERIDIEN
GASCOGNE
LANGUEDOC
Avignon
Montpellier
Aix
Bayonne
Narbonne
Montpellier
Narbonne
GNE

CHAPTER 1

Here Be Dragons

"And the countless tribes of men built the whole temple of wrought stones, to be sung of forever... nearby was a sweet flowing spring, and there with his strong bow the lord [Apollo], the son of Zeus, killed the bloated, great she-dragon ..."

The Homeric Hymns, 7th century BCE[13]

This quote from a Homeric Hymn to the solar god Apollo tells of the slaying of the great dragoness Pythia, the spirit guardian of the spring at Delphi. Before the usurping by Apollo, the priestess-oracles of Delphi received messages from the python-dragoness during vapor-induced trances for all manner of guidance, for the common people and for the rulers of the region. The Greek myths and epic poems say that when Apollo replaced the female oracular orders at Delphi, he became the single most important prophet, and his cult endured for centuries. I have witnessed some of the *Talking Heads* of Apollo in southern France. At a hilltop sanctuary near Le Puy, a sculpted head of the god in the temple garden was connected to the interior of the sanctuary by an audio-conducting passage, where the priests of Apollo would prophesy from a hidden recess, a tradition far removed from the oracle priestesses of Delphi.

Apollo and Artemis Attic cup, c. 470 BCE, Louvre.

Apollo was said to be the twin of the great goddess Artemis, and she would never have allowed this usurping by her brother. How was this allowed to happen? Artemis had nothing to do with this shift to male-dominant culture, which coincided with the entry into the age of Aries, the two-thousand-year era of the Mars-ruled god of war Aries, from approximately 2000 BCE to the birth of Christianity and the beginning of the age of Pisces. Unfortunately, humanity did not receive the memo that the age of Aries ended more than two thousand years ago.

Myths are reflections of humanity's evolution, or in some cases, devolution, and the age of Aries coincided with the rise of the patriarchy and suppression of ancient goddess traditions, feminine equality, and basic freedoms for more than half of humanity. And to be clear, these female and male-dominated cycles have little to do with gender but with ways of being and respect for life. Epic myths are metaphors for humanity to reflect on archetypal patterns of behavior, and in the current global events, we can see the result of the long suppression of the feminine and wisdom traditions. This included the demeaning of serpents and the slaying of dragons, which has been a favored pastime of male-dominant cultures and religions.

After spending many years traveling to sites on the Dragon Path and becoming familiar with the terrestrial serpentine force that was moving between the ancient sites, it was inevitable that I would encounter one of these great dragon guardians. It was late November in the village of Rennes-les-Bains, and the turning of the foliage had transformed the valley into a golden paradise. The windows of my home where I write face east with the salty Sals River running directly below. The Sun was rising over the mountain, bringing everything to life, transforming recent rain on the leaves into glittering diamonds, rubies, and sapphires. Sunlight can be a rarity in November, especially in this moist river valley in the foothills of the French Pyrenees.

Taking advantage of the light and warmth, I took a cup of tea outside and began a morning breathing exercise, drawing in and circulating the solar light, followed by silent meditation. After some time, I became aware of a grand presence of immense power and expansive love, the kind of love without limits that totally consumes. The being identified itself as a female dragon and said that she was the guardian of the hot spring in the center of the village called *Bain Fort* (meaning "Strong Bath" in French), which flows with the hottest water of all the springs of the valley. According to one local friend and researcher, the old name of the spring was *Pisc Isis,* "Pool of Isis," which makes sense, as the Romans who developed the site adored Isis. The dragon communicated that she dwells mostly in the deep magma and aquifers of the Earth, yet she arises from these depths from time to time to kiss the stars and receive the celestial light.

Interestingly, dragon goddesses are often associated with water locations, and in China, there are references to the tradition as early as 1350–1027 BCE. According to Buffy Johnson in *Lady of the Beasts*, the Chinese female dragons were overseers of rain and fertility and ruled sites such as lakes and streams, often taking the form of a beautiful woman with a serpent body below the waist:

> *"The Dragon Goddess's shadow flits through ancient poems and stories, still visible in the delicate Dragon Ladies and Shamankas [female shamans] . . ."*[14]

Since the dragoness appeared "out of the blue," there must have been a good reason, and I asked how I might assist her. She communicated that the dragons and elementals need humanity's help in balancing the elements on the Earth and that we must work together more consciously with the guardians in the subtle dimensions. She explained that the dragons are overseers of the elements and work to maintain the balance between earth, air, fire, and water and ensure the fertility of the ecosystem. With the current climate extremes increasing, it seems essential to reach out to these guardians. Even though humanity does not normally acknowledge these unseen realms, nevertheless, they exist, and the elemental kingdoms work tirelessly on behalf of all beings who inhabit the Earth. As my friend Dan Winter commented during conversations regarding our work with the Pyrenean weather dragons,

> *"The elementals are weakened and confused with the spread of urban areas and decimation of nature. The survival of magnetic lines is essential to their survival and for attracting rain. They need us as much as we need them ... Let's collectively evoke the spirit of Gaia ..."*

I agreed to work with her, whom I shall call "Mag-Ma," since she indicated that much of her time was spent within the realms of Earth's hot molten iron magma. The dragon's immediate request was for a new song to support her work in balancing the elements. She was quite specific about the tones to use, which resulted in a new tuning for the harp. Following her guidance, the song emerged instantly and effortlessly, which is always a clear indication that the music is a gift, a transmission with a specific purpose. The song "Mag-Ma of the Deeps"[15] has a regal, expansive quality, and I can imagine her rising from the depths of inner Earth on the ascending tones to circle and soar in the elegant fields of the universe. She is a dragon of fire and water and one of the many *Shining Ones* beginning to reveal themselves to humanity so that we can once again cooperate in the guardianship of the Earth. At the end of that first visitation, the dragoness reminded me of the plaque next to the entry of my home, inspired by a French medieval sword inscription:

> *"Guarded by a dragon who does not sleep, in the name of truth."*

During the years of explorations in the region, I would encounter other dragon guardians, and one in particular appeared in the Py Wilderness, a river valley in the French high Pyrenees on the western slopes of Mount Canigóu (Canigó in Catalan).[16] An ancient pilgrims' and smugglers' path passes through Py and leads up through the valley and over the mountains, and true to the emerging pattern, Py, alternately spelled Pi, marks the Paris-Magdalena Meridian. Another coincidence is that Pi is 22/7, the ratio of the circumference of a circle to its diameter, marking two halves of the whole. This ratio gives us the Feast Day of Maria Magdalena, the 22nd day of the seventh month of July. Pi and Phi (the Golden Ratio) both form the basis of the geometry, mathematics, and music of the perfect harmony of the universe.

The "Dragon of Py," who I simply call *Drac*, communicated telepathically that music is needed to sustain their kind, and of course, he requested a song. (I can hear your mind spinning with the question, "How does one communicate with a dragon?" For me, it's simply being present, quiet, and receptive—nothing fancy.) When I inquired who he was, Drac responded that he has been a guardian of the Eastern Pyrenees and the sacred mountain since before the time of Atlantis. He had lost track of exactly when he first arrived. He had a grand presence and was an important guardian of the Eastern Pyrenees, yet he said that it has become a lonely job, and rarely does anyone notice him. I was traveling with a small harp and composed a song to hopefully inspire and support Drac and played it for him in the valley of Py. The piece is called "Dragon's Serenade,"[17] and perhaps when you hear the song, you will think of Drac and how we can assist the dragons in their eternal dedication.

Seven Dragons, Seven Sounds

"The seven vowels celebrate me, the great imperishable God ... I am the imperishable lyre, having tuned the lyric songs of the celestial vortex."

EUSEBIUS OF CAESAREA, *PRAEPARATIO EVANGELICA V*, FOURTH CENTURY CE[18]

Every world culture has at least some knowledge of the inherent power of the seven vowels and their use in accordance with specific harmonic signatures and resonant effects. The vowels have always been an integral part of the sound science used in mantras and magical invocations, and their effects on matter and energy are well known by many ancient traditions. But most are not aware of the association of vowels with dragons and the creation gods. In the 1800s, the great mystic and Gnostic teacher Helena Petrovna Blavatsky claimed to have come into possession of a mysterious text in the Himalayas called the *Book of Dzyan*. She describes the manuscript in her classic *The Secret Doctrine*, first published in 1888, and says the Tibetan word *Dzyan* is from the Sanskrit "Dhyāni," referring to the Buddhas of creation. Blavatsky says this lost text features seven dragon deities who inseminated our world with the seven vowels.[19]

I can remember one of my Tibetan teachers speaking of the Dhyāni Buddhas that created the world by emanating specific sounds. Blavatsky claims the "Primordial Seven" dragons breathed the seven sounds, the creative fire, into the void, and the various worlds appeared. The Dzyan text describes a "Blazing Divine Dragon of Wisdom," who sounded forth the Logos.[20] This sounds like the opening line in the Gospel of John, "In the beginning was the Word." In fact, Blavatsky quotes another portion of the Bible from John's Revelation 10.4, with her addition in parenthesis:

> *"The (Serpent of the) Seven Thunders uttered these seven vowels," but "seal up those things which the seven thunders uttered, and write them not."*[21]

In John's reference, it appears that the seven thunders, the seven vowels were part of a secret esoteric tradition, yet this knowledge somehow made it into the Bible. The vowels were often purposefully left out of the Hebrew and Egyptian languages used by the masses, as the vowels contained a hidden, secret power that was not available to all. (The seven vowels are used differently in various languages, but for English speakers, they can be written phonetically as: ah, ay, eh, ee, ih, oh, oo.)

We find this same mystery tradition of the magical use of the vowels in the Gnostic text *Pistis Sophia*, in which Jesus tells an inner circle of disciples:

> *"There is no mystery which is more excellent than these mysteries [the seven voices] ... in that it will lead your souls into the Light of the lights, into the regions of Truth and Goodness, into the region of the Holy of all holies, into the region in which there is neither female nor male, ... but a perpetual indescribable Light."*[22]

In a ritual called the "Treasury of Light," Jesus invokes a specific formula of vowels that would, in effect, create a garment or robe of light around each disciple. The invocation is given as, "iaō iouō iaō aōi ōia." Jesus tells the disciples that he is offering them "Keys to the Kingdom of Heaven" with this chant, after which they were surrounded with an unearthly light.[23] He says,

> *"I will give you the mystery of the kingdom of heaven, in order that ye yourselves may perform them for men."*[24]

In other words, Jesus is encouraging the disciples to use this secret knowledge for not only their benefit but to help others and lift the frequency of the world. The vowel formulas are a powerful creative tool used in prophecy and to open the doors to many dimensions of consciousness that he most likely learned during his time spent in Egypt and India. You can hear the "Treasury of Light" chant in a video filmed in a medieval French château linked in the footnote.[25] Was this science of sound that could raise one's consciousness to the realms of the gods part of the secret teachings received by John the Evangelist, and symbolized in his "Golden Dragon Grail"?

In her *Secret Doctrine*, Blavatsky relates the dragons of creation to the Egyptian adoration of Sobek, the crocodile god, and the Constellation Draco. For the Egyptians, the crocodile was their dragon deity, and in some zodiacs Sobek was illustrated on the back of the hippopotamus goddess Taweret (also written Reret and related to the goddess Neith), with the two representing Draco in the heavens. The astronomical painting from Dendera depicts the goddess holding a "mooring post" or axis stabilizer, which is tied by a cord tethered to the circumpolar stars of the north.[26] As we have already seen, Draco was at the northern axis, and Thuban (Alpha Draconis) was the pole star during the time of building many of their monuments, including the Great Pyramid. We will find this same northern star used in the orientation of numerous megalithic sites in Catalonia.

During a recent return to Egypt, more pieces of the dragon sound connection fell together. I had arrived on the Full Moon in February of 2022 to bring specially prepared music for my friend Kathleen McGowan's tour. Kathleen is a *New York Times* bestselling author, well known for her ground-breaking *Magdalene Line* series. I had a couple of days before the tour, so planned a brief exploration into Sobek's territory, the Fayoum desert, about 60 miles (96 kilometers) south of Cairo. Before setting off, breakfast was being served on the upper deck of the family-run hotel, which looked across to the three Giza pyramids. I was sipping good dark Egyptian coffee when the owner approached and introduced himself, and I invited him to join me. I described being a harpist and singer with a long dedication to the temple music of Egypt. Mohammed grew excited, and we dove into a deep exchange about ancient sound traditions. He was a retired Egyptologist and when I mentioned heading to the Fayoum, heart of the "Dragon God's" region, Mohammed shared many things, but one thing stood out as it related to this story.

Queen Tiye and Seven Cobras, Brussels Royal Museum.

He said that, according to Egyptian tradition, the creation of this world was accomplished by seven cobras, each making specific hissing sounds. As already mentioned, dragons and serpents are often interchangeable in ancient traditions. He associated these seven voices with the creator goddess Neith, with each of the tones relating to a human chakra. (Chakras are seven energy fields portrayed as wheels or many-petalled flowers in Vedic and Tantric systems.) He described the hissing sounds as being like the notes of a flute, each serpent breath creating one of the seven musical tones and the seven dimensions. Mohammed completed our conversation by saying that these tones also related to the stars. Perhaps he was referring to the stars of Draco as the "Fiery Dragons," emanating their frequencies into the Earth and resonating with the ancient stone temples.

My guide arrived and we departed in a 4x4, heading to the Fayoum desert. After driving through the desert where dinosaurs roamed millions of years ago, exhibited by their bones still visible and strewn across the land, we arrived at a small, remote temple called Qasr el Sagha. The temple was most likely built during the 12th Dynasty reign circa 1800 BCE of Pharaoh Amenemhet III (also spelled Ammenemes), and his daughter, the Queen Pharaoh Sobekneferu. Currently, the temple location is a lonely, arid landscape; however, during the time of Qasr's active use, it would have been a garden paradise overlooking the expansive Quarun Lake fed by the Nile. The temple stones are uniquely cut irregular shapes reminiscent of Egypt's Valley Temple or Peru's Saksaywaman, so the site may be much older!

Qasr el Sagha, Fayoum desert.

Qasr el Sagha's Seven Chambers.

I entered the temple through its single south-facing door and paid homage to the gods, especially Sobek and the extraordinary Sobekneferu, who may have overseen the temple rituals. With a small harp, I slowly progressed through the seven small shrine rooms, sensing the presence of a serpent guardian in each one. A spontaneous song arose from the central chamber with lyrics honoring the "Eye of Eternity," which I sensed referred to the star Eltanin, eye of Sobek in the constellation Draco, marking the northern axis of the temple. The following is what Andrew Collins writes regarding the seven cobras of creation in his 2023 release, *The First Female Pharaoh: Sobekneferu, Goddess of the Seven Stars*. He cites the Coffin Texts that describe the seven cobras containing the magical force called *hekau*, "the sounds of creation" ingested by the Goddess Hathor:

> *"TO BECOME HATHOR. How happy are those who see the festival in this place of mine! I am seated on the throne of Khopri [or Khepri, the scarab beetle and proto form of Ra], I give judgement in company with the seven cobras . . . I have swallowed the seven uraei, [cobra guardians] because I am Hathor, Mistress of rams, the serpent who laughs with Edjo [Wadjet the cobra goddess] . . ."*[27]

Mohammed's information on the seven cobras and this Coffin Text spell reminded me of a significant dream that occurred in 1992, the night I had completed an intensive training in Voice Analysis. Very simply, this diagnostic system studies the voice frequency patterns of an individual, which reveal physical, emotional, and spiritual sound keys for well-being. This sound science is rooted in Sufi and Egyptian wisdom traditions and is currently being used in medical diagnostics and by corporations to identify an individual's character and potential based on their voice pattern and is what I call *Sound Alchemy—Bio-Acoustic Medicine*.[28]

Cobra Goddess Renenutet, Isis-Thermouthis, Medinet Madi Museum.

After the three-day training, I was exhausted and fell into a deep sleep. The dreamscape was in the Egyptian desert at night, with a dark silhouette of mountains in the distance, and superimposed over the indigo sky were seven large black cobras. There was no message, just the image, with the sense that this represented an ancient sound tradition which would be influencing my future sound therapy practice. Upon reflection, the dream makes total sense.

Stories of dragons can be found in children's stories and modern fantasy books and films such as George R. R. Martin's American HBO series *House of the Dragon*, but we are told these magical beings do not *really* exist. Unfortunately, when Christianity spread its mantel of protection across the world, it came at a great cost that included a divorce from the magical creation realms of dragons and ancient wisdom traditions. The subsequent separation between the material and subtle, metaphysical realities created a terrible schism between humanity and the Earth and a resulting loss of the imaginal realms. Author and Christian educator Cynthia Bourgeault describes the access to this realm being possible when we simply expand our bandwidth of perception:

> "*The imaginal realm is* a meeting ground, a place of active exchange between two bandwidths of reality."[29]

In this quest across the Pyrenees, I would discover remnants of not only a belief in dragons, but also an entire matrix of sites, including megalithic temples, rivers, and mountains aligned with terrestrial and celestial dragon paths that appeared to have been established in prehistoric times. And how was it that the numerous ancient sites located along the north-south axis of the Pyrenean Dragon Path are aligned with the same axis known in modern times as the Paris Zero Meridian?

Measuring a Meridian on the Dragon Path

> *"It was intended that the [Paris] observatory would ... function [as] a laboratory, not only for astronomy, but also for meteorology and physics such as the determination of the speed of sound."*
>
> Paul Murdin, astronomer[30]

Paris Zero Point.

It was November of 2016, and I was eager to finally visit the Paris Observatory, where the modern meridian mapping of France began in the 17th century. But before describing the extraordinary observatory tour, a little background on the meridian will set the scene of why it is of such importance. It is much more than an invisible line drawn between the north and south poles, passing through the heart of Paris, across the Pyrenees, and superimposed on a globe.

The Paris Meridian project began in 1666 CE, when the French King Louis XIV authorized the establishment of the Paris Observatory to measure the longitude from the northernmost point of France at Dunkirk on the North Sea, continuing due south to the southernmost point of France in the Pyrenees. The measuring was later extended

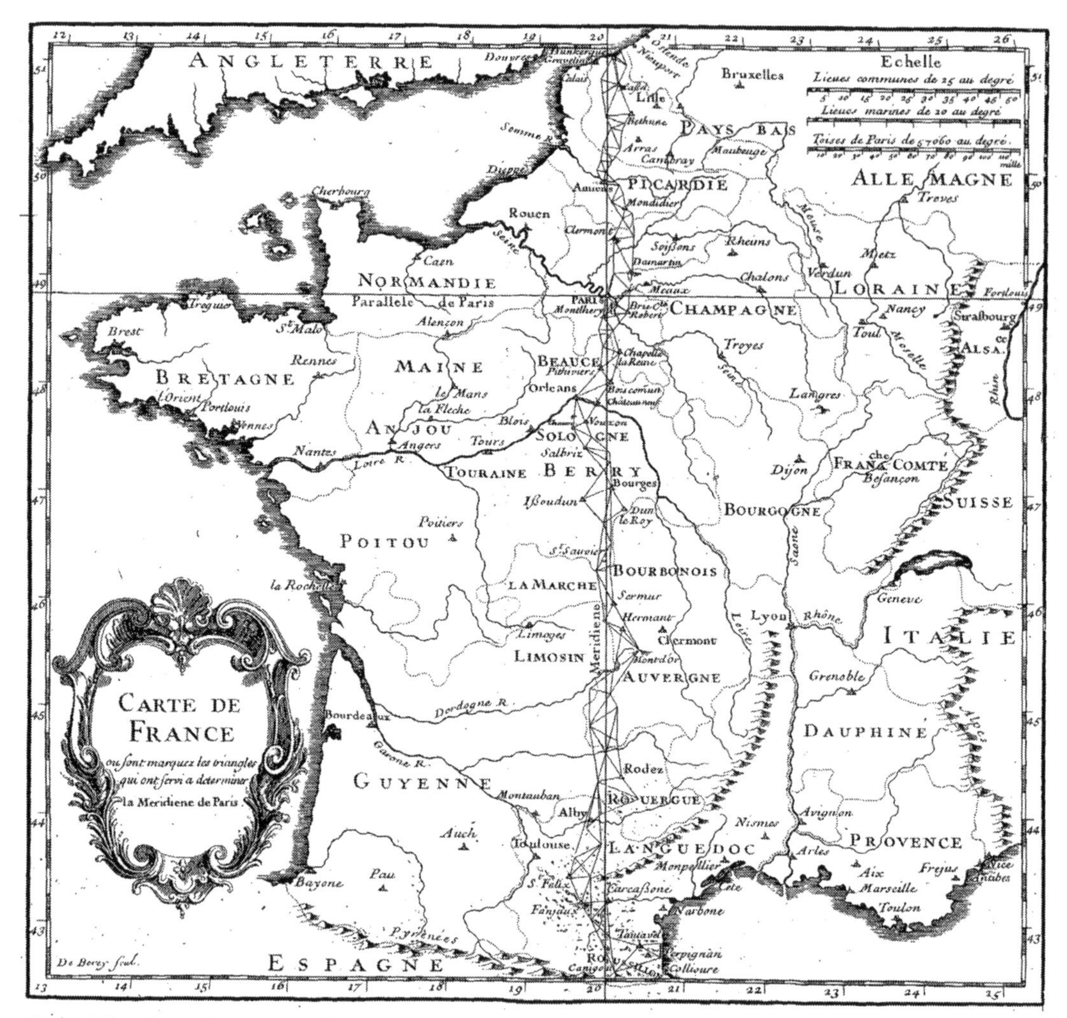

Paris Meridian, Picard and Cassini 1720.

across the Pyrenees to Barcelona and beyond to Majorca in the Mediterranean Sea. The king's motivation must have been his knowledge that establishing a north-south meridian (longitude) is essential for navigation on sea and land and crucial for trade and the survival of a country. And, of course, the prestige of establishing France as the Zero Meridian standard for global time and travel, used for navigation by sea, land, and in our current time, by air.

When astronomers from the Paris Observatory began their measurements based on the position of the stars, they were measuring time and space across the Earth. France was the first country in the modern world to successfully measure and map Europe, America, and Africa. In addition to establishing longitude, the astronomers from Paris were able to measure the speed of sound, using triangulations on the Earth based on the star positions. This is an extraordinary discovery, to imagine that the measurements revealed the movement of sound and the gravity of our solar system. Astronomer Paul Murdin says:

"The accurate Prime Meridian survey of Paris enabled the astronomers to measure the speed of sound! ... The Paris Meridian was a construct that tested the theory of gravity, the same theory ... that shapes the earth, holds the planets in their orbits and, indeed, decides the fate of the Universe."[31]

The scientists' measurements also established the meter (3.28084 feet or 39.3701 inches), which is based on a fraction of the distance between the North Pole and the equator. The meridian measure of our planet relates not only to the speed of sound but the meter relates to the distance traveled by the speed of light![32] After moving to France, I was resistant to using the metric system, but after discovering that it corresponds to the speed of light, sound, and the measurement of the Earth, it began to look much more attractive. And I mused at the linguistic similarity of the term *meter* that the scientists chose for their measure and the Greek word *mētēr*, meaning mother, or the Latin word for mother, *mater*. (The word meter derives from the Greek *metron*, meaning "measure.") The term meter was a perfect choice!

It was a cold overcast day in November when I arrived at the gate of the Paris Observatory, and being well into writing this book, coincidence was playing a strong hand. I waited in the small reception area, refusing to give up after being informed that it was impossible to enter the observatory. It was exactly one year after the 2015 Paris terror attack in which 130 were killed and more than 400 wounded, and the city was still on high-security alert, with many sites closed to the public.

I had waited a good hour before an official-looking man entered the room, looking very much in charge with his black suit, glasses, and briefcase. I stepped forward and introduced myself in rather rough French and explained that I was writing a book on the Paris Meridian, and would it be possible to visit the Cassini Room? This man turned out to be Dr. Stéphane Mazevet, the astrophysicist heading the exoplanet research at the observatory, the search for other planets in the universe that might support human life. He responded by smiling with amusement at my accent and, to my relief, answered in perfect English, offering a private guided tour.

We ascended the elegant old wooden stairs worn smooth over the hundreds of years of footsteps of scientific pioneers. We entered the long Cassini Room and Stéphane pointed out the oculus, the circular opening in the high wall that allowed the entry of the Sun's focused rays, like a *camera obscura* projector. The movement of focused light across the floor along the north-south meridian axis was marked by a copper line and mosaic images of the twelve signs of the zodiac. As we viewed the current solar path, it illuminated the constellation of Leo.

It is important to note that this copper line originally marked the Zero Meridian, but this was adjusted in 1884, when world leaders decided in favor of Greenwich, England, as the new prime meridian location. Henceforth, the longitude of the Paris Meridian became 2°20'14" east of Greenwich, although the longitude of the Paris Observatory is also given as 2°20'11". (The difference between the two longitudes is less than a city block.) This adjustment to 2°20' longitude for France's Zero Meridian is most interesting, as the number has significance in our story. The day chosen long ago for the feast day of Maria Magdalena was the 22nd of July. The number 22 has many important correlations and can be found coded in Magdalena's chapels, especially at Rennes-le-Château, as we shall see. Additionally, there are 22 major arcana in the Tarot, which some believe is a symbolic journey of the Grail. There are 22 letters in the Hebrew alphabet, and the list goes on and on. The 22nd of July is also the date that the Sun enters the zodiac sign of Leo. (Due to the Earth's elliptical orbit and the tilt of its axis, the date of the entry into Leo changes between the 22nd and 23rd of July.)

The resonant connection between the longitude of the Paris Meridian and Magdalena will be confirmed by her numerous sites being located along this north-south axis of 2°20' longitude on the Dragon Path. This was more than a coincidence. As mentioned, Magdalena's feast day equates with the well-known approximation for pi, written as 22/7, the ratio of the circumference of a circle to its diameter. In other words, the division of a circle into two equal halves, which conjures all sorts of symbolism relating to duality and oneness. This ratio was known by the Babylonians and Egyptians and used in temple design, and often called an infinite number of "transcendence."

My guide then pointed out the spot where Foucault's Pendulum was originally suspended in 1851, the amazing mechanism that perpetually swings to the rhythms of the orbiting Earth. Foucault's pendulum is named for Léon Foucault, who designed his device to move with the oscillations of the distant stars and galaxies of the universe and the rotation of the Earth. The original pendulum is now at the Musée des Arts et Métiers (Museum of Arts and Crafts), and a copy is also keeping time with the Earth and cosmos at the Paris Panthéon.

The Cassini Room was named for Jean-Dominique Cassini, the first in a long line of astronomers in the Cassini family to pioneer the measurement of the Zero Meridian. The Paris Observatory was designed to be a highly accurate instrument to measure the movement of the Sun, thus establishing longitude, the north-south axis of Zero Point. As we walked in the garden within the observatory grounds, stepping over the Arago bronze plates marking the meridian, I thought of the intrepid François Arago, who mapped the southern portion of the meridian from the Pyrenees to Isla Dragonera, Majorca. Arago endured tremendous challenges getting exact measurements of the southern meridian during the Napoleonic Wars (in the early 1800s) in Spain. He was even thought by local Majorcans to be a foreign spy, and barely escaped with his instruments and his life!

Stéphane pointed to the lower level of the observatory, where archives of ancient texts and maps were housed in the crypt. He casually mentioned a Black Madonna altar that once guarded the precious archives, a place that would certainly be well worth exploring. At one time, the crypts under cathedrals and temples housed not only statues of the Black Virgin but sometimes she was worshipped as Isis. There seemed to be a link between the hundreds of Black Madonnas in Europe and the ancient cults of Egyptian Isis, Maria Magdalena, and we could include black Artemis of Ephesus. Temples dedicated to these Eastern Goddesses were established across Gaul and Iberia before the time of Christianity, and, as was the habit of the Church, these dark mothers were absorbed and venerated in Europe's cathedrals and chapels as the Black Virgin. Camille Flammarion, the 19th century French astronomer, wrote of seeing the Black Madonna altar in the crypt of the Paris Observatory in September 1871. He said that engraved at her feet was the title *Notre-Dame of the Underground* and that she was placed in the crypt in 1671.[33]

Notre-Dame de Dessous-Terre, 1671, Observatoire de Paris.

This little-known Madonna and the date of her placement is highly significant. Establishing her altar in the underbelly of the Paris Observatory at the time marking the beginning of the grand project of measuring the meridian, places her as "Mother of the Meridian," grounding and holding the seed of birth within her hidden temple. Notre-Dame de Souterraine, Our Lady of the Underground, was one of many wisdom guardians of the Dragon Path, forming a matrix of dark mothers who I could imagine were communicating down the path, from Paris in the north to Isla Dragonera in the south at the Mediterranean. There are numerous references of discoveries of Black Virgins and Isis statues and shrines in Paris. One significant Isis was once guarding the southern gate of the old city, which *just happened* to be located on the yet-to-be measured meridian:

> *"In 1512 ... French historian, Lemaire de Belge, reported that an idol of the goddess Isis had been worshipped in a temple immediately outside the southern gate of Paris, where now stood the Abbey of St. Germain des Prés."*[34]

Even the name of the city of Paris could be derived from *Par-Is*, as the Egyptian word *par* or *per* means house or temple. The syllable *Is* is the root in the name for the Egyptian Mother Goddess Iset or Auset, called Isis by the Romans, who were her well-known admirers and built many temples to this goddess. This lady of magic, word power, and Queen of Egypt for all time, we shall hear more of in the coming pages. The Romans adored Lady Isis and established her temples across the Empire. Before they arrived in 52 BCE, Paris had been a thriving city in Celtic Gaul founded by the Parisii tribe, the most likely origin of the name. But no matter what the origins of the name, Paris has always loved Isis, the Black Madonna, and later, Marie Madeleine.

Since the tour was drawing to a close, I asked Stéphane about his exoplanet discoveries and if there were any planets that might support life similar to Earth. He responded that they have identified nearly five thousand exoplanets so far and that this is a small number, considering that there are most likely planets orbiting around most stars. Their search so far has revealed the uniqueness of our home planet to provide life in the way humanity currently requires. So much for sailing off to brighter planetary horizons. This planet is precious, and we need to treat it so. As we departed the observatory, Stéphane said regarding my interest in meridians, "Remember, that the country knowing longitude rules the world." I pondered his statement.

Establishing longitude requires complex measurements of star positions and marking these patterns on the Earth. One can observe meridian markers from the northeastern corner of France at Dunkirk all the way to the Pyrenees. These markers were placed in 2000 to celebrate the entry into a new millennium, with trees planted along the entire length of the meridian. Once the north-south meridian in a region is known, concise maps can be created for navigating across land and sea, allowing more efficient trade and communication, as well as an advantage in conquering nations, hence ruling the world.

But more important than imperial quests, and on a more personal level, knowing the movements of the cycles of nature surrounding us, we know where we stand. We can find our center within the circles and turning points created by the movements of the Earth and heavens, the Sun and Moon, and the six directions of east, south, west, north, above, and below. In addition to measuring the Earth from pole to pole, meridians are also currents of terrestrial and celestial energy moving and interacting with all living forms. Awareness of these subtle pathways on the Earth and in ourselves helps us to maintain a state of coherence in our lives, ideally, residing in the center of our Compass Rose. A Compass Rose is a series of concentric circles printed on a map or chart from which bearings can be taken. It establishes our location and can symbolize the four winds or directions not only of north, south, east, and west but also present, past, future, and the infinite possibilities when we abide in the center.

Compass rose from: Catalan Atlas by Abraham Cresques, circa 1370, Majorca. Library of Congress.

Meridians were known long before the first 17th-century longitude-measuring project was launched in Paris. Cycles of the Sun, Moon, and Stars were observed and measured, and meridians were used for thousands of years and provided the coordinates for not only travel but the placement of megalithic monuments, temples, and sanctuaries. In Egypt, it was the goddess Seshat, who, with Thoth, was called on to perform the stretching of the cord ritual to establish the foundation measure and orientation of a temple. The pre-Mayan Olmec civilization of Mesoamerica also used a cord to establish the measure of time and space.

In the Pyrenean region, medieval sanctuaries dedicated to Maria Magdalena and earlier temples to the mother goddesses of the Eastern Mediterranean were built on ancient routes and meridians that had been used for thousands of years. These same paths were marked by Neolithic stone temples arranged in a cross pattern to reflect the patterns in the heavens. There are too many of these alignments to be mere coincidence, and these monuments are aligned to mark the paths of light and the turning points of the year, such as summer and winter, sunrise and sunset, and the equinoxes.

As the perfection of these patterns became evident, one site at a time, I realized that these alignments were marking the currents of force that breathe and move with the Earth and stars. Often guided by dreams, my journey across the Pyrenees was like a treasure hunt, gathering fragments of the stories and traditions of the guardians of the land. The cultures that established their temples and trade beyond the Pyrenees in Iberia left their indelible impression on the region we know today as Catalonia, and in remembering these traditions, we gather the scattered fragments of the sacred feminine, to reanimate and breathe the living enchantment back into our world.

CHAPTER 2

Pyrenees—Mountains of Visions, Valleys of Dreams

"The Spirit of the Valley never dies.
It is called the Mystic Female.
The Door of the Mystic Female
Is the root of Heaven and Earth."

Lao Tzu, *Tao te Ching*[1]

Flying over the Pyrenees from Toulouse to Barcelona in November, the airline flight path was surprisingly low, and I could easily see the rugged details of the mountains that were glistening with fresh snow. I was following the Paris Meridian south from the Languedoc region of southern France to Barcelona in Catalonia, my final destination at the southern end of the meridian, Isla Dragonera, Majorca.

Dragon of the Pyrenees.

The Languedoc is a region extending across southern France from the Pyrenees to Provence, a land of mystery and allure, and once you have visited the region, you will want to return. The word *Languedoc* means "Language of Oc" or the "Land of Yes," as the Occitan word *Oc,* means "yes." This is the heart of Cathar country, *Pais de Cathar,* a land of enchanting châteaux, with Cathar and Templar fortifications built on top of daunting stone precipices. The Cathars were a medieval group of peaceful Christians operating independently of the Church, who professed "The

Way of Love." They believed that Maria Magdalena was the beloved of Jesus and that she brought an original and pure form of teachings into the region. This is a tradition that honored women as equals and allowed them to be priests, called *parfaits*, "perfects."

Every small village across the Languedoc has its own church, often filled with mysterious symbols that require knowledge to decipher. This is a land of fiercely independent, passionate people, a land that was considered part of Catalonia long before it was claimed by the French crown in the north. In fact, the old Occitan and Catalan languages are very similar, and the resonance of this tongue unites the spirit of the people on both sides of the Pyrenees. Languedoc was the region of the troubadours and the poetic tradition of "Courtly Love," which set forth the codes of behavior that elevated and demanded respect and honor for women. This is a land that gave birth to the early Grail legends and received some of the first exiles and apostles from the Holy Land. This is a land that continues to love and honor Maria Magdalena.

"Echoes of the troubadour's song can still be heard across the lands of Oc, ringing in the silence and the song of the nightingale, in the melody of flowing springs, and sometimes a chanson from a modern minstrel. Since the beginning of time, the music of nature and of muse wove a spell that sustained the harmonious patterns across the landscape and between earth and heaven. Enchantments woven by the troubadour poetry and their songs nourished the land and all its creatures."[2]

As I looked out the window of the plane, the jagged granite peaks of the Pyrenees pierced the sky and emitted a daunting force. It's hard to imagine the challenges that faced the scientists sent to measure the meridian over the Pyrenees! This range is the result of the two enormous terrestrial plates of Iberia and Europe colliding and pushing the Earth up millions of years ago. One can see in the geological formations of the region the unusual vertical angle of the crust of the Earth, the visual proof of a violent thrust that created these mountains. Sixty-five million years ago, the two great land masses of Iberia and Europe raised an ancient seabed up 10,000 feet (3000 meters), creating a massive stone wall that forms the natural divide between modern France and Spain. One can still find seashell and ammonite fossils formed from ancient sea creatures embedded in the mountains.

"These mountains reveal to me almost the entire history of the successive periods in the terrestrial crust ... the prodigious force which has rent the terrestrial crust in a fault of eighty leagues [240 miles, 390 kilometers] in breadth, which has upheaved ... enormous masses of limestone that once formed the basin of

seas succeeding each other at different epochs ... What a terrible cataclysm must that have been which thus reft and upset the globe, changing an extensive plain long submerged into a gigantic wall of granite ..."

J. H. Michon, archeologist and novelist[3]

This upheaval and change of orientation of the Earth's crust also created geomagnetic field anomalies, producing such strange effects as "Earth lights," and energetic portals. The Pyrenees range has numerous areas where the veils between the dimensions are thin, and where altered states of consciousness can occur—places for dreaming. These magnetic anomalies drew the attention of ancient people, including the builders of megalithic stone monuments that mark the path of the fault line and mirror the movement of the stars from east to west. The Way of the Stars is an ancient initiation path marked by stone circles, dolmens, menhirs, and sanctuaries that follows the southern flanks of the Pyrenees, which will be discussed in future chapters.

Beneath these mountains are great subterranean rivers and extensive cave systems that have provided places of refuge and ritual for ancient civilizations for at least the last 37,000 years. The Paleolithic (Old Stone Age) cave art that these people created, dated between 35,000 and 11,000 BCE, included drawings of prehistoric animals and humans. There are numerous Pyrenean grottos, such as Altamira, Mas d'Azil, Bedeilhac, Niaux, and Grotte des Trois Frères, that exhibit images of impressive, sophisticated artistic skill, as well as indicating shamanic rituals.

Perhaps the oldest known example of art representing a shamanic being is at Grotte des Trois Frères in the French Pyrenean region of the Ariege, dated to circa 13,000 BCE. *Dieu Cornu* (Horned God) is a dancing deer shaman, bearded and surrounded by various animals. The painting is in a section of the cave that is difficult to reach, indicating its hidden, sacred nature. Another example is the enchanter-shaman entitled *Petit Sorcier a l'arc musical* (Little Sorcerer with the Musical Bow) in the form of a flute-playing bison.[4] The ecstatic altered states of both ancient and modern shamans are often precipitated and heightened with music and dance, and in the Pyrenees, this was enhanced by the strong magnetic anomalies of the granite rock and the fault line energy.

"Little Wizard with the Flute" engraving by Henri Breuil, 1930.

Visiting these sites and experiencing the ancient paintings firsthand, one has the impression that this cave art must have been created by artist-shamans during altered states of consciousness. They not only made their art on flat rock walls, but they painted on uneven surfaces, blending their oracular visions with the stone crevasses and shadows created by the torch light, producing a three-dimensional effect. The Magdalenian Era of prehistoric culture (circa 11,000–17,000 BCE) paintings at the Grotto of Niaux in the Ariège included bison, ibexes, stags, and horses, all animals that were endemic to these mountains.

During one visit to Niaux, I began to chant to the Earth Mother in an inner cathedral-sized chamber decorated with prehistoric rock art. For those few moments, the reverberating and amplified sounds recreated a magical atmosphere, similar to the acoustical effects that must have inspired those ancient artists, and their shamanic encounters with the spirit world. These were the same caverns used by people throughout the ages, and the magical dimensions induced by incantations and music could be heard by the gods of the Earth and sky:

"The waters spoke into the ear of the sky:
You stags have leapt across the thousands of years,
From the darkness of rock to the caresses of the air.
The hunter driving you, the spirit watching you ...
And what if, in a moment of hope, I had [their ears] their eyes?"[5]

The spectacular beauty of the Pyrenees is enough to enchant us. Yet, in addition to the magnetic field anomalies created by the meeting of the two great terrestrial plates, there is an abundance of iron and quartz in these mountains. The presence of these elements creates effects that can precipitate altered states of consciousness and various interdimensional phenomena. At the very least, people visiting the region feel inspired and uplifted, and some report visions and life-changing epiphanies. Entire sections of stone and soil in the Pyrenees and the surrounding region are deep, blood red with high concentrations of iron, which ancient people viewed as sacred. Iron is magnetic, and some of the Pyrenean peaks are so charged that they have altered the sensitive instruments of aircraft.

These magnetic anomalies occurring in the Pyrenean fault can create gravitational reversals and portals, locations where the veil between dimensions is thin. The great Saint Teresa of Avila, Spain (born 1515 CE) is documented by the Catholic Church as having levitated on many occasions. Her case is not isolated, as there are numerous documented reports of other saints levitating. St. Teresa's episodes were witnessed by bishops, nuns, and many others, much to her humble dismay. One local legend says that when she was in the Pyrenees and over the fault area, she couldn't help but continue to levitate. In St. Teresa's words, although she was afraid when it first occurred, she became filled with deeply consuming love:

> *"One sees one's body being lifted up from the ground; and although the spirit draws it after itself, and if no resistance is offered does so very gently, one does not lose consciousness—at least, I myself have had sufficient [awareness] to enable me to realize that I was being lifted up."*[6]

Anti-gravity effects are one of the many anomalies found in the Pyrenees. Unusual moving lights and unidentified flying objects have been witnessed by many locals, and one good friend reported seeing orbs of light or balls of electricity moving back and forth above one of the iron and granite peaks. Prolific British author and ancient history researcher Andrew Collins commented on the geomagnetic and electromagnetic phenomena that are enhanced when iron, quartz, and copper are present. During his dialogue with author Erich von Däniken, Collins spoke of certain window areas or portals where communication between the dimensions can occur more easily. (These sites had concentrations of the same elements and fault lines as those present in the Pyrenees.) Collins also mentioned the findings of field researcher Paul Devereux, who discovered that many of the sites with unusual sightings, Earth lights, and energies precipitating altered states of consciousness, were also the chosen locations for the ancient builders of megalithic monuments.

> *"When you looked at the geology of these locations, they were all very similar. They all had very intense geologies associated with fault lines, magnetic and gravity anomalies, along with the presence of very specific minerals like copper, iron, and quartz... types of materials that could cause electricity and the flow of electrons. These electrons would come out of the ground into the air and under certain circumstances produce manifestations of lights and objects which we would call UFOs... the ancients were interacting with these lights and intelligences associated with them."*[7]

The Pyrenees is not just a place of visions and phenomena, but these mountains have also witnessed epic dramas of survival, countless wars, and the mass exodus of millions of people. Flying over these mountains en route to Barcelona, all looked peaceful, yet daunting in the jagged ice and snow-covered peaks. I tried to imagine how those escaping France during the various revolutions and wars in winter could have survived. At least half a million people, including men, women, and children, fled the brutality of Franco's 1930s regime in Spain over the Pyrenees toward France, but only the strong survived. And shortly after, during the 1940s, Jews and resisters of Hitler's invasion of France were fleeing over these same mountains in the opposite direction. These are only the more recent examples. The medieval Cathars were escaping the French Inquisition, and then the Jewish diaspora of 15th-century Spain had sent Jews fleeing in every direction.

One of the lucky survivors of those escaping the Nazi occupation of France was Mike. I met him when I was working in an art gallery in Sedona, Arizona, and he used to come in and gaze at the works of some of the fine twentieth-century artists, such as Chagall, Dali, Picasso, and Miro, who had all lived and painted in his homeland near the Mediterranean. Mike told me of when he was a ten-year-old Jewish boy living in Southern France in the 1940s, and sadly his entire family had been taken to prison camps or killed. His only option was to cross the rugged Pyrenees alone in winter. It suddenly made sense that he had become a volunteer hiking guide through the wilderness areas surrounding Sedona. I will never forget his story of endurance, courage, and will. Thankfully, through the compassion of various people living in the remote Pyrenean valleys, he survived to tell his story.

From the window of the plane, I could see the high mountain lakes and small villages tucked into the valleys, villages where Mike and countless others might have found refuge. The people in these remote areas have many stories to tell, of times when it was not so peaceful. Of times when they risked their lives to assist refugees fleeing in one direction or the other, through the old passes, the same routes used by Princess Pyrene, Hercules, Hannibal, early Christian missionaries, and later Cathars and pilgrims on the Camino. Now the sprawling vineyards in the lower foothills lay dormant following the annual grape harvest in September and October. These vineyards have been cultivated for thousands of years, fed by the great rivers that flow from the heart of the high Pyrenees.

Montserrat—Her Blackness is Wisdom

"Nigra sum, sed Formosa—I am black but beautiful."

Song of Songs (1:5)

As we drew closer to Barcelona for a change of planes to Majorca, the pilot circled low above the white stone spires of Montserrat. I felt a glowing warmth inside from the power emanating from the great white dragon-shaped mountain, and a feeling of returning to a familiar beloved friend. Montserrat is home to one of the best-known of the more than four hundred Black Madonnas in Europe. Montserrat means *serrated mountain,* and the unusual formations of stone spires have always been recognized as sacred. Three of the highest white peaks are named for Magdalena, her white towers rising in contrast with the deep red earth valleys below. In traditional alchemy, red and white represent life's duality, male and female, and their ultimate union within the alchemical vessel. Visiting the Black Madonna of Montserrat is like an alchemical infusion of spiritual strength from her dark, fathomless wisdom.

Montserrat's Magdalena Peaks.

The Madonna holds her infant son, an archetypal image finding its roots in Isis holding Horus and again in Mother Mary holding Jesus. The Great Mother images return in every age, yet her origins are ancient. Barcelona researchers familiar with the caves of Montserrat say that they discovered shrines to the ancient Mother Goddess inside the belly of the mountain. And who is this Black Mother of Montserrat? Robert Graves paints a poetic image and, gives her a magical tongue and the alchemical language traditionally associated with Isis:

Black Madonna of Montserrat.

"... an unveiled woman, black as
Mother Night,
Teaches him a new degree of love
And the tongues and songs of birds?"

ROBERT GRAVES, 'THE HEARTH'[8]

People often ask, why is the Black Madonna black? Is she black from centuries of candle smoke as the nun tried to convince me during my first visit to the powerful Notre-Dame of Rocamadour, France? Is she related to the Queen of Sheba who is "*Nigra sum, sed Formosa,*" black but beautiful as in the Song of Songs? The wise and beautiful Queen and beloved of King Solomon who came out of Ethiopia, the land of the origins of the Nile?

My sense is that Our Lady of Montserrat's blackness represents primordial origins, the divine intelligence and void that existed before the birth of this world. She is dark like the inner recesses of the Earth and the wombs of mothers. She is the wisdom needed to carry, birth, and care for new life.

She is a creation mother like old Black Stone Woman of the Yavapai-Apache creation legend of Arizona. Pukmukwana sings as she grinds round and round with her metate (volcanic grinding stone), creating manna, creating new worlds like the black holes in deep space. As she hummed, light appeared, the people were healed, and the stars were woven by her songs.[9] I see these timeless black mothers as a matrix of wisdom keepers, who work together as guardians of all life, of space, and time.

According to the Christian legend *La Moreneta*, "Little Dark-Haired One," the Black Virgin of Montserrat was carved in the first century by Saint Luke and brought to Montserrat. According to Catalan legend, the Black Madonna was rediscovered in 880 CE by shepherd children, who witnessed lights and heard music emanating from La Cova, a small cave in the white rock cliff. The children also reported strange lights moving down the mountain, and these lights and the singing guided them to the cave, where they found the ancient Black Madonna and carried her down the mountain.

There was an early hermitage of Santa Magdalena on the mountain, and the Catalan people speak of an ancient temple dedicated to Venus having been at the current site of the monastery. The 19th-century French archeologist Francesc Jaubert de Paça confirms that a temple of Venus had long been established at the location of the present cathedral of Montserrat. He says that rather than destroying the previous pagan temple, the earliest Christian founders often utilized the same foundations:

> *"[Christians] hastened, here to replace it with their own worship… without contradicting or totally destroying the original temple. This is at least what happened to the temple of Venus, in Montserrat, during the time of Emperor Felipe, in the year 253 [CE]."*[10]

The Black Madonna is currently having a revival, with many attracted to her blackness, which can equate to her depth of origins and wisdom. For too long, the feminine wisdom traditions have been intentionally suppressed, and people on the quest for awakening are hungry for her return. We need the wisdom of these black mothers now, their silent roar, their thunder perfect minds.

> *"The fanatical zeal of the priests, who denied, subjugated, or tried to transcend nature altogether, was in bleak contrast to the healing and nurturing powers of the Black Virgins. Behind this dark female face was hidden a Catharic leap in*

consciousness... A new image of love sung by their troubadours had its real roots in the alternative church of Mary Magdalene and the Black Virgin."

Malcolm Godwin, *The Holy Grail*[11]

Was the prevalence of Black Virgins in Europe a continuation of the first-century arrival of a boat on the shores of Provence carrying Maria Magdalena and Saint Sara? Sara-Kali, as she's called by the Gitane, the European gypsies, is the dark one they celebrate at the end of May at Les-Saintes-Maries-de-la-Mer. Some believe that Sara was the daughter of Magdalena and Jesus, and it is interesting that the name Sara in Hebrew means "Princess." Or was the Black Madonna a continuation of much earlier arrivals of dark mother goddesses in the form of Isis or Artemis of Ephesus? Some accounts say that it was in the temple of Artemis in Marseilles, that Magdalene, Saint Sara, the other Marys, Saint Lazarus, and their companions took refuge on their arrival on the shores of Gaul.

Music always accompanied the goddess, and hymns to Artemis were sung in the processions celebrating her in the new temples in the new lands in the western Mediterranean. In Ean Begg's compendium *The Cult of the Black Virgin*, he states: "the patroness of every Massiliot [people of ancient Marseilles] from [the] founding of the city in 600 BC was the black Artemis of Ephesus that the Phocaeans brought with them from Asia Minor; [the] BV [Black Virgin was] invoked in [the] first hymn for Candlemas procession as 'Virgin of light.'"[12]

And whether she is known as Venus, Artemis, Isis, or the Black Madonna, every goddess loves a song in her honor. I had scheduled a couple of days at Montserrat with my pilgrimage group. Often before visiting one of the Madonna shrines, I would receive a message from Our Lady with the request that I compose a new song in her honor. Just days before the arrival of the group, I was speaking with a receptionist at the Montserrat Hotel, making final arrangements. She knew that I played harp and asked if I had ever thought of playing for the Black Madonna in the chapel behind the altar of the cathedral. I said that I would love to and was surprised to know it might be possible. The receptionist promised to get back to me after checking with the cathedral authorities. The next day, she had an affirmative reply, that I would have an hour of private time for our group in the circular Knights Templar chapel of Saint Michael with a passage open to the ancient Black Madonna. I was elated.

Immediately after the conversation, I had the distinct impression of Our Lady of Montserrat saying, "Well, if you are invited into my sanctuary, I want a new song." (Perhaps Aphrodite or Artemis had tipped her off that I often write songs for the goddesses). Right, with only two days before the pilgrimage, through vivid intuitive impressions, she directed a specific tuning of the harp and a melodic style with which I was unfamiliar. The song necessitated more practice, but I was out of time. Oh, and one more detail she required, that the lyrics should be in Latin. I don't know Latin, but

I courageously agreed again. The song, which I call "Regina de Montserrat" (Regina meaning "Queen" in Latin), was beautiful in the resonant chapel, which interestingly had a fire-breathing dragon in the floor mosaic near the altar. Here are the Latin and Spanish lyrics:

Regina Terram, Regina Coeli
(Queen of Earth, Queen of Heaven)
Dirigi nos in sapientia tua
(Guide us in your wisdom)
Dirigi nos in caritate tua
(Guide us in your love)

Reina de la Tierra, Reina del Cielo
(Queen of Earth, Queen of Heaven)
Guíenos, en su sabiduria
(Guide us in your wisdom)
Guíenos con su amor
(Guide us in your love)
Stella Maris
(Star of the Sea)
Brillas siempre, brillantemente[13]
(You always shine, brightly)

CHAPTER 3

An Awakening—Our Body, the Earth

"'Mother, I come from you, you carry me, you nourish me, and you will take me after my death,' is a phrase still heard in European villages."

Marija Gimbutas *The Language of the Goddess*[1]

I was ready to board the flight that would take me from Barcelona to Majorca, but I should back up a few days and explain how the journey had suddenly taken a new direction. Just three days before my scheduled research trip to the end of the meridian, which had been planned for months, all of France was in mourning and shock following another terror attack in Paris. This time it was several coordinated attacks across the city, all in a day's work, leaving 130 people killed and more than 400 wounded.

It was a dark November, Friday the 13th, 2015. A candle was lit in the window of my upstairs apartment, and as I looked across the darkened tree-lined village square of Rennes-les-Bains, France, other windows glowed golden, also illuminated by candles honoring the many fallen. I could feel the shock, sadness and fear piercing the atmosphere in an eerie silence that permeated the night. Gone was the normal friendly activity in the center of the village. Quiet was the café normally filled with lively conversation, music, and flowing wine.

The ominous silence reminded me of one of my music tours, which I had completed the night before 9/11, 2001. I was driving along the empty California highway that morning after watching the news and the atmosphere was consumed by a similar otherworldly feeling. The Paris attack was certainly not the most horrific event in the world, but it was bad enough and it struck a chord close to home. I was in the midst of writing this book on the meridian that connects Paris with the village where I lived and runs southward to Majorca, my destination, which made the event significant and visceral.

I wept and prayed for the end of senseless suffering. I could imagine the Mother of the World weeping for the innocent ones in Paris who were at the wrong place at the wrong time. I prayed for the perpetrators of violence who could do this to other human

Henry Lincoln, Castelfranc, France.

beings. I wept and raged for the people who live far removed from the code of love and compassion, who are driven by self-righteous hate. I chanted and played the harp, calling on the Great Mother to bring her solace to the departed souls and the families, husbands, wives, mothers, fathers, children, and friends who lost their loved ones.

The following day I went with my close friend and neighbor, the late British author Henry Lincoln, to a church in the nearby town of Quillan. The old château on the hill has kept watch over the town for a thousand years, and the steep hills of the lower Pyrenees surround the valley. This is the heart of Cathar country and the land of troubadours. The last Cathar stronghold of Montségur is nearby, and the region is no stranger to persecution and suffering. Up the road from Quillan is Château Puivert where troubadours gathered during the Middle Ages from Provence and Spain for the annual festival featuring the finest bards, poetry, and music.

Henry had worked at the BBC in the 1970s, producing films on the Cathars, Egyptian archeology, and the mysteries of Rennes-le-Château. His books on the Holy Grail and Mary Magdalene, and his discovery of a geometric pattern in the landscape surrounding the enigmatic Rennes-le-Château, were some of the factors that drew me, as well as thousands of others, to the area. (See following Venus Pentagram illustration 15) During the writing of this book, Henry sadly passed away and I made a short film in homage to our friendship and his incredible body of work, "Quest for Invisible Treasure."[2]

Henry and I entered Quillan's medieval church of Notre-Dame des Monts de la Haute Vallée (Our Lady of the Mountains of the High Valley) and we were immediately drawn to a window where the sun was illuminating the image of Mother Mary. She was reaching out her opened arms, and the effect produced by the morning sun appeared to be sending light streaming directly toward us from her loving hands. I began to sing, petitioning the Great Mary to help us all, to bring love into the dark places of fear, to bring healing where families were broken. And to awaken the hearts of those so consumed with hate that they kill people they have never met, simply because they are driven by a different story. They are all stories after all, stories that created stark divisions between people, cultures, and religions.

I needed to give a voice to the helplessness, sadness, and frustration that we were all feeling. Henry and I were alone in the church, so I allowed the raw emotion to emerge in a fierce lament. It was a voice of pain and outrage—a calling for a return to sensibility, for healing. It felt like the only thing to do with all the shock and tension hanging heavily in the atmosphere like a dark cloud. Spontaneous keening and wailing have always been a natural response to outrage and pain.

Animals and children naturally express their feelings in sound, but what can we do when the natural connection between voice and emotion is discouraged and even broken? We are told over and over not to voice our feelings, programmed to be polite, correct. Giving a voice to an emotion, creating a sound that is linked with the feeling, can liberate the tension held within. It can also clear the atmosphere around us and be healing and restorative. The Austrian biophysicist Manfred Clynes discovered a universal language in the emotions of people around the world. Clynes' years of study in neuroscience and neurophysiology proved the sound-emotion connection which he termed the science of *sentic forms*.[3]

Keening, howling, expressing raw emotion, or even sighing, putting a sound to a feeling is therapeutic. A song, an expressive dance, art, or writing can be a direct link to not only express an emotion but also to set it free. Some of the creative art arises from poignant or painful experiences, when we reach deep to pull forth the notes and shapes from a place that is authentic. In the words of Nigerian writer and storyteller Ehime Ora:

> *"You gotta resurrect the deep pain within you and give it a place to live that's not within your body. Let it live in art. Let it live in writing. Let it live in music.*
>
> *Let it be devoured by building brighter connections.*
> *Your body is not a coffin for pain to be buried in. Put it somewhere else.*[4]

In other words, we can put our emotions into action, not let them become like stagnant waters. After all, the word emotion can be seen as "energy in motion." My heartfelt lament in the church had filled the dormant sanctuary with expanding harmonics, reverberating through the old stones and carried beyond. Henry and I both felt a bit lighter as we walked out into the sunny village street to look for a sidewalk café for a warm drink. Henry repeated what I would hear him say many times over the years, "This world will not be as we know it. Nothing will be the same." We spoke about our thoughts and feelings about these changes that were all around us. There was a mixture of despair and yet hope for a better world.

Two days following the Paris attacks, the collective fear and trauma of the event still hung heavily in the atmosphere. Did we really need such shock and violence to awaken and transform? Was the pain and suffering necessary to awaken humanity out of its slumber? The process of the planetary breakdown before breakthrough was daunting, and it felt like we were all in the awesome passage of a collective birth canal. Although expressing the lament in the church helped, along with continued prayers, I could still feel the oppressive cloud of fear and shock in the collective psyche.

I booked a session with a woman who came highly recommended for her healing gifts and ability to clear energy. The location for the session was in the heart of a sacred valley near Rennes-le-Château called Lavaldieu, meaning "The Valley of God." The lush green hills and forests of Lavaldieu are home to fields of grazing horses and sheep, and an occasional shepherd blocking the road with his flock. Long ago, this verdant valley was a favorite location for Druids and there is evidence of an ancient Drunematon (Druid ritual and gathering site). Lavaldieu also has stone ruins from perhaps the Templars and an earlier goddess temple, which some say was dedicated to Isis. This is possible, as the Roman settlements in the region brought the cult of Isis, which was popular throughout the Mediterranean, including in Gaul and Iberia, until at least the 5th century CE. It is no wonder that the valley has always been a magnet for mystics, as the Valley of God is a place of great beauty, and the land seems to emanate a subtle, luminous glow.

It was a perfect place to experience healing, and as the therapist progressively worked more deeply during the massage, I began to sense multiple waves of energy moving throughout my body. I had received many alternative treatments and therapies over the years, but this time there was a potency beyond anything I had ever experienced. The pulsations of subtle energy were moving from my crown down through my feet, like powerful waves of the ocean washing and cleaning. I had an overwhelming sensation of my body as the Earth's body. I began silently repeating a Tibetan purification mantra, *Om Ah Hum Vajra Guru Padme Siddhi Hum*,[5] that I received from the late Bardor Rinpoche. During the transmission of the mantra, Bardor said that the mantra brings not only purification but also radiance into the region where it is repeated. He added that doing the mantra in a sacred place amplifies the benefit a thousand times. (A lyric book with the meaning of this mantra and a video of how chanting it lit up the stones at Stonehenge are both linked in the footnote.)

The mantra was noticeably accelerating the movement of energy, and I suddenly remembered that we were less than two miles (three kilometers) west of the Paris Meridian. It was also significant that the location for the session was very near the center of the Venus Pentagram discovered by Henry Lincoln, a geometric alignment of ancient sites, including those dedicated to Maria Magdalena and the Knights Templar. As the practitioner continued, the waves increased, and I realized that opening and allowing this movement of energy was also helping to clean and clear the collective trauma. I had the sense of a channel of energy running from Paris, traveling down the north-south axis, which became my spine, and there was no separation between my body and the Earth. I sensed the movement of energy through the land, waters, and psychic atmosphere to the southern base of the Paris Meridian, emptying into the purifying salt of the Mediterranean.

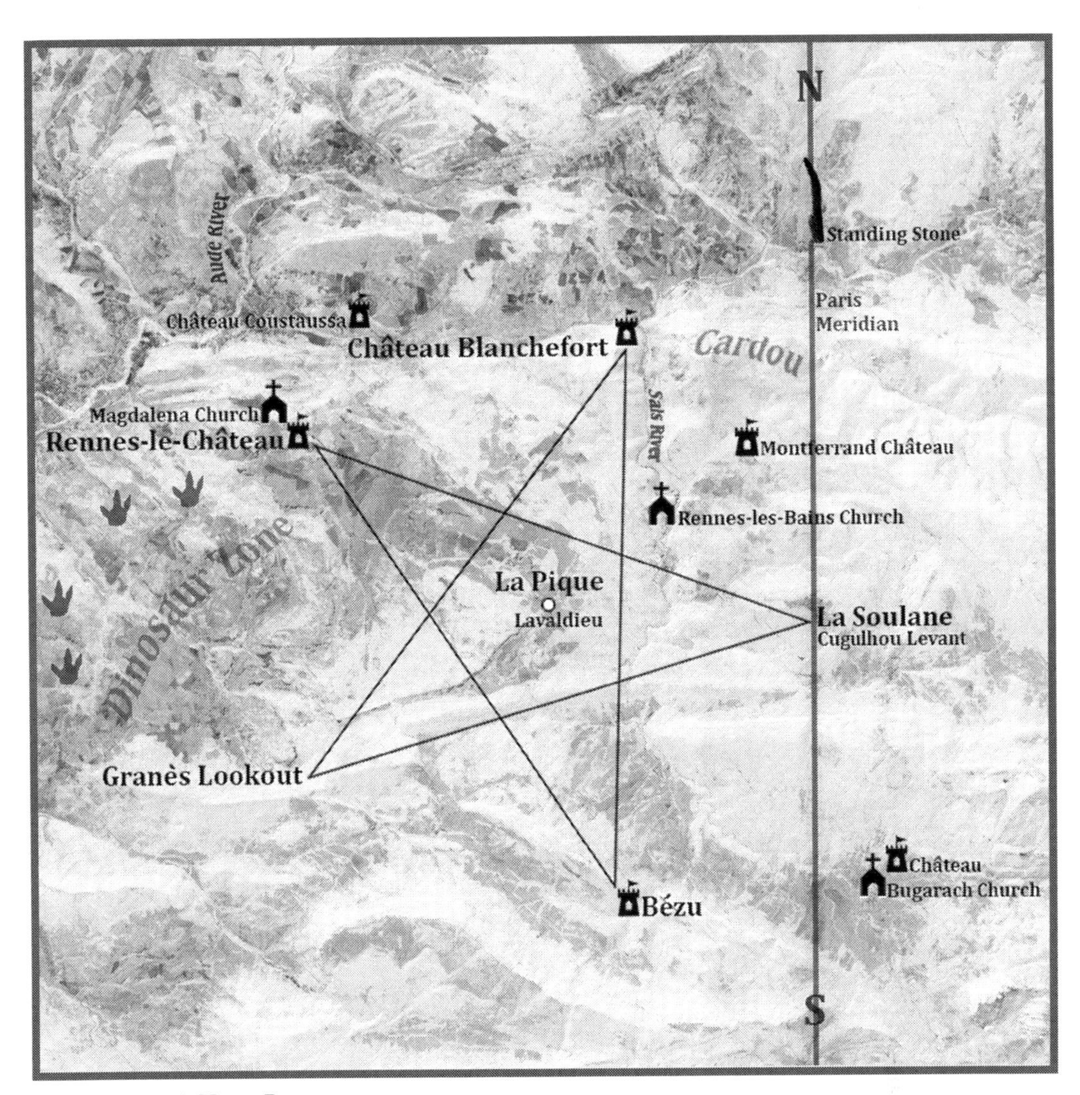

Illustration 15: Venus Pentagram

> *"... the Earth, like you, has an internal anatomy, with veins and channels, fluids and gases that circulate beneath our feet ... The Earth as a living being has a process that keeps her alive, producing energy, producing waste, and generating ..."*
>
> Ferran Blasco and Elyn Aviva, *Where Heaven and Earth Unite*[6]

This concept of our physical body mirroring the world outside of us is nothing new. Ancient people saw the Earth as part of themselves, as evidenced in the Hermetic tradition of "As Above, So Below," or in this case, "As Within, So Without." The ancient Taoist practices of clearing the internal and external meridians are an example. The Chinese science of placement, termed Feng Shui (meaning "Wind Water"), works with "Dragon Currents," the flow of terrestrial energy, clearing where the energy is stagnant, polluted, or blocked. These "Dragon Currents" are also influenced by celestial energies, including the Sun, Moon, and stars. This Earth science has been in use for thousands of years for creating a more harmonious landscape, in worked stones and hills, and in temple design. This same science is practiced within the energy field of the human body temple, as in Chinese medicine, acupuncture, and numerous alternative therapies. John Michell speaks of a Chinese Emperor working with astronomers and Feng Shui priests surveying the Chinese north-south meridian, which ran through the heart of the region:

> *"Every year ... they made a ritual survey of the great meridian line which divided the kingdom from north to south. On the accurate determination of this line the whole sacred geometry of the country depended... The entire Chinese landscape was irrigated by a network of invisible canals, along which flowed the dragon current, the fusion of the terrestrial current with the influences emanating from the heavenly bodies."*[7]

The Serpent-Dragon's Invisible Power

This invisible energy is moving across the Earth and within our bodies. The Sanskrit word *nadi,* meaning "channel" or "flow," can be seen as the serpent or dragon paths of energy in motion. Ancient cultures the world over saw the serpent and dragon as representing the wisdom teachings, regeneration, medicine, and the movements of creative life force. We can find a similar root syllable in many languages that refer to this dragon energy and universal current. In Sanskrit, the syllable *na* as in *nadi* means "serpent," "meridian," or "dragon current," and we see this in depictions of serpent-tailed *naga* deities. Significantly, the syllable *na* appears in the Sanskrit word *nada*, meaning "sound current." The Hebrew word spelled either *nahash, nāḥāš,* or *nachash* means "serpent." The Mayan syllable *na* means "serpent," which we find in the older name for the pyramid site of Palenque, *Na Chan*, meaning "Serpent House," or as we could say, "House of Knowledge." The term for a medicine person or magician who is wise as a serpent is *Na-gual*, a word deriving from the Nahuatl (Aztec) language of the people of Mesoamerica. According to Gerald Massey, the

Caduceus, Saint-Lasare Church, Avallon, France.

19th-century English poet and writer on ancient Egypt and linguistics, the Egyptian word *nas* means "fire-breathing serpent."[8]

We can see how the dragon and serpent energies share a common linguistic root, most likely originating in an ancient primordial language. As a further example, the word *Nahuatl* was most likely derived from *nāhuatlahtōlli,* meaning "clear language" or "serpent wisdom language." One theory is that after the fall and dispersal of Atlantis, knowledge, traditions, and language spread across the Atlantic, toward the east and the west. I remember the impact of seeing, for the first time, the Egyptian-appearing symbology in Mayan temple art, such as the Eye of Horus at Tulum, Yucatan. And, of course, the Nahuatl creator god was the plumed serpent Quetzalcoatl, called Kulkulcan by the Mayans. Deities combining the bird and snake imagery can be found in the Egyptian goddess Wadjet, the winged cobra, protectress of pharaohs.

The universal image used by most cultures to symbolize this dragon current is a wavey or spiraling line. We can see this in the serpent movement around the staff of a caduceus, the commonly accepted symbol of medicine. The staff can be seen as the "Tree of Life," and this same serpentine shape can be seen winding up the human spinal column in the representation of Kundalini movement. In Taoist as well as Tantric meditation techniques, one can imagine the internal circuit of the serpent rising from the root up the spine to the crown and back again to the root, ascending and descending as one follows the breath in a cyclic manner. This dragon path is internal as well as external, existing in the rhythms and resonance moving within us and across the Earth and in the heavens.[9]

The *nadi* neural currents that carry energy through our bodies are mirrored in the electromagnetic currents moving across the Earth. The veins and arteries carrying our blood are like the Earth's rivers and streams. Visible currents of serpent-dragon energy can be observed in the growth patterns of nature, in how a tree trunk will shape itself and bend to allow an invisible current of terrestrial energy to pass unobstructed. This can be seen in trees located near a church or a megalithic dolmen, which grow around an energy field emitted by the sanctuary.

One example is the ancient cedar rose tree that grew next to the church of Maria Magdalena in Rennes-le-Château. At a certain height, the trunk suddenly bent at a right angle and then, after several feet, continued to grow straight up again. The area where the tree bent and changed direction was measured by dowsers to be where a dragon current was flowing through the church and into the garden next to it. (Dowsing is a form of *geomancy,* "Earth science," in which subtle energies are measured, often with copper dowsing rods. Dowsing has been used for eons to find water and mineral sources and is still implemented across the world, especially in rural areas. This measurement technique is one that I used at many ancient sites that will be discussed.)

Nature is shaped by subtle energies and can take on the appearance of the activities that have occurred in the environment. These mirrorings in the patterns of natural forms and their energetic imprints are called *simulacra*, meaning "likenesses in form."

For example, in Tibet, where mantras to the Buddha or Tara are repeated hundreds of thousands of times at a shrine, the leaves and bark of the surrounding trees are often imprinted with images of the Buddha or Tara. I have personally seen examples of these remarkable imprints caused by mantras and prayers from my Tibetan teachers. These visible and invisible pathways and currents are moving in an interactive, animated dance of life.[10]

As mentioned, the Sanskrit term *nada* refers to sound currents, the sonic vibrations related to creation and manifestation. The ancient science of mantras is designed to precipitate the movement of nada waves to create harmonious and coherent forms, with each vowel emanating a unique harmonic signature. The coherent sound patterns from mantras not only affect matter but cause changes in subtle energy fields. For the person uttering a mantra and for those who hear it, there are measurable changes in the brain state,[11] thus changing sensory perception and causing an altered state of consciousness. In *nada,* we find once again the root syllable *na,* meaning the serpentine, or wave movement of sound, used to arouse the serpent of wisdom and awareness. Ajit Mookerjee, the late Indian scholar of ancient texts, comments in *Kundalini: The Arousal of the Inner Energy* on the activation of the nadi currents with mantras:

> *"According to the Tantras, to 'awaken' a mantra is to activate vibration channels ... The very sound of a mantra has the capacity to arouse the divine forms or their energies ...Hum is the root vibration or atomized form of sound representing the essential nature of Kundalini Shakti ..."*[12]

Out of the drums of our hearts, and carried on our voices, new energies are born, resonant seeds that ultimately shape our realities. We are literally informing the world how to respond to us by the sounds we choose to utter. This is the same teaching mentioned earlier, as given in the *Book of Dyzan*, with the seven creation sounds voiced by the seven dragon deities. This is the same ancient science taught by Jesus in the *Pisits Sophia*, in which he instructs the disciples to use the vowels that he has given them, as *Keys to the Kingdom of Heaven*. Current science and astrophysics are confirming these ancient traditions, describing the universe as a symphony and matrix of frequencies. (Universe is from the Latin *unus versus* meaning "turned into one," or we could say, "one song.")

> *"The universe is a symphony of strings. The mind of God is cosmic music resonating through hyperspace."*
>
> Michio Kaku, physicist[13]

The powerful effects of subtle sound waves, *nada*, affect the movement of *nadi* currents of vital force that are coursing through every living being and across the Earth, which we could call "rivers of song." Ideally, these currents are not stagnant but moving, changing, and regenerating, creating a vital system symbolized by the cyclic shedding of the serpent's skin. If the Earth is healthy, the people tend to be healthy, and vice versa. We can easily see the negative effects of pollution on the Earth and all biological forms. Pulses of great telluric and celestial force move through and across the Earth, which we could call the *humming of the dragons*. This music of creation is pulsing through all of life, in the songs from the stars streaming as subtle energy impacting the Earth and all living things. It was time to put this ancient science into practical action with the intention of cleaning the Dragon Path at Majorca.

CHAPTER 4

Majorca, A Long Time Coming

"If you do not render corporeal substances incorporeal, and incorporeal substances corporeal, and if the two are not made one, nothing will be achieved."

Mariam the Prophetess, 1st century CE Hebrew alchemist[1]

What I originally planned as a research trip at the southern end of the Paris Meridian had taken on new meaning. The shock of the Paris attacks had shaken and awakened something in my body and in the psychic body of the Earth and it felt necessary to do something tangible to help. The alchemical process referred to by Mariam the Prophetess in the quote above, can be used in a very practical way by acknowledging and cleaning both the seen and unseen realms. Salt is one of the three primary materials used in the alchemical transmutation process of turning lead into gold or transforming dense matter into illuminating life energy, and the salty waters of the Mediterranean would be ideal for performing a purification ritual for the Dragon Path.

After changing planes in Barcelona, the short flight descended and circled low on the approach to Majorca's Palma Airport, flying directly over Isla Dragonera, *Illa de sa Dragonera* in the native Catalan language. We were low enough that I could see the ridge of the dragon's spine, and as mentioned, the name translates as "Island of the Female Dragon," named for the numerous dragons in the form of thousands of lizards that live on the island. I pondered the meaning

Isla Dragonera.

and importance of the Paris Meridian ending here at the lair of the "Female Dragon" in the vast sea of Aphrodite.

In the small rental car, I headed from Palma to Sant Elm on the westernmost tip of Majorca, which is the closest point to Isla Dragonera. I had hoped to be physically on the island, but since it was November, the tourist boats that normally run to Dragonera were on winter holiday, so this was the closest position from which to commence the work. I found a remote pine-covered hill overlooking the narrow sea between mainland Majorca and the small island. Sitting on the wooded hillside across the narrow channel from Dragonera, it looked close enough to swim across, on a warmer summer's day.

They say that when two or more are gathered, the universe hears our call. But sitting alone and gazing at the island, I realized that I would need to call forth spiritual helpers from the etheric realm to assist in clearing the Dragon Line. I settled into a meditative state and asked for my allies and guides to join the circle. I began by calling and thanking the five elements and the six directions, East, South, West, North, the Above and Below. After asking permission to offer a cleaning of the meridian, I called upon the love and light of the Creator, the local guardians, elementals, and Earth dragons to assist in cleaning the clouds of shock and heaviness along the meridian. I sensed others joining the circle, and I began chanting the powerful *One-Hundred Syllable* purification mantra of Tibetan Buddhism.[2] I imagined the Dragon Path as an illuminated current in the body of Gaia, like a spinal column stretched across the Earth.

As I visualized the meridian from Paris to Isla Dragonera, I experienced the flow of energy through my body and through the Earth, like the strong current of a river, from north to south, releasing the trauma and suffering into the sea. The purifying and transmuting qualities of salt are in our tears, in our blood, and in the waves that were washing against the shore. I gave thanks to all the directions, elements and guides who assisted and to those who would continue this cleansing process, and formally closed the circle. I sat quietly gazing at the dance of sunlight on the sea, reflecting like diamonds and the shape of the island that looked like the spine of a great dragon mama, swimming in the salty currents.

"In every culture and in every medical tradition before ours, healing was accomplished by moving energy."

Albert Szent-Gyorgyi, biochemist and Nobel Prize winner[3]

Majorca, Theater of the Extraordinary

After completing this segment of work with the Dragon Path there was still time to explore the magic of Majorca. But before embarking on my short tour of several sites, it is important to illustrate a bit of the colorful and often wild history of Majorca and her sister island Minorca. With their strategic position off the coast of Barcelona, Spain, marauding pirates, Carthaginian conquistadors, and Phoenician and Greek traders all used the islands as a waystation for either trade and rest, or conquest and plundering. At least one of the pirate ships still lies at the bottom of the sea near Isla Dragonera.

Beginning in the 8th century CE, Majorca was inhabited and ruled by the Moors, and one can still visit their beautiful architecture and gardens in the capital city of Palma. In September of 1229, the young King James I of Aragon, with the help of the Knights Templar, departed the Spanish coast with 155 ships, 15,000 foot soldiers, and 1,500 mounted knights, and arrived on the southern shore of Majorca near Isla Dragonera, successfully liberating the island from more than 300 years of Moorish rule.[4]

James (Jaime in Spanish, Jaume in Catalan) was born in Montpellier, France, son of King Peter (Pedro in Spanish) II of Aragon and Marie of Montpellier, and when only a toddler, he was used as a political pawn to secure peace between France and Spain. The two-year-old had been placed in the care of Simon de Montfort, the ruthless French military leader who was leading the campaign to exterminate the Cathars across the Languedoc. Peter petitioned Pope Innocent III, and James was thankfully released back to Aragon. The young boy was placed under the care of Guillem de Montredó, the head of the Aragon and Provence Knights Templar, and with his noble education, James absorbed the strength and legacy of the Templars and went on to become King James I, "The Conqueror." He established the great and powerful Kingdom of Majorca, which ultimately ruled Aragon, Catalonia, and portions of Provence.

Majorca had long been an important region for Arabian science and astronomy, scholars of Jewish Kabbalah, and early Christian missionaries. In its remote location, it was a hotbed of mystics and heretics of every persuasion. Remember, the root of the word heretic comes from the ancient Greek *hairetikós*, meaning "able or free to choose." One of the most influential medieval visionaries was Raymond Lull, otherwise known as Ramon Llull or Raymund Lully in Spanish and Catalan. Lull was born on Majorca circa 1235 of a noble family and was raised in the magnificent courts of Aragon as personal page to King James I. Following a vision of Christ, Lull, the courtly troubadour, became a Franciscan priest and dedicated the rest of his life to establishing peace and unity through education.

Luckily, my visit to Majorca corresponded with the 700-year anniversary celebrating Lull's life and works, and one of the exhibitions was at his Monastery of Miramar. The Franciscan retreat sits on the spectacular western cliffs of Majorca, overlooking the Mediterranean to the north of Isla Dragonera. Raymond was often called the "Illuminated" or "Hermetic Doctor," and the display of his works included rare documents and illustrations on alchemy, magic, Islamic astrology, Kabbalah, geometry, and philosophy that he termed *"Ars Magna Sciendi"* (Art of the Great Science). He became known throughout the Mediterranean, England, and beyond as the visionary who would attempt to unite the three major religions, Christianity, Judaism, and Islam. He ultimately

Monestir de Miramar.

established numerous academies throughout Europe dedicated to linguistic and religious education with the goal of bridging the differences and creating a peaceful realm in the West.

Lull's enormous legacy is a perfect example of the wealth of mystical and Hermetic knowledge that was flowering in medieval Spain and concentrated on the small island of Majorca. The presence of Christian, Hebrew, and Islamic scholars, scriptoriums, and libraries during the 11th-15th centuries produced a tsunami of ancient knowledge that still exists today in the fiery passion and the arts of Catalonia, an echo of Lull's "*Ars Magna*." Inspired by Lull's vision for a peaceful world and co-creation through education, I wrote the song "Ode to Ramon Llull," combining Hebrew and Arabic chants, linked in the note.[5] His legacy is a reminder of a time in Spain when the major religions of the world coexisted and thrived in an illuminated atmosphere of higher learning.

"Tree of Philosophy and Love," Raymond Lull exhibition.

Centuries later, during the 1800s and early 1900s, freethinkers arrived from the north, attracted to this beautiful island surrounded by turquoise waters and its eccentric history. Majorca became a favorite retreat destination for Parisian elite artists, authors, and musicians who gathered in Paris' famous private salons, sharing their music, poetry, revolutionary ideas, and theater. Were they all sensing the potent telluric currents moving through the Dragon Path between Paris and Majorca and as influential, creative, freethinkers following the places of power to inspire their works? This circle included notables such as Ernest Hemingway, Gertrude Stein, Anaïs Nin, Robert Graves, George Sand, her lover Frédéric Chopin, Franz Liszt, novelists Turgenev and Gustave Flaubert, and artist Eugène Delacroix, to name just a few. Delacroix was

Tree of Life Unity by Raymond Lull, 2015 exhibition Miramar.

known for his evocative paintings of Mary Magdalene, such as *Madeleine dans le Desert* (*Magdalene in the Desert*), in which she has an all-knowing expression, as if the viewer does not know her secret.

I was excited to explore some of the favorite haunts of these characters who had colored and inspired my teenage years as an avid, curious reader of Paris' 19th and early 20th-century scenes. After a restorative lunch and fine Majorcan red wine, I made a beeline to the medieval Valldemossa Monastery, where George Sand (the pen name of Amandine Aurore Lucie Dupin, Baroness Dudevant) and Chopin had spent a winter in 1838. They had arrived on the Barcelona-Palma steamship that made regular crossings to Majorca and made their way to their temporary home in the remote monastery. The rooms where they stayed are now open as a museum. In Chopin's music room, I stood before his piano, viewing the original music sheets, on which scribbled notation was often crossed out and updated with new melodic lines and timing. His music has always inspired me.

In Sand's writing study, I gazed at her original handwritten manuscripts, soaking up as much creative inspiration as possible. She could turn out an entire book in just a week, and her views on equal rights for women, sexual freedom, and revolutionary ways of thinking helped influence our views today. One theater piece entitled *"Le Drac"* (*The Dragon*) is a story about a magical being of Provençal legend, perhaps inspired by Majorcan dragon tales she may have heard from the locals. One of her lesser-known plays, *"Les Sept Cordes de la Lyre"* (*The Seven Chords of the Lyre*), speaks to women of all times and traditions, and reveals George's love for Egyptian and Pythagorean Hermetic principles of love, music, and harmony:

> *"The spirit of the Lyre is speaking: Awaken, Oh daughter of men ... This lyre is my body; sound is divine, harmony is God. Daughter of men, your being is divine, your love is God... All is harmony, sound, and color. Seven tones and seven colors intertwine and move around you in eternal nuptials. There is no silent color. The universe is a lyre."*[6]

During the winter of 1838, George Sand often chatted with the locals and heard fantastic stories about the mysterious man sent from the Paris Observatory who had arrived on the island. His name was Dominique François Jean Arago, who was commissioned by Napoleon Bonaparte to map the Prime Meridian beyond Barcelona, to Isla Dragonera. Arago was born near the Pyrenees in Estagel, France, where everyone also spoke Catalan, which would prove to be a lifesaver. He had departed Paris in 1806, and little did he know his adventures would last many years, and several times, he would barely escape with his life. There were at least two factors slowing down Arago's progress in making proper measurements in Majorca. In addition to Spain's 1808–14 Peninsular War with France, Isla Dragonera was surrounded by the Mediterranean, which limited Arago's normal mode of establishing signal fires on nearby mountains or church towers to make exact measurements on the land.

Napoleon's army had recently invaded Catalonia as far as Barcelona, which caused Majorcan locals to be very suspicious of the foreigner Arago. It is interesting that Napoleon sent Arago to Majorca and then proceeded to invade the region and cause the scientist endless problems in doing his job. Majorcans assumed Arago was a French spy, and bandits and armed farmers were stalking him continually, assuming his instruments installed on their mountaintops were enemy spy stations. Knowing the Majorcan Catalan dialect helped him escape numerous times, but finally, he was imprisoned in a castle at the capital city of Palma to appease the angry locals, but mostly for his protection.

As the story goes, Arago escaped from the prison and, with his friend, boarded a boat headed for Algiers. All was going well until they were almost at Marseilles when they were captured by a Spanish ship and taken all the way back to Catalonia. Arago and his friend were imprisoned once again, first in a windmill and then a fortress near Roses, where they almost starved to death. He was eventually released, and with a strong, persevering Pyrenean spirit, Arago was able to finally map the Paris Meridian at its southernmost point in Majorca. The meridian is marked still today with Arago's long line of stones on Isla Dragonera.

Arago Meridian Plaque Paris.

Arago would also be remembered for discovering a prehistoric cave at Tautavel, near his family home at Estagel on the French side of the Pyrenees. The cave named Grotte de Arago was later found to contain early human *homo erectus* remains dated to 450,000 BCE! (*Homo erectus* was an upright human that lived throughout most of the Pleistocene Epoch.) Included in the cave were bones of saber-toothed tigers, wooly mammoths, and bears that roamed across the foothills of the eastern Pyrenees nearly half a million years ago. Interestingly, the skull found in Arago's Cave designated as the "Tautavel Man" is currently housed in

Paris at the Museum of Natural History, located near the meridian, 1.24 miles (1.995 kilometers) to the west.

Arago had an important friend in the 19th century French fantasy writer Jules Verne, and they often met in Paris for long discussions on Arago's adventures in mapping the meridian. Verne was fascinated with the scientific measurements of the Earth and the altitude of stars, including the discovery of the meter. He eventually wrote several novels based on their lively conversations, including *Measuring of a Meridian,* inspired by the extraordinary perils that Arago had endured while calculating the Paris Meridian from the Pyrenees to Isla Dragonera.

Dragons and Pearls

"Awake and rise from your sleep.
Listen...
Remember...
Recall the pearl for which you were sent to Egypt."

"The Hymn of the Pearl," *Acts of Thomas, 2nd–3rd century CE*[7]

There were more dragons to discover on Majorca. *Las Cuevas del Drach*, meaning "the Caves of the Dragon," are located at Porto Cristo (Port of Christ) on the island's eastern coast, and include extensive natural caverns and underground lakes renowned for their production of luminous cultured pearls. The caves are a popular venue for classical music concerts, and the superb acoustics amplify the musical harmony into the inner Earth—the water, pearls, and stones all resonating. The harmonic field created by sacred or classical music is a form of subtle energy, acoustical nutrition, bringing benefit to the region, and I could imagine, a favorite food of dragons. (See illustration 6 Magdalena Meridian So., p. 218)

Multiple sites named for dragons on the island indicated the presence of a potent, vital, terrestrial life force. This is evidenced in the numerous megalithic stone temples, including dolmens, ritual enclosures on Majorca, Minorca, and Ibiza. With the concentration of ancient sites, and dragons honored in the location names, I could easily see why I had envisioned the north-south axis of the Paris Meridian as the spine of a dragon. (These two islands are spelled Mallorca and Menorca in Catalan, but I have chosen to use the familiar English spellings.)

Dragons have long been considered guardians of caves and treasure, or in this case, a priceless pearl of enlightenment. There is a wonderful story told in the Gnostic apocryphal text "The Hymn of the Pearl," an allegory of the human journey of forgetting and remembering, and ultimate awakening. Often called the most elegant account in early Christianity, the text is found in the 3rd century CE *Acts of Thomas*, but most scholars agree that it was composed earlier.

Indonesian dragon, author's collection.

"The Hymn of the Pearl" begins with a journey undertaken by a boy of noble lineage, who is sent from his homeland to Egypt by his father and mother, the king and queen. His quest is to find a precious pearl guarded by a fierce dragon. The location of his home is not clarified, but there is a clue in the Hymn's text when he is returning home from his quest in Egypt and reaches the great seacoast of Meson. There are numerous sites with the name Meson, most of which are on the coasts of Spain and Majorca. The word *meson* comes from the Latin *mansiō* or *mansiōnem* meaning "abode" or "home." The term in modern Spain has come to mean an inn or tavern. The boy's home could have been anywhere near the coast in the region of Spain, but given the themes, let us imagine for now, that it was Meson, Majorca. (Interestingly, a *meson* also refers to a type of subatomic particle in physics, some of which were created during the Big Bang, giving a cosmic flavor to our hero.)

The prince departs his homeland with instructions to retrieve the precious pearl, the quest engraved on his heart. When he enters Egypt, he disguises himself by donning the garments of the local people, so that he appears to be "one of them." And, over time, the young man begins to blend more with the local people, taking on their beliefs and customs, and forgets his identity and original mission: "I forgot the pearl for which my parents had sent me. And I fell into a deep sleep..."[8]

His parents eventually realize that their son has fallen into forgetfulness, and they send him an urgent message:

"From your father the king of kings and your mother, the mistress of the East ...
Awake and rise from your sleep.
Listen to the words in this letter. Remember you are the son of kings, You have fallen beneath the yoke of slavery ...
Recall the pearl for which you were sent to Egypt."[9]

Here it is important to mention that in Eastern spiritual traditions, the seed of consciousness or Buddha nature is often referred to as a pearl. The Indian guru Swami

Muktananda said that the Blue Pearl resides in the Sahasrara center in the crown of the head, the pineal gland. It is the doorway of light through which the seed of life from the heavenly realms first enters the body. Muktananda describes the Blue Pearl as:

> *"... blue light, the size of a tiny seed, that appears to the meditator whose energy has been awakened. The Blue Pearl is the subtle abode of the inner Self."*
>
> SWAMI MUKTANANDA, *DOES DEATH REALLY EXIST?*[10]

In "The Hymn of the Pearl," the message sent by the boy's parents reminds him of his lineage and mission to retrieve the pearl, which is guarded by the great dragon. He awakens from his long dream, remembering his quest, which was engraved upon his heart. Now a young man, he sets out once again and finds the cave of the dragon. By intoning the resonance of his father's name, a mantra, perhaps one of the seventy-two Sacred Names of Judaic Kabbalah, the dragon is subdued, and the young man retrieves the pearl. On the hero's journey home, he sheds his worn and soiled garments, leaving his forgetfulness behind. Further along the long road, he meets a woman who initiates him with her enchanting voice. Her voice lifts him up, and the resonance of her song becomes a guiding light, leading him to a place of deep splendor.

> *"And on the road, I found a female who lifted me up.*
> *She awakened me, giving me an oracle with her voice, and guided me to the light."*[11]

This female guide sounds like a reference to Sophia, who sings her praise songs in search of the Beloved, as described in the *Pistis Sophia*. Or perhaps it is a reference to a priestess of the order of oracles, the *Bath Kol*, meaning "Daughters of Voice" in Hebrew. During the time that "The Hymn of the Pearl" was written, the Bath Kol tradition of oracles was active. These Daughters of Voice used their voices and instruments such as harps, drums, and tambourines to open the gateway to heaven to receive wise guidance for the temple and the people. The similar tradition of Sibylline oracles was also active at this time across the entire Mediterranean. The Sibylline orders of priestesses were a continuation of the ancient Magna Mater (Great Mother) Cybele of Anatolia.

After the young prince receives his awakening from the chantress-oracle and is guided to the light, he passes through a great labyrinth, and then, floating before his eyes, there appears a glorious, radiant garment. Through this garment or new awareness, he is now able to perceive his true unified essence:

"I perceived in it my whole self as well ...
For though we originated from the one and the same,
we were partially divided.
Then again we were one, with a single form ...[12]

This passage sounds Hermetic and alchemical, with the basic duality of creation, or two (male and female) becoming as one, the transformation of separate beings into wholeness, the Hermaphrodite, in the alchemical process of "Becoming Gold." The young man received his garment of light, which was woven of gold and pearls, trimmed with deep blue lapis lazuli. When he put it on, he was immediately swept up into the land of "peace and homage." As he arrived at his heavenly home, multitudes were singing hymns in harmonious voices, celebrating his successful quest and his retrieval of the pearl of awakening.

"The Hymn of the Pearl" is one of the most beautiful and poetic texts from the non-canonical gospels, hardly requiring any explanation in its simple and direct symbolism. As mentioned previously, "The Hymn" was discovered in part of the *Acts of Thomas*, one of the Apocryphal Acts of the Apostles. Since Thomas is the apostle known for bringing the teachings of Jesus into India, it is not surprising that we find the connection with the pearl of Eastern tradition.

"Through regular and prolonged meditation on the blue pearl or the seed of consciousness, one gradually experiences one's true nature, which is called the 'Buddha Nature' in Buddhism."

Master Choa Kok Sui,
Om Mani Padme Hum: The Blue Pearl in the Golden Lotus[13]

Did "The Hymn of the Pearl" refer to Majorca, or did the people who named the island's sites have this story in mind? Finding Las Cuevas del Drach, the Caves of the Dragon, at the Port of Christ, where they produce pearls, and sites named Meson on the island certainly are important ingredients of this Gnostic gospel. Additional links are in Egyptian relics found at the megalithic sites on Majorca's sister island Minorca, indicating a long tradition of trade, travel, and cultural exchange between the Eastern Mediterranean and these islands. The whole allegory seems to fit perfectly with Majorca, so could it have been composed here? This is entirely possible as there was a great dispersal of Jews following the Roman attack on Jerusalem in 70 CE, and many of these refugees found their way to Catalonia and Majorca. The following is an extract from the lyrics of my song "Dragon and Pearl," inspired by Majorca and "The Hymn of the Pearl":

"The pearl shall be revealed,
In the numinous cave of your mind
A dragon guards the path,
To a treasure you may find.

Sleepers awaken
To magic long denied.

Secret Dragon and Pearl
Sleeping deep within
Follow the golden path
Of your breath to begin."[14]

Minorca's Enigmatic Megaliths

"Colossus, sculpted by the hand of Time,
What mystic secrets of the Universe
Are crystalled in thy form!
...Fire-mist an Age; an Era, crust of stone;
An Epoch, soil, slow silted to the sea..."

HENRY SMITH WILLIAMS, "COLOSSUS"[15]

Minorca has more sacred temple enclosures in a concentrated small region than almost anywhere on Earth. There is a sense of mystery here, reaching back thousands of years. The local families tell of legends of a race of giants that once lived on the island, and these stories have been handed down through many generations. One friend told me that, while visiting the island with a group of researchers decades ago, one of the members claimed he saw the mythological sirens while swimming in the sea at one of the rocky coves, and that these half-bird, half-woman creatures spoken of by Homer still exist in some dimension. Perhaps these are the same sirens that enchanted Odysseus during his long adventures across this same sea, when he stopped at numerous islands that may have included Minorca. This is possible, as the island had one of the most splendid safe harbors in the Mediterranean, according to the great third-century BCE Carthaginian family of Hannibal, who sometimes overwintered in its shelter.[16] There are many layers to Minorca's mysterious past and much that is lost to historians, but the island remembers.

The most amazing signatures of Minorca, still extant, are the ancient T-shaped standing stones. Are they an Iberian clone of Göbekli Tepe and Karahan Tepe in

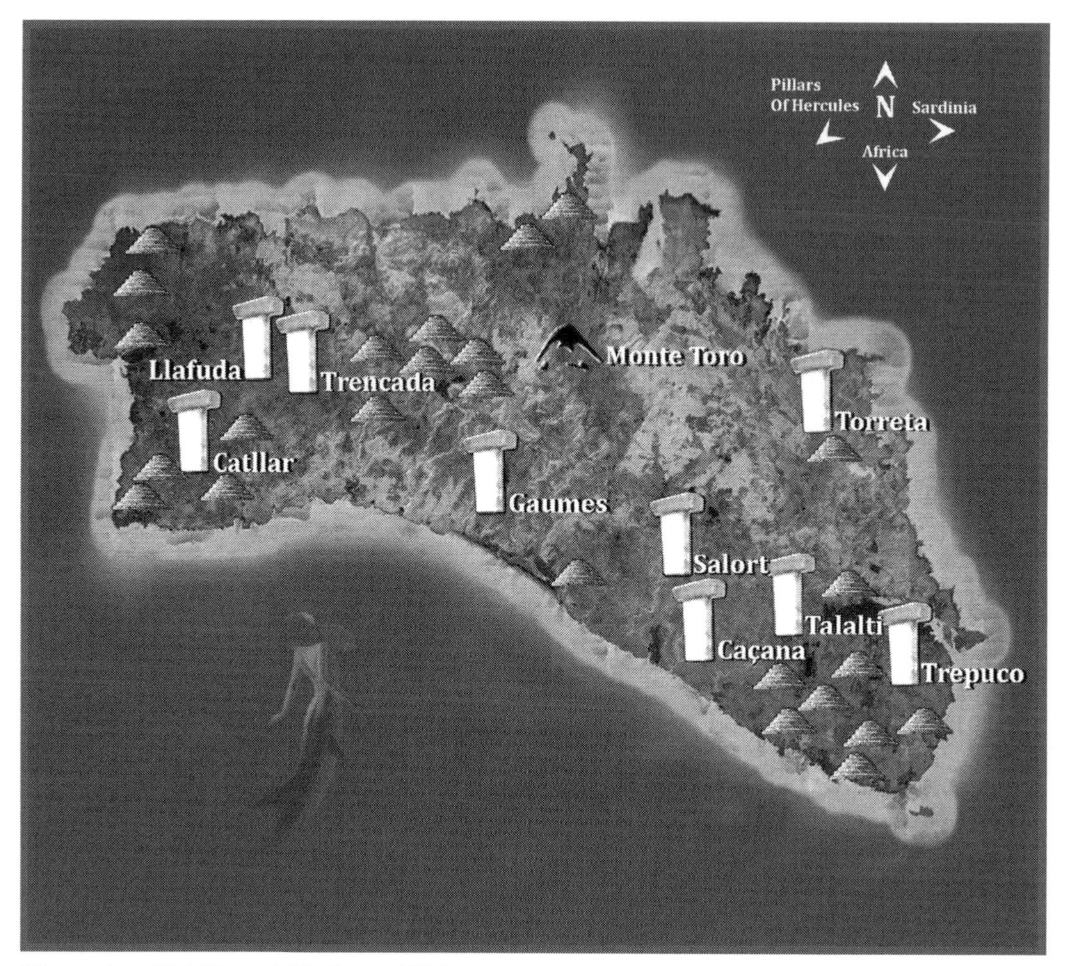

Illustration 12: Minorca's Taulas and Talayots

Turkey? They certainly look similar and are uniquely shaped among the world's megalithic structures. Thirteen sites featuring these signature T-shaped standing stones have so far been identified in Turkey; however, there are eleven enclosures exhibiting similar stones on the small island of Minorca, and a dozen more which are in a ruined state. Turkey's extraordinary sites are much older, being dated to at least 9500 BCE, making them the oldest known megalithic temples on Earth.[17] Although the great standing stones look identical, the environments of the two locations are very different, with Turkey's arid desert terrain as opposed to Minorca's more feminine setting, with each enclosure purposefully situated with an unobstructed view of Aphrodite's Sea.

But let's back up a little before we discover these enigmatic stones of Minorca. In the southern shrine at the base of the Paris Meridian, there are remains of numerous ancient cultures and their temples, spanning thousands of years. The Balearic Islands, which include Majorca, Minorca, Ibiza, and several smaller islands, were often a resting place for ships heading for Iberia, arriving from Phoenicia, Egypt, Greece, and the many island cultures of the Mediterranean. These islands have a colorful and fascinating past, with relics from the Near East, stone watchtowers, and numerous impressive megalithic structures that mark alignments with the stars. Both Minorca and its larger neighbor, Majorca, have evidence of human habitation for at least the last 9,000 to 10,000 years.[18]

Minorca is a small, rocky island only 30 miles (48 kilometers) long and about 10 miles (16 kilometers) wide, about one-fourth the size of Majorca. Yet Minorca has 1,574 inventoried archaeological sites concentrated in its small land base. So why does the smaller island have more than all the other Balearics put together? What was the mysterious "X-factor" that attracted ancient temple builders to Minorca? There is certainly more space available on Majorca. I began to look at any features that would give ancient arrivals the impression that "here is a sacred land worthy of our temples and worship."

Minorca has many unusual geological qualities that set it apart from the rest of the Balearic chain. This island has an abundance of quartz in the extremely ancient Paleozoic stone that is scarce on its sister island Majorca, and non-existent on Ibiza. The Paleozoic was a period between about 539 and 252 million years ago when dramatic geological and climatic changes occurred in what is often called the "Biological Big Bang," when many forms of life began to appear.[19] If we think of the unique property of quartz to retain memory, similar to the crystal component in a computer, what stories remain in Minorca's Paleozoic formations? The local Minorcans consider their stones to be living and sacred. Like the line in the poem above, "What mystic secrets of the Universe are crystalled in thy form!" And how is it possible that tiny Minorca received most of the ancient stone dating from this evolutionary leap, yet it mostly eluded the other islands?

It could have something to do with Minorca's unique drift away from the landmass along Spain's southern coast. According to one geological study, during the millions of years of the Earth's movements and rising sea levels, Minorca became like a lonely traveler, and drifted beyond its Balearic neighbors, settling at its ideal location to the east.[20] Another feature of the island is the fault that divides the northern and southern sections, which runs at the same angle as the Pyrenees range (WNW-ESE). As we have seen, faults can create electromagnetic anomalies, which attracted megalithic builders to the slopes of the Pyrenees. Additionally, there is an abundance of magnetic iron, which has prompted some to call the island "Red Minorca," adding magnetic effects and a visual allure as well as an association with sacred earth.

For arrivals to ancient Iberia, Minorca would have been the first landmass for ships coming from the Eastern Mediterranean, and its southern shore hosts a large port that could hold entire fleets of ships. Some ships would have carried pirates, smugglers, and potential conquerors, although Minorca's people had a unique method of defense. They were skilled slingshot warriors who could hit a target at a long distance and were hired by Carthaginian armies who overthrew the Greeks in Sicily in the 6th century BCE, with these same warriors participating later in the Punic Wars against Rome. The name of their island chain most likely derives from these "slingers," in the Greek word *Balears* meaning "to throw." The first-century BCE Greek historian Strabo describes Minorca and its peaceful inhabitants, who could also be fierce defenders of their island paradise:

"... owing to the great fertility of the country, these people have always had enemies plotting against them. Although naturally disposed to peace, they bear the reputation of being most excellent slingers, which art they have been proficient in since the time that the Phœnicians possessed the islands. [1000 BCE most likely] ... They were accustomed to go into battle naked, having a shield covered with goat-skin in their hand, and a javelin ... The long sling they use for hitting at far distances, the short one for near marks, and the middle one for those between. From childhood they were so thoroughly practiced in the use of slings, that bread was never distributed to the children till they had won it by the sling."[21]

Who were these clever people who settled this island? They were called the Talayotic, named for the numerous signature towers they constructed, from the Arabic *talaia*, meaning "watchtower." Where they came from is a subject of ongoing debate, with some experts saying they arrived from southern Gaul or northeastern Iberia, and others from some of the Mediterranean islands to the east, such as Sardinia, Malta, and Sicily, where similar towers were built. Whatever their origins, in about 2500–2300 BCE, the Talayotic culture arrived on the Balearic Islands and began extensive construction of megalithic monuments, including its 33 watchtowers. (The full count of talayots has been given as nearly 200.) These towers, which were constructed in tiered levels like a Mesopotamian ziggurat or an Egyptian stepped pyramid, formed a matrix across the island, where watchers could observe any approaching vessels. The towers also enabled the people to quickly send messages from one end of the island to the other with signal fires and mirrors in this clever communication network.

Additionally, the Talayotic people built burial chambers called Naviforms, which look like overturned ships, hypogea (underground temples)—some measuring 10–15 meters (30–36 feet) in length—and numerous dolmens. But most impressive are the T-shaped standing stones called *taula,* meaning "table" in Catalan. At least eleven remain standing, some reaching 5 meters (16.4 feet) high, and as mentioned, looking strangely similar to those found at Göbekli Tepi and Karahan Tepi, Turkey.[22] The taulas on Minorca are of a similar height to the Göbekli T-shaped stones, which measure up to 5.5 meters (18 feet) high.

Although Minorca's taulas are believed to have been constructed sometime during the 1st millennium BCE, much later than Göbekli Tepi, the similar shapes are intriguing, to say the least, and must be an echo of the earlier sites in Turkey. A researcher from Istanbul University, Mehmet Özdoğan, wrote that the people from Göbekli Tepi migrated westward, eventually bringing their culture to Spain circa 3000–2500 BCE.[23] There seems to be a universal significance in the T-shape, which appears in various regions across the world. We find the T shape symbolizing male organs, the horned bull, and fertility, a tradition found in Egypt, Crete, and throughout the Mediterranean. Certainly, the bull cult arrived in Spain and is evidenced in modern times with bullfighting and the well-known running of the bull rituals.

The T or Tau shape is also a symbol of the "Tree of Life," and for the Mayan and Aztec cultures it represented the source of all nourishment and growth, the creative force. The old Mayan word for tree is *te* and the Mayan and Aztec names for their creator gods are Teol and Teotl, respectively.[24] Was the Mesoamerican understanding of the T shape similar in the Taloyotic and Göbekli Tepi cultures? In the Egyptian language, we find the syllable *Ta,* meaning "Earth," as in the creator goddess Taweret, the hippopotamus deity, who is illustrated in the Egyptian zodiac as she stabilizes the northern axis of the sky. The letter T also designates a term to be feminine, as in the Egyptian words *neter* and *netert*, meaning "god" and "goddess," respectively.

Could these shared symbols, language, and cosmology from the far-distant Mayans and Egyptians have originated from a single culture and then spread out in all directions following the Flood? We don't know the answer, but we certainly find similar traditions and shared symbology emerging from isolated regions of the planet. The following is an explanation of the Aztec god Teotl as the essential generating force and movement of universal life energy embodied in the T symbol, from James Maffie of the University of Colorado:

> *"... continually active, actualized, and actualizing energy-in-motion... It is an ever-continuing process, like a flowing river... It continually and continuously generates and regenerates as well as permeates, encompasses, and shapes reality as part of an endless process. It creates the cosmos and all its contents from within itself as well as out of itself."*[25]

The Balearic Islands, mainland Spain, and Portugal saw the influence of migrations from areas such as Malta, Sardinia, Cyprus, Crete, and beyond, as we will continue to see. The presence of hypogea on Minorca may share a common tradition with the hypogea in Greece and Malta, such as the use of underground resonant chambers for oracles and ritual chanting. Archeoacoustics research carried out at Malta and other earthen chambers such as Newgrange, Ireland, found that in both these sites, there is a dominant resonance within the chambers of 110–111 hertz (cycles per second), which corresponds to an A tone in the octave of a male chanting voice.[26]

And, similar to other megalithic sites, Minorca's monuments are oriented to the stars, with each taula shrine built at locations where the southern horizon and sky were clearly visible. An interesting study on Minorca's taulas was published in a 1985 paper in the journal *Archaeoastronomy*, "The Talayotic Culture of Menorca: A First Reconnaissance," by Michael Hoskin, Cambridge University historian of astronomy.

The article discussed the research of German archaeologist Waldemar Fenn, who came to Minorca in the 1930s and spent much of his life researching the enigmatic taula enclosures, and eventually moved to the island. Hoskin wrote that Fenn believed he had discovered a ground plan in the stone monuments that mirrored the stars:

> *"Convinced that he was dealing with cultures with a developed interest in astronomy and the ability to represent the movements of the celestial bodies, he derived from the ruined taula precincts an idealized master ground-plan and interpreted this as a representation in stone of the movements of the heavenly bodies ..."*[27]

In reviewing the diagram created by Waldemar Fenn in the *Archaeoastronomy* paper, what caught my attention was the orientation of his compilation study of the eleven best-preserved Minorcan temples, which shows a north-south orientation. While a few of the enclosure entries faced south-southwest, most faced due south. The view the Talayot people would have seen from their taula precinct enclosure would have been the Southern Cross near the Centaurus Constellation.

Archaeologists from Minorca's Museum have proposed that the taula entry from the southern direction represents a portal to access the "north room ... an entrance to the sacred space."[28] The inner sanctum, the ceremonial area in the north of the taula enclosures, is one more example of the many sites on or near the Paris Meridian, with a similar northern orientation of the inner temple to the circumpolar stars, called the Imperishable Stars by the Egyptians. These are the stars that do not appear to set, and through the ages, have marked the northern axis orientation for temples around the world, the stellar destination in the afterlife journey of souls.

This important north-south orientation was in evidence not only at the taula sites on Minorca but also the similarly shaped megaliths at Göbekli Tepi, according to Andrew Collins in his groundbreaking study of that site. Collins indicates that the northern stars are a doorway to the realm of the gods and for human souls before incarnation as well as the place of return after death.

> *"The North was seen as the source of light and power, as well as the Primal Cause, which was eternal. From the North emanated the 'cosmic existences.' These were thought to manifest through the seven planets, which were seen as individual deities under the rule of the North."*[29]

Illustration 13: Minorcan Taula and the Southern Cross

For the people lighting fires, making offerings, and performing their ceremonies in the northern section of Minorca's taula enclosures, their view through the southern opening at night would have revealed the Southern Cross. Originally known by its Latin name Crux (cross), this constellation lies at the southern end of the Milky Way and would have been used for navigation. However, the visibility of its stars over the centuries varies according to the precessional drift of our view from Earth's Northern Hemisphere. Even when the Southern Cross is visible at Minorca's latitude, its lowest star most closely marking the Earth's southern axis (named a-Crucis, or Acrux) is only visible during May.

Cruz, or Cruces de Mayo is an ancient pagan festival that emerged out of this annual reappearance of the star Acrux, which is still celebrated on the 3rd of May in some areas of Spain. However, like many pagan traditions, it was absorbed into the Church and had a rebirth as Constantine's vision. When the Emperor was at war in 312 CE along the Danube, he had the vision of a great cross in the sky, and the words "*In hoc signo vinces*" ("With this sign, you shall conquer"). I am wondering how many celebrating the cross every year in May remember how this tradition began, with ancient people watching the southern night sky and the return of a special star in another eternal cosmic cross.

There were amazing discoveries of relics at the Minorca taulas, including a bronze bull, 6.69 inches (17 centimeters) long, which indicates bull worship at these temples, with its association with fertility, virility, and strength, common across the Mediterranean. Bull worship has been found in Minoan Crete, Egypt, Anatolia, and the veneration of bulls can be seen in Spain as early as circa 13,000 BCE in the cave art at Altamira. This must be why the island's highest hill, located in the geological center of Minorca, is called Monte Toro. On the summit of the hill is the sanctuary of Mare de Déu del Toro, Mother of God of the Bull, a perfect example of the assimilation of pagan traditions into Church iconography. In discussing the bull cult connection on Minorca with Andrew Collins, he said he believes the shape of the taulas represents the bull's cranium and horns. This association of the bull with fertility and life force is in keeping with the ancient meaning of the letter T mentioned above.

For me, the most notable and surprising discoveries were at Torre d'en Galmés (also spelled Gaumes) in 1974, during excavations by Guillem Rosselló Bordoy. Several items were found in the northern section of the taula sanctuary, the area used for rituals in the direction related to the sky gods of the afterlife: a small statue of the Egyptian god Imhotep, two bronze lancets, and a quadrangular stone that could have been used for mixing libations during rituals. Also found was the helmet of a warrior goddess figurine: an Iberian Amazon? The bronze Imhotep was 5.9 inches (15 centimeters) high, and it was made in Egypt. Is this the reason that well-known Egyptologist Margaret A. Murray came to the Balearics for archeological excavations in the early 1900s? Murray was a long-time student and assistant in Egypt to English archaeologist and Egyptology pioneer Flinders Petrie. In her *Egyptian Religious Poetry,* published in 1949, Murray says *I-em-hotep* means "Come in peace" or "Welcome" and that he was a great sage and magician who was deified.[30]

Imhotep was the chief architect for Pharaoh Djoser's stepped pyramid at Saqqara, built circa 2700 BCE and Egypt's first pyramid. He was also a high priest at Heliopolis, a physician, and the author of numerous texts on Egyptian wisdom and healing. As high priest, Imhotep was well aware that specific sounds produce magical effects, and as chief architect of Egypt's temples, he would have known how to produce healing, transforming acoustical effects in designing the pyramid as a burial chamber for Djoser. After visiting this pyramid numerous times, in 2022, I was finally allowed to play my harp in the heart of the structure, overlooking the pharaoh's tomb far below. The resonance took on a transcendent quality as I dedicated a spontaneous piece to the gods and to Imhotep.

> *"Received by the Harpist of the Gate, the Adept has entered by the virtue of music into the domain of spiritual festivals... And here is a magic whose fragrances liberate the initiated hero's soul from all the bonds accumulated by reason...*
>
> *By the irresistible force, rightly directed, of the harmonics of sound ... he can flatten the menace of Jericho's impregnable walls, or raise serenely, like Amphion with the sound of his lyre, the walls of Thebes whose stones came and placed themselves in rhythm and in meter, one on top of the other. By the science of the rhythm of the universe, he has become the equal of the Demiurge on the first day of creation."*
>
> JOSEPH-CHARLES-VICTOR MARDUS, ORIENTALIST AND POET,
> *LA TOUTE-PUISSANCE DE L'ADEPTE*[31]

Not only was the great Imhotep a master architect whose designs produced perfect temple harmonics and a temple priest of Ra, but Egyptologist Sir Alan Gardiner, in his "Egypt of the Pharaohs," mentions that Imhotep was identified with the Greek god and father of medicine, Asclepius.[32] And true to Imhotep's association with the god of medicine, the discovery of his statue at Minorca's taula enclosure also included the libations stone and two lancets, which look very much like surgical instruments. The bronze statue of Imhotep is typical of Egypt's late period of the seventh–sixth centuries BCE.

Imhotep, Metropolitan Museum, NY.

Was this taula enclosure being used as a temple of healing? Did someone with knowledge of funerary traditions dedicated to Imhotep arrive on Minorca carrying these votive objects used in Egypt's temples? There is a reference to Imhotep in an Egyptian funerary ritual from circa 1390 BCE in which the priest would traditionally offer libations and recite specific invocations to release the Ka of the deceased:

> *"The wab-priest may give offerings to your ka. The wab-priests may stretch to you their arms with libations on the soil, as it is done for Imhotep with the remains of the water bowl."*[33]

Is the Ca Ka?

Another possible connection between Majorca and Egypt is in the origin of the names. I have often pondered the meaning of the names Majorca and Minorca, which etymologically break down to *major ca* and *minor ca*. But what was the origin of the syllable *ca*? Did it relate to Ka, the Egyptian word for the etheric double of the Pharaoh? In the Catalan language spoken on these islands, the word *ca* means dog, not, as we will see, irrelevant for ancient travelers who navigated by the stars.

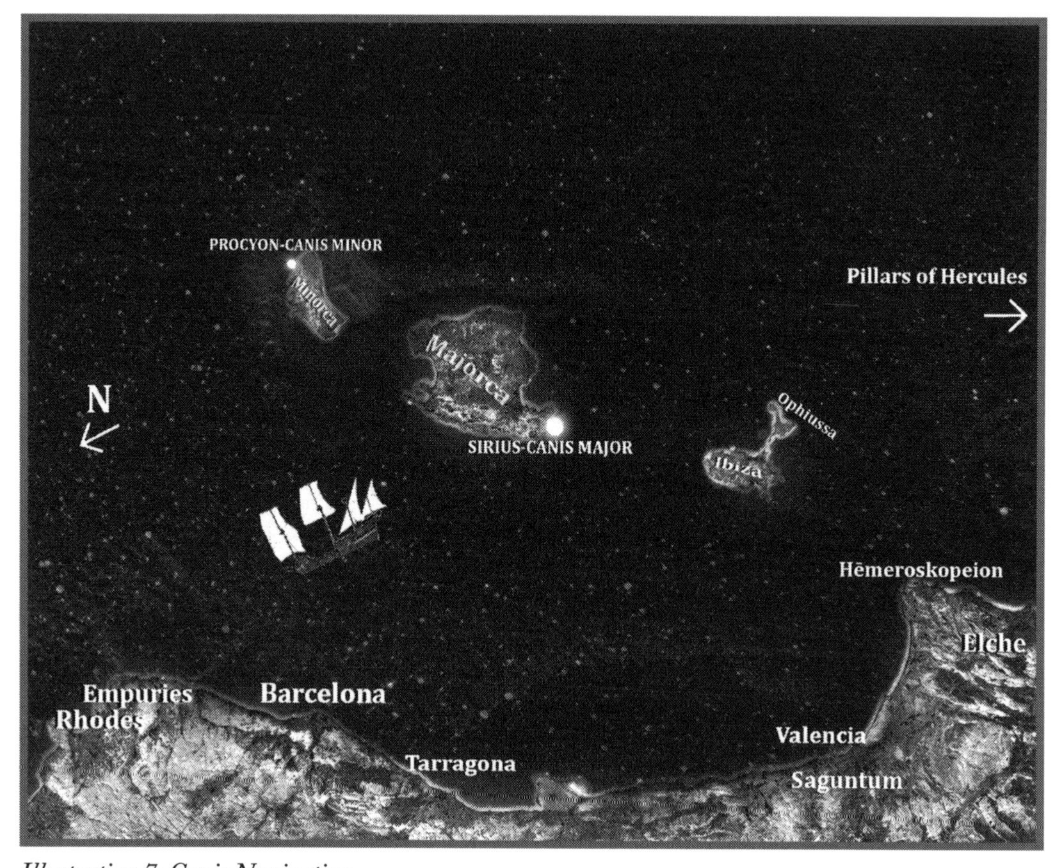

Illustration 7: Canis Navigation

For ships departing from Iberia's major trading ports of Empúries and Rhodes, or further south from Barcelona, during winter the relative positions of Majorca and the smaller island Minorca can be seen mirrored as the brightest star in the night sky, Sirius, and its neighbor Procyon. Sirius is in the constellation Canis Major, the Latin name meaning "Major Dog." This is why Sirius is often referred to as the "Dog Star." Procyon is the brightest star in the constellation Canis Minor, "Minor Dog." Hence, *major-ca* and *minor-ca*. In illustration 7, you can easily see how the two bright Dog Stars in their relative positions in the sky overlay perfectly on Majorca and Minorca.

The Goddess Isis was the protectress of mariners on the Mediterranean and her star is Sopdet, or Sothis (Sirius). For those whose lives depended on correct navigation across the sea, especially in winter, the magnitude of Sirius dominating the evening sky would have provided a guiding light from afar:

"Daughter of the Sun, with flame and fury
Flashing from the prow upon the foe;
Safely sails the Boat with thy protection
Passing scatheless where thy fires glow."

HYMN TO SEKHMET-BAST,
BOOK OF THE DEAD[34]

There is yet another possible source for the naming of the two islands based on ancient inscriptions recorded on the temple walls of Edfu, Egypt. Referred to as the "Edfu Building Texts," they tell of an ancient civilization from a time long before the building of the great temples along the Nile that we know today. According to British author Graham Hancock's *Magicians of the Gods*, these texts speak of a sacred island inhabited by prehistoric gods:

"... and these gods, it transpires, were not originally Egyptian, but lived on a sacred island, the 'Homeland of the Primeval Ones', in the midst of a great ocean."[35]

To paraphrase Hancock and the texts, long ago, a great flood inundated the sacred island and its people, and those who survived boarded ships and set out in several directions with the purpose of establishing civilizations in new worlds. In addition to the Edfu inscriptions, there is an Egyptian papyrus currently in Moscow that tells a strange account known as the *Tale of the Shipwrecked Sailor*.[36] In this story, a ship is engulfed in a huge wave, and there is but one survivor who washes ashore on an island filled with fruits and abundance of every kind. One day he is greeted by a dragon-serpent guardian who informs him that he has arrived at the sacred "Island of the Ka."

> *"Then I heard a thundering noise ... Uncovering my face, I found it was a snake that was coming. He was of thirty cubits (15 meters or 50 feet) ... His body was overlaid with gold; his eyebrows were of real lapis lazuli ..." [Then the serpent tells the sailor] "It is a god who has let you live and brought you to this Island of the Ka. There is nothing that is not upon it; it is full of good things ..."*[37]

Hancock continues in his review of the two sources and compares these tales with Plato's account of Atlantis. In *Timaeus*, Plato describes the Greek statesman Solon (circa 630–560 BCE) visiting Egypt, and his discussions with the temple priests. The priests tell Solon that the location of Atlantis was just beyond the Pillars of Hercules, and that the princes of Atlantis conquered many islands of the Mediterranean Sea.[38]

Did princes from Atlantis truly conquer islands in the Mediterranean? Was one of these the sacred island of Ka described in the *Tale of the Shipwrecked Sailor*? Could this have been "Major-ka" or "Minor-ka" in the Balearics, the first islands that ancient mariners, and possibly Atlantean refugees, found after passing the Pillars of Hercules (Straits of Gibraltar) from the Atlantic? Were Majorca and Minorca the islands referred to in the ancient texts of Egypt, telling of the lands of the ancient guardians and gods? Could the serpent guardian in the *Tale of the Shipwrecked Sailor* be remembered in the naming of Isla Dragonera, the island of the female dragon on the Atlantic-facing coast of Majorca? These are things that history may never be able to prove, but these legends live on in the psychic memory in stone, in the salty brine of the sea, and the dragon guardians who still watch from the invisible realms.

CHAPTER 5

Egyptians in Iberia

"... the close relationship of the early Iberians with the Afro-Semitic races ... included the Egyptian or Copt ... The language of the Iberians is lost, but enough of it remains on coins ... to prove that it had a common root with the Egyptian and the Saharan tongues ..."

HENRY SMITH WILLIAMS, *THE HISTORIANS' HISTORY OF THE WORLD*[1]

WE OFTEN THINK OF THE HISTORY OF VARIOUS COUNTRIES AND REGIONS OF THE world as having developed as separate, unique entities. However, in the Mediterranean, there was a high degree of acculturation. There has been active trade from one end of this sea to the other for at least the last four thousand years, and ancient Iberia was rich in resources, receiving visitors and cultural influences from Egypt, Phoenicia, Anatolia, Greece, Carthage, the islands of Sardinia, Malta, Cyprus, and Celtic tribes migrating from the northeast.

Many of these cultures sent trade ships to Iberia in search of its precious metals, mainly silver, tin, and iron, and most arrivals founded new communities and built temples to their gods and goddesses. Perhaps some of these explorations even ventured into the Atlantic, hoping to discover the fabled land of Atlantis. Later arrivals brought Romans, early Christian missionaries, Jewish refugees, Visigoths, and Moors. Each came with their religion, art, music, and knowledge, and these mutated over the thousands of years to emerge as the Iberian culture and ultimately the Spain we know today.

The Egyptians came to Iberia circa 2000 BCE, according to according to Cairo-born researcher Moustafa Gadalla in his book "*Egyptian Romany: The Essence of Hispania.*"[2] Gold was plentiful in Egypt, but they needed tin for the manufacture of bronze alloys for tools and weapons, and there was a well-known tin route on Iberia's western coast which Gadalla says was used by the Egyptians. There was another precious metal that the Egyptians did not have in their homeland, which was silver, and this was plentiful in Iberia. The combination of gold and silver produced electrum, which created a magical shining effect for the temple statues of the Egyptian gods and goddesses. The brilliance of electrum gave temple devotees the sense that their deities were alive and reanimated with their prayers and music of adoration.

The fifth century BCE Greek historian Herodotus in his epic *The Histories* tells us of the ships built by Egyptians and the great amounts of silver amassed by certain kings. Since Iberia was one of the best sources of silver, this seems to confirm early trade and excursions into the far West. In one story, a legendary Egyptian King Rhampsinitus (Rhampsinit) accumulated a great treasury filled with silver, and Herodotus relates that silver was a common import to Egypt.[3]

The following account from Herodotus tells of the Egyptian King Necho II (circa 610–594 BCE) hiring Phoenicians on a mission around Africa. Necho ruled from Sais, the ancient city in the Nile Delta, famous for its abundant trade and temples to the creation goddess Neith. On their return from the long journey, the king's ships sailed through the Pillars of Hercules and past Iberia, likely trading for silver and tin before heading back to Sais:

> *"... he [King Necho] sent Phoenicians in ships, instructing them to sail on their return voyage past the Pillars of Heracles until they came into the northern sea and so to Egypt. So the Phoenicians set out from the Red Sea and sailed the southern sea; whenever autumn came they would put in and plant the land in whatever part of Libya [term used for Africa] they had reached, and there await the harvest; then, having gathered the crop, they sailed on, so that after two years had passed, it was in the third that they rounded the pillars of Heracles and came to Egypt."*[4]

The Phoenicians had also established a metal trade with Iberia from at least 1100 BCE,[5] and likely traded these metals with Egypt, along with other countries. Spanish archeologist Benjamin Collado Hinarejos gives evidence for items from the Eastern Mediterranean coming to Iberia on Phoenician ships from the 14th century BCE, much earlier than the normally accepted dates. Hinarejos cites pottery fragments found at Cordoba and Granada that have been dated to 1300–1100 BCE.[6]

The Spanish archeologist also cites a much earlier account of Egyptian excursions under the Fifth Dynasty pharaoh Sahure (Sahu-Re), who reigned circa 2460 BCE, and who ordered forty ships of cedar from the Phoenicians.[7] Where were the Egyptians going besides south on the Red Sea to Punt? Most likely to Iberia for precious silver at a much earlier date than most documented evidence has revealed. Sahure was well known for his international trade, having some of the first seagoing ships in Egypt.[8]

Diodorus Siculus, the first century BCE Greek historian, claimed that Spain had so much silver that the clever Phoenicians made their anchors of this precious metal instead of the normal lead, which allowed them to carry more across the Mediterranean.

"... the Phoenicians, as they pursued their commercial enterprises ... purchased the silver [from the Iberians] in exchange for other wares of little if any worth. And this was the reason why the Phoenicians, as they transported this silver to Greece and Asia and to all other peoples, acquired great wealth."[9]

It has long been established that Phoenicia had a strong presence in Iberia, founding some of the earliest colonies, but who were the Phoenicians? Beginning in about 3200 BCE, Phoenicia began its evolution out of Mesopotamian, Syrian, Babylonian, and Egyptian influences from the constant invasions and ongoing trade with these cultures. Phoenicia's location along the eastern shores of the Mediterranean had always been enticing to its neighbors, and throughout the centuries, it was periodically ruled by either Egypt or Babylonia. The importance of linking Egypt's long history with Phoenicia is that when the Phoenicians settled in Iberia, circa 1000 BCE, they brought with them numerous Egyptian influences. The following story, found in various texts, illustrates an interesting connection between Isis and Phoenicia.

Isis Sails to Phoenicia

"Behold the excellent sistrum-bearer! ...
Behold me seeking for thee—I am searching for thee to behold thee!"[10]

The legends of Isis and Osiris say that after Seth tricked his brother Osiris into entering a wooden sarcophagus, the evil brother had the coffin sealed up and dropped into the Nile. After being pushed by the tides beyond Egypt, the coffin floated across the sea to Byblos on the coast of Phoenicia and landed on a wooded shore. After some time, a large and marvelous tree grew up around the coffin, and when the Phoenician king saw the beauty of the tree, he was enchanted and had it cut down and installed as a pillar to support the roof of his palace.

Isis was tipped off by Anubis regarding the whereabouts of the now-concealed coffin. As "Mistress of Mediterranean navigation," Isis was no stranger to the sea, and she immediately hopped on a ship to Byblos in search of the remains of her beloved. Unbeknownst to the king, Osiris was now holding up his domain—quite literally. Isis used her magic to connive her way into the palace and explained to the queen that her husband was boxed up within the palace's pillar. Using her feminine persuasion, the compassionate queen convinced her husband to cut down the pillar for the powerful Egyptian goddess.

Osiris' Ascension with Isis and Nephthys, Dendera.

Now in possession of the coffin, Isis sailed back to Egypt, where a magical and elaborate temple funerary ritual was enacted. One of the striking aspects of this was the ritual transformations of both Isis and her sister Nephthys into kites (a type of hawk). The association with birds can relate to shamanic journeys to the spirit world and accessing subtle dimensions. The two sisters beat their wings over the body of Osiris, and this powerful rushing sound, along with their magical incantations, conjured the crucial missing piece, the phallus of Osiris, whereby Isis could conceive Horus.

The Burden of Isis: Being The Laments of Isis and Nephthys, found in several papyrus texts, describes the two goddesses enchanting Osiris with their sistrums (rattles) and their words of power to come and receive the revivification and divine breath of life.

"Behold the excellent sistrum-bearer!—Come to thy temple! Lo I, thy sister, love thee—do not thou depart from me!"[11]

The shaking of the sistrum by temple priestesses was associated with reanimating the fecundity of the pharaoh or the god. When Isis and Nephthys stood on either side of the body of Osiris shaking their rattles with focused intention, powerful reverberations filled the temple chamber, altering the atmosphere. These sounds, along with their whispered invocations called *Hekau* (meaning "magical words"), conjured Osiris' missing member, and ultimately opened the path for him to ascend to the Imperishable Stars. The sounds of the chants, the beating of their wings, and the shaking of their sistrums would have created acoustical waves called *phonons,* which have antigravity properties, allowing matter to become more malleable. The *Egyptian Book of the Dead* describes Osiris also becoming a hawk in "The Chapter of Changing into a Hawk of Gold":

Sistrum Dendera Crypt.

"I fly, I alight (or, flutter in the air) like a hawk ... I have risen, I have gathered myself together like a beautiful golden hawk ... the Field of Offerings is before me."[12]

The myth of Isis' journey to the island of Byblos to retrieve Osiris not only tells us of the strength of her love, determination, and magical skills but is also an example of the influence of Egypt on the cultural development of Phoenicia and the historic ties between the two cultures. And this influence would be carried by the Phoenicians into Iberia. As we shall see in chapter 22, rituals featuring Isis and Nephthys would be incorporated into summer mystery plays in Spain blended with the Christian Marys. These ritual traditions inspired the song "Tears of Isis," and the cultural blending of Egyptian and Spanish flamenco styles is evident in the song. Further bridging of these two lands occurred when I played the piece at the ruined temple of Isis in Catalonia and in the temple of Dendera, Egypt, where this resurrection ritual is depicted in the wall reliefs.

"Tears of Isis Nephthys weeping,
Fill the Nile with love's lamenting,
Flame of Isis Nephthys burning
Fill the realm with love's returning—
Anointing the Earth with your tears,
Anointing the Sky,
Awaken Osiris with your love!

The beating of your wings,
Awakens your king—
Golden sistrum shaking,
Enchantments you bring—
Anointing the Earth with your song,
Anointing the Sky,
Awaken Osiris with your love!"[13]

Elissa Sails West with Priestesses of Astarte

The enchantments and song knowledge of Isis were well known in Phoenicia and across the Mediterranean. And the Babylonian knowledge of the stars contributed to the tradition of priestess-astrologers and oracles that arrived with the Phoenicians when they founded temples in North Africa and Iberia. In 814 or 813 BCE, Elissa (Elissar Dido),

Astarte, 7th c. BCE, Archeological Museum, Seville.

sister of the Phoenician king Pygmalion, fled to North Africa and founded Carthage,[14] called *Qart Hadath* in Phoenician, meaning "New Town." I will relate a short version of the epic according to known history.

In about 820 BCE, Matten, the king of Tyre, handed his kingdom to his son and daughter, Pygmalion and Elissa, with the son inheriting the crown. But when Elissa married the powerful and wealthy high priest of the temple of Melqart (Heracles), she gained a status equal to her brother, and a familial and political struggle ensued. We can see this same dynamic between the royal and religious sectors played out over and over, and true to the pattern, Pygmalion had his sister's husband assassinated. Elissa's life suddenly hung in the balance, and she secretly made her escape with her dowry and a portion of the temple treasury on a ship bound for Africa, which included some of the royal assistants, servants, and temple priests.[15]

Along the way, the ship stopped for supplies at Cyprus, and the priests kidnapped eighty priestesses of the temple of Astarte to establish a new temple in the land of Carthage. It's hard to imagine a kidnapping on such a grand scale, but so the story goes. Astarte is one of the oldest mother goddesses of the Middle East and is mentioned as early as 2300 BCE on Sumerian cylinder seals.[16] She is known as Asherah or Ashtoreth in the Bible, Attart, Ashaa, or Ishtar by the Hurrians, and Athtar-Venus by the Arabs. One myth says that following her marriage to El, the Semitic father of the gods, she threw her crown into the sky, which became the constellation Corona Borealis. And ever since, Astarte has been called "Queen of the Stars," and linked with Eastern astronomy and astrology:

> *"Astarte ruled all the spirits of the dead who lived in heaven wearing bodies of light, visible from earth as stars. Hence, she was known as Astroarche,* 'Queen of the Stars'"[17]

Elissa's story illustrates the arrival of the astrologer-oracle priestesses in the western Mediterranean, although given the earlier dating of Phoenician settlers in Iberia, these traditions may have already been established in the West. Punic religion favored their divine consorts, with Astarte and Melqart (Herakles), Tanit and Baal, being two of the most popular pairs, and images of Tanit have been discovered in Phoenician temples on the island of Ibiza. Additionally, Egyptian Bes, Bastet, Isis, Osiris, and Ra all made their way into Carthage and Iberia and their images found in temple ruins can be seen in Spain's museums. Let's look at Astarte's consort Herakles (Hercules), called Melquart by the Phoenicians, and his Egyptian roots before arriving in Iberia.

Hercules the Egyptian Comes to Iberia

Most have heard the Greek myth of the Twelve Labors of Hercules, and his wild escapades, in which he eventually crossed the Pyrenees into ancient Iberia. Hercules was reenacting the annual journey of the sun through the twelve signs of the zodiac during his twelve labors, progressing across the length of the Mediterranean into the place of the setting sun. These twelve labors were monumental tasks symbolizing the journey through the twelve archetypes of the zodiac and the evolutionary path of humanity. Spanish legends say that Hercules accomplished two or three of his labors on their terrain, which corresponds to place names on the Catalan coast, but more on this in later chapters.

Hercules in Bronze, Amiens, France, Saint-Germain-en-Laye Museum.

The hero's name is spelled variously as Hercules, Herakles, and Heracles, meaning "Glory of Hera," signifying that the power and might of this god was rooted in the Great Mother. According to Greek myth, the goddess Hera was the wife of Zeus and stepmother of Hercules. However, there is strong evidence that Heracles existed in Egypt long before the Greeks created their stories about the god. The Greek historian Strabo described the northern Egyptian city of Thônis-Herakleion in 450 BCE as located in the Canopus Branch of the Nile Delta with the temple of Herakles standing at the mouth of the Nile.[18] Herodotus visited the site and wrote in his *Histories,* that Heracles was first an Egyptian deity associated with the god Shu or Khonsu and was worshipped in Thônis-Heracleion now submerged off Egypt's northern coast.

> "... *it was not the Egyptians who took the name Heracles from the Greeks. The opposite is true: it was the Greeks who took it from the Egyptians—those Greeks, I mean who gave the name [Heracles] to the son of Amphitryon. There*

is plenty of evidence to prove the truth of this, in particular the fact that both parents of Heracles—Amphitryon and Alcmene—were of Egyptian origin."[19]

Historian William Smith (1870) writes that sources in addition to Herodotus and Diodorus agree that Hercules was an Egyptian god predating the Greek:

"Herodotus tells us that he made inquiries respecting Heracles: the Egyptian he found to be decidedly older than the Greek one; ... The Egyptian Heracles, who is mentioned by many other writers besides Herodotus and Diodorus, is said to have been called by his Egyptian name Som or Dsom ... This Egyptian Heracles was placed by the Egyptians in the second of the series of the evolutions of their gods."[20]

As well as the temple on the Nile Delta, temples dedicated to Heracles were at Herakleopolis Magna in Upper Egypt (in the south), and according to Gadalla, temples of Heracles were in use throughout the Pharaonic era. Hercules became a cult hero throughout the Mediterranean and had temples from one end to the other, from the Levant to the Atlantic. Legends recorded in numerous sources tell of Hercules arriving in the Pyrenees and receiving the hospitality of the Celtic King Bebryx. The king had a beautiful daughter, Princess Pyrene, and within no time, a fated tryst ensued, a love story known to all in this mountain region. But the oft-heard tale has a fresh and surprising twist and conclusion in chapter 8, "Pyrene and Pyrrha the Princess and the Queen."

After Hercules continued over the Pyrenees into the west across ancient Iberia, it is said that he came through the narrow mouth of the sea between Africa and Iberia, the Pillars of Hercules, now known as the Straits of Gibraltar. Legend says that he continued into the Atlantic and headed north to the site known as Cadiz (called Gadir by Phoenicians), just 50 miles (80 kilometers) north of the Pillars of Hercules. The legendary temple to the god was founded here, and it may have been discovered underwater in the Bay of Cadiz. The announcement on "*The Archaeologist*" website posted on the winter solstice, 2021, revealed that a monumental stone structure has been identified at the bottom of a channel in the bay:

"... finding the temple [of Hercules] has become something of a holy grail for historians and archeologists, who have been searching for it for centuries."[21]

In addition to the Egyptian god Hercules being in Spain, numerous artifacts have been found as evidence of Egyptian religious traditions migrating to the furthest western shores of the Mediterranean. This includes the small statue of the architect Imhotep on Minorca mentioned earlier, and numerous relics of the Egyptian deity Bes found at Ullastret, Roses, and other sites in Catalonia. (Bes is related to fertility, and he is often depicted playing a harp in Egyptian temple reliefs.) In later chapters, we will discover the spectacular temples of the Egyptian Isis and Serapis, founded on the coast of Catalonia by Alexandrian traders. Iberia comes alive in historic accounts and legends, revealing its importance to the cultures from the eastern end of the Mediterranean. Traders from Carthage, Egypt, Phoenicia, Greece, and Anatolia had arrived in the far western lands to forge a new and unique culture, and those arrivals may have included the daughter of Pharaoh Akhenaton!

Did Egypt's Royal Princess Come to Iberia?

There are amazing reports from several sources that a royal party, including the daughter of a pharaoh, departed Egypt and arrived in Iberia. Unrest and plague threatened the region, prompting the pharaoh to send the royal princess Scota to safety in the far distant land of the setting sun. The following quote from Walter Bower's *Scotichronicon* (*Scots Chronicle*) of 1447 describes her journey:

> *"In ancient times Scota the daughter of Pharaoh left Egypt with her husband Gayel by name, and a large following. For they had heard of the disasters which were going to come upon Egypt, and so through the instructions or oracular responses of the gods they fled from certain plagues that were to come. They took to the sea entrusting themselves to the guidance of their gods. After sailing in this way for many days over the seas with troubled minds, they finally were glad to put in at a certain [Iberian] shore ..."*[22]

Researchers have recently identified the pharaoh as Akhenaten, dating these events to circa 1320 BCE. If this is true, it would establish Egyptian royalty in the far west at an earlier date than archeologists have thus far documented. Egypt was in a period of radical unrest between the ancient traditions upheld by the temple priests and Akhenaten's new religion of the "One God."

Ralph Ellis writes in "*Scota, Egyptian Queen of the Scots*" of Akhenaten's daughter, her husband, and entourage fleeing the capital Amarna, and after many stops along the way arriving at the river Ebro, south of modern Barcelona, Spain. Here they discovered a rich alluvial soil similar to the Nile Delta and established a settlement they named Brigantia, where they lived, bore children, and prospered for several generations before their descendants finally continued north to Ireland. Ellis concludes that Scota's husband, named in the *Scotichronicon* as the Greek prince Gytheolos or Gayel, became Pharaoh Aye after his marriage to the Egyptian princess, who he identifies with Ankhesenamun.[23]

According to Ellis, the royal family arrived circa 1320 BCE, correlating the time of their flight from Egypt with a second Exodus, (the first being 250 years earlier with Moses). Ellis argues that the Ebro River was named for the Hebrew people, with Ebro and Hebrew phonetically alike. The other similar name, Hibernia, referred to both Ireland and Spain as the "Land of the Hebrews" or "Hibers," hence the name Iberia.[24]

Ellis again refers to the *Scotichronicon,* which says that the Egyptian settlers often sailed to the nearby Balearic Islands. They called these waters between Majorca and the mainland the Sea of Hibernia, which is now known as the Gulf of Valencia. Is this how the Egyptian relics arrived at Minorca? Numerous stone urns and vessels have been discovered in Spain featuring Egyptian hieroglyphic inscriptions. One vessel discovered at Puerto de Santa Maria on the north side of the Bay of Cadiz bears the inscription of a Theban priest. An alabaster burial pot found at Granada was inscribed with the name of Pharaoh Takelot II of the 22nd Dynasty (850–825 BCE), who ruled Middle and Upper Egypt. Another stone vessel was discovered in the region of Barbate, south of Cadiz and close to the Pillars of Hercules, with a hieroglyphic inscription around the top of the jar, but the deteriorated state has not allowed its translation.[25]

As we can see, there have been numerous Egyptian artifacts found on Spanish soil with an attribution to Egyptian royalty and its priesthood; I have only listed a few examples. We don't know if these items were trade items or brought to Iberia by Egyptian visitors such as Scota, and as an Egyptian princess, we can assume that she played the harp.

There is historical evidence that the lyre (an early form of harp) was known in western Iberia. A stele was discovered at Valpalmas, Spain (north of Zaragoza in Aragon), dated to about 700 BCE, which features a beautifully decorated lyre with fourteen strings, similar to the Egyptian harps that were in use during the 18th dynasty, and in Ur circa 2500 BCE.[26] In another discovery at a sepulcher at Murcia, a 4th century BCE terracotta portrays an enthroned queen or goddess playing a small harp.[27] Moustafa Gadalla claims that the Bronze Age people in Iberia (c. 2500–1200 BCE) created music with double pipes, tambourines, and lyre, much like instruments used in Egyptian temple music.[28] When Scota arrived in Iberia it is highly likely that she would have brought at least one harp, as this was an essential temple instrument.

During the Bronze Age, there was a strong cultural exchange across the Mediterranean world and into the northern isles, and instruments such as the harp, normally associated with the Egyptians, Sumerians, and Greeks (such as Apollo and Orpheus, who both played lyres) became known in the western lands. The working in bronze across the Mediterranean required tin and copper, and during the Bronze Age trade in these metals increased the exchange of ideas, culture, and traditions between the eastern Mediterranean cultures and sites with an abundance of tin in Iberia, Cornwall, and Ireland. The story from the *Scotichronicon* adds that after spending some time in "Hibernia" (Iberia), the descendants of Scota continued to the northern Hibernia, Ireland, and ultimately Scotland, which was named for the Egyptian princess.[29]

Goddess playing lyre, terracota, 4th–3rd c. BCE, Museo Arqueologico de Murcia.

Interestingly, an almost identical tale of the history of Princess Scota exists in Irish tradition, only this time her name was Princess Tea Tephi. Various accounts say that Tea was a "Princess of Zion," born of the House of David, and was the daughter of the last king of Judah, Zedekiah. She too had come from the eastern Mediterranean and had spent time in Egypt and Iberia before heading north to Ireland, arriving at the Hill of Tara (*Tea-Múr* in Irish).[30] The legend says that Tea brought precious relics from Jerusalem, including the famous harp of King David. These stories of princesses bearing harps may explain how the harp arrived in Iberia and the Northern Isles, and we will discover yet another version in the legends of Orpheus and his lyre coming to Spain's eastern Pyrenees in later chapters.

Suffice it to say, the evidence for ancient voyages from Egypt and the Near East to Iberia is documented by respected Greek historians, recorded in Scottish and Irish chronicles, and can be found in numerous legends. Many sense the colorful and rich cultural history of Iberia when visiting modern Spain and Catalonia, but few realize its Egyptian roots. Now we have set the stage for meeting many of the goddesses who arrived in the west from Egypt, Phoenicia, Anatolia, and Greece, and were honored in Iberia, the ruins of their temples remaining today. But first, I must relate an important dream concerning the lighting of a series of ritual fires, that would ultimately lead to the discovery of an ancient landscape cross over the Pyrenees.

Part II
The Four Fires and the Cross

CHAPTER 6

Four Fires Dream

"We light fire on the mountain—our breath stirs the air,
Our feet beat the rhythms of Earth's ancient prayer,
With cauldron of fire—Moon on the sea,
We dance for the old ones, we chant for Pyrene."

Ani Williams "Fire on the Mountain"[1]

It began with a dream. I had returned to the United States for a few months, but in the dream, I was back in Catalonia and gazing at the majestic snow-capped peaks of the eastern Pyrenees. The voice in the dream said, "Traditional fires have been lit on these peaks over the centuries to mark the season into summer. And you also must light four fires as part of your journey to meet the guardians of this land."

There was no indication of where these four fires should be lit, but it seemed that the quest to locate the sites would be an essential aspect of the story I would soon be writing. And through this process I would experience a deeper connection to the land, its history, and stories. The locations for each of the fires began to reveal themselves slowly and naturally during numerous journeys across the Pyrenees.

The first site that drew my attention was a 5500-year-old megalithic dolmen in northeastern Catalonia, where the Pyrenees range meets the Mediterranean Sea. The place felt alchemical, at the meeting point of the yang up-thrusting peaks of the Pyrenees, named for fire, and the yin, receptive salty waters of the sea. The power produced by this meeting of elemental forces infuses this region of the Pyrenees with vital energy.

Dolmen Creu d'en Cobertella.

The dolmen Creu d'en Cobertella (meaning "Covered Cross" in Catalan), is the largest such structure in all of Catalonia and is located above the town of Roses, ancient

Rhodes or Rodes, founded in the 7th–6th centuries BCE by the Greeks and Phocaeans (from what is now Turkey). A series of dolmens marks a path from the sea to the great Pyrenees range that divides modern-day France and Spain, which I would discover forms the eastern segment of an ancient pilgrimage path. As mentioned, a dolmen is basically a "stone house" constructed of vertical stones for the walls and usually a single roof stone. These stone slabs can be more than two or three meters long and most dolmens are large enough to enter by stooping low. Cobertella sits on a hill in view of both Mount Canigó and the Mediterranean. (Canigó is the Catalan spelling, which I will use since most of the journey is in Catalonia.) It is one of the many dolmens, menhirs, tombs, and huts located along the walking path called Ruta Megalithica (Megalithic Route) above the town of Roses.

I sensed that this path of ancient stone temples marking the landscape between the Mediterranean and the Pyrenees peaks was holding the entire region in balance, in a resonant coherent field. My friend Juan Saez, a Catalan Earth mysteries author, says the path of dolmens constructed along the slopes of the southern Pyrenees is an ancient initiation route. When the people interacted with the stone monuments, they became harmonious with nature and the subtle energies of each place, and as they journeyed from site to site they underwent a gradual transformation of consciousness. He said the life force emanating from each monument can extend for several kilometers. Juan says the following regarding the purpose of dolmens in his book *Lugares de Poder* (*Places of Power*):

> *"From the Neolithic times, the builders tried to stabilize the special moments of light, like solstices and equinoxes, in their works. These seasonal alignments define axes that create the energetic structure of the temple together with subterranean waters and faults."*[2]

This emanation of beneficial energy from the ancient megaliths can create what we could call a "Radiant Zone," especially when there is a concentration of dolmens and menhirs in one small area. We can often observe this radiant emanation affecting the biofield, creating more vibrant plant growth, more nesting birds and their accompanying songs, and a feeling of wellbeing for those who live in or visit the area. I have often observed this effect, and at Creu d'en Cobertella, we find abundant olive groves surrounding the dolmen, plants called "Ombligo de Venus" (Umbilicus, Navel of Venus), and the healing herb Yerba Santa, which I have often found growing at ancient ruins in the American Southwest.

This is a region that had been calling me to return again and again. I had already explored several of the other dolmens and standing stones located a short distance to the north on the same promontory called Cap de Creus (meaning "Cape or Head of the

Cross" in Catalan). This landmass juts into the Mediterranean, forming the easternmost point of mainland Spain, and the Cobertella dolmen lies on the southern edge. The repeated "cross" theme in the names of these two sites was the first clue regarding the importance of a cross pattern in the region. But what cross and what did it signify? The mystery would be revealed during the process of lighting the four fires.

I rented a room overlooking the sea in Roses and headed to the local tourist office to stock up on maps. They had several that showed the network of paths connecting the megalithic monuments, which include dozens of dolmens and menhirs. Heading up the winding road bordered to the north by sheer granite walls, I found the small parking area and made the short climb up to Cobertella. It was winter solstice and late afternoon, just before sunset, with the western golden light illuminating the dolmen. I stood transfixed, feeling as if I was meeting an old friend. Having a strong feeling for a pile of stones may sound strange, but those of you out there who have been on the Earth mysteries trail will understand.

Using my compass, I noted that the structure is aligned due north and south, with the entry facing south. I stood outside the enclosure and connected with the site and its guardians, asking for permission before entering the dark chamber. But an important warning about entering: The site is fenced off to protect the historic landmark, and people who might enter, as the stones forming the roof are extremely heavy and could become dislodged. It is possible to connect with a site without entering, by simply projecting one's attention and sensing the response. However, on this occasion, it was important to enter the dolmen to discover something unexpected.

The inside of the eastern wall is inscribed with six distinct deep cup marks, with a less distinct seventh indent above forming a pyramid, the symbol for fire. The shape points heavenward and can indicate celestial star or solar alignments, or features on the land, like a map, providing ancient people with important locations or alignments for their ritual calendar. I offered prayers to the guardians of the site and the six directions, east, south, west, north, above, and below. I lit a candle, asking for this light and the solstice Sun to illuminate the hearts of all beings. After completing the prayers and offering a song, I noticed that a sliver of light had appeared through a narrow opening between the stones to the southwest, pointing at the lowest of the cup marks. The "Sun Dagger" slowly moved upward to point at the uppermost cup mark at the exact moment of the winter solstice sunset. A few minutes later, another dagger formed on the northern

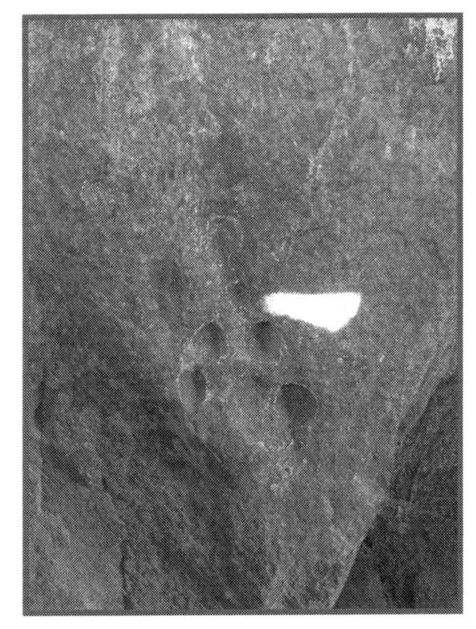

Sun Dagger December 21, 2022.

wall, pointing to a brilliant, winged sun bird in the northeastern corner, to the left of the cupules dagger, creating three light effects!

This was extraordinary, and to my knowledge, no one has noted this Catalan "Sun Dagger" phenomenon at Creu d'en Cobertella. This effect also occurs at numerous sites in the American Southwest, where a similar sliver of light illuminates special petroglyphs on the summer and winter solstice. Petroglyphs are images etched in stone, and some sites also include pictographs, which are painted images. One site is at Fajada Butte in Chaco Canyon, New Mexico, where a summer solstice Sun Dagger was discovered in 1977 by artist Anna Sofaer. Through her repeated visits, photographing and sketching the shapes created by the Sun, she discovered the site was marking the summer and winter solstices as well as the equinoxes. Interestingly the Catalan and Chaco Sun Daggers were both discovered by curious female artists, and not archeologists.

Another Sun Dagger solstice marker occurs in the American Southwest at Crane Petroglyph Heritage Site in the Verde Valley near Sedona, Arizona. (The site was previously known as V Bar V Ranch). The extensive petroglyph panels are located within the heart of a large concentration of archeological ruins established circa 800 CE by the Sinagua, ancestors of the Hopi tribe. The nearby Sacred Mountain is a hilltop settlement with a ballcourt similar to those found at Mayan sites to the south. Red Tank Draw, perhaps two miles (three kilometers) to the west, contains some of Arizona's most prolific rock art. And Montezuma's Well and Montezuma's Castle, both with impressive cliff-hanging settlements, are a few miles to the south.

Sun Bird NE corner.

I have witnessed the Sun Dagger at the Crane Heritage site several times on the winter solstice. Moments before the exact solstice, a dagger of sunlight begins to move across a petroglyph panel that is covered with symbolic images. At the exact moment of the solstice, the Dagger points to the center of a petroglyph of concentric circles representing the center of the sun, the solstice moment, the turning point of the seasons. The Hopi, Zuni, Yavapai, and other tribes used these solar markers as a calendar for their planting and ritual cycles. Some of the rock art images in Arizona and New Mexico are 12,000 years old, although each succeeding age of habitation added its layer of markings. These can be symbols for the Sun, Moon, stars, waterways, springs, animals, reptiles, deities, humans, and even beings from other dimensions.

The dolmens in Catalonia are often oriented north-south and mark all four cardinal points and the solstices and equinoxes (meaning equal night, when day and night are of equal length). The temple builders were dedicated Earth keepers and sky watchers, who knew the value of creating a harmonious grid across the landscape to maintain the well-being of all species in the region. Some of these monuments are energetically dormant, or sleeping, but most are still creating energy fields of varying degrees, communicating with the elements, mountains, and stars. The indigenous people believe that certain stones are singing or speaking with other stones and mountains in the region, maintaining the resonant field.

Petroglyphs Red Tank Draw, Arizona.

The inscribed cup marks at Creu d'en Cobertella and nearby dolmens may also be emanating waves of energy that form part of this communication. Cup marks appear around the world, and researchers in Britain have mapped a network of cup mark sites across the landscape. David Cowan and Chris Arnold write in *Ley Lines* and *Earth Energies:*

> *"The [cup mark] carvings are ... a pattern of telluric or Earth energies, with the petroglyphs transmitting telluric energy between standing stones, stone circles, burial-grounds ... in an astonishingly highly evolved manner."*[3]

Cowan and Arnold did extensive dowsing of both straight ley lines and cup mark paths in Britain and discovered the cup mark paths often follow both underground water flows and the contours of rivers, indicating a more yin or female path:

> *"The energy emitted from the cup-marked stone in the Sma' Glen follows the contours of hills and valleys. It does not travel over the hills as straight leys do and has similarities to the Chinese ch'i, which flows along the 'dragon paths' ..."*[4]

Similar to the Sun Daggers and cup marks at Cobertella, researcher Ronald Morris, author of *The Prehistoric Rock Art of Galloway and the Isle of Man,*[5] has confirmed that cup marks on stones in Britain indicate astronomical alignments and can even show the location of nearby copper and gold mines. Cup marks have been found to emit waves of positive energy that affect the environment and mark astronomical and seasonal alignments, such as at Cobertella on winter solstice. Cup marks form a network of energy lines connecting mineral and water sources and other megalithic stones in the region.

The First Fire had been lit at winter solstice at dolmen Creu d'en Cobertella, the covered cross, and upon reflection, this was the perfect site and timing. Not only was the location overlooking the Mediterranean Sea near the easternmost point of Spain, but this dolmen is in view of Mount Canigó, the most sacred mountain for the people of Catalonia. We shall also discover in future visits that Cobertella marks a northern axis alignment to the Pole Star, which at the time of the dolmen's construction, would have been Alpha Draconis (Thuben) in the constellation Draco the Dragon. Winter solstice is the time of light inception, the beginning of a new solar year, and the return of increasing light. It was a good beginning for the mission of lighting four sacred fires.

The Medallion

"Crux Sancta Sit Mihi Lux—May the Holy Cross be a Light for Me"

English translation of the letters C.S.S.M.L., Latin inscription on the vertical line of the medallion cross of Saint Benedict

During the years of journeying and discovering the extraordinary history and sites on both sides of the Pyrenees, I was often wearing a silver medallion bearing an equal-armed cross. Little did I realize at the time, that this cross would become a guiding symbol, helping to reveal the locations for the remaining sacred fires. I mentioned the piece briefly earlier, with its striking Grail serpent image. I found the medallion in a small open market in Coyoacan, Mexico, or I should say, it found me. *Coyoacan* is a Nahuatl (Aztec) word meaning "Place of many Coyotes." Indigenous traditions of the Americas see the coyote as a trickster, and it felt as if the magic of old coyote was at work.

As I walked past the gift shop, a silver disc reflected the late afternoon sunlight, dazzling brightly like a mirror. It drew me closer, and I was intrigued by the strange symbols around the cross, which appeared to be a coded message, indicating something magical. My concert tour sponsor saw my enchantment with the medallion and bought it as a gift, which made it more meaningful. The piece was the ancient amulet of Saint Benedict.

This traditional medallion has a remarkable history and is known to offer protection to the wearer. As mentioned earlier, on one side, it is inscribed with symbols set into an equal-armed cross within a circle, like the Celtic cross, a common symbol found on ancient rock art in France and Spain. As mentioned in the quote at the beginning of this chapter, the vertical line of the cross is inscribed with five letters, C. S. S. M. L., standing for *Crux Sancta Sit Mihi Lux*, Latin for, "May the Holy Cross be a Light for Me." But on the medallion, it is not the traditional crucifixion cross that is indicated as holy, but the equal-armed version used by Cathars, Templars, and ancient pre-Christian cultures across the world.

Saint Benedict Medallion Cross.

The horizontal line of the cross is also inscribed with five letters, N. D. S. M. D., standing for *Non Draco Sit Mihi Dux*, Latin for "Let not the Dragon be my Guide." As mentioned in the introduction, this mantra did not at all match my journey along the Dragon Path, hence I removed the "Non" from my intention. As you can see on the version used on this book's cover, "Non" has magically disappeared. Although I understood the Church's intention and their association of the dragon with the "devil," my work was focused on the elemental and benevolent dragon energies and guardians in the Pyrenean lands. Hence, my motto became: *Draco Sit Mihi Dux*, "Let the Dragon be my Guide."

On the opposite side of the medallion, a heavily bearded Saint Benedict is standing surrounded with rays of light, spiritual fire, and holding the same equal-armed cross in his right hand and an open book in the other. An open book normally symbolizes exoteric knowledge, and in this case, it is the well-known Benedictine Rule which became a foundation for Christianity, still followed today.

Saint Benedict Medallion.

Benedict was born in Nurcia, Rome, in 480 CE, along with his twin sister Scholastica, who left an important legacy for the education of women in the Benedictine orders worldwide. The twins were born of noble parents, and both received an advanced level of education. Before founding his monastic order, Benedict found life in the heart of Rome's intrigue too decadent for his taste, and he chose to live as a hermit in a cave outside of the city. He is reported to have had healing gifts and extraordinary powers, and there are accounts that he practiced alchemy and magic. Pope Gregory the Great (circa 540–604 CE) mentions Benedict's ability to perform miracles, such as making broken things whole, causing a new spring to flow from rocks, and raising a young boy from death.[6]

Inscribed on the medallion to Benedict's left (left being the feminine, intuitive side) is a crow, often associated with shamanic realms and magic. Below his right hand is a chalice containing a serpent, an image normally associated with Saint John the

Evangelist. One can see numerous portrayals of Saint John with the chalice and serpent in paintings and sculptures in churches throughout the world, occasionally with the serpent depicted as a winged dragon. The story given by the Church for both Saint John and Saint Benedict is similar, that they both banished the serpent symbolizing Satan's poison.

Yet, the esoteric and pre-Christian meaning of the "Serpent Grail" symbolizes wisdom, medicine, regeneration, and the resurrection mysteries. Indeed, the Serpent-Bearer constellation known as Ophiuchus is said to be the ascended body of the wise god of medicine Asclepius. Greek myth says that Zeus became jealous of Asclepius' power in healing and resurrecting the dead, so the god sent a thunderbolt to make an end of him. But Asclepius continued his healing ministrations from the heavens as Ophiuchus, who protects one against poison. That certainly contradicts the Church's later overlay that the serpent *is* the poison, and we know that snake venom can also be used for healing. In ancient cultures and Gnostic tradition, the Serpent-Bearer is the wisdom and knowledge required for healing and regeneration, like the snake that is renewed by shedding its skin. The chalice containing the serpent associated with both Saint Benedict and Saint John the Evangelist indicated that they both carried this gift of wisdom and healing.

And is it a coincidence that three of the figures on Saint Benedict's medallion also appear in the heavens in the constellation Hydra? In this group of stars, we find the images of Corvus (crow), Crater (cup or chalice), and Hydra (serpent). These three symbols in Hydra provide a clue, perhaps not perceived by many, that Saint Benedict was privy to Hermetic knowledge and its motto that harmony in the heavens reflected on Earth, is the key and the law of nature: "*As above, so it is below. That which has been, will return again. As in heaven, so on earth.*"[7]

CHAPTER 7

Search for the Second Fire Site

"Mary briefly soundeth forth
Strange things like Thunder round the Earth...
Mary the Light of dew...Pluto's daughter...
Joyned with three seeds she does aspire
To be exalted in the Fire."

Mary the Prophetess on becoming gold, '*The Dialogue of Mary and Aros on the Magister of Hermes*,' 1st century CE

Saint Benedict's Cross medallion had become my guiding symbol for the locations for lighting the sacred fires. As I studied the maps, it became clear that the four fires were to mark the ends of an equal-armed cross, N-S-E-W. The first fire site at dolmen Creu d'en Cobertella, the Covered Cross, marked the winter solstice sunset with a Sun Dagger and is located at latitude 42°N15'25". I checked on Google Earth to calculate the distance from Cobertella on the Mediterranean westward to the Paris Meridian, and it was 44.31 miles (71.31 kilometers). Using the meridian as the central axis seemed logical for the north-south foundation of the landscape cross, especially, as it formed the Dragon Path that began my quest. Little did I know at that time, but the number of sites dedicated to Maria Magdalena and ancient megalithic sites located on the meridian far surpasses the realm of chance. I recalled Henry Lincoln saying many times that the Paris Meridian was a cromlech (megalithic stones) intersection marker from ancient times. The center point of the cross on the meridian appeared to be in the southern foothills of the Pyrenees, but it would require a future exploration to discover the extraordinary and perfect site that was hiding in those hills, holding the heart at the center. This will be revealed in its extraordinary detail in future chapters.

Since I would be heading south to Barcelona soon to explore the possible site for the Second Fire, I measured 44.31 miles south along the Paris Meridian from where it was crossed by the east-west latitude line from the dolmen. Just over one mile short of the 44.31-mile point (42.73 miles, 68.77 kilometers), and located on the meridian, is a site called Cardedeu. Continuing about three miles (five kilometers) south of Cardedeu on the same axis, there is a large concentration of megalithic monuments, including

Cardedeu Wayside Cross.

dolmens, menhirs, and stones marked with equal-armed crosses. An obvious pattern began to emerge, with the eastern and southern arms of the cross marked with not just one, but multiple dolmens, menhirs, and megalithic sanctuaries!

The town of Cardedeu marks the Paris Meridian with a very unusual wayside cross inscribed with multiple carved equal-armed crosses. Cardedeu was a medieval village, dating according to historical records to 941 CE, but surrounded by much earlier Iberian and megalithic sites going back thousands of years. It is close to the Mediterranean and just northeast of Barcelona. The cross at Cardedeu is called "Creu de Terme a Cardedeu." *Creu de Terme* is a Catalan term meaning "a wayside cross marking an ancient track," often the intersection of three trackways. This is an ancient tradition and one can find these wayside crosses throughout Europe. However, this cross marks not only the intersection of three roads but also, more importantly, the Paris Meridian.

Creu de Terme is a stone pillar, perhaps 4 meters (about 13 feet) high, with a serpentine spiraling column and an equal-armed stone cross at the top. The serpentine design fit well with the Dragon Path theme that was evolving. The marker was built in the 17th century, just when the Paris Observatory was beginning to measure the Paris Meridian in the north of France. The scientists from Paris would not be mapping the southern end of the meridian in Catalonia until 1823–1825, supervised by François Arago. This tells us that the meridian cross is marking a more ancient track that was already established on the Dragon Path. This is also indicated by the series of megalithic sites marking this same north-south axis less than three miles (five kilometers) to the south.

Cathar tombstone, Maison Déodat Roché Museum, Arques, France.

There are strange symbols carved in the square base of Creu de Terme, including a large diamond encasing an equal-armed cross. This symbol is identical with a Cathar tombstone that I had photographed in the Maison Déodat Roché museum in Arques, France, and most likely indicates the strong Cathar presence

Cardedeu Base.

that was in Catalonia. Wayside markers are part of an ancient mapping system, and the engraved symbols record more of the story of the region. When the Romans entered the Iberian Peninsula circa 220 BCE, they marked the measure of roads with stone pillars called milestones. (The Roman mile was 1000 paces, each pace being about five feet, so about 5000 feet or 1500 meters.) These roads were often tracks already established by the Celts, Iberians, and various other Mediterranean cultures who had come to establish trade, including Egyptians, Greeks, Phoenicians, Carthaginians, and most likely used by earlier Neolithic builders. Let's look at the meaning of Cardedeu and meet Goddess Cardea, guardian of meridians, hinges, and doorways.

Axis of Goddess Cardea

The name Cardedeu is most likely a Roman term, with *Cardo* a Latin word meaning a north-south meridian or axis. The word *Deu* in Latin means God, hence, "Meridian of God," or perhaps, "Axis of the Goddess." The numerous sanctuaries dedicated to Magdalena that I would discover located along this meridian indicated a female Dragon Path, in addition to the southern end being at Isla Dragonera, Majorca, "Island of the Dragoness."

Cardo, in its meaning of hinge, can indicate a key or cardinal point marker, such as those used in delineating the equinox Sun's rising and setting points. The ancient people often oriented their settlements and temples to the cardinal directions, east-west or north-south. The Greeks and later Romans who came to this region also based the layout of their settlements and temples on a cross or wheel formed by north-south longitudinal lines (*cardos*) and east-west latitudes (*decumanus*). Designing our cities, homes, and temples to align with the celestial axis and solar movements enhances the harmonious resonant field, precipitating health, prosperity, and a feeling of connection with the natural rhythms of time and space.

The name of the town Cardedeu could also be an old association with the goddess Cardea. She is the Greco-Roman goddess of the hinge; in other words, she is a gatekeeper and guardian of doorways. Robert Graves wrote of Cardea in his insightful books on the Greek myths and goddesses during his many years living on Majorca, which is no accident, given he was at the southern end of the Paris Meridian's north-south axis. Graves says that she is the White Goddess of the hinge, on which the world swung on its polar axis:

"The White Goddess Cardea was in charge of the four cardinal winds; mythologically the most important was the North Wind at the back of which she had her starry castle, close to the polar hinge of the Universe."[1]

Since the wayside cross of Cardedeu marks the north-south meridian, we can follow this axis north to the circumpolar stars, Cardea's starry castle. There is another association with the goddess Cardea and the millstone or grinding stone of the universe. The name of the town next to Cardedeu is Granollers, from the Latin word *Granullaria*, meaning "grain or grain sellers." We can find the goddess of grain and her task of grinding to create sustenance and life in almost every world culture. One example mentioned previously is Black Stone Woman, called Pukmukwana, in the Yavapai Apache tradition of the American southwest. In the Yavapai language, *puk* means "Black Stone," which was considered magical and created good luck. *Mukwana* means "to grind," as on a metate, a traditional grinding stone. These stones were often volcanic and dark gray or black, with a deeply textured surface perfect for grinding.

In the Yavapai creation story, Pukmukwana ground round and round, and with her magical speech and song, and her grinding, she created First Woman, Komwidapokuwia. First Woman sang for all beings, and wherever she sang, everything around her changed and became filled with light:

"She came out and sang like this: 'My talking and singing are life. I bring it out [speak] for spiritual life all over the world.' ... [a] cross she made on each shoulder four times like burning fire. That fire reached up from her shoulders to heaven like lightning ... Her words went forth like lightning and the heavens were illuminated in the four directions... Then she said, ... 'I am the one who understands everything.'"[2]

This creation story from the Yavapai-Apache contains many of the basic elements that are important in this story and would be one of many times that the indigenous traditions of the Americas corresponded with Pyrenean traditions. In the Yavapai legend, Komwidapokuwia made a cross four times that was like burning fire that reached to heaven. Her rituals and songs illuminated the sky to the four directions—and I began to realize that I was reenacting an ancient tradition. The clues were confirming the importance of a cross reaching over the Pyrenees, which would be discovered through the long journey of lighting the four fires.

Cardedeu's wayside cross had revealed one more guardian of the Dragon Path in Cardea, goddess of the hinge, gateways, and the starry castle at the northern axis. There is a universality in the stories and the ways that the creative feminine matrix works. The late Marija Gimbutas makes a reference to the Axis Mundi turning to the song of the Great Mother as she weaves creation, in her classic book, *"The Language of the Goddess,"* referring to a section from Plato's *Republic*:

> *"In the tale of Er, the concentric spheres of the heavens turn around a spindle, like a vast spindle whorl. Each sphere is associated with a siren (Bird Goddess), who sings its particular note creating the Music of the Spheres."*[3]

It is wonderful to imagine the universe and all the celestial spheres, including the Earth, turning to the tunes of women with wings. At times during walks in remote canyons, in my mind's eye I would glimpse grandmothers sitting in a circle, in some subtle realm, continuing to grind round and round, conjuring creation with magical black stones. The old creation stories are metaphors, and we can see them mirrored in space in the black holes, spinning and not only absorbing galaxies but birthing new star systems. And do these creation mothers with outstretched wings continue to turn around the center in a great celestial dance, singing as they turn? In the end, it is up to us to re-enact these timeless traditions.

Neolithic Mother Goddess from Sardinia.

In *"Language of the Goddess,"* Gimbutas features several female figures whose bodies are forming a cross, dating from 5000–3000 BCE, and she comments that the cross or X shape represents inherent regenerative energy.[4] We can also imagine these goddesses forming the cross as celestial sirens, with their arms becoming wings. The image above of Dea Madre is dated to circa 4500 BCE and was discovered at Senorbi, Sardinia.[5]

The Cross as Sacred Unity

The equal-armed cross is a symbol of perfect equilibrium and life in balance and can be found in every world culture. An entire book could be written just on its multidimensional symbology. For the Druids and other ancient cultures this cross was the key to the science of the universe and can be a reference to the four directions, the four winds of the gods, and the four elements. It is also a calendar wheel, marking the cardinal points of the year and the greater cycles in the turning of the heavens, termed a "Medicine Wheel" by indigenous Americans. It is a reminder for each of us to live in balance on the Earth, and to move from our own center so that our actions reflect and maintain that balance. This cross would become a repeated theme on the journey of the Four Fires. These crosses can be found etched in stone monuments built more than five thousand years ago, and I would ultimately discover that they appear at each end of the four arms of the Great Cross that was being revealed across the Pyrenees. They also appear in the shapes of medieval fortified castles, in church windows, and in the names of the sites that mark the landscape cross. It was considered holy and the chosen symbol for, the Celts, megalithic builders, and later Templars and Cathars. What are these crosses telling us, and what do they symbolize? The following is one example.

My ex-husband and British Earth mysteries writer Nicholas Mann and I would often discuss our dreams and their possible meanings during morning tea. One morning, Nicholas described what he felt was a significant soul remembering. In the dream he was a temple builder in an ancient land in North Africa, perhaps early Egypt. He was inscribing a symbol on a stone wall, an equal-armed cross within a circle. As he was carving the symbol, he sensed it would be important in the future, so that he and others would always remember the ancient knowledge it symbolized.

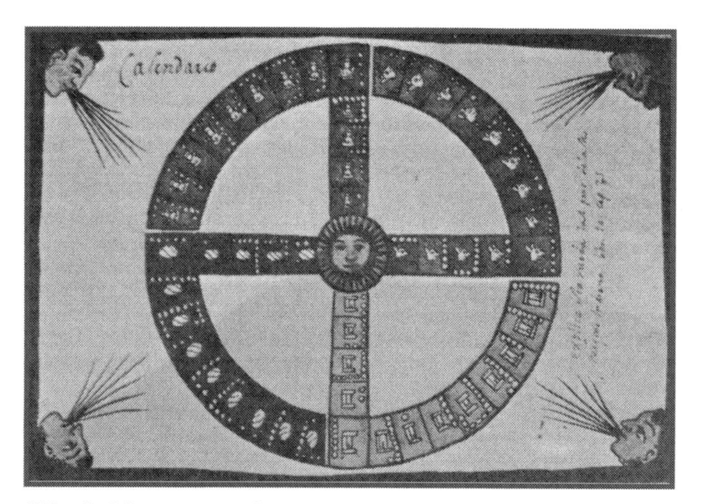

Wheel of Space-time, Aztec 52-year calendar, Tovar Manuscript, Archaeoastronomy Journal, Vol. VI, January-December, 1983.

But what was this knowledge? There were numerous sites in Catalonia that had used the wheel or cross within the circle. We can find a variation of this symbol in the Chacana cross found in Peru, near Lake Titicaca and the Bolivian border, and its symbolism gives some good insights into the dynamics of the equal-armed cross. The Chacana is made up of 9 cubes, with one additional cube at each of the four sides, making the thirteen cubes of the cross. Incan tradition says this cross represents the four directions, *Tawantinsuyu,* a Quechua term meaning "Realm of the Four Parts." The center is an open hole, which the local people claim is a portal to other dimensions, a doorway to travel through time and space.

We can imagine that the center of this cross is the center of our own awareness, and from this still point, we can travel forward and backward in time. The word *chacana* is derived from the Quechua word *chaka*, meaning "to bridge" or "to cross over." This magical, shamanic view of the equal-armed cross is a portion of the great body of natural science used by megalithic builders to create a magical living landscape aligned with the Earth and cosmos. As we have seen, many of the cities, temples, and megalithic sites in Catalonia were aligned to the four cardinal points. And these master builders knew the correct placement of their monuments as markers at places of power, placements that allowed the song of the stars to resonate and amplify the subtle energy of the stones throughout the dragon paths.

It was time to light the Second Fire at the southern gate of the Great Cross at the Creu de Terme wayside cross at Cardedeu. Silently connecting with the Dragon Path marking the north-south meridian, and the Mediterranean just to the south, I thanked the guardians of the six directions, north, south, east, and west, the heavenly above, and the Earth below, then lit the Second Fire at the southern arm of the Great Cross. The First Fire had anchored the east at the dolmen of the "Covered Cross," and the Second Fire now anchored the south at the stone cross of Cardedeu, axis of the Guardian Cardea. The cross appeared to be intentional, and once again, it seemed that I was a pawn on a chessboard, repeating a timeless ritual and that lighting the fires was an act of hallowing the landscape and, of course, myself.

Ancient Stones at the Southern Arm of the Cross

"The first principle was to identify the main axis of the territory, the longest line that can be drawn between its two opposite extremities. Preferably, this should be the north-south axis, emphasizing the symbolism of a world-pole."[6]

JOHN MICHELL, *THE SACRED CENTER*

This main axis referred to by John Michell describes perfectly the original boundaries for calculating the Paris Zero Meridian. The northernmost point of France is at Dunkirk, and the southernmost in the eastern Pyrenees, and the north-south axis of the Paris Meridian marks the longest possible line drawn through mainland France. As mentioned, the southern end was later extended and measured across the Pyrenees through Catalonia and is marked by numerous sanctuaries of Maria Magdalena and megalithic monuments ending at Isla Dragonera off Majorca. (See illustrations # 1 and 2.) To keep things in perspective, the measuring of a meridian is not an isolated line drawn on a map. Measuring the meridians involved complex trigonometry and calculating the movement of the Sun and other stars to establish longitude, which has enabled us to navigate on land, sea, and air. And the Dragon Path that runs along the Paris Meridian also guided ancient travelers, and can be seen as a living field of terrestrial and celestial energies, marked with numerous ancient sites.

I would soon be visiting a large concentration of dolmens, a Ruta Megalithica located on the Paris Meridian just 2.79 miles (4.49 kilometers) south of Cardedeu. *Roca del Vallès* (Rock of the Valleys) is a prehistoric archeological park and nature reserve, with stone structures built 4000–2500 BCE. The monuments lie along forested paths along the meridian axis and one can visit at least seven of the dolmens in an afternoon's walk. The monuments were constructed up to 6000 years ago, and some are decorated with large inscribed equal-armed crosses, cup marks, and carved basins. How is it that the dolmens were built on the Paris Meridian nearly 6000 years before the meridian was measured? This is extraordinary and indicates an ancient awareness of the Dragon Path north-south axis. In addition, there are seventeen more dolmens and menhirs, including a stone circle, within a six-mile diameter. This is an extremely high number of megalithic sites in a small area and comparable to the megalithic routes at Cap de Creus, where we find Dolmen Creu d'en Cobertella. This was exciting, as it meant that there were major concentrations of megalithic structures at both the eastern and southern arms of the cross.

The first dolmens on the Paris Meridian at the northern end of Roca del Vallès are located 45.52 miles (73.26 kilometers) south of the intersection with the east-west axis which forms the center of the Great Cross. (See Great Cross Illustration.) The east-west axis is based on the latitude of dolmen Creu d'en Cobertella, 42°15'25" N. The length of the southern arm marked by the dolmens at Roca del Vallès is only one mile longer than the eastern arm, which seemed an acceptable symmetry when working in such a large landscape. Each axis is about 90 miles (144.8 kilometers) long.

It was the perfect time to visit the site, as the following day would be a lunar eclipse that included a powerful alignment of planets. At these celestial moments when the Sun, Moon, Earth, and additional planets form an alignment, stone temples can become activated, and tremendous dragon energy (telluric currents) can surge between the sites. It felt important to light another fire for the southern arm of the cross in the stone temples, which were established thousands of years before the 17th-century Cardedeu cross. Additionally, this megalithic route maintained a greater degree of vital energy in its more remote and natural environment, as the wayside cross is at an intersection of busy roads and traffic.

I contacted my friend Dani Valdés, a professional photographer and author from Barcelona. Dani grew up exploring these valleys and he would be the perfect guide. I knew from experience that many of the megalithic routes are not well marked and having a guide is often very helpful, sometimes essential. (Cobertella dolmen to the north is well signposted and easy to access, but that is rare. Often, megalithic sites are in wild, remote areas.)

I was in luck, as Dani was available. We arrived at the trailhead at the southern end of the prehistoric route and headed into the forest, which was gorgeous with recent rain creating myriad prisms shining like jewels on the moss and grass. It was a good thing that I had my guide, as there were many branches of paths through the forest, much like a labyrinth. We laughed at the few signposts, as they had become dislodged from their original positions, and the arrows often pointed between two paths, or in the opposite direction!

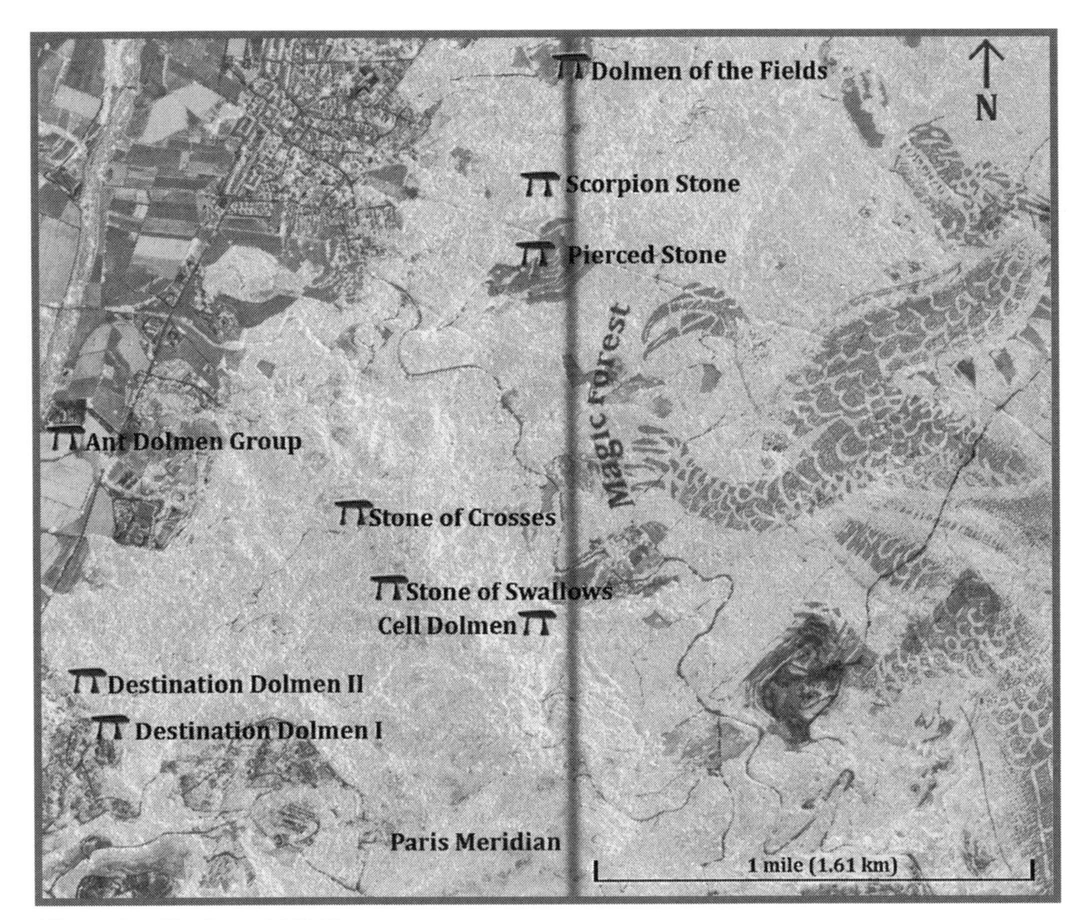

Illustration 22, Roca del Vallès

The first megalith on the route was appropriately named Pedra de les Creus (Stone of the Crosses), a large solid granite stone, perhaps five feet (1.5 meters) square. Multiple large equal-armed inscribed crosses covered the stone, and one cross was enclosed in a circle. Pedra de les Creus also had a stone basin carved on top, filled with water from recent rains. These basins are fairly common on megalithic stones in the region, but this basin was unique as it was marked with a large six-pointed asterisk carved in the center. It was difficult to know the age of the star symbol, but it was well-weathered and may be ancient. If so, was the water-filled basin used as a mirror for observing the stars? The asterisk in addition to the engraved crosses indicated that Pedra de les Creus may have been the nexus, focal point in the entire complex. It was incredibly exciting to discover the large crosses at the southern arm of the landscape cross, on the Dragon Path of the Paris Meridian.

I quietly connected with this unusual stone and the north-south axis which it marked. The multiple crosses and asterisk may well indicate an intersection of currents, pathways connecting with other granite stones in the region. Granite contains abundant quartz, which has a piezoelectric field that emits an electrical charge. This natural effect is the same technology used in computers to transmit and communicate information.

Pedra de les Creus.

At Pedra de les Creus, I felt a sense of centeredness, of being at a still point within the complex of dozens of megaliths. The anticipation was building to discover what additional sites were at the southern arm, and what might lay beyond at the other points of the equal-armed cross.

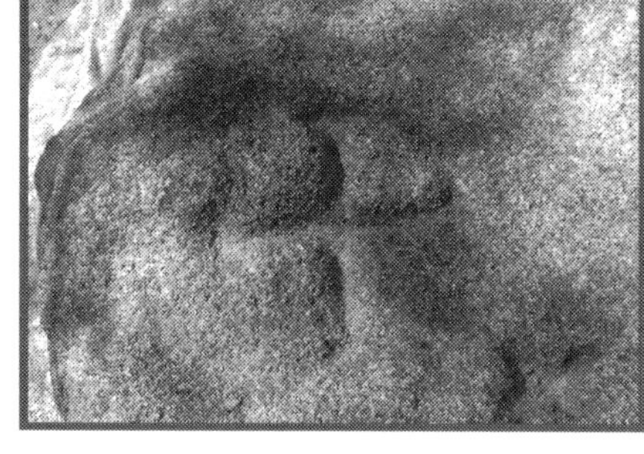

Pedra de les Creus detail.

Departing Pedra de les Creus, and its crosses, the continuing archeological route left the gentle paths of the valley floor, and the ascending trail narrowed and became rocky and steep. Finally, we arrived at Dolmen de Céllecs, and since it was January 10, there was still a Christmas creche decoration, complete with baby Jesus and all the animals. It was well-meaning, but somehow incongruous with the ancient pre-Christian stones. But then again, what we celebrate as the birth of Jesus is during the ancient holy days of the winter solstice. The name Céllecs may derive from *cel*, the Catalan term for sky, and *celístia* means starlight, or more likely, *cella*, meaning cell. The dolmen was in good shape with all the stones intact, and a small altar of stones had been created just inside the doorway, which was perfect to place a small tealight candle.[7]

White Tiger and Green Dragon

With the lunar eclipse, the energy of the dolmen felt strong, and I reflected that its name may relate to the sky. To add to the potency of the eclipse, the Moon, in the zodiac sign of Cancer, was in opposition to the Sun, Mercury, Saturn, and Pluto, all conjunct (appearing together from the Earth's perspective) in the sign of Capricorn. Jupiter was also in Capricorn, but a few degrees away. This strong line-up with five luminaries in the constellation Capricorn on one side of the heavens and the Moon sitting alone in Cancer in the opposite side of the sky meant that the Moon was holding a precarious balance. Cancer is a water sign, often related to nurturing, home, and mothering, and since it was alone this reminded us of the thousands of years of male-dominated cultures, with the feminine voice often struggling to be heard. It felt like an ideal time for an intention of balance between the Sun and Moon, male and female principles.

Roca del Vallès, Dolmen de Céllecs.

These stone monuments were built during the late Neolithic period, meaning the "New Stone Age," circa 4000–2000 BCE. This was the Age of Taurus when that constellation was rising due east at the spring equinox. This was the age of the Mother Goddess cultures, the development of agriculture, and an era of relative peace before the Age of Aries and the Iron Age, beginning circa 2000 BCE. The Age of Taurus was when many great temples were constructed across the Earth, including the Giza Pyramids, Stonehenge, Avebury, and the dolmens on this prehistoric route. I sang for the Earth Mother, circumambulating the stone temple, and gave thanks for the beauty and abundant life energy that prevails in these hidden forest places.

After checking the compass for the orientation of the north-south axis running through the dolmen, Dani and I took our respective east and west positions on each side of the meridian. It felt auspicious to do prayers and mantras for the harmonious balance of the female and male energies at the southern end of the Dragon Path with the celestial polarities mirrored above. In the Chinese system of Earth energy, Feng Shui, the west relates to the female White Tiger (yin) and the east to the male Green Dragon (yang). Dani and I both sensed a current of energy moving through the meridian, from north to south. These currents can change size and direction, depending on the time of the year and the activity in the heavens, and are also influenced by human interaction. Our intention and focus was to balance the male and female energies within the Earth and humanity, and that the Green Dragon and the White Tiger would dance in harmony and balance along the Dragon Path meridian.

Scorpion Stone and Dancing Women with Red Serpents

It is no wonder that so much energy is buzzing through this archaeological park. Roca del Vallès is a concentrated matrix of megalithic structures more than 17 miles (28 kilometers) long, which will take much more time to explore fully. This complex is impressive as its dolmens and marked stones follow the Dragon Path and mark the southern end of the landscape cross. La Pedra de l'Escorpi (Scorpion Stone) could have been named for the constellation Scorpio on the southern horizon for travelers arriving from the north.

It was a very strange occurrence that drew my attention to the Scorpion Stone involving another total lunar eclipse on May 26, 2021. The Sun was conjunct the giant red star Aldebaran in the constellation Taurus and the Moon was conjunct the giant red star Antares, in the heart of the constellation Scorpio. During eclipses, it is my habit to pray and do a mantra practice for purification, but this eclipse felt more potent, and the experience was amplified. I sensed a deep connection in my heart with the star Antares, as it aligned with the Moon, Earth, Sun, and Aldebaran, the "Eye of the Bull."

Two days later, I was on another research journey in the Pyrenees, and I had walked to the Monastery of Saint Martin, high on the majestic flanks of Canigó. Walking in these mountains gives a fresh view of the power and magnificence of these peaks. That night I stayed in Vernet les Bains, the thermal springs town just below, but still in view of the monastery. The town is just 2.74 miles (4.41 kilometers) east of the Paris Meridian. At 3 am, I was awakened by what sounded like a bell being struck three times. The sound brought me out of a dream in which I was observing a red rock petroglyph with concentric circles, a common pattern in ancient rock art, which can indicate a celestial alignment point. (See image page 79.) But a voice in the dream said that this design also represents sound harmonics. When I awoke, I searched for the source of the bells, and no electronics or phones were on. I opened the windows and looked up at Canigó, to see Antares radiating like a ruby jewel in the south, just before setting over the Pyrenees. The Scorpion Stone lies due south from Canigó on the Dragon Path, and I could imagine Antares serving as a southern celestial marker for people journeying from the megalithic routes in the north.

Scorpion Stone, Francesc Baldris.

In addition to the strange occurrence with Antares, what also drew my interest in the Scorpion Stone was a potential connection with Egypt. The stone temples at Roca del Vallès were established circa 3500–3000 BCE, when the first known predynastic king, Scorpion, ruled Egypt. There were two predynastic pharaohs of this name, Scorpion I circa 3200 BCE and Scorpion II circa 3100 BCE. Several inscriptions have been found bearing this pharaoh's name, but the main evidence is the "Scorpion Tableau," discovered in 1995 southeast of Abydos. I realize this is a long shot, but names can be clues to lost history. There are more questions than answers. Is the name of the Scorpion Stone an ancient assigning or modern? And did the Egyptians, during the fourth millennium

BCE, venture as far as Iberia to procure silver or other metals? We have already learned of the Fifth Dynasty pharaoh Sahure (circa 2460 BCE), who was well known for his Mediterranean trade. The answer remains unknown.

Two dolmens in the Roca del Vallès complex, Can Gol I and Can Gol II, have interesting names and, because of their size, seem to have been sites of enormous importance in the complex. *Can* is a Catalan word that generally means a place, and *Gol* means goal, so *Can Gol* is "the final place or destination." Can Gol I is the largest dolmen in the entire prehistoric route of Roca del Vallès, and luckily it is well documented, as it is located in the garden of a private estate. It is about 30 feet (9 meters) long, and the original surrounding circular mound is 49 feet (15 meters) in diameter. This grand size is impressive relative to the other megalithic structures across Catalonia. The entrance is to the south, which means the inner altar stone faces the North Star axis, similar to the Pole Star alignment at dolmen Creu d'en Cobertella. We also found south-facing doorways at the Taula enclosures at Minorca.

Since this was a burial site, the inner sanctuary orientation to the northern Imperishable Stars relates to the destination of souls, as in many afterlife traditions. (Reminding the reader, the Imperishable Stars are the stars in the constellations circling the Pole Star that appear to never set, hence called by the Egyptians "imperishable.") Interestingly, *Can Gol*, as a "destination place," could have been a site for launching the journey of the soul to its final resting place in the stars. Excavations at Dolmen de Can Gol I revealed axes, flint, pottery, and human remains dating to circa 2500–2100 BCE. The entire complex at Roca del Vallès would have been an initiatory path, with each site having a unique purpose in the life journey of the people. There would have been a ritual order and progression connecting the stone temples, with specific prayers, chants, and alignments to be honored at each.

Another site in this megalithic route worth mentioning is La Pedra de les Orenetes ("Stone of the Swallows" in Catalan). This is a block of granite 8 meters (about 26 feet) long, covered with paintings and petroglyphs, and located on the western slope of a long ridge listed on maps as Céllecs Massif. The paintings include more than thirty red-orange images of female figures, serpents, and curved lines. Many anthropomorphic forms are depicted, meaning images combining human attributes with those of animals or supernatural beings. Red serpents and swallows are related to Isis, and it is indeed interesting to find her symbols on the Paris Meridian, with serpent glyphs, the perfect symbols to mark and confirm once again the ancient knowledge of this Dragon Path.

The Stone of the Swallows clearly appears to be a female shamanic site. Did the figures of dancing red women indicate that they had painted themselves with red earth, or perhaps even their menstrual blood for a fertility ritual? Like the Selk'nam indigenous women of Tierra del Fuego (Earth of Fire), Argentina, in the following quote, did the women at the Stone of the Swallows also paint their naked bodies for an eclipse? It was no accident that it was during a lunar eclipse that we lit the Second Sacred Fire at this complex at the southern end of the landscape cross.

"The shaman, xo'on, knew from his dreams when the Moon would eclipse ... The women painted their bodies with red clay, their faces with bands of white clay from the nose to the ears, while they beat the ground ... and chanted to appease the fury of the Moon."

"Where are the women who sang like the canaries? There were many women. Where are they now?"[8]

Where are these women now, doing the rituals and dancing with the Moon? After spending a good part of the day hiking at Roca del Vallès and doing our ritual for the Full Moon eclipse, Dani and I were starving and found a restaurant in the next town. When I returned to the hotel, I brought up Google Earth and was amazed to find more ancient constructions and geological patterns in this mega-complex at the southern end of the cross. This added to not only the antiquity of the Dragon Path meridian but also the importance of the sites marking the great landscape cross that was being revealed.

The Céllecs Massif ridge stands out as it rises above the megalithic complex and the Stone of Swallows, shaped like the back of a large green dragon. This fit perfectly with the ritual for the White Tiger and the Green Dragon. The north-south crest of the dragon's spine is aligned exactly to the Paris Meridian and is punctuated with two high hills, *Turo de Céllecs* and *Turo de Rodó* (*Turo* means "Hill" and *Rodó* means "Round" from the Latin *rotundus*). Turo de Céllecs has an ancient Iberian hilltop settlement, perhaps dating to circa 800 BCE. Another important site marking the spine of the dragon on the meridian is *Castell de La Roca* (Castle of the Rock). This castle was documented from 932 CE, and from the 11th century, it was owned by the famous knight Arnau Mir de Tost, considered the El Cid of Northern Spain for his role in liberating Catalonia from the Moors.

It was fantastic to discover a castle owned by Arnau de Tost at this site, marking the southern end of a developing landscape cross. What I would soon discover is that this famous knight had built his principal residence at a castle far to the northwest. The location of Castell de Tost marks the western arm of the landscape cross that would soon be revealed as the site of the Fourth Fire, one more strange synchronicity in the perfection of the pattern.

In the wooded valley below the dragon ridge was a site called *Bosc Magic de la Roca del Vallès,* the "Magic Forest of the Rock of the Valleys." Strangely, it was spelled in

English, not the normal Catalan or Spanish *Magia*. This southern end of the landscape cross was entirely magical, with an Earth dragon, inscribed stones with crosses, shamanic rock art with dancing red women and serpents, and a funerary dolmen aligned with the Imperishable Stars. With the discovery of two castles owned by the same well-known medieval knight marking and connecting the southern and what I would discover to be the western arm of the cross, the area surpassed my wildest dreams. The medallion had provided the first clue for the location of lighting the four sacred fires, but it felt like the journey was just beginning. I was hungry to discover more of the feminine roots, sites, and traditions of the region.

Roca del Vallès, Magic Forest.

CHAPTER 8

Women of the Pyrenees

LA DAMA DE ELCHE

I was headed to the Archeological Museum of Barcelona, where there is a beautiful replica of La Dama de Elche or Elx in Catalan, meaning "Our Lady of Elche." (The original is in Madrid's Archeological Museum.) This extraordinary Goddess graces the cover of this book and is one of many Iberian female deities found at indigenous sites in Spain. I will mention just two of the others: Dama de Oferente (Lady who Offers, pictured throughout this book), who carries a vase much like the Mesopotamian goddess Mari, and Dama de Guardamar, who wears large ear ornaments similar to Our Lady of Elche. These Iberian deities date from circa 800–300 BCE.

The curator informed me that La Dama de Elche was in the museum's upper-level library, so I headed upstairs before exploring the lower level. Our Lady of Elche was discovered in 1897 at Elche in the region of Alicante, Spain, originally the site of an Iberian settlement now called La Alcudia. (See illustrations #4 and 7.) The Lady of Elche is dated to 426–376 BCE, and some researchers believe that she represents the Phoenician-Carthaginian goddess Tanit. She was a popular goddess across the Mediterranean and her worship may find its origins in the Phoenician great goddess Astarte. She may also be related to Asherah, the great Mother Goddess of the Levant, or the Mesopotamian Ishtar. According to

Dama de Elche copy, Archaeology Museum of Catalonia, Barcelona.

Barbara Walker, Tanit is most likely related to the biblical Ashtoreth and Asherah, and one of her titles was "Queen of the Stars."[1]

As Buffy Johnson relates in her *"Lady of the Beasts,"* Tanit's temple priestesses were renowned astrologers, whose prophesies were consulted by many, including the royal rulers of the land. We often hear of the Babylonian priests who studied and mapped the stars, but rarely do we hear of Tanit's priestesses who did much the same. Was Our Lady of Elche also a priestess of the stars and a practicing oracle? It is highly possible, as these temple traditions were not isolated to one region of the Mediterranean. As we have already seen, the Phoenician royal princess Elissa Dido brought priestesses of Astarte and their astrology-oracle gifts to Carthage in the 8th century CE. The Phoenician goddess Tanit was most likely absorbed from much earlier Near Eastern traditions, and then spread to Carthage and the Iberian Peninsula. Cult images of Tanit have been found in Spain and on the Balearic Island of Ibiza, and interestingly, Elche is near the promontory that is only 55 miles (88 kilometers) from Ibiza.

Could the name of Tanit refer to the ancient Egyptian creation goddess Neith? It is a common occurrence that popular goddesses adopt different names as their cult of worship moves across land and sea. When a deity is absorbed by different cultures, the people sometimes change or alter the name to fit their own language. The root *Ta* and the letter *t* in ancient Egyptian hieroglyphic notation indicates the female gender and the root *nit* is related to Neith, the ancient creator goddess associated with weaving, as in combining the threads to weave something into existence. We also find another Egyptian goddess of weaving in Tait, mentioned in the Pyramid Texts' Utterance 415, where it says Tait will:

> *"... gather together the King's bones, lest they become loose, and put the love of the King into the body of every god who shall see him."*[2]

She is the one who weaves and gathers. Tait gathering the bones of the king is similar to Isis gathering the fourteen pieces of her beloved Osiris. And it is the goddess Tait who clothes the king in fabric she has woven and lifts him up to the sky to the goddess Nut.

Gerald Massey states in his *Book of the Beginnings* that the more ancient name for Neith found in records from the First Dynasty Egypt is Anit, written 'Anit-neb-her', and he relates Anit to her aspects in the heavens as Neith in Ursa Major and Isis in Sirius.[3] We can see how the progression of the identity of aspects of an ancient creator goddess have mutated through time: Anit, Tait, Neith, Tanit. The goddess Tanit has her probable origins in Neith, she who weaves and clothes the kings with the stars, she who is associated with the starry realms and her oracular astrologer priestesses. As I gazed at the perfect replica of Our Lady of Elche in the Archeological Museum,

I wondered if she was one of the star priestess-prophets of Tanit. I marveled at her exquisitely detailed head decoration and her powerful presence. She is often described as an Iberian priestess, but she has the countenance of a Queen Mother. (See image.)

La Dama de Elche's unusual wheel-shaped ear coverings, called rodetes, have been interpreted in many ways. The intricately detailed grid geometry on these wheels looks like a complex calendar or star map. Some are convinced that the Lady of Elche is an echo of the powerful advanced culture of Atlantis, and that these wheels depict Atlantean technology. (Possible remnants of Atlantis have been found in Spain both inland and off the southwestern coast, near the Straits of Gibraltar.)[4] Perhaps these wheels represented the Lady of Elche's connection with the entire wheel of life. Or perhaps, as they cover her ears, "She who listens and hears the All."

Before leaving the museum's upper level, I perused its unusual library, which included copies of the journal *Archeoastronomy*, published in the US. Since I had just arrived from Arizona, it was surprising to find articles on Hopi, Zuni, Navajo, Aztec, and Mayan sky watcher traditions here in Barcelona. The journals featured numerous examples of the equal-armed cross in American indigenous cosmology as symbols of the heavens mirrored on Earth. Although this history was not what I was expecting to find in the Barcelona Archeological Museum, the theme fit perfectly with the landscape cross that was revealing itself in Catalonia.

One example in the collection of journals was an Aztec cross entitled "Wheel of Space and Time." Another featured the great medicine wheel calendars that were constructed on the Earth, mirroring the heavenly cycles and the four directions. But by far the most interesting was a Navajo sky map with the four direction lines of the cross drawn as corn stalks that depicted the positions of the stars. The image entitled "The Female Revolving One"[5] featured the constellations of the Pleiades, Scorpio, Ursa Major, and Cassiopeia, as well as the North Star in Ursa Minor, all significant for the Navajo sky-watchers. We will be discovering Cassiopeia mirrored on the Earth in the landscape cross in future chapters. Magic and synchronicity were certainly afoot.

La Senyora de les Muntanyes

All this unexpected information from the Americas fit perfectly with the theme of the developing Great Cross of the region, but I was anxious to discover the archeological history of Catalonia. The exhibitions in the lower level of the Archeological Museum of Barcelona included a brilliant collection of reconstructed models of megalithic dolmens and stone burial sites. Many of the dolmens were originally covered with earthen mounds and surrounded by a circular enclosure. Over the thousands of years of erosion and weathering since their construction, only the inner stone structures remain.

However, it was *La Senyora de les Muntanyes* (The Lady of the Mountains) who held me captive. I knew nothing about her before coming to this museum, and quickly realized that she was one of the main reasons I had come. La Senyora is displayed in a replica of

La Senyora de les Muntanyes by Dibuix F. Riart, Archaeology Museum of Catalonia, Barcelona.

a sepulchral cave burial from the 15th century BCE. Her skeletal remains were discovered in *Cova sepulchral de Montanissell* in Alt Urgell, in the foothills of the Iberian Pyrenees. When she was discovered, she was still wearing her finely crafted metal bracelets and necklace on her skeletal remains. As I stood in front of her bones, I suddenly began to weep, and am still deeply moved whenever I think of her.

The archeologists studying La Senyora said that her jewelry was of the type from the northern side of the Pyrenees where legends say Pyrene had lived. The refined quality of her adornments indicates a woman of high standing, perhaps royalty. The Barcelona Archeological Museum's dating for the Lady of the Mountains burial is 1400 BCE, during the late Bronze Age. This is the possible time that Greek historians estimated for the lifetime of Hercules, the legendary lover of Pyrene. As mentioned previously, Herodotus wrote in the 5th century BCE about Hercules being an ancient Egyptian god who was adopted by the Greeks much later.

Herodotus says that the city of Thonis-Heracleion was established to mark where Hercules set foot on the coast of Alexandria.[6] Although the ancient city is now submerged under the sea, archeologists date it to before the 12th century BCE. Another clue lies in the numerous legends that the beautiful Queen Helen of Sparta and her lover Paris of Troy visited Egypt's temple of Heracles at the Egyptian port city of Heracleion before the start of the Trojan War. The beginning of the war is given as 1250 BCE by Herodotus, and between 1750–1300 BCE in Homer's Iliad.

This background history and timeline is important in reference to an underlying feeling that arose when I stood before the bones of La Senyora de les Muntanyes. I sensed that she could have been the legendary Celtic Princess Pyrene. (The Celts were only known in Iberia from circa 900 BCE, so perhaps Pyrene's identity as Celtic was a generic term referring to a woman of the Bronze Age.) I noted the experience of

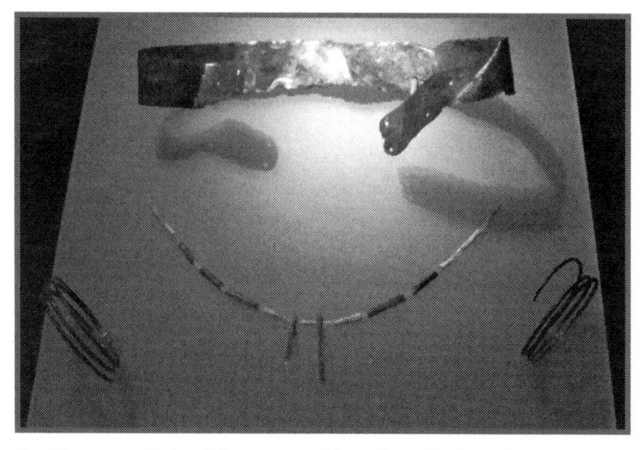

La Senyora de les Muntanyes' jewelry, Archaeology Museum of Catalonia, Barcelona.

La Senyora in my journal that night in the Barcelona hotel: "I feel a connection with the bones of the woman of the mountains and having very emotional memories. She was found in the Pyrenees cave with her bracelets from Gaul still clinging to her arm. Could she be our Pyrene?"

As we shall see, the legends of Pyrene normally place her on what is now the French side of the Pyrenees. And the jewelry that was still encircling the bones of La Senyora de les Muntanyes was also from the French side of the Pyrenees, according to archeologists.[7] The remains of legendary Pyrene were never found. Was that because she crossed the mountains to Iberia? It is not far and totally feasible, and the old roads and passes over the mountains were well-used by ancient people.

When I checked the maps, the cave burial site at Montanissell in Alt Urgell is only 2.49 miles (4 kilometers) southwest of a large group of megalithic dolmens that I would eventually discover mark the end of the western arm of the landscape cross. It seemed beyond coincidence that key sites in this story were all located in such proximity. Could the Lady of the Mountains found in the cave of Alt Urgell, really be the Princess Pyrene, daughter of King Bebryx of the French Pyrenees?

Mysterious Princess Pyrene

"In the Pyrenees, he [Heracles] courted and buried the Bebrycan princess Pyrene, from whom this mountain range takes its name ... near a city also named in her honor."

Robert Graves, *The Greek Myths*[8]

Legend says that Pyrene was the daughter of King Bebryx in the region of Cerdagne, in the French Pyrenees, and perhaps the royal family lived in the city named for Pyrene near the sea (the current city of Elne, France). In other accounts, the King and Princess lived in the Ariege near Tarascon in the Lombrives cave. Either way, most of the purported locations of Pyrene's homeland are in what is now the French side of the Pyrenees. When the great Hercules was making his way west on his twelve labors, legend says he stopped to rest and receive hospitality at the castle of King Bebryx, which included a tryst with his beautiful daughter.

As is the case with myths and legends, there are variations to the story. Most accounts say that Pyrene was a beautiful young woman and Hercules immediately fell in love. Many male writers say he seduced her, but we will discover that this may not have been the case! Popular traditions say that after his love conquest, Hercules continued into the west of Iberia on his twelve labors. When Pyrene realized she was pregnant, she didn't want to tell her father, and to avoid his wrath, she escaped into the nearby mountains.

Some accounts say that she gave birth to a serpent. This is interesting as there is also a Scythian serpent version of the Hercules story. The Scythians were a nomadic people in the region of Kazakhstan, Siberia, and Eastern Ukraine. A version told by Herodotus says that Hercules married a Scythian serpent-tailed Earth Goddess. Was she a "Drakaina," a female dragon, typically illustrated with her lower half as a serpent and her upper half as a woman? The presence of the serpent with the goddess most likely indicates the wisdom traditions and is also a reference to regeneration and rebirth. Most of the Pyrenean versions of the legend of Pyrene also relate her to the serpent, one more example of the cultural melding between the Levant and the Pyrenees.

By the time Hercules returned to the Pyrenees on his way back from the Pillars of Hercules (Gibraltar), his beloved Pyrene was gone. Did she escape to the other side of the Pyrenees and create a new life for herself and her child with friends or relatives? The legends say that Hercules roamed the mountains, calling her name, searching throughout the rugged valleys and peaks, and that the sound of Hercules calling Pyrene still echoes in those mountains.

The Latin poet Silius Italicus (circa 28–103 CE) wrote an epic poem comprising seventeen books, entitled *Punica,* in which he tells the tales of history's heroes. In Book III he recounts Pyrene's encounter with Hercules, which is one of the oldest versions of her story:

"From the eminence of their [Pyrenean] rain-swept peaks they command a wide prospect and divide Spain from Gaul, making an eternal barrier between two great countries. These mountains took their name from Pyrene, daughter of Bebryx and victim of Hercules. For Hercules, in the course of his appointed Labours, was travelling to the distant land of three bodied Geryon, when he was mastered by wine in the savage court of Bebryx, and left Pyrene robbed of her maidenhood; her beauty was a cause for mourning.

The god (if it is not sinful to believe it), was the cause of the poor maiden's death. For when she gave birth to a serpent she fled at once from the home she loved, in horror and dread of her father's wrath. Then in lonely caves she mourned for the night when she lay with Alcides, and told his promises to the dark forests; till at last, as she mourned the ingratitude of her ravisher, and stretched forth her hands, imploring the aid of her guest, she was torn in pieces by wild beasts.

When Hercules came back victorious, he wetted the mangled limbs with his tears; and when he found the head of the maid he had loved, he turned pale, distraught with grief. Then the high mountain-tops, smitten by his cries, were shaken; with loud lament he called Pyrene by name; and all the cliffs and haunts of wild beasts echoed the name of Pyrene. Then, with a last tribute of tears, he laid her body in the grave. And time shall never eclipse her fame; for the mountains retain forever the name that caused such grief."[9]

What a sad and poignant love story. Hercules called his beloved Pyrene and all the mountains resounded, echoing her name. There are many variations of the legend of Pyrene in numerous books on the region, and it is understandable, as the tragic love affair between two popular personages would have made headlines in today's news.

Pyrene, St. Augustins Museum Toulouse "La femme au serpent."

The legend that Pyrene gave birth to a serpent is illustrated on a mysterious stone carving, the *Pierre d'Oô* (Stone of Oô, a village in the Pyrenees), which is displayed in the Augustine Museum in Toulouse, France. It was discovered in the remote high Pyrenees and was kept for some time in a local chapel, and is reminiscent of other Pyrenean Romanesque art. This portrayal of a serpent fertility goddess is found in other Romanesque churches in France, which include women feeding snakes.

The Oô stone depicts Pyrene birthing a serpent who is suckling at her breast. This can symbolize Pyrene giving birth to a magical being of wisdom and regeneration, rather than the typical interpretation of her birthing a devil. She gives birth to new life and then nurtures her creation, which sounds like the myriad manifestations of the ancient Mother Goddess.

In Egypt, the predynastic goddess Wadjet, whose lower body is a cobra, was one of the oldest female guardian deities who protected the pharaohs. Wadjet is mentioned in the Pyramid Texts as representing nature and growth in the rising up of a new papyrus plant.[10] And Renenutet, whose name in Egyptian means "snake who nourishes," is the lifegiving serpent goddess of fertility, regeneration, and rebirth. Here we find a similarity to the image of the carving of Pyrene giving birth to and suckling the serpent. The serpent is also the ally of Hygeia, the Greek goddess of medicine who is often depicted feeding her healing snake a cup of elixir or milk. Serpents are often associated with healing elixirs and immortality, as they regularly shed their skins in a symbolic regeneration and rebirth.

Serpents were honored resident-healers in the Asclepian temples of healing throughout the Mediterranean, including the one near the Pyrenees at Empúries, Spain. The preferred symbol of Hygeia's cup and serpent, signifying medicine, still appears as pharmacy signatures across Europe. We can find many examples of feminine deities combining the wisdom, regeneration, renewal, and healing of serpent medicine.

Pharmacy sign, Czech Republic.

The location of the discovery of the Pyrene stone, the village of Oô in the region of Bagnères de Luchon, is near the Spanish border. Oô is just 55.5 miles (89.3 kilometers) northwest of the cave burial site of La Senyora de les Muntanyes at Montanissell in Alt Urgell (south of Andorra). Other Pyrenean sites such as the Ariège, Cerdagne, or the city of Pyrene where the princess may have lived with her father, are all within range of a reasonable escape route for her. Who exactly was Pyrene, whose story became famous throughout time? We don't know, but the clues are in several sites that carry her name, in addition to the Pyrenees.

An ancient city called Pyrene most likely existed on the hill of the current village of Elne, France, until the 9th century BCE, according to information at the Terrus Museum in Elne's cathedral cloister. Pyrene was once a thriving center on the Mediterranean and would have been on the old trade route between Gaul and Iberia, used by Greeks, Celts, Iberians, and perhaps earlier Phoenicians and Egyptians. The Terrus Museum has an illustrated timeline of the various names of the city.

The timeline suggests that sometime around the 5th century BCE, the city of Pyrene became Illiberis, likely named for the Iberian people in the region. The word *ille,* meaning 'island' in Catalan, indicates that perhaps the site was once surrounded by water. During the time of Emperor Constantine in the 4th century CE, the town was renamed in honor of Helene his mother. During the Visigothic presence in the 6th century CE, it became Helna, and finally, its current name of Elne, now a village known for its abbey and museum. Pyrene of the 9th century BCE was most likely an island with a lighthouse, a beacon for arrivals across the Mediterranean, but the water levels have receded.

One thing is certain. The Celtic Princess Pyrene garnered the attention of the world's most well-known historians, poets, and authors. But every account of Pyrene was interpreted and written by men, and the era of these accounts was not known for supporting the dignity and equality of women, and female authors were few and far between. The story presenting a poor Pyrene, a victim of a fleeting affair, a wanton woman birthing an evil serpent, weeping and remorseful, reminds us of the portrayal of Maria Magdalena as a weeping, sinful, penitent woman, another story interpreted by male historians and Church Fathers. But what if Princess Pyrene was not a victim of an overpowering Herculean seducer, but a brilliant and wise Celtic medicine-woman?

Pyrene's serpent gives us the strong clue that there is an ancient wisdom and a medicinal association with her.

The Iron Age traditions of Pyrene's era most likely included knowledge of the stars, medicine, music, and elemental magic, the same principles that would be taught in the later Druid academies. Most likely these traditions were practiced in a continuing thread by Pyrenean medicine women, and as a princess Pyrene would have been educated in this knowledge. The Bruixas and Brujas (Catalan and Spanish words meaning witches) were maligned for millennia on both sides of the Pyrenees, and they are a reminder of the healing traditions that have long existed in the region. These medicine women knew the natural magic of the elements, healing plants, and, according to many legends, even weather control and time travel. This tradition is still strong in the Pyrenees and many caves, mounds, and springs still carry the Bruixas names (called Breiches or Breychos in Occitan).

What if when Pyrene met Hercules, she recognized the opportunity of a lifetime to create a powerful lineage mixing her royal Celtic blood *sang roial* (meaning "royal blood" in Old French, a play on *sant graal* meaning "Holy Grail") with that of an Egyptian god-king? As Herodotus wrote, "Concerning Heracles, I heard it said that he was one of the twelve gods ... a very ancient god in Egypt ..."[11]

And what if that Egyptian lineage seeded the future generations of the people of the Pyrenees? There are some people in these mountains who still claim to be descended from Pyrene and Hercules. According to the 17th-century French priest and poet Jean-Géraud d'Astros, the people of Gascony claim to carry this royal bloodline. And to counter the idea of popular legend that Pyrene was a victim of seduction by the powerful Hercules, Barry Cunliffe, in *The Ancient Celts,* writes:

> *"Women clearly occupied a more significant position in Celtic society than they did in the Graeco-Roman world ... The Poseidonian tradition notes the beauty of Gallic women, describing them to be as tall and as strong as their husbands ... a Celtic woman raised to anger, ... as a fighter she is more than equal to the male."*

Cunliffe continues citing 1st century BCE historian Diodorus of Sicily on the sexual morals of the Celts and the strong passions of the beautiful Celtic women:

> *"They generally yield up their virginity to others and this they regard not as a disgrace but feel themselves slighted when someone refuses to accept their freely offered favours."*[12]

Calling Pyrene album cover.

Was it the beautiful and clever Pyrene who seduced Hercules, who could not resist her charms? According to Celtic sexual customs, it is highly possible. And in due time, Pyrene would have given birth to a magical child, symbolized by the serpent of wisdom. Remember, serpents in earlier times were considered as powerful guardians and messengers of the spirit world. Could Pyrene's royal Celtic bloodline combining with Hercules' Egyptian royal blood have birthed a dragon lineage (symbolized by the serpent) in the Pyrenees?

It is no wonder that legends of dragon consorts are still remembered in these mountains, and the phantom voice of Hercules calling Pyrene's name still echoes throughout the Pyrenees. Her fascinating story inspired the album and title track "Calling Pyrene," and tributes to her are sung in the various languages that were spoken in the region. The songs on the album focus on the ancient Pyrenean traditions and the cover art features Pyrene's creative breath as a fire dragon. As a medicine woman, she is depicted next to her dolmen ritual site, a woman of wisdom and beloved of Hercules, always remembered as Princess of the Pyrenees, the mountains named in her honor.

Pyrene Pyrene, I'm calling
Pyrène Pyrène, la femme de la montagne, Je vous appelle
(Translation of the French:
Pyrene, woman of the mountain, I'm calling you)

Chorus: Celto-Iberia, land of our dreams

Piréno Piréno, llamándote, la doña grande de la montaña
(Translation of Spanish:
Pyrene, I'm calling you, the great woman of the mountain)

Pirè Pirè, deessa grega
(Catalan translation: Pyrene, Greek goddess)
TTυρεVIO Καλώ
(Greek translation: Pyrene, I'm calling)[13]

Did Queen Pyrrha Sail to the Pyrenees?

"She [Pyrrha] and her spouse repopulated the earth after the Flood by the instruction of the Goddess Themis, magically creating human beings out of stones. Pyrrha... 'fiery red,' may have been the magic ingredient of the charm, embodying the Blood of Life."

BARBARA WALKER, *THE WOMAN'S ENCYCLOPEDIA OF MYTHS AND SECRETS*[14]

Queen Pyrrha shares a resonance with Pyrene in the etymology of their fiery names, linking both with creative, vital energy. Pyrrha was married to Deucalion, the king of Phthia, Greece, the son of Prometheus, who had gotten into heaps of trouble with the gods for giving the gift of fire to humanity. Pyrrha was the daughter of Pandora, who was born in the fiery heavenly forges of Hephaestus and was given knowledge and wisdom by Hermes. Pandora means "all-giving," but unfortunately, she has been maligned for millennia in her portrayal as the brainless woman who unleashed all manner of suffering on humanity. Robert Graves cites the eighth-seventh century BCE Greek writer Hesiod, who rewrote the story of Pandora:

"Hesiod's account of Prometheus, Epimetheus, and Pandora is not a genuine myth, but an anti-feminist fable, probably of his own invention...Pandora (meaning 'all-giving') was the Earth-goddess Rhea, worshipped under that title at Athens and elsewhere..."[15]

The early goddess Pandora was depicted carrying a honey jar, but this was mistranslated by 16th century Dutch theologian Desiderius Erasmus. He, most likely intentionally, mistranslated the word *pithos*, Pandora's sacred vessel as *pyxis*, meaning "box," which was also a slang term for female genitals.[16] We can see how changing one word in a story changes everything. And so it went, and Pandora has been blamed along with women in general for unleashing sin, seduction, and all manner of suffering on the world.

With Pyrrha's name meaning "Fiery One," her mother being created in a fiery forge, and her husband Deucalion being the son of the one who stole the secrets of fire from the gods, they made a fine fiery pair. It seems they needed this vital fire element to navigate a long journey during a time of calamity, perhaps becoming the pioneers of a new world in the Pyrenees, the mountains named for fire.

According to Robert Graves in *The Greek Myths*, Prometheus was exceedingly intuitive and wise and foresaw a great flood coming. (His name means "foresight.") He warned his son Deucalion and daughter-in-law Pyrrha to create an ark to prepare for the deluge. Graves calls them the Greek version of Mr. and Mrs. Noah. Indeed, many cultures have similar stories of the great flood, which may have occurred circa 10,000 BCE with the destruction of Atlantis. When the waters flooded the Earth, the ship carrying Deucalion, Pyrrha and their consortium from Greece floundered on the raging sea for many days, constantly being pushed westward by the strong winds.

The ship and its survivors finally landed in a mountainous area that I strongly believe was the Pyrenees. Although different versions of the myth say that they landed at sites in Greece, such as Mount Parnassus, it is unlikely that the ship made it no further than where they started after being driven west by strong winds and currents for many days. Robert Graves, in *The White Goddess,* says that Deucalion sent out a dove to bring back signs of land, and the ark finally came to rest on a mountain far to the west. Upon their arrival in the foreign land, the god Hermes came to counsel them, instructing Deucalion and Pyrrha to go to the temple of the wise goddess and oracle Themis. The oracle instructed the royal couple to gather the "Bones of their Mother" (Stones of the Earth), and create a new world. As Barbara Walker writes:

> *"Classic myth made Themis the spirit of the post-diluvian creation. After the Flood receded, Themis taught the survivors Deucalion and Pyrrha how to repopulate the earth by magic. They were to fling 'the bones of their mother' behind them as they walked ...By the grace of the Goddess, new human beings rose up from these stones."*[17]

Themis as the goddess and overseer of Earth magic guided the postdiluvian creation of a new world. Manley Palmer Hall comments on this legend in his classic book, *The Secret Teachings of All Ages*:

> *"Entering a ruined sanctuary to pray, they [Deucalion and Pyrrha] were directed by an oracle to depart from the temple and with heads veiled and garments unbound, cast behind them the bones of their mother. Construing the cryptic message of the god to mean that the earth was the Great Mother of all creatures, Deucalion picked up loose rocks and, bidding Pyrrha do likewise, cast them behind... From these rocks there sprang forth a new and stalwart race of human beings, the rocks thrown by Deucalion becoming men and those thrown by Pyrrha becoming women."*

> *"In this allegory is epitomized the mystery of human evolution; for spirit, by ensouling matter, becomes that indwelling power which gradually but sequentially raises the mineral to the status of the plant; the plant to the plane of the animal; the animal to the dignity of man; and man to the estate of the gods."*[18]

The ensouling of matter by the gods described by Hall is the archetypal story of creation, and it is possible that following the flood, the great Pyrenees range was named in memory of the Greek Queen Pyrrha. Their strong lineage from alchemical fire certainly gave them the power needed to create a new civilization in the west.

Pyrrha and Pyrene can be seen as two of the legendary founding mothers of the Pyrenees. Their stories were rewritten and retold hundreds of times by male historians and theologians, until the feminine thread in the weaving was barely visible and often totally disappeared. But the traditions of the Magna Mater, the Great Mother, can never die, as she lives in our deep memory, in our blood, and in the remnants found in legends, language, artifacts in the corners of museums, and our dreams. The "Fiery Ones" Pyrrha and Pyrene had become metaphors in my journey of reclaiming fire.

CHAPTER 9

Reclaiming Alchemical Fire

I was a single-celled life form, living in isolation, but aware of other cells. The only existence we had known was the current place we called home—a great sheet of ice during one of the great Ice Ages. Finally, one day the voice of a Great Presence said, "You know the way of ice, and now you must learn to create fire."

THE SCENE ABOVE OCCURRED IN A DREAM PERHAPS FOUR DECADES AGO, AT A TIME in my life when it was necessary to make a change, take the next step, walk into the unknown. In retrospect, this turning point was a shift into a life of greater opportunities, playing in a larger field of possibilities. Along with that change came greater responsibilities, challenges, risks, doubt, and pain, requiring a degree of courage and passion that some would call irresponsible, or even crazy. The repeating message was, "The way out is the way through, into the heart of matter," something that I had always resisted. This was the reclaiming of fire, following deep-seeded dreams to break open, seeking the yearning that was slowly gestating within.

The new direction meant quitting a stable job with a regular income and pursuing the life of a modern troubadour. This often required traveling alone across the world, to places about which I had only basic knowledge. It required a presence of knowing deep inside that I was not alone, and somehow trusting that all would be well... eventually. It was not always easy. I was a single mom at that time, with no outside financial support. Sometimes the path was hard, and doubts arose. But there was a glimmer of inner fire and fortitude, a determination to always keep going and take the next step, no matter what.

"In the great work of alchemy... fire does the work, fire is the process, fire is the medium, and fire finds the gold. Nothing happens without fire or without desire. Nothing melts. Nothing evaporates or circulates. Our habits stay solidified; our perspectives remain hardened and cold."

MANLY P. HALL[1]

The fiery power center related to courage and will in the human energy system is located below the diaphragm at the solar plexus, meaning the "solar network." The solar plexus is not only the intersection of a network of nerves and meridians, but also a connecting point with subtle fire, called "chi." In the Taoist traditions this energy center is illustrated as one of the cauldrons of fire and in Sanskrit it is called Manipura. The solar plexus is related to building self-confidence and taking control of our life, moving from being a victim of circumstance to being a conscious creator.[2]

Looking at some of the extreme challenges that our story's key characters endured, what would we do if we played the role of Prometheus or Pandora? Would we suffer endlessly because of what some jealous god decided in a fit of rage? Would we carry that burden of guilt or shame lifetime after lifetime? Or would we decide to break the chains of domination and reclaim our fire, our autonomy?

And the voice in the dream said, "You must now learn how to create fire." This meant diving deeper into the fire of the heart, the heart of life. It meant finding the seed of illumination within and recognizing this seed within others. This is an ongoing process and just when we think we are complete with this alchemy of the soul, the journey is just beginning again. The Tibetans call this living fire *Ground Luminosity*, recognizing the true golden seed essence within every being. Underneath the layers of mistaken identity, cultural limitation, and negative perceptions, lives a radiant being containing jewels of potentiality. This is the true gold and goal of alchemy of the soul.

Flame of Canigó

"Lighting a sacred fire is nothing less than elemental alchemy. This is the Alchemist's Covenant."

Again, the messenger had appeared in my dream, and the following morning I pondered the term *Alchemist's Covenant*. A covenant is a promise, an agreement, and involves trust. And this promise to light four sacred fires involved alchemy, transformation, both personal and, I assumed, at each of the four fire sites. Lighting sacred fires is an ancient ritual enactment. This often occurred at the eight turning points of the year: solstices, equinoxes, and the four mid-points called the cross-quarter days. These four fire festivals are: Imbolc (Candlemas) in February, Beltane (May Day) in May, Llamas (Harvest) in August, and Samhain (Halloween) in October. Fires were lit on mounds and hills and ceremonies were enacted to give thanks and welcome a new cycle. These rituals kept society in harmony with the seasonal rhythms, which helped regulate all of life.

A perpetual flame was maintained in the great cauldrons of fire at the Greek temple of the Goddess Hera, whose temple flame eventually became the Olympic flame. This torch would be carried to every corner of the world, in the name of excellence and endurance. Perpetual fires in the Greek temples were overseen by Vestal Virgins, priestess guardians of the sacred fires of Vesta, the goddess of the hearth and home. There is a perpetual fire burning at the Arc de Triomphe in Paris, called the Flame of Remembrance, in honor of the unknown and fallen soldiers who risked everything to fight for freedom. This Parisian perpetual flame is only 1.87 miles (3 km) west of the Paris Zero Meridian. In Catalonia until recently, the census taken for the population was counted in the number of hearth fires, not individuals.

On both the Catalan and French sides of the Pyrenees there is an ancient tradition of lighting a fire on summer solstice, celebrated at Midsummer's Eve, also in honor of Saint John the Baptist. In Catalan, it is called *Focs de Sant Joan* (Fires of Saint John) and in French, *Fête de Saint-Jean* (Feast of Saint John). The ritual at Mount Canigó in the eastern Pyrenees is also called *Flama del Canigó* (Flame of Mount Canigó). This is the mountain considered sacred to people on both sides of the eastern Pyrenees and is located near the Paris Meridian. This ritual fire is a *Grand Fête de Lumière* (Great Celebration of Light), rekindling the vision, hope, and spirit of the people for the coming year. The fire lighting at Canigó is a purifying, healing fire that keeps the spirit alive in the land and is a unifying force for the people living in villages below the great mountain.

About a week before summer solstice, members of the villages surrounding Canigó meet at the Refuge Cortalets on a plateau below the peak for *La Trobada* ("The Gathering Meeting" in Catalan, from *Trobar*, to find). People from all over the region come together to gather bundles of firewood and dried vines for a bonfire. *La Trobada* symbolizes the unity of the people residing on both sides of the Pyrenees, a time when they gather with a common purpose.

The source fire is kept at Le Castillet, a medieval castle in Perpignan built by the Kings of Majorca in the 14th century, and the castle entry formed the old main gate of the walled city. The ceremony to retrieve the flame draws thousands of people, who gather at the castle to celebrate the lighting of the torch, called "Regeneration of the Fire." Afterward, this flame is carried up the steep ascent of Canigó on June 22nd, and a bonfire is lit at Cortalets. The following day runners carry lanterns or torches lit by the fire down to many of the villages on both sides of the Pyrenees. One can witness from a distance these lights appearing like a great serpent winding down the mountain at night.

The first time I had the opportunity to witness Saint John's Fire was in the French Pyrenean town of Mosset, which was originally part of Catalonia, the people there still speaking Catalan as well as French. It is located on the Paris Meridian, just north of Canigó. I had booked a room at a farm near Mosset, and with my friend headed up to the village for the festivities. A small group was singing old Catalan chants in front of the church dedicated to Saint Julien, and their harmonies filled the village square. Everyone had a complimentary glass of local red wine in hand. I wandered into the church and marveled at the numerous stone carvings of cauldrons filled with fire. This is a theme that is found in the décor of churches and castles across the region, a symbol of the eternal fire and passion of the Catalan and Pyrenean people.

A tall pyre of logs had been prepared for the bonfire in the village square. As it became dark, the children of the village carried lanterns that had been lit from the central fire on Canigó and wove their way through the old cobblestone streets, illuminating every corner of the village. They sang as they made their procession of light, finally gathering in a circle around the bonfire. The tradition of having the children begin the ritual fire procession was impressive, and it was also the children who lit the sacred fire for the annual blessing of the region. We have much to learn from these people and their ancient traditions honoring sacred fire. And including the children with prominent roles in the ceremony is something that I would witness at every village that celebrated these solstice fires.

The village of Mosset's southern gate is an ancient stone archway that opens to face the sacred mountain. Above the arch is a medieval Madonna silently watching, smiling, another guardian of the Dragon Path. This gate is called "Porte de Madeleine" (Door or Gate of Magdalena) and marks the Paris Meridian before passing Canigó to cross the Pyrenees into Catalonia. What silent voice had guided those who named this southern gate, the same voice that caused the placement of numerous sanctuaries to Magdalena along the same meridian? Remember, these Magdalena-named sites were established before the Paris Meridian was measured. This was one more confirmation of her importance on this ancient alignment, and again, I sensed the magnitude of the love for this "Apostle to the Apostles" on both sides of the Pyrenees.

The ex-mayor of the village was sitting next to us, and I took the opportunity to ask him about the Madonna. He explained that the medieval Virgin was originally in a Cistercian abbey at the top of Col de Jau, just north of Mosset. The Col (meaning neck or mountain pass in Catalan) is at an elevation of 4950 feet (1509 meters) and forms the natural boundary between the Aude and the Pyrénées-Orientales départments of Southern France. When the Abbey of Sainte-Marie de Jau was abandoned, the Madonna was brought to Mosset for her preservation. She was set over the Magdalena meridian gate facing south, but every morning the villagers would discover that she had turned herself around to face north. This went on for a couple of weeks, until the people realized that Sainte-Marie had a mind of her own. And thus, she remains facing north to keep an eye on the abbey ruins as another Guardian of the Dragon Path, a watcher of the northern gate toward the northern stars.

Flama de Canigó is not the only mountain peak where the Pyrenean people light the solstice fire for their region, but this occurs on several peaks and cols, and indeed throughout Catalonia and Spain. I would eventually witness the Fire of Saint John as far west as Andalusia, where the tradition is to jump the bonfire and throw written prayers and wishes, *Las Esperanzas*, into the flames. Summer solstice is the longest day of the year, the time of greatest light, and this tradition of lighting fires has endured for thousands of years. This ritual consistency gives the region a vitality that is palpable.

One major Saint John festival is at Vernet-les-Bains, France, on the western flank of Canigó below the monastery of Saint Martin de Canigó. Another festival is at Col de Ares on the Catalan side, at one of the main ancient paths used for thousands of years to cross the Pyrenees. (Ares is named for the Roman god, one of the many cultures who used and guarded this path.) The flame brought from Canigó to Col de Ares is rekindled in a bronze cauldron suspended in a large sculpture shaped in the image of flames. This looks out from the Col over the other peaks and valleys to the south into Catalonia. Next to the cauldron, there is a commemorative plaque in white marble, engraved with the dedication: "A la Flama del Canigó, simbol d'unio del Paisos Catalans" ("To the Flame of Canigó, symbol of union of the Catalan Countrymen").

On the marble plaque below the dedication is a short extract from the epic poem "Canigó," composed by one of Catalonia's favorite poets, Jacint Verdaguer. He was an extraordinary priest, prolific poet, and mystic of the 19th century. He had a lifelong love for these mountains and was known to walk barefoot through the Pyrenees, and he made several ascents to the summit of Canigó, in addition to the other highest peaks of the eastern Pyrenees. I visited Verdaguer's hermitage retreat at Santuari Mare de Deu del Mont (Sanctuary of Mother of God of the Mount) in the eastern Pyrenees. The small window of his simple monk's quarters looks directly across to the snow-capped sacred mountain, providing the constant inspiration and proximity to heaven that fed his lofty poems.

"Lo Canigó es una magnolia immensa
Que en un rebrot del Pirineu se bada:
Per abelles té fades que la volten
Per papallons los cisnes i les áligues."[3]

(The Canigó is an immense white magnolia flower
That in a flowering of the Pyrenees is opened:
For the bees you have fairies that spin around its peak
For butterflies there are the swans and eagles.)

Cardou
Sals River
Bain Deux
Rennes-les-Bains
Bain Fort - Isis Pool
Las Breiches
Le Cercle
Isis Throne
Sals
La Madeleine
Fontaine des Amours
Blanque River
Paris
Meridia
La Soula
Cugulho

CHAPTER 10

Looking North

"Men were created to tend the terrestrial garden ... according to the divine knowledge inherent within each member of the human race. This quest for perfect order ... was the inspiration for the monumental works of antiquity."

John Michell *The View Over Atlantis*[1]

I had followed the "Voice" in the dream and had begun to light four sacred fires. This became a journey of both self-discovery and an awakening to a magical landscape, abundant with mystery, history, and remembering. The journey evolved naturally over a period of almost two decades and the recognition of an overall pattern emerged slowly. Often I discovered the sites before realizing that they were the perfect location for the next sacred fire. The lighting of the First Fire at dolmen Creu d'en Cobertella was in the heart of a megalithic route, meaning that the site had not just one ancient standing stone or dolmen, but numerous monuments grouped in a condensed area, in this case, in view of the sacred Mount Canigó and overlooking the Mediterranean Sea. From the first visit to this dolmen, I sensed an affinity with the site and its importance in antiquity.

As mentioned, the Paris Meridian formed the north-south axis of the developing cross. This meridian was chosen as the central axis, because during the many years of living on this alignment I had discovered numerous ancient ritual sites and medieval sanctuaries of Maria Magdalena located on the axis and sensed it was a much more ancient path. The lighting of the Second Fire to the south, near Barcelona, would be done in three stages, with the first at the wayside cross on the Paris Meridian called Cardedeu, meaning "Meridian of God."

The second was at Dolmen de Céllecs within another major megalithic route just over two miles (3.2 kilometers) south of Cardedeu at Rocas de Vallè on the Paris Meridian, which added a perfect mirroring with the group of megalithic monuments at the site of the eastern First Fire. The third enactment of the Second Fire would come a year later at a dolmen called Can Planes, located on the Paris Meridian and on the same megalithic route. I would discover that this dolmen was exactly equidistant from the future site of the northern arm of the landscape cross, yet to be revealed. The journey continued to be a process of refinement and discernment of the perfection of a great landscape cross. Not only were numerous megaliths marking the eastern and southern arms of the cross, but the site names and inscribed stones featured equal-armed crosses.

An ancient grid pattern was revealing itself, that to my knowledge, had not yet been discovered in this era. Would the other two fires confirm this pattern of megaliths and crosses? Was this grid pattern established in some long distant time and, over the thousands of years, forgotten? Since the Paris Meridian formed the north-south axis of the landscape cross, I was curious what would be marking the northern end of the of the equal-armed cross, mirrored in the medallion of Saint Benedict that I continued to wear through the discoveries.

To search for the location of the Third Fire, I began at the same latitude of 42°N15' of Dolmen Creu d'en Cobertella, which formed the east-west axis. Using Google Earth, I calculated the distance north 44.31 miles (71.31 kilometers), the length of the eastern arm of the landscape cross. 44.31 miles north landed in a wooded area about one mile south of the village of Rennes-les-Bains and two miles short of Pech Cardou, *Pech* meaning mount and *Cardou* most likely referring to the Latin word *cardo*, meaning north-south meridian or hinge. (Cardo also means "thistle" in Latin and French, but the meridian definition fit much better.)

Having a mountain at the northern end of the cross named Cardou certainly fit the developing pattern, and the Paris Meridian passes along the eastern side of the mountain. But I needed to find a site that more closely matched the distances and themes of the first two fire locations. I don't want the reader to get lost in numbers and calculations, so before we discover the location for the lighting of the Third Fire, let's explore the amazing landscape surrounding Cardou, and the Celtic settlement of Rennes-les-Bains. When we discover the many facets of this jewel, we can better appreciate the mysteries that the ancient architects have left for us here.

Druid Stone Circles

> *"The circles traced by the standing stones had a profoundly religious meaning for the Celts. The Druids, just like the ancient philosophers, regarded the circular figure as the most perfect. It represented to them Divine perfection, immense and infinite, having neither beginning nor end."*[2]
>
> Abbé Henri Boudet[2]

The thermal village of Rennes-les-Bains ("The Queen's Baths") lies in the narrow valley of the Sals (Salt) River, surrounded by ridges that are strewn with the stone foundations of Celtic villages. Henri Boudet arrived in the village in 1872 to serve as parish priest. After years of hiking and exploring the hills he envisioned the entire valley as a great circle of standing stones crowning the surrounding hills, which he

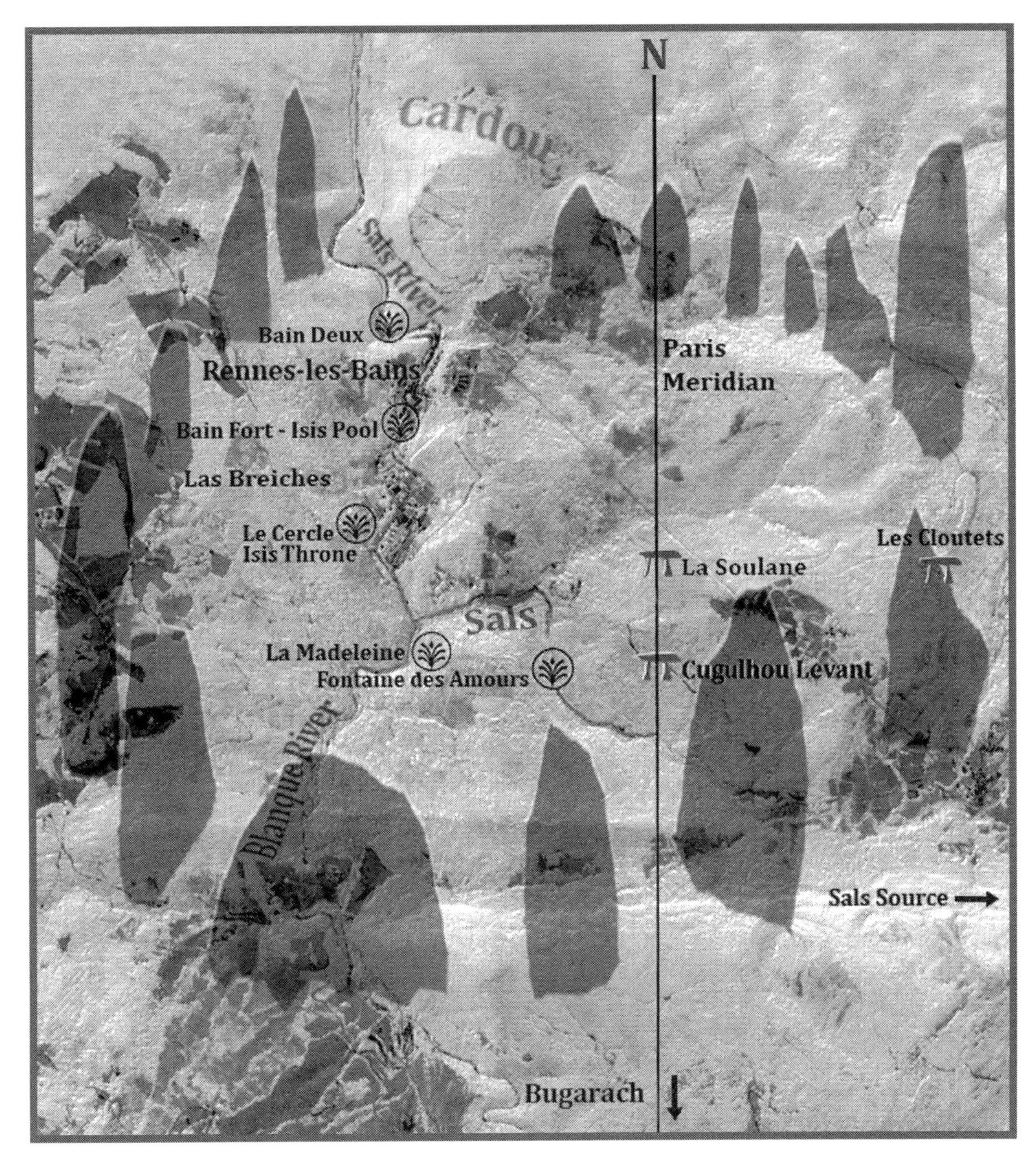

Illustration 11: Cromlech of Rennes-les-Bains

called a *cromlech,* a word meaning "stone circle" from the old Welsh and Breton languages. Boudet said that this stone circle was between sixteen and eighteen kilometers (10–11 miles) in circumference.

The valley was formed by the river, surrounded with steep hills, creating a cauldron that is moist, feminine, and magnetic in nature, a place for dreaming. (Sals is spelled Salz in Occitan, also meaning salt.) On the hills on both sides of the valley, we find the remains of Celtic villages and shrines with numerous menhirs, worked and inscribed stones, and natural monoliths that were used for rituals and as astronomical markers.

This valley that I have called home for fourteen years has attracted many artists, musicians, filmmakers, writers, and visionaries who have given birth to numerous creations, one of whom was my dear friend, the late Henry Lincoln. Another Henri who used the mystical inspiration of this valley was the priest Boudet, who wrote about the history of the valley in his strange, encoded book in 1886.

Henri Boudet was no ordinary backcountry priest and spoke not only the local Occitan language and French but had a university degree in English, knew Latin and Greek, and had a basic understanding of Hebrew. In addition, he had a comprehensive knowledge of ancient history and archeology and was guided to explore the valleys and hills with an eye for mystery. Born under the sign of Scorpio, he had an acute intuition and a propensity to dig beneath the surface in his quests.

There is reason to believe that the priest was privy to sensitive secret information regarding buried documents, relics, or treasure. Boudet was one of a trinity of village priests in this region, along with Antoine Gélis of Coustaussa, and Bérenger Saunière of Rennes-le-Château. Strangely, all three priests may have died under mysterious circumstances, with Gélis being brutally murdered. Gélis' gravestone in Coustaussa displays a Rosicrucian Cross, which is certainly unusual for a priest, indicating esoteric knowledge. The area was no stranger to stories of intrigue and hidden treasure, since the Visigoths and Templars had been in the region, and both had access to items from the Holy Land.

My local source indicated that Boudet's cromlech, crowning the hills above the village, corresponds to a zodiac pattern of thirteen signs, perhaps related to the thirteen astrological poems in a text called *Le Serpent Rouge* (The Red Serpent). This mysterious document was deposited in the Bibliothèque Nationale in 1967 and contains a Merovingian genealogy, maps of France, and a ground plan of Saint Sulpice in Paris, with its own meridian line running through the church. The thirteen signs of the zodiac include Ophiuchus, the Serpent-Bearer, and Maria Magdalena and Isis are featured in the Leo poem, coinciding with her feast day in July. My source continued to explain that each point on the zodiac wheel marked the location of a cache of relics and information placed there during the medieval era by the Knights Templar. He described some of the sites having standing stones with nearby remote caves that would lend themselves to concealing items of import. He added that specific rituals are still carried out at certain intervals of the year, also corresponding to larger calendar cycles. Mysterious indeed!

The cromlech had been inhabited by the Celts and their wise Druids. Some of the enormous stones marking the landscape were natural, but many were worked, carved, and moved into positions to form important alignments. The Celtic villages on the western slopes of the valley were built on tiered levels, and the stone steps connecting them are still intact, as are the ancient spring enclosures. The valley has at least a dozen red and white springs, and salty healing waters fed by a nearby natural salt spring.

The Romans revived the thermal village, which they called *Aquae Calidae*, Latin for hot waters, with the hottest spring currently called *Bain Fort* (Strong Bath), but as mentioned earlier, the older name may have been "Pool of Isis." We know that the Romans and late Egyptians carried the cult of Isis into the west, so this is certainly possible.

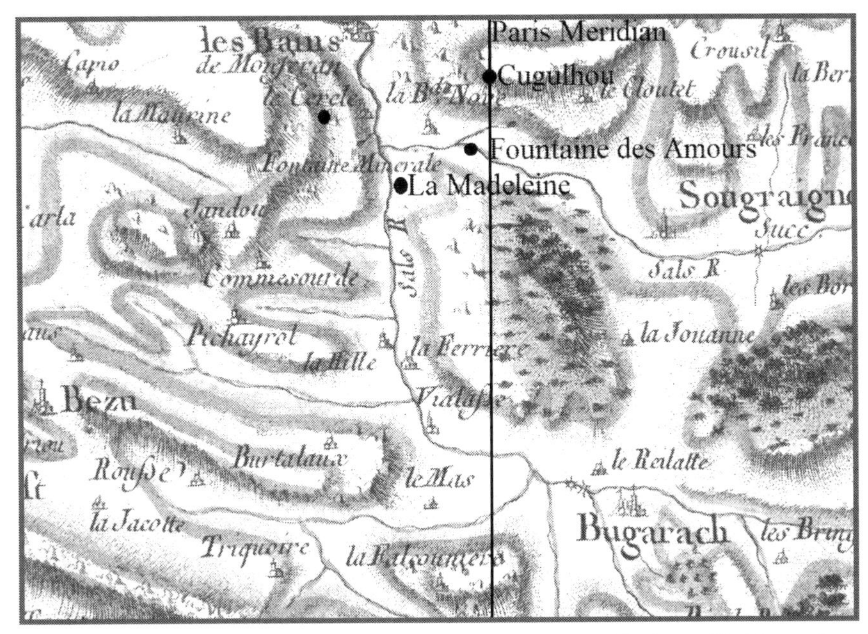

Illustration 14: Cassini map Rennes-les-Bains, 1700s, with sites added by author.

Temples were constructed to their deities, which included one to Jupiter, which stood on the slight rise opposite the village square, the temple columns still visible. My local source says that just to the south of the Jupiter temple was another to Venus, and Boudet purportedly discovered a large statue of the goddess but reburied it for fear of reprisals from the local god-fearing congregation.

Regarding Rennes-les-Bains' many springs, author Gérard de Sède says in his forward to Boudet's *Le Vrai Langue Celtique* that the village was originally called *Regnes*, a Celto-Germanic word meaning "Red Waters." From the 14th century to at least the 17th, the village was called Bains de Montferrand (Baths of the Iron Mountain), and this is the way it is listed on the Cassini maps that measured the Paris Zero Meridian, beginning in the 17th century.

Montferrand is a hamlet up the hill from Rennes-les-Bains, on the flanks of Mount Cardou, and there are crumbling stone remains of a medieval château, so the site held some importance. The view is spectacular from the site of the old château looking southward along the Dragon Path toward Mount Bugarach and the Pyrenees in the distance. An old equal-armed wayside cross marks the meeting of three trackways, which Henry Lincoln said marked important ancient routes, and as we have learned, another marks the meridian at the southern arm of the Great Cross at Cardedeu. Relevant to our developing landscape cross, during the 18th century and perhaps earlier, Rennes-les-Bains was also called *Val Crux,* meaning "Valley of the Cross."

The Celts and Romans were known to have mined the rich iron in Cardou that gives the deep crimson hue to the terrain. The plentiful gold, silver, and copper in the valley had been mined throughout the ages by Celts, then Romans, and later by the Knights Templar, and the open mine shafts are still visible. These elements are known to affect the telluric energies and enhance electromagnetic phenomena. Another precious element is the extremely rare salt spring at Source de la Sals, which flows through the valley from the east and turns north at Rennes-les-Bains. The salt content of this spring is greater than seawater, and salt was considered so valuable that it was compared to gold.

Salt, Sophia, and Maria Magdalena

"For everyone shall be seasoned with fire, and every sacrifice shall be seasoned with salt ... Have salt in yourselves and have peace one with another."

MARK 9:49–50 (KJV)

If we have salt in ourselves, the wisdom and light of Sophia, the Mother of the World, is present. Salt is a primary ingredient used in alchemy, not only in the classic work of turning lead into gold but in the transformation of the soul. Salt is purifying and necessary for life, and we are born from the salty amniotic waters of our mothers' wombs. And in death, salt was used in embalming the dead, such as in Egyptian mummification. Clearly, it is essential in the transitions of birth, life, and death. Salt has always been considered an essential element in rituals and prayers, and its ancient connection with wisdom is made clear in the Gospel of Philip, from the Nag Hammadi codices:

"The apostles said to the disciples, 'May our entire offering obtain salt.' They called Wisdom (Sophia) 'salt.' Without it, no offering is acceptable."[3]

The Greek word *Sophia* means "Wisdom," and in the Rabbinic tradition of the first century CE, salt symbolized not only wisdom but also indicated one who is a "seer," one with clear vision. These qualities certainly fit with Our Lady, Maria Magdalena. Many years ago, I wanted to know her true essence, as there were endless ideas and legends circulating. In a quiet moment, I posed the question, "Magdalena, who are you, really?" And immediately I heard, "I am the salt of the Earth." The response didn't make any sense at that time, until I remembered the same exact phrase from the Gospel of Matthew 5:13. And in the following verse, he adds: "You are the light of the world." Salt, light, and wisdom created a perfect portrait of Magdalena's essence, and inspired the song "Salt of Earth."[4]

In a conversation with Henry Lincoln, he pointed out an extremely interesting, coded message in one of the parchments purportedly discovered hidden in Magdalena's church in Rennes-le-Château. He explained that when the irregular letters are reassembled, it reads in a combination of Latin and Greek: "Panis Δ Ω Sal," meaning "Bread-Alpha-Omega-Salt." Bread relates to Corpus Christi, the body of Christ;

Alpha represents the male, the blade; Omega is the female receptacle, the inverted chalice or womb; and Salt is Magdalena, the wisdom of Sophia. Hence, "Bread-Jesus-Magdalene-Salt." Alpha and Omega are the bridegroom and the bride, and is it a "coincidence," that the 22nd verse in John's Revelation says:

"I am the Alpha and the Omega, the Beginning and the end,
the First and the Last."

We find the similar Alpha-Omega phrase in the "Thunder Perfect Mind" text from the Nag Hammadi codices, and here, it is clearly the feminine voice and in particular, Maria-Sophia speaking:

"For I am the first and the last.
I am the honored one and the scorned one.
I am the whore and the holy one.
I am the wife and the virgin ..."

With the clues provided by the Rennes-le-Château parchments and the presence of salt as a sacred element in the region, it is not surprising that many visitors sense Magdalena's presence. At the southern end of the village of Rennes-les-Bains flows an ancient red "blood" spring called Source de Madeleine, known by this name at least since the time of Henri Boudet. The older Celtic name was *Gode*, meaning cup, but again, a feminine symbol.

I reflected on several other sites associated with Our Lady and Salt: Les-Saintes-Maries-de-la-Mer, where French legend says that the Three Marys, Mary Jacobi, Mary Salome, and Mary Magdalene came ashore; Sainte Marie-la-Mer, another Mediterranean port just south of Rennes-les-Bains, where alternate legends say that Magdalena arrived. At both seaside villages, salt has been dried and traded for eons. And the only cathedral dedicated to Magdalena in North America is in Salt Lake City, Utah, site of an enormous ancient salty sea.

Searching for the Site of the Third Fire

"Then began the ritual process of hallowing the country. This included the lighting of bonfires around the borders of the lands they occupied."

JOHN MICHELL, *THE SACRED CENTER*[5]

The process of lighting the first two fires had opened doorways of communication with the land, with the elements, and had revealed unexpected alignments of the sites with stars and the cycles of time. Creating an intimate relationship with fire opened a sensitivity to subtle dimensions of the natural kingdoms, seen and unseen, audible and inaudible. Before this quest to know fire, my focus for many years had been on the elements of water and earth, especially the sacred water sources. These holy wells often formed the origin and heart of an older sanctuary, which later became Celtic and Druid meeting places and ultimately, churches and cathedrals. I wondered if the site for the Third Fire would be at a spring or water source, since the first two fires were not, and this region is certainly a land of many waters.

To locate the site for the Third Fire, I used Google Earth to measure 45 miles (72.4 kilometers) north of the east-west latitude path of 42°N15', which ends up in the woods below Pech Cardou. The mountain rises above the ancient Celtic settlements and the village of Rennes-les-Bains and seemed a likely location. Not only is the eastern side of Cardou on the north-south meridian, but another prominent marker in the regional landscape, Mount Bugarach, is on the meridian just to the south. One can see both Cardou and Bugarach dominating the landscape for many miles. It was becoming increasingly apparent that this is no accidental meridian and has most likely been known and worked for eons. As Henry Lincoln would remark many times regarding the perfection of sites on the meridian, "It ain't no accident," using American slang for my benefit.

The landscape surrounding Pech Cardou is enchanting, with the numerous healing springs in the thermal village, Celtic settlements, and worked stone sites. This region is rich in history but finding the exact location for the Third Fire remained elusive. Just east of Rennes-les-Bains on the Sals River, and a third of a mile west of the Paris Meridian is a site called Fontaine des Amours (Fountain of Lovers). Even though it was not exactly on the meridian, it was close, and was the first site that seemed a likely location for the Third Fire.

Fontaine des Amours.

This magical place features a series of pools and small waterfalls, and looks like a scene straight out of a fairy tale. The waters of the Sals are fed by the salty Source de la Sals a few miles up the valley, with salt providing the alchemical, purification element. An old mill powered by a water wheel was once at the site, but only ruined stone walls remain. Above the stream, a tiny spring with tangy effervescent-tasting water flows during the wet seasons in an ancient sanctuary enclosure, with niches in the stone walls for lighting candles and making offerings. Even the trees above the spring grew in two separate directions to allow a dragon current to flow freely through the sanctuary down to the salty stream. Others have noticed this terrestrial current, as there is a dragon carved on one of the rock faces near the old mill and over the deepest of the pools of the lovers.

Dragon-Serpent at Fontaine des Amours by Renick Turley.

Interestingly, there is a 16th-century French alchemical tale called "The Fountain of Lovers of the Science," referring to the Hermetic science of the transmutation of the soul. Scottish historian of alchemical images and texts Adam McLean claimed that the earliest edition that he had seen was issued in Paris in 1561. Not only is this allegorical text Hermetic, but one of the main characters is a dragon! In the story, the author describes a most noble thing contained in the fountain, which is used alchemically. This obviously refers to salt, one of the three essential elements in classical alchemy, the other two being sulfur and mercury. The following is extracted from the larger text:

> *"In it the fountain has a thing, which is most nobly contained. He who shall know it well, will love it above all other things. He who would seek and search it out, and being found put it afterwards into the earth and dry it to a most subtile powder, then again dissolve it in its water ... then gather the parts together ... Thence there will a maiden breed, bearing fruit at both her breasts ... For she mounts into the air flying on high; afterwards descending down gliding in the valley, and in descending down she fawns the fawn which Nature gives to her. It is a Dragon ..."*

The allegory continues: "... you would be pleased to tell me, how they do call this Fountain, which is so amiable and wholesome. She answered; Friends behold, since you desire to know it; It most properly is called, the Fountain of the Lovers. How it must be known to you, that ever since our Mother Eve, that I have governed all the world, as great as tis in all the Circle, nothing without me can rule unless God would inspire it. I who am called Nature O environed the Earth, without, within and in the middle."[6]

The Fountain of the Lovers of the Science, written during the Renaissance or earlier, features alchemical salt and is, to my knowledge, the only written reference to a dragon in this valley other than my encounter mentioned earlier. And true to the name of the site, there is a local legend that if two beloveds bathe nude in the salty turquoise pools the enchantment of love will bind them together forever. Henry Lincoln reported in *Key to the Sacred Pattern* that the priest Bérenger Saunière of Rennes-le-Château came to the Fountain of Lovers on a tryst with, some say, his lover Emma Calvé. She was a well-known opera star from Paris who visited the priest on occasion, and Henry found her name and a large heart carved on one of the stones above the pools, and a photograph appears in his book. (It has since been rubbed out, by someone who didn't want the story circulated of the priest having a love affair.) But her name strangely still appears in Rennes-les=Bains, on the large cross with Jesus overlooking the river. At the bottom of the cross dedicated "Mission 1885" by the enigmatic parish priest Boudet, it says "E. Calvet," an alternate spelling of her name. Most who stop there to gaze at Jesus don't notice the coded signature below.

Mysterious Circles in the Forest

"We are not overly astonished that the Celts had such extensive knowledge. They had brought from the Orient the most precise ideas about the Divine Being and they fixed in the ground, by means of standing stones, their thoughts and belief in God ..."

HENRI BOUDET[7]

Although Fontaine des Amours is a magical place, I kept searching for the perfect site located exactly on the Paris Meridian for the Third Fire. As you can see, the search often led through a labyrinth of sites, and yet it was not a project to be rushed or taken lightly. I remembered visiting, years previously, a strange megalithic worked stone site in the forested hillside just to the northeast of the Fontaine. A friend had taken me there during my early years of living in this region. Trebha always had a finely attuned ability to find obscure Celtic and megalithic sites that most people visiting the region would never know existed. The locations often required scrambling up steep wooded terrain and forging a new path where the original way was long forgotten and overgrown. Trebha was of Irish descent and the ancient Celtic cultures were very much alive and resonating in his blood.

I didn't know the name of the site in question but recalled the first time he had taken me there. We climbed up a steep hillside, thick with underbrush, passing larger than normal fallen stones that appeared to be ancient dolmens or tomb enclosures. Finally, the terrain leveled out, and in a clearing surrounded by thick forest stood a large rectangular stone table with two carved circles, perfectly symmetrical. One circle was smaller, with a narrow opening connecting to the larger circle, which was nearly three feet (just under one meter) in diameter. How were they created with such precision?

The circles appeared to be intended to hold water, perhaps for mirroring the stars or oracular use. Either way, this was an ancient ritual site. We cleaned the forest debris out of the circles and Trebha suggested I tune into the ancient guardians and listen for a song. The language that emerged was unfamiliar, rough, and guttural, and as I was chanting, the wind picked up and circled around the grove, causing the leaves to tremble. Trebha pointed out equal-armed "Greek" crosses engraved in the stones on the opposite edge of the clearing.

Cugulhou Levant.

When I remembered this site, I was hopeful that this might be the location for the Third Fire. It had engraved crosses and megalithic stones, which certainly matched the pattern of the first two fire sites. I contacted another friend in the village, Danish author and master Mason Kaj Lilliendal and asked if he knew the site. Kaj said it was Cugulhou Levant, and I was elated to discover that it is located exactly on the Paris Meridian. And better yet, the distance from Cugulhou Levant to the east-west axis of the Great Cross was 45.52 miles (73.26 kilometers).

This was amazing, as the site of the Second Fire at Dolmen de Can Planes in the megalithic route near Barcelona was also exactly 45.52 miles to the south of the east-west axis.[8] Thus, the northern and southern arms of the Great Cross were exactly equidistant from the center, revealing an extraordinary perfection to the developing pattern. Additionally, the site of Cugulhou is located directly below one of the five points of Henry Lincoln's landscape pentagram, the peak of La Soulane, also on the Paris Meridian. (See illustration 15 Venus Pentagram on page 33.) The peak is crowned with about eight large stones, six having fallen. The site appears to be basically a natural formation that has eroded over time, and the two remaining upright stones are aligned north south, both about 13 feet (4 meters) high. There is a natural perfection here, with the two slabs marking both the Dragon Path and the eastern point of the Venus Pentagram. And based on the number of menhirs and engraved stones in the surrounding landscape, the site would have been used for rituals. My local source confirmed La Soulane as one of the ceremonial sites in the cromlech surrounding Rennes-les-Bains. Soulane, or *soulan*, is a French Pyrenean term referring to a geographic site exposed to the Sun, and in this case, a solar temple.

Were the ancient people who worked the stones in this region also marking the Venus cycles? Mayan and Babylonian sky watchers calculated the cycles of Venus, including the eight-, thirty-two-, and sixty-four-year cycles of the planet. And every 128 years or so, Venus makes an exact conjunction with the Sun and passes across its face, which I had witnessed in June of 2012 from a high peak (La Pique) at the center of the Venus landscape pentagram below Rennes-le-Château. I would discover later that even the Camino de Santiago also has an interesting connection to the cycles of Venus and Maria Magdalena, and I remembered Henry Lincoln saying many times, that Venus' cycles in heaven are reflected in this land as the pattern of secret revelation of Maria Magdalena. There definitely seemed to be a master plan in both the natural arrangement and human placement of sites forming star patterns and a Great Cross centered in the Pyrenean landscape, and I wondered when this ancient grid pattern was laid out on the Earth. I reflected on the St. Benedict medallion that I had been wearing throughout the years of these discoveries and how perfection was unfolding. (See film on Henry Lincoln's pentagram and the Venus transit, "Quest for Invisible Treasure," in footnote 2, chapter 3.)

In re-reading Boudet's book on this Celtic region, I would discover more about the name of the megalithic carved circles. To paraphrase his description of this site:

Within the great Cromlech, stone circle of Rennes-les-Bains, there is an enigmatic pair of ancient circles carved in stone at a site located on the Paris Meridian to the east of the village called Cugulhou Levant.[9]

Boudet says that this name means "carved and set upright," and we will soon discover an interesting double meaning in the name. (*Levant* derives from the French *lever*, meaning to rise). Boudet's language and names are coded, and I'm not exactly sure what he intended here, as upright does not describe the circles that are carved into a flat, horizontal stone table. Perhaps there were upright standing stones at this site that have since fallen. Or perhaps *lever* refers to the abnormalities in the electromagnetic energies, or the rising of a particular star aligned to the site, which we shall discover is Sirius.

Lighting the Third Fire

"O ignee spiritus laus tibi sit
qui in timpanis et citharis operaris"

Praise be to thee O spirit of flame
who speaks through lyre and tambour [drum] ..."

Hildegard of Bingen[10]

Cugulhou Levant was the perfect place for the lighting of the Third Fire. The two perfectly symmetrical circles were unique in the entire region and formed what was obviously an important ritual site. Additionally, near the two circles were engraved stones with equal-armed crosses, this location being equidistant from the large Neolithic engraved crosses to the south near Barcelona. Both the northern and southern ends of the landscape cross were located on the Paris Meridian and Cugulhou was on the eastern edge of the valley that had been called Val Crux, Valley of the Cross! The perfection in the coherent repeating patterns never ceased to amaze.

To light the Third Fire, I returned to Cugulhou with Trebha and another friend, Nancy Safford, who has since passed away. It's strange to be writing these memories now, when so many people that were part of these stories are no longer here. Nancy was the first person to invite me to come to this region, saying that she sensed that the elementals of the forests wanted to hear the music of the harp, and almost twenty years ago I found myself answering the request. It was a beautiful warm spring day at Cugulhou, and the birds were in full force with their melodies. The songs of the nightingale during late spring reverberate through these valleys, often with one singer answering another in their extensive repertoire.

Arriving at the site after another steep climb up the wooded hillside, we cleaned the circles and filled them with salty water from the Sals River that runs below. As an offering to the place, we sang a piece that matched the magic of the forest, "Earth Mother."[11] This is a chant that I heard issuing from the stones of another ancient monument many years ago, on a summer solstice at the megalithic burial chamber of West Kennet Long Barrow near Avebury, England. The song begins with an ancient Celtic chant which we sang together to the accompaniment of my small lyre and Nancy's drumming on the stone. The wind picked up and caused the leaves to dance around the two circles, and we sensed the elements and invisible guardians signaling their approval.

Nancy called in the four directions, the above and below, and we lit the Third Fire for the northern end of the Great Cross. It felt like we had ignited the *ignee spiritus*, spirit of the flame, that Hildegard of Bingen spoke of in the previous quote. I had placed the medallion of Saint Benedict on the stone, aligned with the four cardinal points, and we faced the north toward the Imperishable Stars, the stars that never set, continually circling the Earth's axis. We imagined the flame of our candle between the two circles igniting the Dragon Path to the north. We turned to the south and visualized the flame of our love streaming southward along the meridian all the way to Isla Dragonera as she floats in the salty sea. We acknowledged the guardians of the site and the elements, fire, air, earth, and water.

There was a hushed silence in the grove, and we sensed invisible presences acknowledging our symbolic act and intentions. There was a distinct ringing in the air of multitudes of harmonics. Nancy perceived it as light particles and colors. Trebha remained silent. Even the birds had stopped singing during the ritual. As we closed the circle, the birdsong suddenly resumed, knowing the work was complete.

Yin-Yang Stones and the Language of the Birds

"Nothing is completely yin nor is it completely yang. All things in the material universe contain the seed of their opposite force... Therefore, yin can become yang and yang can also become yin, though both yin and yang are needed for the whole to be complete."

Chang Sok Suh, *Acupuncture Anatomy*[12]

My friend Kaj Lilliendal had measured the two circles at Cugulhou Levant and found that the diameters are in the same proportion as the size of the planet Mars to Venus. (Mars is about half the size of Venus.) The two circles also vary slightly in depth and are connected by an intentional hole between them so that water in the elevated smaller circle (Mars) flows into the slightly lower and larger circle (Venus). This was highly suggestive of fertility, with the water from the male circle flowing into the female. And the village priest Henri Boudet may have suspected that this site was related to fertility rites. He was prone to writing in the punning "Green Language," also called the "Language of the Birds," in which words can have multiple meanings, with the magical meaning discernable only to those knowledgeable in the mysteries. Boudet wrote that Cugulhou also means "to cock, to raise up ..."[13] Cock is slang for phallus, and perhaps Boudet had heard some of the old people of the village recalling stories of mysterious gatherings at the strange circle stones on the hill.

Could this site located on the Paris Meridian have been a ritual site for balancing the female (yin) and male (yang) energies of the Dragon Path? We live in a world of duality, and in Gnostic tradition, as well as in most world religions, all deities have consorts, sacred allies, termed *syzygies,* meaning a pair or couple. In astronomy, *syzygy* is a conjunction of pairs, such as the Sun and Moon, which occurs monthly, or the conjunctions of Venus and Mars, which occur in groups about every 32 years, based on the orbits of Venus. I pondered the perfection of these ancient, engraved circles on the hill overlooking the "Lovers Pools" of Fontaine des Amours. Could these two circles be serving this function of maintaining a balance in these polarities? This would be an important function for the Dragon Path.

As mentioned previously, my friend Dani Valdés and I had done a meditation for balancing female and male energies along the Paris Meridian at the site Dolmen de Céllecs during a lunar eclipse, with the Sun and Moon at opposition, and the Earth between. As stated earlier, the balancing of the Earth energies was a dedicated and ancient Chinese art called Feng Shui, and two of the basic energies were female yin in the west and male yang in the east, represented by the female White Tiger and the male Green Dragon, respectively. During the work at the dolmen, Dani and I had stood on the eastern and western sides of the "Dragon Path," and we both sensed a current of energy moving

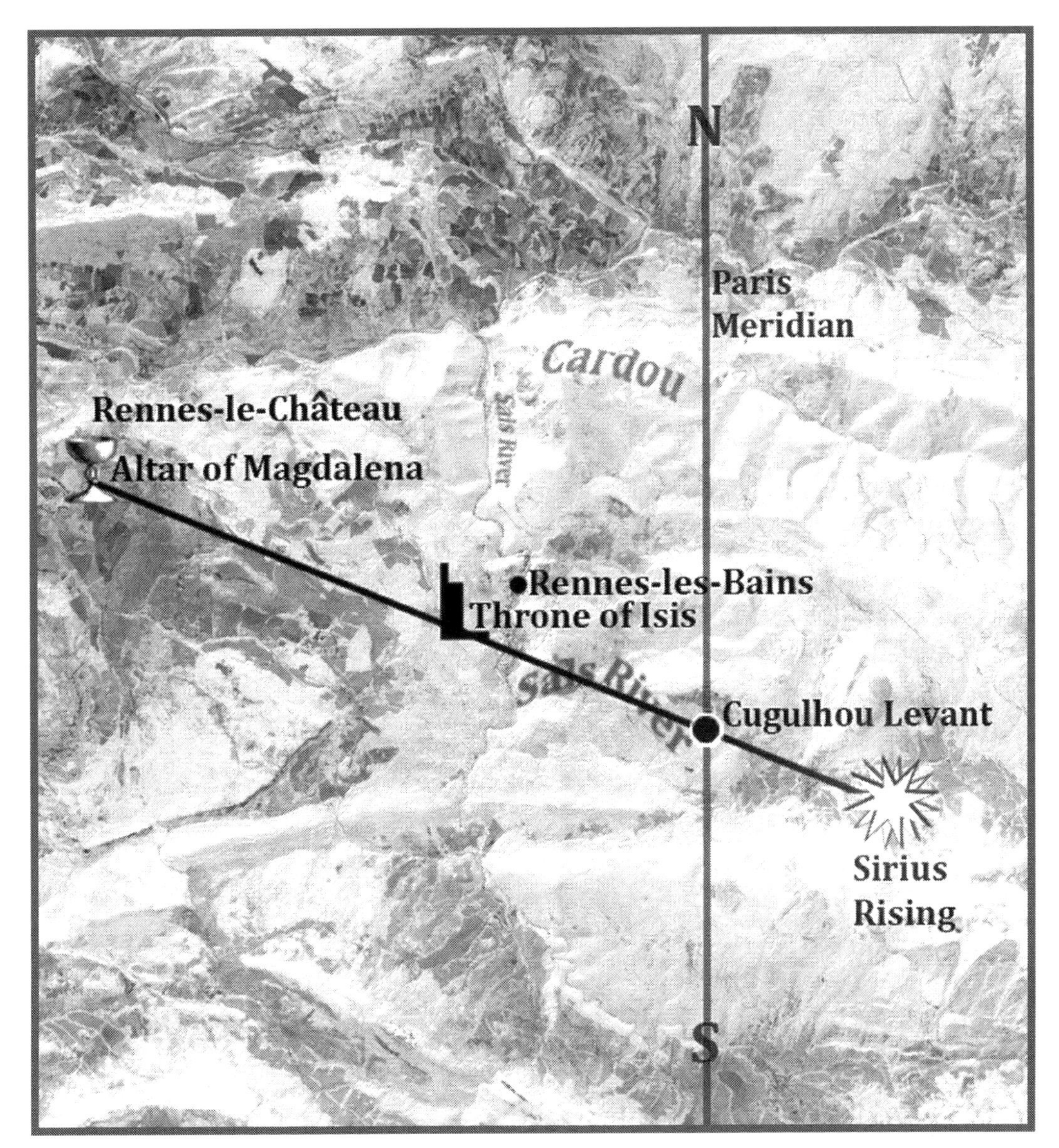

Illustration 17: Sirius Alignment

through the meridian, from north to south and within our internal *nadi* pathways, the ancient work of geomancy, or natural magic. It appeared that this yin-yang balancing was one of the purposes of the enigmatic circles at the northern arm of the Great Cross.

Additionally, there is an important star alignment through the circles at Cugulhou, connecting the two Rennes. According to Kaj, there is a line that runs from the altar of the church of Maria Magdalena at Rennes-le-Château, through *Le Fauteuil du Diable*, the "Devil's Armchair," to the circles of Cugulhou Levant to align with the rising point of the brightest star in the night sky, Sirius.[14] The Devil's Armchair is popularly known these days as the "Seat or Throne of Isis," and at first glance, this new name seems arbitrary. But given the alignment with Sirius, the name is perfect, since the Egyptians identified Sirius (which they called Sopdet, or Sothis) as the star of Isis. This alignment linking Magdalena and Isis is one more confirmation of the synastry between the two Rennes, the "Two Queens." (See illustration 17 Sirius Alignment.)

During a later return trip to Cugulhou Levant we were filming songs for the Earthling Project, an international effort to gather many voices from around the world to be sent to the Moon. (See the link for some of the songs filmed at Cugulhou.[15]) Earthling Project is part of the Artists in Residence program of the SETI Institute, founded by astronomers Drs. Carl Sagan and Jill Tarter. (Dr. Tarter's work inspired the film *"Contact"* and SETI stands for the Search for Extra-Terrestrial Intelligence.) During the filming, our cameraman lost contact with the drone when it was directly over the circles. The control device said, "Connection lost, magnetic interference." It is not unusual to have similar anomalies with electronic equipment at sites with powerful electromagnetic or abnormal telluric energy. Another common experience at ancient shrines in the region is a sense that one is entering a zone of silence, a portal to other dimensions, thus enhancing altered states of awareness. During later film projects at nearby sites between Rennes-les-Bains and Rennes-le-Château, this magnetic interference reading with the equipment kept repeating.

Henri Boudet may have had another elusive meaning in mind for his name of Cugulhou Levant.[16] Was he also indicating, by the word Levant, that the site has elevated, antigravity properties? Cugulhou certainly has an otherworldly ambiance. The priest used the "Green Language" to describe the megalithic sites surrounding his village, using words that have multiple meanings. The late author Vincent Bridges related to me that this language is a phonetic wordplay, like a spoken, mystical cabala, and that it can reveal subtle associations. This Hermetic language, also used by the Druids, served to mask the occult mysteries known only to the initiated. The 20th-century French scholar René Guénon, in his article "The Language of the Birds," gave the following examples from the Koran and a Norse legend of the dragon as the guardian of the language of the birds, and of immortality:

> *"We read, for example, in the Qur'ān: 'And Solomon was David's heir. And he said, O mankind! Lo! we have been taught the language of the birds ... and have been given abundance of all things' (27:16). Elsewhere we read of heroes who, having vanquished the dragon, like Siegfried in the Nordic legend, instantly understand the language of the birds; ... Victory over the dragon has, as its immediate consequence, the conquest of immortality, ... which is guarded by the dragon ..."*[17]

Was the Rennes-les-Bains priest Henri Boudet also thinking of Isis when he used the Language of the Birds in his encoded descriptions of this region? Egyptian Isis was honored in this landscape, as evidenced by place names and ancient ruins that locals claim were the foundations of her temples. There is archeological evidence of shrines and temples to Isis in this region, constructed by the Greeks and Romans who settled in Gaul and Iberia, which will be revealed in future chapters. Isis was an enchantress, a mistress of magical words, and she was said to have been coached by the great teacher Thoth in the powerful language of creation. Isis, lady of magic, was known to speak this secret Language of the Birds, in other words, the Language of the Gods and Goddesses:

> *"Thoth wrote the Book with his own hand, and in it is all the magic in the world. If thou readest the first page, thou wilt enchant the sky, the earth, the abyss, the mountains, and the sea; thou wilt understand the language of the birds of the air... And besides this, thou wilt see the sun shining in the sky with the full moon and the stars, and thou wilt behold the great shapes of the Gods."*[18]

Part III

Discovering Magdalena at the Center

CHAPTER 11

Black Stone Calling

"[Nicholas] Roerich speaks of Mongolian traditions which state that the Lord of the World once gave the Dalai Lama a magic black stone ... This black stone wanders the Earth."

Elizabeth Van Buren, *The Sign of the Dove*[1]

The recurring dream was always calling me back to the same ancient monastery. During the first dream, I had entered a large medieval monastery that had been transformed into a museum. As I wandered through the various rooms of extraordinary artifacts, I was pulled by an irresistible force to the museum's upper level and a small chamber to the left. The only other person in the room was a museum curator. It was 5 pm, nearly closing time, and she was in the process of lowering a large black basalt stone from its hidden and secure place from the level above. It was strange that, although it was closing time for the museum, the woman lowered the stone for visibility. Apparently, this was something I needed to see.

The rectangular stone was settled into a wooden display case, and I was left alone for some time to observe it. The stone slab was about 6.5 feet (2 meters) long and inscribed with symbols that looked like Egyptian hieroglyphs. I heard a voice that seemed to emanate from the stone say, "Ka Ba." Then the curator returned to hoist the mysterious relic back up into its hidden chamber. The museum considered it to be a very rare and priceless piece and I sensed the stone provided an important clue for my work, but what was it?

Subsequent dreams took me back several times to the same old monastery-museum. Each time I was hoping to view the mysterious inscribed black stone, but I was only able to see it one other time, though with no additional information. In one of the sequences, I returned to this same side room, and the black stone was replaced with a chalice and a footprint of Maria Magdalena. Interesting clues. In Celtic legend the Grail took the form of a magical cauldron, and in his *Parzival* Wolfram von Eschenbach describes it as a stone. Some say that Magdalena herself was the Holy Grail.

But what was the black stone in the dream telling me? My meditations didn't produce any more details, other than it was a crucial piece of the Catalan story of Magdalena.

I began to research important black stones, which have held a certain mystical allure throughout history. The Chintamani was a mysterious black stone wandering the Earth according to Mongolian legends and was purportedly given to the Dalai Lama. In Buddhist tradition, the Chintamani is said to be one of four *terma* or sacred relics that fell from the sky during the fifth century CE reign of the legendary Tibetan King Lha Thothori Nyantsen.

The Chintamani is a wish-fulfilling jewel, a magical tool for manifesting and healing, sometimes inscribed with a mantra, such as *Om Mani Padme Hum*. The Mani Stone, as it is more often called, was said to be a palm-sized meteorite that fell from the region of the constellation Orion and landed near the Altai mountains of Mongolia (an Orionids meteor most likely). For the 20th century Russian mystic and artist Nicholas Roerich and his wife, Helena, the region where the Chintamani stone landed was also the location of the legendary Shamballa, the heavenly city on Earth. Shamballa is mentioned in the *Vishnu Purana* Vedic text as being the site of the kingdom of the Maitreya Buddha, who will signal the dawning of a new age, called the Satya Yuga.

When the Roerichs went to Mongolia and Tibet in search of the mysterious black stone in the 1920s, they met with many wise teachers and heard various accounts. But it was when they returned to Europe that they were given a treasured Chintamani stone by a secret society in Paris, where the stone had been kept after arriving from the East. The letters MM inscribed on the casket containing the stone could have indicated the secret society was either Martinist or Masonic.[2] Some have speculated that they were the initials of the great ascended teacher of the Far East Master Morya. Or did MM relate to Mary Magdalene, linked in some way to the Black Stone dreams and the single reference to Magdalena in one of the monastery scenes? Could the stone from Shamballa and the realm of the gods be coded with knowledge that can help humanity awaken from our state of unconsciousness, and remember our greater destiny?

Tibetan Mani Stone.

In the American Southwest, meteors were considered by indigenous cultures to be messengers from the gods. A giant meteor crashed in Northern Arizona more than 50,000 years ago during the Pleistocene epoch, scattering heavy black stones across the landscape. The crater created by the impact is almost 4000 feet (1200 meters) wide. Archeologists have located numerous sites where these meteor fragments landed and have discovered stone shrines that were built by local tribes to protect these stone messengers. Interestingly, several of the shrines look like small megalithic dolmens shaped like stone houses, miniature examples of the hundreds of monuments found across Europe. Prayer offerings of local blue crystal salt and prayer feather sticks, called *pahos*, were found surrounding the black stone shrines.[3]

The black stone mystique reaches throughout history, but what was the black stone inscribed with hieroglyphs in my dreams? The search had produced some interesting stories, but the stone from the museum-monastery seemed to be a different sort of relic. I wondered about the words "Ka Ba" that I heard whispered during the first dream. Could it relate to the Kabbalah and the esoteric mystery traditions of Judaism? Or was the message indicating the enigmatic Hebrew term for a mystical chariot, a Merkaba? Or perhaps the dream referred to the black stone housed in the Ka'ba shrine at Mecca, which was also said to have been a meteorite fallen from heaven. The Arabic term *al-Ka'ba* means "the Cube."

Could the Ka Ba message be a clue to the multi-dimensional aspect of the Great Cross that stretches across the Pyrenees? Certainly, one-dimensional shapes can produce corresponding three-dimensional shapes and beyond. If the cube was indicated, this is indeed interesting, as this was the shape of the inner sanctuary of the Holy of Holies in the Temple of Solomon, signifying it as the true dwelling place of God. The Book of Revelation 21:10–22 describes a similarly shaped new heavenly city on Earth, descending with a great light like a precious stone, with twelve gates, facing north, south, east, and west. Each gate was an illuminated pearl, and the entire city was a cube, measuring one hundred and forty-four cubits, and adorned with twelve gemstones. This provided a strong possibility for the meaning of the whispered message.

Esther Harding, in her book *Women's Mysteries,* mentions that it is believed that originally the Ka'ba Black Stone was used in ancient goddess rites in Chaldea, and that Magna Dea, the Great Mother, was worshipped in the form of this stone, black like the dark of the Moon, and guarded by priestesses.[4] And there was said to be a black stone, *"Lapis Niger,"* engraved with the Greek goddess Themis' divine law that the Black Sea Amazons worshipped. The images of Artemis at Ephesus and of Venus-Aphrodite at Cyprus were said to be Black Stone meteorites in the shapes of the goddesses that fell from heaven. A stone that fell from heaven is sounding once again like the early Grail legends.

This was all very interesting, but what about the Egyptian hieroglyphics inscribed in the Black Stone of the dream? I began to search for monastic buildings that became museums, which was the scene in the dreams, and one that also exhibited a stone inscribed with Egyptian hieroglyphics. The black stone was rectangular and shaped like a stele. Stelae are rectangular inscribed stone slabs that can be found in many ancient sites around the world, including the great stele in front of the heart of the Sphinx at the Giza Plateau. But none of the stones so far provided an answer to my quest to find the black stone in my dreams.

Black Stone Revealed

Finally, after much rigorous searching online, I discovered what is called the "Palermo Stone" displayed in the Palermo Archeological Museum in Sicily. The building was originally a monastery, so this fit the sequence of the dreams perfectly. The Palermo Stone is

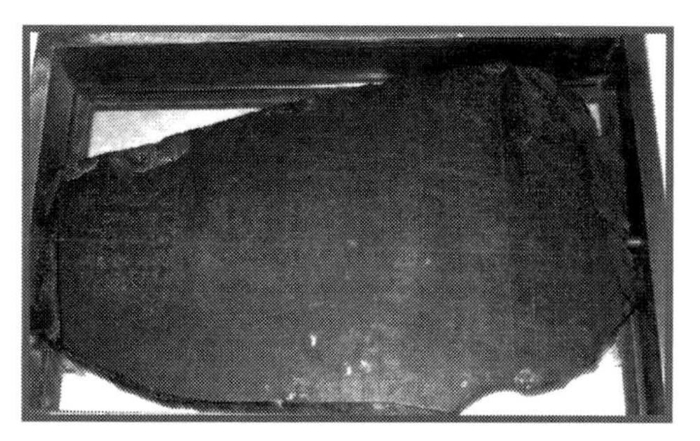

Palermo Stone, Palermo Museum.

the largest of seven fragments of the original stele from Egypt and is inscribed with hieroglyphs. Another perfect fit. The other smaller pieces of the original stone are in London at the Petrie Museum and in the Egyptian Museum in Cairo. And true to the dream, the stone was black, and the reassembled pieces are rectangular and calculated to originally have been 6.5 feet (two meters) long and just over 20 inches (0.5 meters) wide.

What was surprising was that this stele is thought to be Egypt's oldest example of written history! The Palermo Stone's inscriptions are about 800 years older than the oldest known Pyramid Texts at Saqqara, which are dated to 2400–2300 BCE. The Palermo Stone also has a king's list from the Old Kingdom's First Dynasty (3150–2890 BCE) through the early part of the Fifth Dynasty (2392–2283 BCE). This stone is certainly an important key, providing the earliest known source of information from Egypt's Old Kingdom. The inscriptions include the earliest mention of Osiris, the birth of Anubis, and the birth of Seshat.[5] She is an important deity in the Egyptian pantheon and her crown is a seven-pointed star. Seshat was often portrayed with Thoth, as they established the sacred measurements used in temple foundations, called the "Stretching of the Cord" ceremony. Their measurements took into account how the dimensions would create specific resonant effects within the temple, enhancing altered states when sacred music and chant were performed.

Thoth and Seshat, Abydos.

The original location of the whole stele is thought to have been either Memphis or Heliopolis. It is sometimes called by scholars the "puzzle of Palermo," since the seven fragments piece together the history of Egypt's earliest kings, dynasties, and ancient temple traditions. It lists the earliest ruler as King Scorpion, circa 3100 BCE. Interestingly, with the names of each of the kings was included the name of the king's mother, not the father. This remarkable tradition establishes a matriarchal lineage in ancient Egypt, which, according to Moustafa Gadalla, is a tradition that continued to endure in Iberia after the arrival of Egyptians in what he calls Hispania:

> *"The Romany of Hispania love the Virgin intensely. They, like the Ancient Egyptians of Hispania, strictly follow matrilineal practices in their society*

... Throughout Egyptian history, it was the queen who transmitted the solar blood. The queen was the true sovereign, landowner, keeper of the royalty, and guardian of the purity of the lineage. The man who married the eldest Egyptian princess claimed a right to the throne. Through marriage, she transmitted the legitimacy to her husband to become the next Pharaoh—he only acted as her executive agent ... Osiris became the first Pharaoh of Egypt as a result of his marrying Isis. She is the sun—the source of energy/light/ power—and he is the moon—the reflection of the sun/light/authority."[6]

I kept sensing there was something else the stone was telling me. Further research revealed that the Palermo Stone has the earliest known mention of the Opening of the Mouth ritual.[7] This clue seemed to provide the missing piece to the mysterious "Ka Ba" whispered at the museum's Black Stone. The Opening of the Mouth ritual reanimated the pharaoh for entry into the Duat, the realm of the afterlife, so he or she could navigate in their Ka and Ba bodies to the Imperishable Stars. The ritual was performed for a deceased pharaoh by temple Sem priests, who wore leopard skins, indicating their shamanic role as intermediaries to the spirit world. This is similar to the Mayan priests who wear jaguar skins.

Ka Edfu temple relief.

Ba Dendera temple relief.

The ritual prepared the pharaoh's Ka (double, etheric body) and Ba (soul-spirit) for the journey to the stars. Sometimes highly respected individuals connected with the temple also received this special ritual, such as a favored chantress that I would soon discover. In Egyptian iconography, the Ka is represented as two up-reaching bent arms, and the Ba normally by a falcon with a human head. The Opening of the Mouth ritual also opened the other senses, such as the eyes and ears, to enable successful navigation during the ascension journey. The Sem priests used magical incantations, sacred tools for opening, fragrant resins, and natron (a salt solution, always present in alchemical rituals).

"The spells, or 'utterances' ... are primarily concerned with protecting the pharaoh's remains, reanimating his [or her] body after death, and helping him [or her] ascend to the Heavens, which are the emphasis of the afterlife during the Old Kingdom. The spells delineate all of the ways the pharaoh could travel, including the use of ramps, stairs, ladders and most importantly flying."

E.A. Wallis Budge, *The Pyramid Texts*[8]

The Opening of the Mouth normally took place in the "Gold Room" within the temple, which is beginning to sound like a reference to the alchemical process of resurrection, rebirth, and of a soul Becoming Gold, the true goal of alchemy. Lucie Lamy speaks of the soul's rebirth in *Egyptian Mysteries: New Light on Ancient Knowledge:*

"The king's arrival in the sky is a new birth. His mother, Nut, calls him her newborn darling. The divine entities dance attendance on him, reassemble his bones, give him back the use of his senses by opening his eyes and mouth, rituals which are accomplished magically in the 'Room of Gold ...'"[9]

The newborn darling of the great Sky Mother Nut in the Afterlife is welcoming and comforting—we are born from a mother, and to the mother, we return. The natrum salt solution used in the funerary ritual can be compared to the natrum of our mother's womb. The Opening of the Mouth process would enable the pharaoh to breathe, to see, and to communicate, to utter the necessary sacred names, and ensure a safe passage through the dimensions of the Duat to the Sky Mother Nut and the Imperishable Stars in the north. These stars that never appear to set represented immortality for the Egyptians.

Nut Dendera temple relief.

In the following extract from the *Pyramid Texts,* translated by E.A. Wallis Budge, the ascension of the Ka of Pharaoh Unas is welcomed by the enduring, all-pervading goddess of the heavens:

"You did not pass away!
Your Ka does not pass away!
You are a Ka-Soul!
I have come to you, Nephthys.
I have come to the Evening Barge.
I have come to you.
True is She over the (Fields of) Red.
She is my True Love.
She who comes to me over the Fields of Red Barley, is my True Love
I have come to you.
She who remembers the Ka of All the Souls—
I have come to you!"[10]

CHAPTER 12

Down the Meridian to Find Magdalena

Following the series of dreams of the Black Stone, which led me to the Palermo Stone, I was excited to return to Catalonia. The first three fire locations had been discovered and the fires were lit, but the fourth fire site would have to wait, as the roads through the high Pyrenees were still icy. Taking the lower elevation roads from the coast would be another opportunity to scout the Catalan portion of the Paris Meridian and discover the site guarding the center of the Great Cross.

As I mentioned, there was nothing marked on the maps or Google Earth, except what looked like a farmhouse in the Catalan Pyrenees. Just 2.5 miles (4 kilometers) southwest of the center of the landscape cross and the Paris Meridian was the important Benedictine Abbey of Sant Joan de les Abadesses. Sant Joan was founded by the famous Abbess Emma in 885 CE. She was the daughter of the Count and Countess of Barcelona, and her superior education, wisdom, and diplomacy in her dealings with the counts of the entire Catalan region, which included at that time, Toulouse, Carcassonne, Narbonne, and Provence, earned her respect as well as jealousy. Her entirely female-run monastery included one of the finest scriptoriums and libraries with rare texts that were coveted and sometimes stolen by visiting monks.

More than two hundred years of success and prosperity for the monastery and the people of the surrounding region was sadly interrupted by jealous counts and abbots with trumped up charges of "lascivious behavior." Quite simply, they wanted the abbey's land and power, and the women were exiled to Sant Daniel, Girona, and replaced with monks. But the legacy that Emma ignited helped to form the future prosperity, spirit, and independence of Catalonia. As the monastery guide says:

> *"Emma was one of the great figures of new Catalonia and one of the most important women in our history ... Sant Joan is among the oldest and most*

important monasteries in Catalonia, an important influence in the building of the region of Catalonia."[1]

In the church at Sant Joan, there is a stone effigy of Abbess Emma lying in repose, with her right hand shaped like a cup holding the flames of the Holy Spirit, symbolizing the spiritual power and passion of her leadership and devotion. Her cup of fire most likely also relates to the Fiery Grail seen in numerous medieval frescoes in the Pyrenean region featuring a Mary holding a chalice filled with fire, which I will cover in book two of this series. All of this pointed to a history of a fiery, powerful feminine presence in the region surrounding the center of the Great Cross.

A good friend and fellow author Elyn Aviva had mentioned that I should see the numerous paintings of Magdalena in the Vic Episcopal Museum, and quite often museums have information and publications on all the historic sites in their locality. Vic is north of Barcelona and only 4.04 miles (6.5 kilometers) due west of the Paris Meridian. The drive would take me along the east-west arm of the landscape cross, which I will call the Magdalena Path, due to the impressive number of her sanctuaries. Highway 260 from Figueras becomes the A 26 and weaves in and out of the 42°15' north latitude of the eastern arm of the cross like a serpent, passing Santa Magdalena mountains, hermitages, churches, and even a château in her name. (See illustration 3 Guardians of the Eastern Gate on page 274.) We will visit each of these Magdalena sites in Chapter 16, "The Magdalena Path."

The modern highway follows not only numerous Magdalena sites, but also the basic path of an ancient pilgrimage route known as the Way of the Stars. This 6000-year-old road runs east-west along the southern slopes of the Pyrenees on the 42nd degree latitude and is marked by numerous megalithic monuments, built circa 3500 BCE or earlier. This segment of the route is known as *Via Romana Capsacosta*, Catalan terms meaning "Roman Way (of the) Coastal Cape," with *Capsacosta* referring to the eastern end of the route at Cap de Creus "Cape of the Cross," at the Mediterranean. The alternate name Via Annia is sometimes used for Via Romana. This ancient route was traveled by consecutive cultures throughout at least six millennia and was improved by the Romans more than 2000 years ago.

The A 26 road passes the picturesque medieval town of Besalú that, along with Girona to the south, attracted early Jewish communities and scholars of the Kabbalah and other esoteric wisdom traditions. The Benedictine Abbey of Besalú was founded in 977 CE and it's worth stopping at least once to view the Pont Viejo (Old Bridge) over the river Fluviá, originally constructed by the Romans about 2000 years ago and rebuilt in the 11th century. In the past, tolls were collected from anyone crossing the bridge, and the town still has its medieval *mikveh,* a ritual purification bath.

Besalu Pont Viejo.

Continuing west through the southern foothills of the Pyrenees, I passed the Garrotxa region, filled with ancient dormant volcanos. Now the hearts of the calderas are home to churches, strong in the memory of fire, but now intensely green and lush due to the rich minerals that blanketed the region from the inner Earth. We will return to the Garrotxa in future chapters for its important Magdalena and Templar sites. Turning south at the town of Olot, the Serra Santa Magdalena (Mountain Range of Saint Magdalene) rises high from the verdant valley and is crowned with a small white chapel dedicated to Magdalena. Extraordinarily, this Santa Magdalena range is also on the Paris Meridian. The north-south axis of the great landscape cross is marked by additional sites dedicated to Magdalena, which I will call a Magdalena Meridian, reaching from the Pyrenees to Majorca. To the south before arriving at Vic, there is the important medieval monastery of Santa Magdalena de Conangle located on a high hill, also on the meridian, and these sites will be visited in chapter 18, "The Magdalena Meridian." Most of the churches dedicated to her are on high hills, recalling the term *Magdala* in Aramaic, or *Migdal* in Hebrew, meaning "watchtower." Hence, we find Magdalena as the guardian who watches over Catalonia from her high towers. (See illustrations 5 and 6, pages 210 and 218).

With so many sites dedicated to Magdalena on the north-south axis, as well as on the east-west axis of the landscape cross, it was one more indication that there was an intentional pattern to the placement of her sanctuaries. But who established this pattern and when? Her sites were established between the 9th and 12th centuries, more than six hundred years before the Paris Meridian would be measured across Catalonia. This would be a question that I would ask repeatedly on this extended quest. And true to the ongoing pattern, before the Paris Meridian crosses the French Pyrenees into Catalonia, it passes through a medieval city gate called Porte de Madeleine (Gate of Magdalene) in the town of Mosset (described in chapter 9). There were too many meridian alignments related to the landscape cross to be mere chance.

The signs and clues were everywhere. I just had to notice them. Arriving in Vic, I drove to the large seminary on the hill, as this is where the mystical poet priest Jacint Verdaguer was educated. On the gate was a portent of the keys about to be revealed: a chalice at the heart of an equal-armed cross. Magic was afoot. Vic was an important

Grail Gate, Vic Seminary.

cultural and religious center, established circa 1100–800 BCE by the Iberian culture. During the first century BCE, the town was called Ausa, when the Romans built a temple dedicated to Jupiter that is still standing. By the fifth century CE, it became Ausona for the Visigoths, and in front of the current cathedral stood a medieval round church dedicated to Santa Rodona (Saint of the Wheel). She is most likely named for the wheel shape formed by the turning of the Ter River, a few kilometers north of Vic at Roda de Ter ("Wheel of the Ter," with *Ter* referring to the Earth). The Ter carves a magical path, basically following the Paris Meridian and the sanctuaries of Maria Magdalena from the high Pyrenees through Catalonia, then turning east through Girona to the Mediterranean. (See illustration 5 on page 210.)

The Magical Museum of Vic

The Vic Episcopal Museum is a gem, a veritable cauldron overflowing with images of women of wisdom. The museum focuses on Magdalena imagery, as she is depicted in no less than eighteen paintings and sculptures, an impressive number in a small museum. It was striking that the museum's collection of paintings of Magdalena included the originals from important chapels and monasteries dedicated to her across Catalonia, many located on the Paris Meridian. Magdalena is often portrayed in this region wearing a royal red gown trimmed with gold and white fur and carrying a golden vase. A red gown always identifies her as Magdalena, the color worn by people of power, including the cardinals of the Church. She is seated on a golden throne, looking regal and serene as a queen, the throne being her seat of power and the hieroglyphic symbol of her sister Isis. Depicting Magdalena as an enthroned queen seems to be a unique Catalan attitude, as across Europe, we are more likely to find Mother Mary depicted as the queen.

This museum is also host to many of the medieval Madonna statues from churches across Catalonia. They are not black but carved of dark, aged wood, and each has a unique facial expression and character, transmitting her own brand of strength and insight. After pausing at each Madonna, marveling at the potency still emanating from each one, I headed for the Magdalena collection on the upper level. A large Magdalena painting dominates the gallery, again in her royal attire, from the monastery in her name in Palma, Majorca, near Isla Dragonera, which, as we have seen, marks the end of the Paris Meridian. Another large painting of her is from the high altar of her monastery at Santa Magdalena de Conangle, located on the meridian just north of Vic.

There were many more, but by far the most impressive painting was a 15th-century retable (a group of connected altar paintings) of six sections, including five important scenes in the life of Magdalena. I was stunned by the final scene in which she is on her deathbed. The extraordinary part of this image is that it appears that Jesus is performing the Opening of the Mouth funerary rite for Magdalena, which was the "Ka Ba" key and her footprint indicated in the Black Stone dreams. The painting was from Santa Magdalena de Perella, an unfamiliar site, but I would definitely find out the location.

The artist was Bernat Martorell, a leading 15th-century artist from Barcelona and considered one of the most important painters working in the Gothic style in all of Catalonia. Martorell's art was influenced by the great Renaissance artists of Florence,

Altar retable, Santa Magdalena de Perella, Bernat Martorell, 15th c. Vic Episcopal Museum (V.E.M.)

Italy, such as Leonardo da Vinci and Sandro Botticelli. There was an active exchange of artists and artistic styles between Florence and Barcelona during the Renaissance, in addition to the Hermetic sciences and neo-Platonic studies. Let us look at some of those influences that made their way into Catalan art.

Cosimo de' Medici, of the ruling family in Florence, founded the city's Platonic Academy, and was a foremost collector of ancient manuscripts from the far reaches of the Mediterranean, having them brought to be translated at his academy. The academy taught the ancient Greek and Egyptian traditions, which integrated music, medicine, mathematics, astronomy, and astrology. When Cosimo acquired the *Corpus Hermeticum* (Body or Collection of Hermetic texts), he commissioned mystic, priest, scholar, and musician Marcilio Ficino to translate the text from Greek into Latin, the first Latin translation of this collection of Egyptian teachings, based on the wisdom of Thoth-Hermes, and most likely composed in Alexandria. This Hermetic knowledge swept like wildfire throughout the Western world, producing the flowering of Hermetic knowledge and practices that influenced art and medicine, and liberated religious beliefs.

The Platonic Academy in Florence was headed by the extraordinary Ficino, who would inspire many great visionaries after him, such as the brilliant 16th-century Hermetic magus Giordano Bruno, one of many pioneers martyred as "heretics." Ficino acquired a wealth of knowledge while translating Cosimo's rare collections, and one of these was the *Picatrix*, an Arabic text on Hellenistic magic.[2] The text was first translated from Arabic into Spanish in the 11th century, most likely at the court of King Alfonso X of Castile and Leon, called the Wise, who was an avid collector of ancient manuscripts. The king's courts were filled with Jewish, Arab, and Christian scholars, and a rich commingling of knowledge of mystical traditions flourished, including writings that influenced the medieval Grail stories. Many of the precepts of the *Picatrix* texts later appear in Ficino's *Three Books on Life*, a good example of how Hermetic knowledge was circulating back and forth across Europe and across the Mediterranean, influencing art and promoting progressive ideals. The following are titles of chapters in Ficino's *Book Three* that incorporate knowledge from the *Picatrix*:

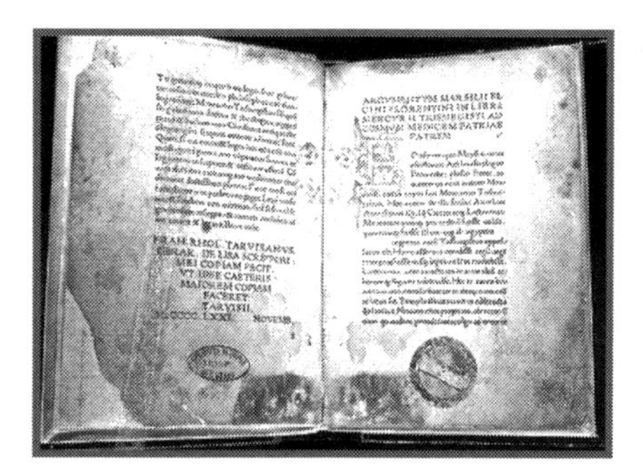

Corpus Hermeticum: first Latin edition, by Marsilio Ficino, 1471 CE, Bibliotheca Philosophica Hermetica, Amsterdam.

"On the Nature of Man according to the Stars.
How to Attract Something from Some One Particular Star."

"On the Power of Words and Song for Capturing Celestial Benefits
and on the Seven Steps That Lead to Celestial Things."[3]

Ficino was not only a priest and scholar, but he was also an astrologer and applied the Hermetic knowledge of music and the stars for healing. In Ficino's writings, there are examples of his patients, who would receive a musical prescription based on their planetary stress and corresponding physical-emotional issues. Ficino's work closely parallels my own practice in Bio-Acoustic Medicine[4], which incorporates Voice Spectrum Analysis, therapeutic sound recommendations and medical astrology. Hopefully, these traditions will continue the legacy of these courageous mystics who preserved this precious Hermetic knowledge. Medical astrology has been used since ancient times in Tibet, China, India, Egypt, and beyond. It was an integral part of Western medicine during the Renaissance, and both astrology and astronomy were required courses in the medical academies in Italy, taught by Galileo (1564–1642), among others.

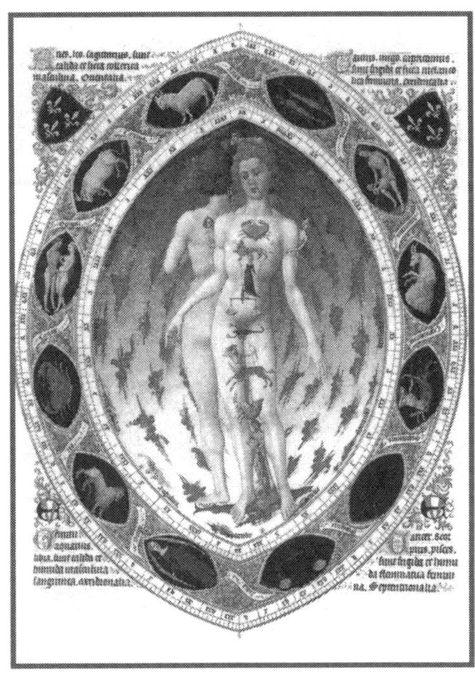

Astroman, LesTres Riches Heures, Duc de Berry 15th century France.

As we can see, the cultures surrounding the Mediterranean continued to be influenced by many ancient traditions. Florence and Barcelona were both flourishing with Hermetic knowledge during the 15th century, and these mystery traditions would have been woven into the great works of art created by those who moved in Barcelona's elite circles. As one of Catalonia's leading artists of that era, this certainly would have included Bernat Martorell, and his paintings were commissioned in locations familiar with these mystery traditions. This included the Sant Pere (Saint Peter) church in the Catalan village of Pubol near the early medieval Jewish Kabbalah center of Girona. Castell de Pubol is where Salvador Dali and his beloved Gala would reside four centuries later, and Gala's castle is now the site of an extraordinary museum of Dali's art.

Martorell was also commissioned to paint the main altar retable in Barcelona Cathedral that portrays Magdalena once again in a royal robe, not a garment for a humble penitent. Martorell's paintings of Our Lady were commissioned for churches, cathedrals, and monasteries on or close to the Paris Meridian: Santa Magdalena de Conangle, Vic, Barcelona, and Santa Magdalena de Palma. Santa Magdalena de Perella seems to be the only unknown, remote site containing Martorell's art: why was it hidden in the Pyrenees? Let us look more closely at his masterpiece from this mysterious chapel.

Six Scenes of Santa Magdalena de Perella

Standing before the magnificent retable from Perella housed at the Vic museum, I marveled at the enthroned Magdalena dominating the center, surrounded by five significant scenes in her story. (See image on page 151.) Beginning at the lower left image and moving clockwise, the first panel depicts Jesus and Magdalena alone in the garden after he has risen from the tomb. Jesus purportedly said to her, *"Noli me tangere"* (a Latin phrase meaning "Do not touch me"). However, in this scene, Jesus appears to be blessing her, not directing her away from him.

Magdalena in the garden, Perella, V.E.M.

It is in this scene that Magdalena is the first to witness Jesus in his body of light. In *The Gospel of Mary Magdalene,* as translated by Jean-Yves Leloup, she tells the disciples, "I had a vision of the Teacher, and I said to him: 'Lord, I see you now in this vision.' And the Lord answered: 'You are blessed, for the sight of me does not disturb you.'"[5] Magdalena is the one who sees, she is able to perceive the subtle dimensions. This ability to *see* beyond normal reality is one of the gifts of Miriam of Magdala, as Leloup refers to her. She then asks Jesus how she and others are able to see him in visions. Was it through her soul, *psyche*, or spirit, *pneuma*? Jesus answers that it is neither through the soul nor the spirit, but *nous,* the intelligence between the two, the bridge that is beyond personality or individuality. This unified field is where true union occurs, in which there is no separate *I and thou.* This gift of seeing from a state beyond separation reveals the true treasure, as Jesus tells Magdalena:

> *"There where is the nous, lies the treasure."*[6]

Church of Maria Magdalena, Rennes-le-Château, photo Stephen Marcus.

The second panel shows Magdalena at the meal in the house of Simon the Pharisee in Bethany, at which she anointed the feet of Jesus with precious spikenard from her alabaster jar. But sadly, the painting is damaged, perhaps intentionally, as hers is the only portion missing, scratched out, in a futile attempt to remove a powerful woman from history. This is one of the most intimate scenes with her lovingly holding Jesus' feet. It also reveals Magdalena as the Myrrhophore, the myrrh-bearing priestess, and the importance of this ritual is verified by its inclusion in all four Gospels, Matthew, Mark, Luke, and John. In Mark chapter 14, verses 3–6, it says:

> *"While he was in Bethany, reclining at the table in the home of Simon the Leper, a woman came with an alabaster jar of very expensive perfume, made of pure nard. She broke the jar and poured the perfume on his head ..." [Then Jesus tells the disciples in defense of her using expensive nard:] "She has done a beautiful thing to me... She poured perfume on my body beforehand to prepare for my burial. Truly I tell you, wherever the gospel is preached throughout the world, what she has done will also be told, in memory of her."*

Wherever his story is told, what she has done will also be told, in memory of her. Powerful words. Magdalena is enacting the anointing role of initiatrix, for the impending life transition of Jesus, as she is the one who sees his destiny. She is also following the ancient tradition of the bride anointing the bridegroom, or the Messianic king, similar to the role of the Queen of Sheba with King Solomon a thousand years earlier. In the *"Rabanus de Vita Mariae Magdalenae,"* commonly attributed to Rabanus Maurus, a ninth century CE Benedictine theologian and writer in Germany, the anointing takes on a much more sensual tone:

> *"Drawing back with her fingers the hair of Almighty God, she broke the alabaster vessel and poured the remains of the nard over the head of the Son of God. Then, massaging his hair with her hands, she dampened his curls with nard. With her delicate fingers, she skillfully spread the consecrated perfume over his forehead and temples, his neck, and adjacent areas ... How sweet-smelling were the hands and lips and hair of Mary from the touch of Christ's feet, whose fragrance surpassed all perfumes! Now was the house filled with the scent of the perfume, as the world would be filled with the fame of this deed."*[7]

We can imagine Jesus melting into this loving, nurturing, intimate embrace. He had been on the road performing healings, ministering, speaking for months on end, always giving tirelessly, and rarely receiving. The text continues with, "Great was the abundance of the gifts of the Holy Spirit in the spirit of Mary when she enjoyed such intimacy with the Son of God ..."[8] We can assume that this was not the first contact that Magdalena had with Jesus. These intimate scenes portraying her in her role of sacred initiatrix inspired the song "Fragrance of Fire." The lyrics are drawn from the Song of Songs and the piece was filmed in a chapel in Southern France and also recorded on the album "Garden of the Magdalene: Banish Me No More."[9]

In the third panel at the top center, Mary Magdalene is standing at the base of the cross at Golgotha, meaning "place of the skull" in Aramaic. Magdalene does not flee when it becomes too painful, difficult, or dangerous. However, most of the male disciples (except John) were afraid and went into hiding during the passion of the crucifixion. In her presence in this scene and later in the garden, she becomes the messenger, revealing to the male disciples what has occurred, and ultimately, she is the one to carry Jesus' message forward. She remains loyal to both Jesus and the teachings. Scholar of Gnosticism Michel Tardieu, says of the *Gospel of Mary Magdalene*:

> *"She is at once the confidante of Jesus, his interpreter, and his replacement: Jesus divulges words to her that are unknown to the other disciples; she occupies the place left vacant by him, and she communicates and explains the secrets that she received from him."*[10]

In the fourth panel at the upper right of the retable, Magdalena is depicted with the angels who are lifting her above the grotto of Sainte-Baume wearing nothing but her long hair. This depiction of Magdalena naked and covered only with her long hair is more in keeping with the one known as Mary the Egyptian, who will be discussed in the following chapters. The 13th century archbishop of Genoa Jacobus de Voragine who wrote the classic *"The Golden Legend,"* comments on the raising of Mary Magdalene:

> *"And every day at every hour canonical she was lifted up in the air of angels, and heard the glorious song of the heavenly companies with her bodily ears."*[11]

Magdalena is "hearing" the music of the spheres, the heavenly song spoken of by Plato and Pythagoras and witnessed by those who live close to the natural rhythms of life. This divine music sustains her and feeds her soul as well as her body and mind. In the first and fourth panels, it shows us that Magdalena has the gifts of *seeing what no eye has seen, and hearing what no ear has heard*, to paraphrase the Gospel of Thomas.

And finally, there is the mysterious last panel in the lower right section of the retable, showing Maria Magdalena on her deathbed. It is this image that held me spellbound, as illustrating her death is highly unusual, and it appears that Jesus is acting as high priest, performing the Opening of the Mouth ritual. Her Ka etheric double has flown free at the moment of death, and the image shows her Ba, her soul, rising out of her mouth. Is the artist Martorell telling us that Jesus was very aware of these traditions? It seems so. In the *Egyptian Book of the Dead*, it states that the god Ptah (through the Sem priests) performed the rite of the Opening of the Mouth, and that he raised up the soul from inertness and gave it life. The following is from an inscription at the temple of Edfu, Egypt:

> *"He [or She] has gone forth from thy mouth. He [or She] has become a god and brought thee every good thing ..."*[12]

Magdalena's death scene, Perella, Bernat Martorell, altar retable, 15th c. V.E.M.

And there is a beautiful reference in Rabanus Maurus' life of Maria Magdalena, when Jesus comes to her on her deathbed, which speaks perfectly to this scene:

> *"The Son of God, the Lord and Saviour appeared to her, and she saw him—Jesus Christ, her only desire—with a multitude of angels calling her to himself lovingly and mercifully: 'Come my beloved, and I shall place you on my throne, for the king desires your beauty, more lovely than any of the sons of men. Receive the reward of heavenly life from him whom you served so faithfully while he was on earth... Rejoice and exult forever amidst the heavenly choirs."*[13]

Let us pause a moment while looking at the image of Magdalena's soul, her body of light rising into Jesus' loving hands, and contemplate those words, "Come my beloved, and I shall place you on my throne, for the king desires your beauty ..." When we view this scene in which Jesus is receiving Magdalena's body of light, we can imagine him speaking those words, welcoming her to his side once again. And Catalonia's portrayal of her enthroned makes perfect sense.

It was this final scene of Magdalena's life that put the final piece of the puzzle in place. The Egyptian black Palermo Stone, more than 4200 years old, haunting my dreams, was inscribed with the earliest known mention of the Opening of the Mouth ritual. And now the discovery of what appears to be this same ritual being performed by Jesus for Magdalena, in an image from a place called Santa Magdalena de Perella. But where was it? I needed to visit the site as soon as possible and discover more about this location and why it was chosen to display this mysterious rare scene.

And to complete the six panels of the retable, the central and largest panel shows her wearing a royal red robe, holding a golden vase of anointing oil, and seated on a throne, again the hieroglyphic symbol of Isis. Once again, this story leads us back to Egypt. Anointing in the Egyptian and other Eastern temple traditions is the role of the anointing priestesses, initiating with precious unguents, such as myrrh, frankincense, and spikenard in preparation for rites of passage. It is also the role of the Bride to anoint the Bridegroom, which we will discover is also illustrated at the Perella chapel. A large equal-armed cross appears on Magdalena's gown, positioned over her heart, which not only provides a clue regarding the important location of the Perella chapel, but also identifies her as Notre Dame of the Cross, the same title used for both Magdalena and Isis that we will discover in the strange Rennes-le-Château document, *Le Serpent Rouge* ("The Red Serpent").

Perella at the Heart and a Chantress in the Crypt

I returned to the lobby of the Vic Episcopal Museum to speak to the curators. I had a map of the region and asked the woman at the desk if she could please point out the location of Santa Magdalena de Perella. I wasn't sure she would know, since there are sixty-four churches dedicated to Magdalena in Catalonia, as listed in the Catalan registry of churches.[14] I was stunned when the woman pointed to a spot on the map located exactly on the Paris Meridian, and at the center of the developing landscape cross (see illustration 2, Great Cross, p. xvi). With Maria Magdalena sitting at the heart of the Great Cross, I could see that the Palermo Stone dreams had provided clear clues to a story that was becoming much more interesting. I began to feel more and more like a pawn on a giant chessboard, which incidentally contains 64 squares.

The curator explained that Perella is on a remote hilltop and on private land, not in any village or town center, hence Google Earth indicating a farmhouse. The question is, why would such a highly esteemed artist such as Bernat Martorell be commissioned to paint an elaborate multi-paneled retable for such a remote and seemingly insignificant location in a small, humble chapel in the Pyrenees? His works were in well-known cathedrals, major monasteries, and churches in Barcelona, Pubol, Lleida, and Palma.

It was a revelation to discover that a chapel dedicated to Santa Magdalena marked the center of a landscape cross spanning the Pyrenees, that was marked by numerous of her sites, and I would discover that Perella sits at the intersection of several ancient pilgrimage routes. The recurring dreams of the Black Stone and the Ka Ba message had included one dream showing Magdalena's footprint and a Grail. Was Perella also related to the elusive Grail mysteries? These connections would be revealed later, relating to the Cathars of Montségur and Majorca.

Almost unbelievably I was about to discover in the same museum an ancient Egyptian temple singer who experienced the same Opening of the Mouth ritual. I wandered downstairs to see what was housed in the crypt. In the center of the room was a coffin of an Egyptian chantress, with her brilliantly painted wooden coffin illustrating the Egyptian funerary rites for the soul's Ka and Ba in the Afterlife. It is dated to the 22nd Dynasty (945–715 BCE) and made of sycamore wood with well-preserved polychrome decoration. Over her heavy wig is the falcon god Horus, protecting her with his wings. The elegant priestess-singer is wearing a large *usekh*, a wide-collared necklace, with a pendant of the lion-headed goddess Sekhmet. These collars are normally worn by Egyptian deities or the elite, so this singer must have been of great renown, a priestess of Sekhmet. She is not named but is identified as the honored singer of Amon.

Chantress of Amun, 22nd Dynasty, V.E.M.

Next to the coffin is a framed portion of an original Egyptian papyrus derived from the Pyramid Texts, listing magical spells to guide the soul's journey in the Afterlife, the same journey which is illustrated on the coffin of the chantress and illustrated in the Opening of the Mouth ritual of Magdalena. These rites were originally reserved for the pharaohs but later were used by others, such as our temple singer. The papyrus is written in hieratic text and illustrated in pigments that are still brilliant. Nearby in the same crypt were busts of the Great Mother goddesses Cybele, Venus-Aphrodite, and Diana-Artemis, all found in Catalonia's ancient shrines and temples.

It was almost too much to take in. In the same Episcopal Museum in a Catalan town near the Paris Meridian, there are three distinct references to the Egyptian Opening of the Mouth ritual. There was an additional personal synchronicity with the Egyptian chantress, as my own life journey has followed this same role, as a singer of sacred songs. This tradition has formed an important part of my life's research in ancient medicine and sound science and resulted in numerous journeys to the Egyptian temples. Since I was alone in the museum crypt, I sang to the chantress' beautiful Ka and Ba and to Magdalena's above, once again threads of Egypt woven into Iberia. The "Nefer Ka Ra" lyrics are drawn from an ancient Egyptian poem, one of the songs on the *Guardians of the Dragon Path* album.

"O Waters of Life
In the Heavens and on Earth
Sky speaks Earth rises
In remembrance of my birth.

In the House of Flame
Lives remembrance of my name
Illuminating flame
Reverberating name.

Chorus:
NEFER KA RA
NEFER BA RA
NEFER KA RA
NEFER SA RA

O Bright Morning Star
Born of night beauty of Dawn
Nefer Ka Ra
Coming forth into One.

In the deep Above
Where the Holy Ones bestow
The Sacred House Above
I shall build here below.

Heavenly abode
Emblems of stars do show
Ursa Major above
Perfection mirrored below.

Hail Ladder of Horus
Unbolt the doors of Sky
Open gates before us
Open the gates of Sky."[15]

CHAPTER 13

The Egyptian Connection

It is very possible that both Jesus and Maria Magdalena had been aware of the ritual of the Opening of the Mouth, as well as many other Egyptian traditions and rituals. Their lives seem to mirror the epic journey of Osiris and Isis and the dying and rising god mysteries. From Biblical references, Jesus lived his early years in Egypt, which would fulfill the ancient prophecy that said he would one day be called out of Egypt for his destined mission. The Gospel of Matthew 2:13-5 says,

"...behold, an angel of the Lord appeared to Joseph in a dream and said, 'Rise, take the child and his mother, and flee to Egypt, and remain there till I tell you; for Herod is about to search for the child, to destroy him.' And he rose and took the child and his mother by night, and departed to Egypt, and remained there until the death of Herod. This was to fulfil what the Lord had spoken by the prophet, 'Out of Egypt have I called my son.'"

My sense is that Jesus would have returned numerous times to the land where he spent his first years, and as a mystic healer he would have had a keen interest in the rich mystery traditions of Egypt. Some would say that as a healer, exorcist, and a regular performer of miracles, Jesus was truly a magician. Morton Smith of Columbia University quotes the second century CE Greek philosopher Celsus on the "Magician Jesus":

"Having been brought up in obscurity, he went ... to Egypt and there acquired experience of some <magical> powers."[1]

The practice of Egyptian-style magic was common throughout first century Israel and a contemporary of Jesus was the Greek Apollonius of Tyana, also well-known for his magical powers. Born circa 15 CE, Apollonius was well-traveled and collected wisdom and mystical practices from many sources, eventually becoming a Pythagorean. Flavius Philostratus (170–245 CE), the Greek author of *The Life of Apollonius of Tyana,* reported that Apollonius lived and studied in Egypt.[2] And according to Morton Smith, he also traveled through Babylonia and India where he learned from wise teachers. Smith compares the supernatural power of these two contemporary wonder-workers, who both had accumulated fame and followers:

> *"... both were believed by their followers to be sons of gods, beings of supernatural power, and both were accused by their enemies of being magicians. For Apollonius, as for Jesus, most of our information comes from his believers and is preserved in documents ..."*[3]

We tend to forget that travel and trade during the first century had been active across the Mediterranean and beyond for thousands of years, especially between Palestine, Egypt, and Greece. The travel routes from the eastern Levant (regions of Syria, Jordan, and Palestine) to the southern Levant (Egypt, Sinai) had been well established since at least circa 3300 BCE. These ancient routes were connected with a persistent recurring dream over the last two or three decades.

The scene always involved traveling over land and sea and finally boarding a barge on the Nile to continue to a destination south of the Delta. This was in the remote past, the land between the temple communities was arid, desolate, and I was wearing what seemed like a simple robe and sandals. Whether a man or woman was not clear, but I was traveling alone, and the journey required courage and stamina. Was I remembering Magdalena's footsteps as she traveled from Palestine to Egypt, or was this a memory of my own journeys long ago? Magdalena may well have traveled to Egypt, given the extensive travel throughout the region.

Jacobus, in his *Golden Legend*, says that Magdalena was of noble lineage, descended from kings, and her father was named Cyrus and her mother Eucharis. He repeats her commonly accepted siblings as being Martha and Lazarus.[4] These three play an important role in the life of Jesus, with their family home at Bethany being a favored refuge and gathering place, and according to legend, their mission would continue in Gaul following the crucifixion.

Why has it taken so long to acknowledge the kingly lineage and wealth of Magdalena's family? Much of the problem lies in the mistranslations and confusion regarding her identity, which began with the conflating of three women by Pope Gregory I in 591 CE. In a sermon known as Homily XXXIII,[5] he combined three of the women mentioned in the canonical gospels of Mark, Luke, and John: Mary of Bethany, the sister of Martha and Lazarus; Mary Magdalene also called Miriam of Magdala in Galilee; and an unnamed sinner, who Gregory assumed was a prostitute. Miriam of Magdala and Mary Magdalene may well refer to the same woman, but it was his conflating the "sinner" with the other two Marys that created a huge schism, which still continues in many minds today.

Did Gregory also conflate the sinner with the later Mary the Egyptian born in 344 CE, a purported prostitute who became a hermit saint? Many paintings supposedly depicting Magdalena throughout the centuries have used the image of Mary the Egyptian, naked, covered by her hair and sometimes draped with a scant, ragged cloth. This conflating of the women has been confusing, to say the least, but as more of the Gnostic gospels were translated, we discovered the truth of Magdalena's high standing as the Apostle to the Apostles and the "High Tower," which is the meaning of her name, as we will discover.

The attributes associated with Maria Magdalena of "sinner" and "prostitute" may also be the result of her likely association with the priestesses of Asherah-Astarte, who still existed in the region. And it is likely that she visited the largest temple to Artemis in the region, which was just across the Jordan River from Israel. Given the inclusive attitudes of Jesus and his disciples, we can imagine they had friendly relations with these so-called pagan traditions, popular in the first-century Levant.

According to French tradition, the three siblings from Bethany, Martha, Lazarus, and Magdalena, along with two other Marys and other disciples, departed from Israel after the crucifixion. Although the popular legend says they came straight to Gaul, it is much more likely that they made many stops along the way, to rest and gather fresh water and supplies. It is quite possible that they stopped in Alexandria, Crete, Sicily, and Sardinia, to rest before continuing across the Mediterranean to Gaul.

Accounts mention that when the entourage arrived on the shores of Gaul, they stayed in a "pagan temple," likely of Artemis, which would have provided a familiar and comfortable refuge. After arriving in the West, the holy family seeded the teachings of love, healing, and the ancient mystery traditions across the land. Beyond all the fragments of history and legend, ultimately, we each need to find Mary within our own hearts, and strive to follow her example as a courageous, loving, and wise woman, a true archetype for women today.

Let us look at the other Mary that was conflated with Magdalena, Mary the Egyptian. Although they were two different women living in different centuries, did the continued conflation arise come from unknown evidence or legends that Magdalena made periodic journeys to Egypt? Travel between Israel and Egypt was common along the well-used trade routes, and it is not out of the question to imagine that she traveled one or more times to Egypt.

Mary Egyptiaca

Mary of Egypt, Convent of Santa Clara, V.E.M.

According to the written accounts, the fourth century CE woman called Mary the Egyptian demonstrated the gifts of clairvoyance and levitation, and could walk on water, as Jesus reportedly did. The first time I encountered the Egyptian Mary was in Paris at the church of Saint-Germain-l'Auxerrois, located at the eastern side of the Louvre. She is the guardian of the gate at the main entrance to the church, with her larger than life-sized image wearing nothing but her hair and carrying three loaves of bread. Bread is a common symbol for the corporal body of Jesus, well-known in the Communion wafers. In the case of Mary, the three loaves were said to be her only sustenance during her years living as a hermit in the desert.

In the *Golden Legend,* Jacobus de Voragine devotes an entire chapter to Mary Egyptiaca, in which he relates a story told by the Abbot Zosimus. Jacobus doesn't make clear the identity of Zosimus other than saying he was "a good, holy and religious monk" who "went through the desert which lieth beyond the flom [flooded] Jordan ..."[6] Jacobus's account describes Zosimus encountering Mary Egyptiaca in the wilderness, whom he said was entirely black all over her body and wearing nothing but her hair. When Mary called Zosimus by his name, he marveled that she knew who he was, and realized that she must be a saint or prophet. He then prayed to her to give him her blessing. While Mary said her prayer, Zosimus observed her spontaneously levitating:

> *"Then she lifted up her hands unto heaven in making her prayer, and Zosimus saw that in praying to God her body was lifted up from the earth well nigh a foot and a half ..."*[7]

According to Jacobus' account, Zosimus returned the following year to visit the Holy Mary. On his arrival, he saw her on the far side of the Jordan. "... the holy woman, which made the sign of the cross upon the water and went on it, and came over to him.

When Zosimus saw this miracle, anon he fell down to the feet of the holy woman ..."[8]

Zosimus reported that when she arrived on his side of the river, her feet were miraculously dry, recalling the episode of Jesus walking on water at the Sea of Galilee. The reference to Mary being black all over her body, recalls the Song of Songs (1:5): "Black am I, and beautiful, O Daughters of Jerusalem ..." Cynthia Bourgeault says in *The Meaning of Mary Magdalene* that this blackness became the classic "Magdalenic signature."[9] And ultimately, this black and beautiful Mary took the form of the Black Madonnas, the matrix of wise guardian mothers across Europe.

Mary of Egypt and Zosimas, St. Nicholas Orthodox Ch. N. Fletcher, Carolina.

It seems obvious that depictions of Magdalena have been confused with the image of Mary the Egyptian, wearing nothing but her hair, a reformed prostitute, who became a reclusive desert mystic. Magdalena's identity is only now being finally rectified. Pope Paul VI retracted her prostitute status in 1969, and Pope Francis officially recognized her as the Apostle to the Apostles in 2017. It is extraordinary that those two acts took two thousand years! But what about the source Magdalena's name?

CHAPTER 14

MAGDALUMA, MAGDALENA—WATCHTOWER AND GUARDIAN

"As for you, O tower [migdal] of the flock,
The stronghold of the daughter of Zion,
Even the former dominion shall come,
The kingdom of the daughter of Jerusalem."

MICAH 4:8, NEW KING JAMES VERSION

THE HEBREW PROPHET MICAH MAY NOT HAVE BEEN SEEING THE FUTURE FOR Maria Magdalena in this verse, but his description of Israel fits perfectly with this daughter of Zion as the watchtower, and the recognition of her importance that would return during our current time. Her name derives from the Hebrew word *migdol*, meaning "tower" or "watchtower," and many believe she was named for the site of an early Jewish temple at Magdala on the Sea of Galilee, hence one of her titles being Miriam of Magdala. But as we shall see, there are no less than fifty-nine sites with names from the same *migdol* root across the eastern and southern Levant, the eastern Mediterranean lands.[1] (Levant is a term meaning east, derived from *lever*, the French word for rising, indicating where the stars rise.) Sites named *magdaluma, migdalîm, magdoloi, migdol, magdala,* could be found from Damascus, across Canaan and along the Nile in Egypt.[2] These sites formed a system of watchtowers guarding the old roads, and played a crucial role in ensuring safe passage, protection of the regions, and trade. These towers were located strategically on high places in the landscape and formed an important communication network using signal fires, and most likely mirrors. We will find these watchtowers as far west as the temples of Greek goddesses in ancient Iberia.

These watchtower sites are referenced in Egyptian papyri and inscribed on the temple walls from at least the 13th Dynasty (circa 1700 BCE), indicating their importance. There is an old city named Magdaluma at the eastern branch on the Nile on the Egyptian Mediterranean coast, and the watchtower at Migdol on the Red Sea is believed to be the site of the Hebrew Exodus. As happens over time, the exact spelling of the names varies as the locations were referred to by different cultures and in many languages. Aaron A. Burke from the Department of Near Eastern Languages and Cultures, UCLA, traces the variations of the names of watchtower sites in the Levant in several languages: *Magdôlos*

Author at Tour Magdala Rennes-le-Château, photo Stephen Marcus.

(Greek), *Migdôl* (Hebrew), *Magdala* (Northwest Semitic), Mktr (Egyptian), and *majadil* (Arabic), all from the original root in earlier Akkadian.[3]

I mention these Magdalūma towers guarding the regions of the Levant as this is a pattern that we are about to discover in the western lands. The sites were lighthouse-watchtowers on the coast at temples of the goddess, then later during the medieval era, the high towers in the landscape were often located at hermitages and chapels dedicated to Maria Magdalena. And true to the traditions in the Levant, the Magdalūma sites in Iberia marked ancient pilgrimage and trade routes, some dating from as early as 4000 BCE, as we will discover. The repeating pattern through thousands of years is truly extraordinary.

Whatever the origins of the name of our beloved Magdalena, she commands a high position. She is a watchtower for our era, guiding us to remember the love that endures through all time. Her name carries a resonance derived from the roots of numerous ancient languages, standing for towers of vision, protection, and guardianship. During the medieval era, the images in the tarot were coded with stories of the Grail and the underground Church of Love, and of course, the Tower card was linked with Maria Magdalena. As the false emblems of power crumble, and truth is revealed, the underlying potency of the divine feminine rises once again. In 2017, Pope Francis made an astounding proclamation to the General Audience in Vatican City when he called Magdalena "an apostle of the new and greatest hope."[4] In her title of "Apostola Apostolorum," I was inspired to write the song of the same name, honoring her as the forerunner and first messenger for the way of love. The lyrics are in Latin:

Apostola Apostolorum,
carisimi sponsum,
spiritus sapiensieh

Apostle of the Apostles,
beloved spouse,
spirit of wisdom and knowledge[5]

CHAPTER 15

WHEELS WITHIN WHEELS

RODA DE TER TO RHODES

"It is also related of the Rhodians that they have been prosperous by sea, not merely since the time when they founded the present city, but that even many years before the establishment of the Olympian Games they used to sail far away from their homeland to ensure the safety of their people... they have sailed as far as Iberia; and there they founded Rode [Rhodes] ..."

STRABO, *GEOGRAPHICA XIV*[1]

THE DISCOVERIES AT THE VIC EPISCOPAL MUSEUM HAD BEEN ENLIGHTENING TO say the least. I departed my pension in Roda de Ter, just outside of Vic, anxious to visit the chapel dedicated to Santa Magdalena de Perella as soon as possible. It was extraordinary that Perella had the rare depiction of Magdalena's death ritual of the Opening of the Mouth, at her "watchtower" hilltop chapel marking the exact center of the great landscape cross! But I would need to delay the journey for two days as I had already arranged for a meeting in Roses the following day at the Ciutadella Museum. Roses is the modern name for the Iberian Greek city of Rhodes on the Mediterranean coast.[2]

Ciutadella is a Catalan word meaning "citadel" or "fortress," and the museum was built over the ancient entrance of the fortified Greco-Roman city facing the sea. Rhodes, (also spelled Rodes) was founded by two waves of Greek settlers, in the eighth and seventh centuries BCE by Rhodians from the Isle of Rhodes and in the sixth century BCE by the Phocaean people of modern-day Turkey. The eastern city gate provided access to the port on the Bay of Roses for ships arriving from across the Mediterranean carrying both goods and passengers. Another busy port was located nine miles to the south at Empúries, a site with temples dedicated to Artemis, Isis, Serapis, Asclepius, and Magdalena, which will be discussed in future chapters.

Who were these early settlers from the Greek Isle of Rhodes? Their island was situated at an intersection of two ancient trade routes, where the Aegean Sea meets the Mediterranean. Rhodes was most likely named for the sea goddess of the same name, sometimes spelled Rhode or Rhodas, who according to Greek mythology was a nymph who bore the solar god Helius many children, all of whom became well-known

Asclepius' staff of healing, gravestone Munich.

astrologers. The island was also home to sects of healers called Therapeutae or Ophites, who were practicing medicine that focused not only on physical ailments but on healing the soul, related to the Asclepian and Pythagorean healing traditions. Many Therapeutae were trained in the medical academies of Egypt and the Hermetic schools of Alexandria, and they viewed healing as a spiritual art. It is significant that women were accepted in this order of healers. However, there were Greek restrictions on women entering their medical academies, so a woman had to travel to the ancient city of Sais, in the Nile Delta, or to Alexandria and other locations in Egypt that accepted women.

A surviving inscription from Sais describes the women's academy there, which incorporated medical skills along with the wisdom of Egypt's female deities, such as Neith and Isis, who had temples at Sais. And these Hermetic healing traditions with origins in Egypt arrived in Iberia with the Rhodians circa 700 BCE. One wonders how humanity could reach such heights of evolution as seen during that time, and then fall into long cycles of forgetfulness.

> *"I have come from the school of medicine at Heliopolis, and have studied at the woman's school at Sais, where the divine mothers have taught me how to cure diseases."*[3]

The Isle of Rhodes was also known to the ancient world for its Colossus, a bronze sculpture of Helios standing 110 feet (33.5 meters) high that marked the entrance to the harbor and was considered one of the seven wonders of the world. Unfortunately, it was destroyed in an earthquake in 224 BCE. The Colossus figure held an enormous cauldron of fire, a tradition which we find in Catalonia, as seen in stone reliefs of churches and castles, and decorating monastery walls. Did the Rhodian settlers also bring this ancient tradition of cauldrons of fire to the western lands of Iberia or was it perhaps a more ancient tradition begun with the fiery founding mothers of these mountains, the Greek Queen Pyrrha and the Celtic Princess Pyrene?

During the medieval era, beginning in the late 11th and early 12th centuries, images of flaming chalices held by a Mary, most often assumed to be the mother of Jesus, began to appear in the frescoes of churches deep in the Pyrenees. These fiery Grails preceded the writing of the popular Grail legends in the 12th and 13th centuries, and although they were not well-known, perhaps they seeded the traditions of the Grail that spread across medieval Europe. This repeating tradition of spiritual fire in the Pyrenees region has endured, and as we have seen, still exists today in the annual ritual of lighting the solstice fires called Flama de Canigó, celebrated every June 23–24, Saint John the Baptist's Eve, and Day. (See chapter 9.)

The Perfect Wheel of Rhodes

"...Plato said, 'The next power to the Supreme God was ... figured in the shape of a cross on the universe.' ... The cross was a sacred emblem with the Egyptians."

GODFREY HIGGINS, *ANACALYPSIS*, 1836[4]

The original foundation design of the new city of Rhodes was an encircled equal-armed cross, and the later medieval city also used a cross design, with the main street named *Calle de la Creu,* "Street of the Cross." As mentioned, *roda* means "wheel" in Catalan and in many other languages, and we find numerous sites across the Mediterranean with this name. The *roda* cross symbol, used in city and temple design as well as appearing on coinage and ritual objects, is highly significant in our story, as we have seen. Symbolically, the cross, square, or cube represents the Earth and manifest reality. The circle represents the whole, oneness, and spirit. The wheel combines the two and thus, it has always been a universal symbol of the union of spirit and matter. This is the symbol found on Saint Benedict's protection medallion, and it is no accident that the wheel of the medallion guided the discoveries of the Great Cross, and the Greek city of Rhodes lies at the eastern end of this cross. This ancient symbol of balance and alignment to the cardinal directions, found in foundation designs, produces a field of harmony, coherence, and well-being, and this effect emanates into the surrounding region.

Wheel of Roses, Rubio Tuduri 1926, Ciutadella Museum.

This pattern of crosses keeps repeating and is not only found in city and temple foundations but also in the names of sites in the region, as we have already discovered in the Creu d'en Cobertella dolmen, meaning "Covered Cross," and the promontory Cap de Creus, "Head or Cape of the Cross." Additionally, the 16th-century Castell

Castell Trinitat, Ciutadella Museum.

de la Trinitat (Trinity Castle) is designed in a four-pointed star pattern and towers above the ruins of Rhodes and the modern city Roses. The Hapsburg dynasty Emperor and King of Spain Charles V built and maintained the castle, which guarded the coast and the entrance to Rhodes.

The site museum features items found at the castle, which included a deck of tarot cards, texts on alchemy, and medical books with information on medical astrology, which is part of the Hermetic tradition and all familiar territory for the Hapsburgs. Charles V had additional fortifications established along the Spanish coast, and his extensive empire included all of Spain, Sardinia, Sicily, most of Italy, and Bohemia. A popular phrase used for the Hapsburg Empire of 1544 was, "The empire on which the sun never sets."[5]

The Iberian city of Rhodes was so important to Mediterranean trade that it was listed in numerous Greek, Roman, and even Egyptian historical texts. Claudius Ptolemy, who lived in Alexandria during the second century CE, was an astronomer, astrologer, and geographer who mapped the known world. He was the first to list the location coordinates (latitude and longitude) on his maps, which were impressively close to being accurate. For example, Ptolemy places the "Pyrenean Temple of Venus" at 42°20' N, and it is actually at 42°19', the site of the current monastery of Sant Pere de Rodes. Ptolemy's calculations confirm the ancient location of the Temple of Venus, and his maps of Iberia in *Geography* are invaluable as he lists the major temples of the goddesses along the coast that figure in our story. He used the same Temple of Venus as a starting point for measuring the entire Mediterranean coast of Iberia to the Pillars of Hercules, basing his precise calculations on the stars. His works included a list of five hundred Mediterranean cities and their astronomical positions in degrees and minutes, with their approximate distances from Alexandria.[6] Ptolemy was a Pythagorean at heart and his advanced theories of music, harmonics, the planetary movements, and their effects on the human soul made a huge contribution that has endured until today.

The founders of Rhodes in Iberia, who arrived from the Aegean Sea, had an amazing navigation device called the Antikythera mechanism, sometimes described as an astronomical computer. This device was discovered in a shipwreck at the bottom of the sea off the coast of the Aegean island of Antikythera in the early 1900s and is dated to 100–80 BCE, although earlier versions of the device may well have existed. It contained more than thirty wheels and plates inscribed with zodiac signs and could show the motion of the Sun, Moon, and most likely the planets, eclipses, as well as the rising points of major stars, a veritable moving model of the solar system and beyond.

Antikythera fragment, National Archaeological Museum, Athens.

The Antikythera device may have been based in part on the extensive knowledge of the second-century BCE astronomer Hipparchus of Rhodes, who is credited with the invention of trigonometry and being the first to scientifically catalogue the positions of stars with his knowledge of Babylonian astronomy.[7] Although, Rhodians must have had this star knowledge long before, given the expert navigation skills needed to found the new Rhodes in Iberia in 800–600 BCE. The modern town of Roses has paid homage to these great pioneers in science, with streets named for Pythagoras, Socrates, Pindar, Archimedes, Aristotle, Pericles, and Euripides. But let us leave the maps, mathematics, and navigation devices and meet the Dragons of Rhodes.

Drakones Rhodioi, The Dragons of Rhodes

Draco Sit Mihi Dux—Let the Dragon Be My Guide.

The quote above is an adjusted version of the Latin letters inscribed on the Saint Benedict's medallion, *NDSMD*, an abbreviation for "Let not the dragon be my guide." However, throughout my research, it would be the wisdom of the ancient dragon traditions that would silently guide the journey to the locations and knowledge of the Pyrenean region. The *non* (meaning "not") had to go. And after making that decision, ancient dragon paths marked with megalithic stones, ancient temples, and Magdalena churches were revealed across Catalonia. And there were islands and caves that were named for dragons, and annual festivals in which people still honor Drac the Dragon that escaped the wrath of Saint Jordi (George), celebrated with dragons on parade and dancing in the streets.

The cities of Rhodes and Empúries became thriving centers of Mediterranean trade from at least the sixth century BCE. The Greek settlers maintained peaceful relations with the indigenous Iberian population, who had already been trading with Phoenician explorers for hundreds of years. Local trade items included silver and other metals, pottery, textiles, grain, etc. The success of the two Iberian ports is confirmed by their minting their own coins, called *drachma* or *dracma*, later called *dragma* by the Romans, from the Greek term meaning "fistful." But the resonance of the word *drachma* is interesting, as in Catalan and other Mediterranean languages, *drac* or *drach* means "dragon" and *ma*, of course, can refer to the seed syllable for "mother" in numerous languages. (The word for dragon in Greek is *drákon*, and in Latin, *draco*.)

Dragons kept appearing in even more strange connections. A Rhodes legend says that the Aegean island's people were terrorized by the *Drakones Rhodioi*, the numerous

Medea's Dragon Chariot, Cleveland Art Museum.

dragons or giant serpents that eventually surpassed the number of people. The residents of the island were fed up and sent representatives to the temple at Delos to find a solution. They were told to consult the oracle, which instructed them how to conquer the invasive *Drakones Rhodioi.* The solution was to place the largest of the serpents in the heavens as the constellation Ophiuchus, the "Thirteenth Sign," located between Scorpio and Sagittarius. The name means "Serpent Bearer," and he is related to Asclepius, the god of medicine, who was known to regenerate the dead back to life. The Asclepian healing temples on the Isle of Rhodes and at Empúries, Iberia (as well as the hundreds of others across the Mediterranean), used serpents as messenger-allies of their god of medicine. The live serpents were free to roam in the temples and were an important aspect of the healing process and honored residents.

In the legend of the *Drakones Rhodioi*, it is likely the serpents represented the prolific Gnostic serpent cults of healing that existed on the island, and that the serpents were actually human *Ophites* (from *ophis*, "serpent"). Ophites were practicing Hermetic traditions, combining medicine, healing, mysticism, and the magical use of words and sound. It is possible that the legend of the people of Rhodes wanting to rid their island of serpents was a later Christian overlay when serpents and dragons became equated with the devil. Even the old name for the Isle of Rhodes was Ophiusa, meaning "Land of the Serpent," and with the Greek influence moving westward, it's not surprising that sites of the same name have been identified on the Iberian Peninsula. According to Ptolemy's *Geography*, the old name for the island of Formentera was Ophiussa.[8] This is a smaller island in the Balearics that lies off the southern shore of Ibiza. (See illustration 7, page 58.)

Galicia and Northern Portugal were populated by the Ophi, "people of the serpent," and the Greek arrivals named the region Ophiusa, as noted by the fourth-century CE Latin poet Rufius Festus Avienius in his *Ora Maratima.* And there may well have been a merging of Greek and Celtic traditions that shared a reverence for the serpent. One notable site is the Serpent Stone of Gondomil, a large, winged serpent relief carved on a granite boulder, with a later triumphant Christian cross mounted over it. This most likely indicates the early presence of serpent cults of regeneration and healing in western Iberia, and the location of Gondomil is striking. It is at the very end of the Camino de Compostela, the "End of the Earth," called Finisterre, the place where the Sun dies and disappears into the ocean to be born again.

Drachma Goddesses

The Greek nymph Arethusa is one of several goddesses on the third-century BCE drachma coins displayed at the Ciutadella Museum of Roses. Other examples featured Tanit, Demeter, Artemis, and sometimes Athena-Minerva. In Greek myth, Arethusa was swimming in a river of Arcadia, which unbeknownst to her, was guarded by a river god named Alpheus, who became madly infatuated and pursued her relentlessly. Arethusa fled to the protection of Artemis, and to show her gratitude to the goddess for saving her she became a temple priestess. Some archeologists believe the image is actually Artemis.

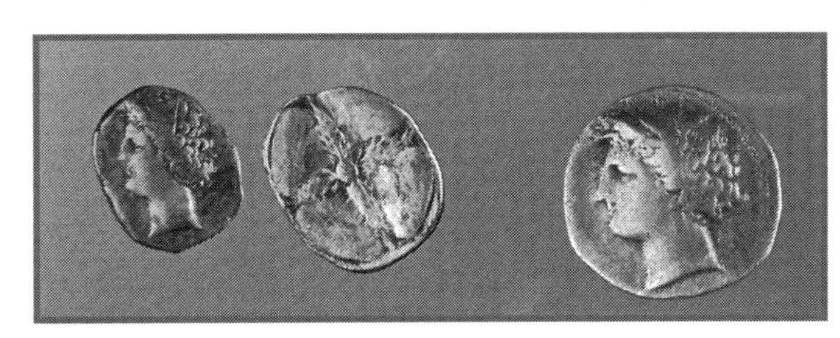

Arethusa coins, Ciutadella Museum.

Her temples were established in the sixth century BCE in Marseilles and Empúries, quite possibly at Rhodes, and further south near Valencia at Hēmeroskopeion, a Greek term meaning watchtower. (See illustration 4, page 262.)

Replicas of drachmas are available in the museum gift shop, and because of the coins' design with a cross in a wheel, I purchased several to take as offerings at the sites of the Four Fires at the ends of the arms of the Great Cross. According to Catalan archeologists,[9] the cross imprinted on the coins had several meanings, including the mystic rose of Our Lady, which will be discussed. As already mentioned, it is the wheel shape termed *roda,* related to the original name and foundation design of the city. This same symbol is featured at all four sites marking the ends of the arms of the great landscape cross and is a symbol of primary importance for all ancient people. Aligning their monuments and cities to the four directions and the turning points of the cycles of time was essential in maintaining the celestial and terrestrial order.

Demeter, Rhodes Ciutadella Museum.

Let's look at other goddesses that were featured on the coins, as this indicated their importance in the religious cults of the region. Demeter is the Greek Mother Goddess related to fertility and prosperity of the land. Terracotta images of her have been found at Rhodes, Empúries, Ullastret, and other Greco-Iberian sites. Her name derives from the Greek word *meter* meaning "mother" and *De* can relate to *Dea,* meaning "goddess" in Latin, hence Demeter, the "Mother Goddess." *De* can also refer to the letter *d* forming the root of the term for door in numerous world languages. (Sanskrit *dwr*, Celtic *duir*, Hebrew *daleth.*)

"Thus, Demeter was ... called the 'Doorway of the Mysterious Feminine'...the root from which Heaven and Earth sprang."

BARBARA WALKER, *THE WOMAN'S ENCYCLOPEDIA OF MYTHS AND SECRETS*[10]

Tanit, who we met earlier, was an aspect of Aphrodite and Astarte for the Carthaginians from at least the ninth century BCE. Some believe that it was Tanit who was adored in the magnificent and enigmatic Iberian goddess, Lady of Elche, who graces the cover. As mentioned, the root *Ta* and the letter *t* in ancient Egyptian hieroglyphic notation indicates the female gender and the root *nit* is related to Neith, the ancient Egyptian Mother Goddess related to weaving and creation. Hence Tanit may have her origins in Egypt. According to Barbara Walker, one of Tanit's titles was "Queen of the Stars":

"Her priestesses were famous astrologers, whose prophecies were circulated throughout the Roman empire ..."[11]

We can see that the Greeks who settled in Iberia adored the goddess, as she was honored in numerous temples and her image, under various names, was chosen to decorate their drachma coins. Ptolemy, in Alexandria, was mapping the western extremities of the known world and using the Iberian coastal temples of the Mother Goddesses as markers for his measurements. These temples also often served as lighthouses and watchtowers in the new lands. We will now discover the impressive integration of the feminine deities at the Iberian city of Rhodes and the many layers of successive temple foundations from the Greek, Roman, early Jewish, and Christian presence.

Monastery of Santa Maria of Rhodes

Catalan archeologists say that the wheel shape on the drachma coins of Rhodes is also the view of the rose from below.[12] What did they mean by this? Did they imagine the Rosa Mystica, the mystic rose of Maria, hovering above their city of Rhodes, which would take the name Roses during the medieval era? Perhaps this is what the surrealist Salvador Dali had in mind when he painted "Rosa Meditative." In this painting, a large red rose is over-lighting the landscape where he lived near Roses, and two megalithic

Rhodes-Roses ruins, Hill of Mary.

standing stones cast their shadows on the land beneath it. Was Dali's Rose painted in honor of Maria Magdalena and the early Christian site at Turo de Santa Maria (Hill of Saint Mary) in the center of Rhodes?

The meeting with the curator at the Ciutadella Museum was complete and many questions that I had from my last visit were answered. I departed the bookshop with additional books for my library to translate from Catalan later. I wandered outside to the expansive grounds of the ancient Greco-Roman city. Green parrots darted through the cedar and twisted olive trees, the bright, colorful birds seeming out of place with snow still covering the Pyrenees in the distance. I headed for the oldest Greek sector of the city, which was now just the remains of low walls that once formed the temples, homes, and the agora, an open area for markets and gatherings. I wanted to check the compass alignments. Sure enough, the main city streets formed a cross with the two axes exactly oriented north-south and east-west.

Walking to the far southwestern corner of the early Christian and later medieval sector, impressive high fortified walls and round watchtowers surround the site of the medieval Benedictine monastery of Santa Maria de Roses. In ancient times, Rhodes was surrounded by two rivers and inland lakes, and the Hill of Saint Mary appeared as an island. The curator had mentioned that the monastery was founded by monks living on nearby Montjuic, meaning "Mountain of the Jews." There is no exact date for when the Jewish people arrived in the region, but we know that following the Roman invasion of Jerusalem in 70 CE, there ensued the Great Dispersal, known in Catalonia as *La Gran Diaspora*, when Jews fled Palestine, and many came to this region. Sadly, this was not the only forced dispersal of these people, that began several centuries BCE. We find numerous hills named Montjuic in Catalonia and a village near Roses is called Villajuiga, "Village of Jews."

The Sibylline Oracles, an apocryphal text from the first century CE refers to the dispersal of the Jewish people: "The whole earth is full of you and the whole sea."[13] And

John William Taylor in *The Coming of the Saints* (1907) claims that at least some of the Jews had arrived here centuries earlier:

> *"...all over the eastern coast of the Mediterranean, we see the Phoenician colonies where Jews, Phoenicians and their descendants had been working together for centuries, singled out as the initial outposts of the Christian effort. And ... we find, in tradition, that [in] all the more distant Phoenician trading ports or colonies at Marseilles, in Sardinia, in Spain and Cornwall, traces may be found of Hebrew missionary effort long antecedent to anything which bears the stamp of actual history."*[14]

Iberia is home to many of the earliest Christian settlements. An important archeological find at the monastery of Santa Maria de Roses is a marble fragment from an early temple altar dating to the fourth century CE. However, we will discover that an even earlier Christian site was established over a temple to Venus at Montserrat in 253 CE. Archeologists say that the Roses monastery site was known as the Hill of Santa Maria before the fourth century. But which Maria? There is a ruined church from the fourth century CE dedicated to Santa Magdalena only nine miles to the south, at the Greco-Roman city of Empúries, and with the strong reverence for her in Catalonia the monastery at Rhodes could have been dedicated to her.

We know from various texts and French legend that following the crucifixion, Magdalena came to the Marseilles region, where there was a temple dedicated to Artemis of Ephesus from the sixth century BCE. And at Empúries, we find another temple of Artemis, founded at the same time, located next to the later Magdalena site. Magdalena would have been familiar with the locations of these Artemis temples, and there would have been communication between the centers, via the active trade route. These sites would have provided a place of refuge for Magdalena in the far western frontier, as referenced by several sources.

> *"Fourteen years after Christ's ascension ... Mary Magdalene, Martha, Lazarus, Saint Maximin and other Christians were put to sea in a rudderless boat by the unbelievers. By the providence of God they arrived safely in Marseilles, where they sheltered under the portico of a pagan temple."*
>
> David Mycoff[15]

Archeologists found tombs and graves at the Santa Maria de Roses monastery dating from the fourth and fifth centuries CE, with tombs lying beneath dating from hundreds of years earlier, including the era of Magdalena's life. This could be one of the earliest Christian sites outside of the Holy Land and contains yet to be discovered ruins beneath the Hill of Santa Maria. Within the cloister, graves were found dating to Greek and Roman times,[16] between 600 BCE and 200 CE. It was common practice to allocate the same site as a sacred temple or necropolis (burial site) throughout the ages. The monastery built on Mary's Hill has certainly been designated as a holy place for at least 2600 years.

I would discover in one of the newly purchased books written by a historian in 1833, that Santa Maria of Rhodes may have been the site of another temple dedicated to Artemis, whom the Romans called Diana. The author, Francesc Jaubert de Paça, mentions archaeological work at the site that indicated a large temple from the third century BCE: "Another temple, dedicated to Diana stood on a hill located to the north of the town," adding, "The location of this other temple is unknown. It is believed that it could be under the foundations of Santa Maria de Roses."[17]

And Strabo, in his *Geography*, confirms Paça's suspicions when he writes, "Here, [in Rhodes-Roses] as in Emporion [Empúries], they worship Ephesian Artemis ..."[18] I discovered this by translating various books written in Catalan, and was amazed that none of the museums or researchers I had spoken with had mentioned this before, most likely because for academics "seeing is believing" and insufficient excavations have been done beneath the monastery. It is a common problem as new temples or churches were built over the earlier structures, preventing further investigation. The museum tourist guide to the Ciutadella (Rhodes City) does, though, mention the Roman and Greek ruins beneath the monastery of Santa Maria, and a road once connected the Greek city to the sacred Hill of Mary. I was happy to find Strabo's account of Artemis being worshiped in Rhodes, indicating a temple or shrine to her must be lying under the current monastery ruins on Mary's Hill. And which Mary was she, is another question that I would continue to ask.

I entered the crumbling walls of the monastery of Santa Maria, sensing the layers of female worship on this small rise of land that used to be an island. In the high-domed elevated level of the original altar, I sang "Mariam Maria," a chant in Greek and Hebrew, honoring all the Marias. A feeling of happiness was present, and a sense that the stones remembered the prayers and songs offered in her name for thousands of years. Santa Maria

Author at Turo Santa Maria Rhodes-Roses, photo Stephen Marcus.

de Roses held a familiar comfort, with the over-lighting invisible "Rosa Meditative" watching and embracing her sanctuary, which has always been called "Mary's Hill."

Here are the lyrics for Mariam Maria, one of my favorite songs composed by my friend Libia Taylor, which is included in the album *Guardians of the Dragon Path:*

"Mariam Maria Sophia Ain Soph
(Mother of wisdom and infinite light)
Agape Theou, Agape Christu
(Love of God, love of Christ)
Mysterioi Theou, Mysterioi Christu"
(Mystery of God, Mystery of Christ)[19]

As I left the monastery enclosure, I noticed abundant fragrant alyssum, also commonly known as "Carpet of Mary," growing near the entry. In Spanish, it is called *mucho miel* (much honey), as these flowers emanate a sweet aroma into the atmosphere. As I leaned in to photograph the flowers, a bee arrived to gather pollen. Science has discovered that flowers open their petals at the sound of an approaching bee, like a lover opening to the beloved. Bees, carpets of flowers named for her, and a hill bearing her name. Throughout the journeys, I would often discover that the flora growing at temples and sanctuaries shared a resonance with the saint or deity honored at the site. This is a beautiful example of simulacra, meaning the pattern of similar forms that mirror the theme of a site or reflect the prayers and songs that were uttered there. My visit to Rhodes felt complete, for now.

CHAPTER 16

The Magdalena Path

Was the monastery of Santa Maria of Rhodes constructed on a site previously dedicated to Maria Magdalena, which was built on the foundations of an earlier temple of Artemis? It seemed likely, given the evidence gathered so far. We see a similar pattern at Rhodes' sister city of Empúries, just 9 miles (14.5 kilometers) to the south, with a temple to Artemis, a fourth century CE Magdalena church, and an earlier necropolis with a watchtower. I could imagine living on the shores of Rhodes, with the elevated island "Hill of Mary" crowned with a temple of Artemis. And across the protected bay at Empúries, the rising Sun illuminating the temples of Artemis, Isis, Asclepius, and the Serapeum. And at night, the lighted watchtowers radiated from both cities, guiding arrivals from near and far. (See illustration 3 Guardians of the Eastern Gate, page 274.)

These Magdaluma-Magdala watchtowers were placed along the major trade routes in the Levant, the eastern Mediterranean, connecting Damascus, Phoenicia, and Canaan to Egypt, and here in Catalonia we find the same pattern of watchtowers guarding not only the coast, but also the towns and ancient roads along the Magdalena Path and the Camino de Santiago. During the medieval era, Magdalena churches were built on hilltops along these routes, guarded by castles often under the protection of the Knights Templar. We will soon learn that the older Camino that runs along the southern side of the Pyrenees is called the Way of the Stars, and dates back 6000 years, corresponding with a similar dating of the Magdala watchtowers in the Levant.

Once again, I departed the Costa Brava ("Wild or Rugged Coast"), named for its spectacular rocky coastline, and drove west along the now-familiar N-260 route, which weaves along the east-west axis of the great landscape cross. As mentioned, this route follows the ancient pilgrimage road Via Annia, more often called Via Romana del Capsacosta. The route, departing from the Mediterranean, forms the eastern arm of

Santa Magdalena de Terrades.

the cross that is marked with no less than fourteen Magdalena sites, all situated on hills and mountain tops, and including hermitages, chapels, mountains, and even a castle in her name. Almost beyond belief, a portion of the N-260 has one section of the route called Carrer Santa Magdalena (Mary Magdalene Street). It seemed that every time I thought I was discovering something new, such as the "Magdalena Path," it became obvious that this was an ancient tradition. We will be exploring some of these Magdalena sites from the eastern end of the Pyrenees at the Mediterranean and progressing westward.

It was a beautiful spring day, and the Sun was shining on the snow-covered peak of the sacred Mount Canigó, the winds swirling the snow around the top creating a visual spinning vortex. Less than five miles to the north, I could see Muntanya de Santa Magdalena, another mountain peak with yet another hermitage, Ermita de Santa Magdalena de Terrades, barely visible, crowning the summit, a watchtower in true Magdala fashion. (*Terrades* most likely means "terraced land," referring to the traditional way of planting.) Viewing these mountains from the north one can see Magdalena's small white chapel crowning the top, which stands out from a great distance, hence a signal fire could be seen from afar.

Santa Magdalena de Montcal:

Near the ancient center of Besalú there is the medieval hermitage of Santa Magdalena de Montcal, and the turnoff toward the north is signposted to the village of Maià de Montcal. Maià is a small river which flows into the Fluvià, one of northeastern Catalonia's most important rivers. The name Montcal derives from "Mountain of Calc," chalk. The region has an abundance of chalk and alabaster mines, the stone associated with Magdalena and her jar of anointing oils. The perfection of the correspondence between nature, the sites, and their names always amazes.

Following the signs to Ermita de Santa Magdalena, up winding unpaved mountain roads, I finally reached the site on the Puig (Hill) de Santa Magdalena. The 13th century Romanesque church is within a working farm that utilized the stone of the

Magdalena Hermitage, Montcal farm guardian.

old hermitage buildings during its rebuilding. An interesting connection with this hermitage is that just 3.5 miles (5.73 kilometers) to the west as the crow flies, is a mysterious and remote monastic site called Sant Sepulcre de Palera, which I had visited years earlier. The church displays a model of a sepulcher with Jesus' eyes wide open, a common depiction in the Pyrenees region, indicating that he didn't die on the cross. As we continue to see, this area of the Pyrenees in the Languedoc and Catalonia is at the heart of heresy, according to the Church of Rome.

Palera is said to be one of the sites where the priest Antoine Bigou (1719–1794) of Rennes-le-Château fled from his Maria Magdalena church with twenty other priests to avoid the French Revolution of 1789. The group escaped over the Pyrenees into Spain, and it is believed Bigou brought with him secret documents regarding the Rennes-le-Château mystery. He had been the confessor of Marie de Blanchefort of the Hautpouls, the noble family of Rennes-le-Château, who was said to have known secrets so powerful that they could unravel the Vatican. Palera has a strange and mysterious ambiance. What secrets did Bigou share with those on the southern side of the Pyrenees? Did he deposit some of the scrolls and secrets that he carried from Rennes-le-Château at one of these remote chapels in Catalonia?

Magdalena Montcal window décor.

I walked around the Montcal farm to view the church, which looked quite plain with a round vault forming the altar area. Then I noticed the multiple small stars and equal-armed crosses carved in the outer walls, which was quite unusual. But what caught my attention was a very unusual window above the western door. The window is framed by two pillars, looking like the twin pillars from the Temple of Solomon, with eight six-pointed stars engraved over each pillar. The six-pointed star is indicative of the Hebrew Star of David, and the local Jewish presence; it is also the symbol of the Davidic bloodline. This star was the first hint of the extraordinary star pattern which would soon be revealed on the Magdalena Path. Five stone spheres crown the window arch, which has twelve stone extensions, or rays. There is a gap where the thirteenth ray may have fallen. The eight stars, five spheres, and most likely, thirteen rays struck a chord, being number progressions in the Fibonacci sequence often used in gothic cathedral design and in musical ratios, better known as Phi, the Golden Mean. Adding each number to the next creates the progression 1+1=2, 1+2=3, 2+3=5, 3+5=8, 5+8=13, etc., to infinity.

In the perfection of things, the numbers five, eight, and thirteen also relate to the cycles of Venus, which is the only planet to create a perfect geometric shape in her orbit. As viewed from the Earth, every eight years, Venus makes thirteen orbits to form a perfect pentagram, a five-pointed star comprised of golden mean angles. Did the designers of the church at Maià de Montcal see our Santa Magdalena as an emanation of Venus? This is certainly indicated just north over the Pyrenees, in the Venus landscape pentagram that includes Rennes-le-Château's Tour Magdala. The carved symbols on the church were a wonderful example of the Hermetic science and the principles of harmony, beauty, and the sacred feminine that can be found embedded subtly in these seemingly simple, remote Magdalena churches that exhibit the ancient science of pre-Christian traditions.

My friend Luiz Pontual Marx knew a member of the family who owns the farm and had been inside the church numerous times. He told me of the interesting painted statue of Magdalena crowned as a queen and holding a child. The statue seems to be from the Renaissance era, and at first glance, we might think she is Mother Mary. However, she is dressed in red with Magdalena's signatures of long hair and a jar of spikenard, revealing her identity as the woman who anointed Jesus. The child is holding an open red book, telling us that all is revealed in this image, with no need for secrets, but who will be able to see her, as the chapel is remote and locked?

One of the things that stands out in Catalonia is the number of Santa Magdalena churches located on private land within small farms or homesteads. It's as if her sanctuaries are hidden from the public eye and guarded by old Catalan families. I have written to the mayor of Maià de Montcal and learned that if anyone wishes to visit the inside of the church, it is possible to arrange this through the mayor's office.

Most of the chapels dedicated to Magdalena in Catalonia have their own signature hymn called a *goig*, a Catalan word meaning "happiness or joy." Here is an excerpt from the lyrics of the song for Santa Magdalena from the church of Santa Maria de Jonqueres in the village of Maià de Montcal. The lyrics certainly matched this remote, unknown hilltop hermitage: "Maria Magdalena, if I could find you." The Catalan original is available online if you want to read the entire text:

"Maria Magdalena, if I could find you;
There at the feet of Christ...
She went from her house to the temple.

To hear the priest who preaches
Is to fall in love ...
He touched her heart ..."[1]

Continuing west parallel to the ancient Via Romana, I thought of all the people who had traveled this route in the distant past, much of the time on foot. And the discovery that a portion of this route is called the Calle Santa Magdalena was beyond my wildest expectations. This is one of the oldest pilgrimage roads in Spain and was traveled by Neolithic and Paleolithic people thousands of years before the arrival of the Phoenicians, Greeks, and Romans. Via Romana connected the Mediterranean with the sites in the valleys below the Pyrenees along the 42nd parallel.

After driving past the medieval center of Besalú, I noticed a small wooden sign on the left side of the highway, *Via Romana*. I was glad to have seen the nearly invisible marker, and immediately turned around, parked, and headed for the path. It was the first opportunity to walk on a section of the old road and the ancient stonework was still visible. Birds were singing, and I joined the choir as I followed the old way of pilgrims singing as they made their long journeys, which I call a *camino de canciones*, a "path of songs." The memories in the stone were palpable, and a sense of timelessness pervaded the scene as I imagined all the feet that had walked here. Even Hannibal, with his train of elephants, was said to have traveled across this route from North Africa to Rome. And later, countless Jewish refugees, early Christian missionaries, and perhaps even members of the Sagrada Familia, the Holy Family, exiles from Judea, including Magdalena.

Santa Magdalena de Montpalau

Just west of Besalú and outside of the village of Sant Jaume de Llierca is Santa Magdalena de Montpalau, guarded by a castle used by the Knights Templar. The chapel and castle sit on top of Muntanya de Magdalena, yet another mountain in her name, located just 3.11 miles (5 kilometers) south of the east-west axis of the Great Cross. The lush riparian zone of the Fluvià River lies below, and its rich soil and volcanic minerals combine to produce a verdant jungle paradise. The site is in the heart of the Garrotxa, a region filled with numerous extinct volcanoes, a land of fire and potent terrestrial force. The area is known as a zone of magic, with stories of fairies, elves, witches, and reports of strange lights, due to its fault line proximity.

The oldest known document on the site says that the land at Montpalau was purchased circa 940 CE by the Countess of Besalú, who built a home there and called it *Villa Palacio*, "Villa Palace." *Montpalau* means "Mountain Palace" in Catalan. The chapel was consecrated as Santa Magdalena de Montepaladio in 1228 by the Bishop of Girona.

Montepaladio is an interesting name, as *monte* means mountain, of course, and *paladio* is a Spanish/Catalan word meaning "palladium." We know *palladium* in English refers to a rare metal element, but the word also means *guardian*, a source of protection. The origins are in the Greek *palladion*, relating to a protective image of the goddess Pallas Athene.[2] The name must have indicated the importance of Magdalena as a guardian from the high places, which is reflected in the *goig* from the Montpalau hermitage:

"Those who go to visit you, on that high rock, [you] always want to help them, glorious Magdalena."[3]

Winding up the Magdalena Mountain, we were driving up the sides of an old volcano, with the Pyrenean fault running along the northern side of the hill facing Mount Canigó. Brazilian-born teacher and investigator Luiz Pontual Marx was my guide, as I had tried to find the church previously but did not know the unmarked small rough track that leads up to the chapel. Luiz has lived in Catalonia for decades and knows the area like the back of his hand. With a keen sensitivity and deep adoration for Magdalena, he gathers wildflowers from her shrines across France and Catalonia to produce flower essences for transformation.[4]

Montpalau castle ruins.

We reached the top of the mountain and found all that remains of the medieval Templar castle that once guarded Magdalena's sanctuary, a single crumbling wall with a window facing west. The chapel is close by and the iron cross above the entrance is entirely unique. A diamond or rhombus design encases the center, which shortens the axis of the crucifixion cross, creating the familiar and more ancient equal-armed cross. The cross within a diamond is a familiar Cathar symbol found throughout the region. The two joined triangles of the diamond can relate to the union of male and female, and heaven and Earth. Also called a lozenge, it is an ancient symbol documented as early as 9000 BCE, referring to female fecundity, regeneration, and pregnancy.[5] We find this shape in every culture, and it is interesting to find it in a prominent position at the entrance, and I wondered if the fertile female message was intended.

We were not able to get the key to enter the church, but it didn't seem to matter, as what occurred at the entry porch was potent regardless. A circular bronze gong is suspended from the eaves facing the Pyrenees to the north, and local people climbing Muntanya de Magdalena often strike it, perpetually sending the sound from her hilltop sanctuary across the valleys. Luiz rang the gong three times to open the energies of the place. This must be a well-known tradition, as my other guide to megalithic sites, Juan Saez, would strike the dolmens three times to open the connection with the site. Additionally, an old Camino tradition says that when the pilgrim approaches a chapel along the way, knocking three times opens an etheric door before entering.

Magdalena de Montpalau.

After Luiz sounded the gong, I experienced my heart opening. He lit the familiar fragrant resins in a brass censer and honored the directions and the guardians of the site. I had a small harp and tuned it to what I sensed aligned with Magdalena of Montpalau. The notes developed into a poignant melody, and the connection with the essence of the site grew to such a degree of emotional intensity that I could no longer play and just wept with the beauty and depth of the moment. Surely, it was Magdalena's essence. This original theme became the prelude to "Guardianes" (Guardians) on the album of songs created for this book, *Guardians of the Dragon Path*. As you will see in the following section, we would discover that the Knights Templar had churches and castles surrounding and guarding Santa Magdalena de Montpalau, forming a perfect six-pointed star, located on the Way of the Stars!

Montpalau gong, Luiz Pontuel.

"They came as Guardianes
Protecting the pilgrim's way,
With an oath to serve Our Lady
And her shrines that shine in the West,
Her towers lighting the Way
of the Stars.

She journeyed across the great waters,
And over the mountains of fire,
With an oath to carry love's promise—
She said, "Set me as a seal upon your heart."
"Set me as a light upon your soul."
They said, "Set you as a star upon our land,"
In remembrance of the Way of the Stars."[6]

Magdalena's Star of David

The Seal of Solomon, known as the Star of David, became the signature for the House of King David, with the six-pointed star symbolizing divine protection. Jesus was of the Davidic bloodline, and when he called himself the "Morning Star" in Revelation 22:16 he must have been referring to the star shield of David and the rising of a new dispensation that he and his beloved would bring to the new world. The Star of David is comprised of two interlocking triangles, and in traditional alchemy the upward facing triangle symbolizes the element of fire, and the downward facing triangle represents water. With the joining of the two triangles, we have the union of the opposites of fire and water, the blade and the chalice, the marriage of male and female, of spirit and matter, and physical as well as cosmic *hieros gamos*.

"Set me as a seal upon your heart,
As a seal upon your arm;
For love is strong as death,
Jealousy is cruel as the grave;
Its flames are flames of fire,
A most vehement flame."

Song of Solomon 8:6

In this phrase from the Song of Solomon, the Shulamite Queen of Sheba is proclaiming herself as the seal upon Solomon's heart, just as Magdalena is the seal upon the heart of Jesus. And we find this six-pointed star in several churches along the

Magdalena Path, including at Santa Magdalena de Montcal and the "Bridal Chamber" chapel of Santa Magdalena de Perella. And the flame of their love finds a resonance in her sites within this "Land of Fire" of the volcanic Garrotxa. Luiz Pontuel explained that Montpalau sits over an enormous crack in the Pyrenean fault, allowing magma to be closer to the surface. This creates a powerful magnetic current, one of the strongest terrestrial currents in the entire Way of the Stars.

The Magdalena seal of protection above is the perfect symbol for her sanctuaries discovered on the Camino, a design developed by my Danish friend and author Lars Muhl, and used with permission. When I was in the final editing stages of this writing, an extraordinary discovery occurred, revealing Santa Magdalena de Montpalau at the center of a six-pointed star, a Star of David. Research is underway with a British astrophysicist, who was inspired by my discoveries of Magdalena mountains and churches in Catalonia, and he has found a perfect hexagram formed by six medieval churches and adjoining castles. He had done fieldwork calculations for the geometry formed by ancient sites in Rennes-le-Château for English authors David Wood and Ian Campbell as detailed in *Geneset: Target Earth*. He used an LGAS-2 computer program to reveal the exact locations of sites in the star. As was revealed with Magdalena de Perella holding the center point of the Great Cross, here we find Magdalena de Montpalau shining from the center of the six-pointed star! And it is no accident that

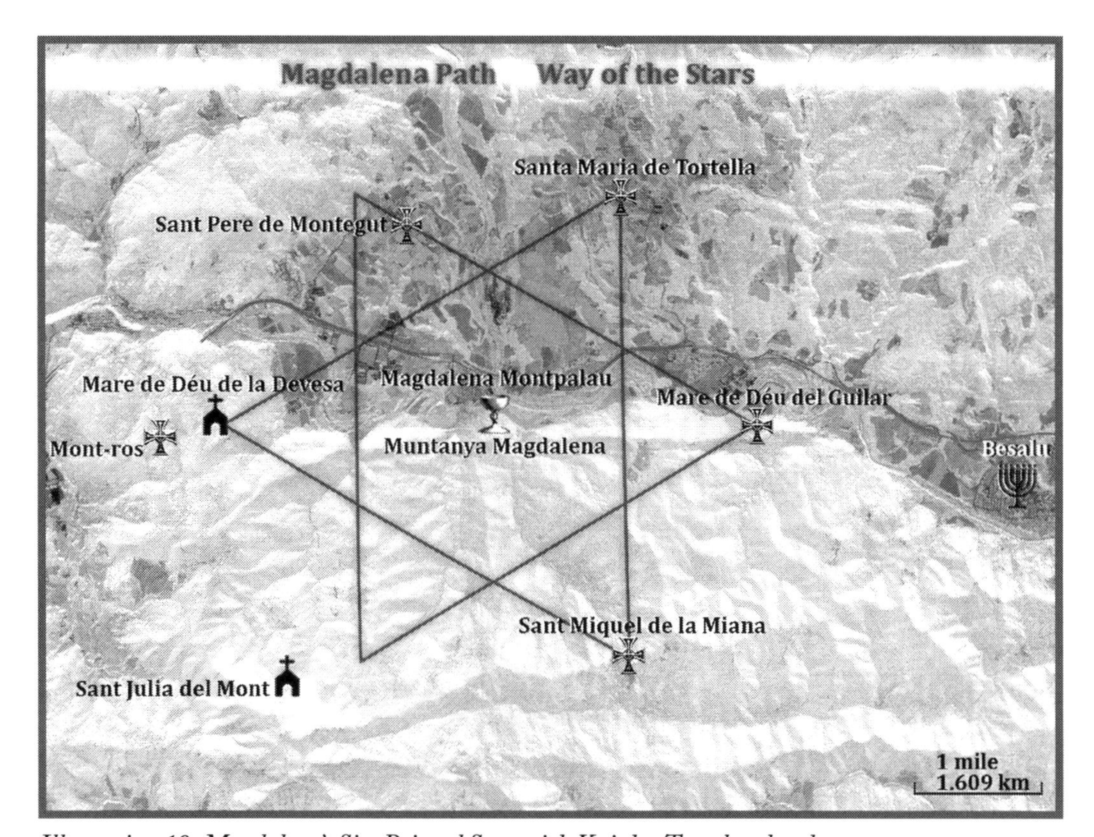

Illustration 19: Magdalena's Six-Pointed Star with Knights Templar churches

Montpalau is 22 kilometers from the Paris Meridian. (As we were going to press, my field researcher, who wishes to remain anonymous, discovered another hexagram pattern involving another two Magdalena churches, which we will save for book two in this series.)

Equally striking are the five Templar churches and their adjoining castles marking the points of the star pattern, which would be serving as guardians of Maria Magdalena at the center. It is significant to remember that the name of the Knights Templar arose from their time at the site of the Temple of Solomon, and their churches forming the Seal of Solomon makes perfect sense. All the sites are located on high hills that could have served as watchtowers for the region and the main east-west route of the Way of the Stars, passing just to the north of the star pattern. Most of the Romanesque churches stand next to ruined castles that were important in Catalonia's history, and well known by popes and the kings of Spain and France.

Santa Maria de Tortella Templar church marks the northeastern point of the star and was a Christian holy site as early as the fourth century. The first official church may have been built in the 8th century and later tombs of knights and noble families were discovered, indicating the site's importance. The octagonal dome rising from the transept identifies the structure as Templar, and the graves of some of the prominent Catalan knights were most likely Templar, given their strong presence in the region.

Sant Miquel de la Miana Templar church marks the southeastern point of the star and was first mentioned in 1279. However, the castle and its watchtower both date from the 9th century. The church has two stone capitals, one of a knight with a Templar cross over his head, and the other is a six-pointed star, common at other Templar sites and forming the foundation geometry of the Flower of Life. The Templars must have been aware of this Star of David landscape pattern formed by these strongholds.

Mare de Déu de la Devesa marking the western point of the star hasn't revealed any Templar associations so far, but just to the west the castle and church of Mare de Déu (Mother of God) de Mont-ros was important in the history of the region. It was owned by various viscounts who fought as knights under the kings of Spain, and it was a healing center run by the Knights Hospitaller, who took over much of the Templar property following the 1307 attempted destruction of their order by the French king Philippe le Bel. Mont-ros was connected to Santa Magdalena de Montpalau through the Viscounts of Besalú (the family who originally purchased the Montpalau land), and all the churches and accompanying castles would certainly have had close dealings for mutual support and guardianship of the Garrotxa region.

Sant Pere de Montagut is most likely a Templar site, just off the northwestern point of the Star of David and its earlier use was first mentioned in 965 by Count Seniofred of Besalú and Cerdanya. (Although the foundation dates of these churches are earlier than the Templar arrivals, they utilized and occupied the older sanctuaries.) The Montagut church has an octagonal baptismal font, and numerous skulls on the holy water fountains, both Templar signatures. Montagut's castle is connected to the nearby Mare de Déu del Cos, which had a 12th-century Marian statue, venerated as Santa Maria de Montagut. My modern Templar friends have said that when a Templar site is named Santa Maria or Notre Dame, it can indicate a secret dedication to Magdalena.

Sant Miquel de la Miana, photo Josep Maria Viñolas Esteva.

And finally, the Templar church marking the eastern point of the star, Mare de Déu del Guilar, also listed as Ermite (Hermitage) de Sant Miquel de Guilar, or Santa Maria d'Aguilario, with *Guilar* and *Aguilario* both meaning "Place of the Eagles." The information posted at the site says that the current chapel was built on an earlier hermitage founded by the knight Simo de Balbs in 1334 and it sits hidden within a lush oak forest and large granite stones, which seemed to emanate the ancient presence of Druids. The area surrounding the church was populated with *Els Albis,* the "White Knights," who used it as a command center for the Knights Templar from the 12th to the 14th centuries, and who were working closely with the Montpalau castle knights and the Magdalena chapel. We can see a possible connection between their name *Albis* and the Cathars, the people from the region of Albi, across the Pyrenees, who were persecuted during the Albigensian Crusades. In the nearby town of Argelaguer, the plaza is called Plaça des Bons, short for *Bonshommes*, the "Good Men," the term often used for the Cathars. Mare de Déu del Guilar was likely a location used by both Templars and Cathars, as more of a spiritual, healing center.

Normally the Star of David is pictured with the apex of the interlocking triangles pointing north and south. But in the orientation of the Montpalau star, the two triangles are perfectly aligned with east and west, putting our attention on the east-west route of the Way of the Stars, the beginning and the end of the great initiation path. (See illustration 19.) This star symbol of unity is calling those who are on the ancient Camino to embrace duality and polarity, healing the wounds of separation. As the star is marked by sites of Maria, the Knights Templar, and with Magdalena at the center, this provides more evidence of the importance of this order of knights and their guardianship of Magdalena's legacy, a repeating theme of the Camino de Santiago de Compostela. It is not merely a coincidence that we find star patterns formed by sites of Maria Magdalena and the Templars on both sides of the Pyrenees, both located close to the north-south axis of the Great Cross and the Dragon Path.

Santa Magdalena de Cambrils

Santa Magdalena de Cambrils, Simon Joan.

If one continues westward several kilometers on the A-26 to the town of Olot, there is yet another chapel of Santa Magdalena, but that would have to wait for another journey. The Serre (Mountain range) de Santa Magdalena towers above Olot and the highest peak is crowned with the small, humble chapel of Santa Magdalena de Cambrils, sitting alone, surrounded by a forest of beech trees. The earliest mention of this Romanesque chapel is 1326, and the altar inside is well cared for, which is impressive given the remote location on the highest peak of the mountains. Visiting this chapel requires a rigorous steep ascent over a rough path. There are two statues of Magdalena at the altar, including an alabaster carving that locals claim is quite old. The following is a line from the traditional goig from Santa Magdalena de Cambrils:

"Hear us glorious one, Santa Magdalena ...
You light up the world with love ..."[7]

The Serre de Santa Magdalena range and the chapel are on the Paris Meridian and Santa Magdalena de Perella is just 6.5 miles (10.5 kilometers) due north on this meridian. The location of Santa Magdalena de Cambrils on the highest peak of these mountains once again follows the ancient Magdala traditions of the Mediterranean with Magdalena as the watcher of the high tower. Cambrils is listed as one of the one hundred highest peaks of Catalonia, part of an ancient network of watchtowers across the land. There are several more sites important to mention before heading north to the heart of the Great Cross at Perella.

Santa Magdalena de Puigsac

Santa Magdalena de Puigsac is a 12th-century Romanesque chapel, and sits on a hill in the higher Pyrenees, just 6.5 miles (10.5 kilometers) as the crow flies to the northwest of Perella. It is sometimes called Santa Magdalena de Pardines and was a popular site for gatherings and festivals of the people living in this remote mountain region. I visited this wonderful chapel during the last days of my stay at Perella. The owner of the hotel at the base of the hill of Perella was born in Puigsac and was very proud of his small village. I could understand why with the picturesque rolling green hills, gardens, and fields of livestock at the foot of the Pyrenees.

I arrived on a crisp, clear day after winding up yet another mountain, on a road covered with patches of ice. The chapel crowns a high hill, but the rugged snow-covered Pyrenean peaks tower high above Santa Magdalena. Located on a popular pilgrimage trail, most of the visitors were hardy sunburned trekkers, carrying serious gear. The Pyrenees are a favorite place for hikers of all ages, often including entire Catalan families, and the Magdalena churches are located on many of the old mountain routes. As we all sat against the medieval stone walls, silently warming in the spring Sun, I wondered what these travelers thought or knew about Magdalena. Did they revere her as a woman of wisdom, a powerful archetype for our time, or did they consider her to be a sinful, weeping penitent? My sense is that being Catalan, they know her true identity, and she still lives in the hearts of the people of this land.

The goig for Santa Magdalena de Puigsac provides some amazing gems, which could be considered high heresy by many. Namely, that Magdalena is the Holy Grail, and that she is Jesus' wife. The first line seems to be a reference to the medieval Grail legend of the *lapis exilis* the stone that fell from heaven in Wolfram von Eschenbach's version of the story, indicating Magdalena as the Grail. Then the Catalan phrase *us fa esposa* meaning "makes you a wife," indicates that she and Jesus were married. The following line must refer to Jesus calling her name Mary in the garden, and finally, her arrival on the shores of Gaul. Granted, these phrases that I have chosen from the goig of Puigsac are out of context, and I have left out the traditional segments regarding her as a penitent, having lived a life of sin, but the following lines paint a profound image of the true, glorious Magdalena.

"Very precious stone of heavenly kind:
Hear us, glorious Saint Magdalena ...
He [God] makes you a wife ...
You embark in a boat without a sail,
In the raging sea without fear ...
This is how you will arrive at the Port of Marseille ...
Hear us, glorious Santa Magdalena."[8]

Templar Churches and a Menhir Mark the Meridian

An old pilgrimage path called *Camino Real,* the "Royal Road," connects Santa Magdalena de Puigsac with a medieval Templar church, *San Miguel de Cavallera*, meaning "Saint Michael of the Knights." The site is in the remote mountains, just 2.49 miles

(4 kilometers) north of Santa Magdalena de Perella and less than half a mile east of the Paris Meridian (.4 miles, .65 kilometers). A menhir stands at the corner of the chapel, with four feet of the stone exposed, but before the soil was built up around the chapel, the stone stood 10 feet above ground level. Normally, up to a third of a menhir's length extends below ground level to keep it upright over the millennia, making the stone's size of perhaps 13 feet even more impressive. My guide surmised that this menhir may have been a marker for an old ceremonial site that has since disappeared. It is indeed interesting that the medieval Templar church and the approximately 5000-year-old menhir both mark the Paris Meridian that was not measured in that region until the early 19th century.

This pattern of certain locations being significant over thousands of years is something that repeats over and over throughout this landscape. And the Camino Real is part of the higher elevation Way of the Stars, which passes between numerous mountains named for the stars. It is impressive that although the site was quite remote, the Templars of San Miguel de Cavallera made thirty-nine significant donations to the Crusades in the Holy Land, according to the information posted at the site.

Another Templar church just 1.94 miles (3.12 kilometers) to the north is Sant Esteve (Saint Stephen) de Llanars, built in the 12th century and located on the river Ter. It is no accident that both Templar sites are on the exact same longitude of 2°20'40" E, which as we have seen, is less than half a mile east of the Paris Meridian. We can see a pattern emerging of not only Magdalena sites located along both axes of the Great Cross, but Templar churches as well. Given more time to research the area's sites, I'm sure that many more Templar sites located near her sanctuaries would be revealed.

Templar Church Llanars reliquary cross.

The old wooden doors of Sant Esteve are carved with dozens of spirals and a bronze dragon on the bolt guards the entrance. Numerous iron Templar crosses hang on the inside walls, so that we don't forget whose temple we are in. A painting of Magdalena in a red robe at the foot of the cross illustrates Jesus pointing to her, letting us know of her importance in his legacy. Most spectacular is the altar reliquary, designed as a large model of the Arc of the Covenant, with two golden-winged angel guardians and, between them, a strange cross.

The anchor at the base of the cross is a signature of the Magdalena mariner's tradition, also decorating the Camargue cross from Les Saintes Maries de la Mer, where the three Maries came ashore in Gaul. Where the Camargue cross has a heart, this cross bears a large X, the symbol of the underground stream of knowledge and the protection of Magdalena's legacy. The X also marks important crossings at this location, the Pyrenean path of Via Romana on the Paris Meridian and the mountain route of the Way of the Stars. We will also discover X's marking the floor of Perella's chapel, which is an ancient symbol of marriage and partnership, formed by the V as the female womb, chalice, and the male blade of the inverted V. A haunting shadow was cast by the candlelight on the stone wall behind, transforming the axis of the cross into a winding serpent path looking like the Magdalena Meridian guarded by the two angels, and certainly during the medieval era, the meridian and her sites were guarded by the Knights Templar.

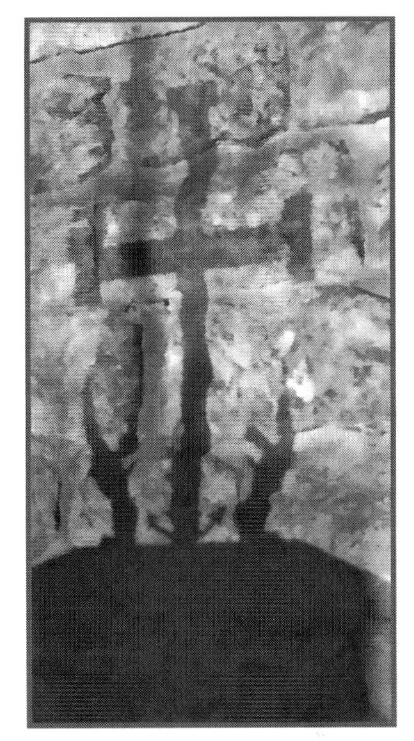

Templar reliquary shadow play.

MON SEVL DESIR

CHAPTER 17

The Queen Bee and Bride of Perella

At the feet of Jesus [you are] prostrated and emotionally moved,
With tears you will wash [his feet],
With ointments you perfume them,
Humbly and with your hair you will wipe [them],
Loose and untied without a braid, Magdalena...

In Perella's inheritance,
You have a humble chapel dedicated to you.
You have been venerated here for centuries;
To all who have invoked you,
Our complete thanks to our Magdalena.[1]

It was finally time to visit Santa Magdalena de Perella, a long time coming. My first view was from the valley below, with the small chapel sitting on a lonely hill overlooking a wide river valley of the Ter. As I approached the narrow old stone bridge over the river, the Sun broke through the clouds, and a large rainbow formed a welcoming portal. Perella, shining like a pearl on the Magdalena Meridian Dragon Path, sitting at the center point of the great landscape cross. After a good meal, fine local wine, and much needed rest at the small family-run hotel below Perella, I began the long morning walk. Passing several small farms along the river, a fine mist was covering the fields and cows with their large brass bells created an enchanting symphony that echoed across the fields.

Santa Magdalena de Perella.

Surrounding the base of the hill of Perella are numerous beehives, and at the bottom of the road leading up to the chapel a warning sign says *Cuidado Abellas!*, "Be Careful Bees!" I enquired later at the hotel to see if this honey was for sale locally. The owner did not know of any, but he did mention that many Catalan beekeepers bring their hives to this location. He said that beekeepers tell him that Perella provides the perfect conditions for good honey. How appropriate to have beehives surrounding her hill—humming and producing golden nectar at the foot of her sanctuary.

I should also mention that on nearly every journey to research Magdalena in the Pyrenees, there were close encounters with bees. On one occasion, I was hiking in the eastern mountains overlooking the sea, searching for an elusive dolmen, and suddenly came upon a series of hives. I tried to tread silently, as the path was next to the bees, with no alternate route. I escaped with only one sting, luckily. On another occasion, I had stopped for lunch at a roadside picnic area. I heard a loud droning sound that kept getting closer, and before I realized what it was, I was entirely enveloped in a swarm of hundreds of bees, who were in the process of moving their queen to her new home. I crawled to the car, keeping below the cloud of hummers, unharmed but dazed by the experience, as bees guarding their queen can be extremely protective. I imagined the bees at the base of Perella as guardians of the house of the "Queen Bee" Magdalena.

Bee symbolism appears in ancient sacred texts and artifacts dating back to the Neolithic period, relating to fertility, bloodlines, oracles, and the Mother Goddess. And apropos to the many mysteries and symbolism at Perella, honey was used in the Egyptian Opening of the Mouth ritual, which Jesus appears to be performing for Magdalena in the altar painting. The honey was said to revive the pharaoh with the golden elixir of Ra, preparing the soul for resurrection.[2]

For the Egyptians, the bee represented the fertility, sexuality, and survival of a royal lineage and was the symbol for the kings of Lower Egypt. Offerings of jars of honey were found in the tombs of pharaohs, including Tutankhamun, and honey was believed to offer protection and revive the sexual power of the kings and gods. The goddess Neith, weaver and mother of creation, had a temple at Sais which was called the "House of the Bee," and bees and honey have been associated with the Mother Goddess as the Queen Bee for thousands of years. The goddess Artemis is portrayed with numerous breast-shaped bee cocoons hanging from her torso, associated with fertility and prophecy. Certainly, Magdalena had the gift of sight as she could see Jesus in his risen light body outside of the tomb. And according to some, for the Merovingian kings, the bees represented the royal Davidic bloodline of Jesus and Mary Magdalene.

"The bee is a perfect model of the perfect symbol ...
The bee celebrates its wedding in the highest flight."

R. A. Schwaller de Lubicz, *The Egyptian Miracle*[3]

The long, winding road up to Santa Magdalena gave me time to contemplate her importance in the Christian mysteries and how the Catalan people have not forgotten her. Looking up toward the chapel, the hillsides were filled with grazing white cows and early blooming wild white roses, reminding me of Dante. His phrase was more perfect than I realized, as I would soon discover:

> *"In form then of a pure white rose the holy host was shown to me, which, in His own blood, Christ made His Bride."*
>
> DANTE, *THE DIVINE COMEDY: PARADISE XXI,* 1–3[4]

As I approached the chapel, there was a single red rose blooming at the outside western wall behind the altar, providing a perfect metaphor for the red and white roses, the male and female in the alchemical vessel of unification and transmutation. The proprietor of the hotel had kindly given me the name of the owners of the property, and I had arranged to meet Jordi, the son. As I waited by the chapel, Jordi approached from the old Spanish-style home with the typically heavy iron, oversized medieval church key and invited me inside her sanctuary. The ancient stone forming the lintel over the entry was original, dated to the 12th century, or perhaps the 9th, according to Catalonia's *Breve Historia Perella.* Perella was mentioned in 887 in the Act of Consecration of the monastery of Sant Joan de les Abadesses.

The chapel is small, simple, there are no brightly colored stained-glass windows, yet this shrine is potent and holy. I slowly walked toward the altar, where a copy of the six-paneled retable by Bernat Matorell decorated the wall. I gazed at the last image of Magdalena's deathbed depicting her etheric body departing her mouth, and Jesus standing next to her, receiving his beloved disciple and bride. Was this image indicating that Jesus was performing the Opening of the Mouth ritual that was also performed on Egyptian kings and queens? The painting shows Magdalena's light body escaping her mouth into the loving hands of Jesus. What subtle body was this? James P. Allen describes the various bodies of the deceased in *The Ancient Egyptian Pyramid Texts*:

> *"The ancient Egyptians believed that each human being consists of three basic parts: the physical body and two nonmaterial elements known as the ka and the ba. The ka is an individual's life force ... each person's ka ultimately came from the creator and returned to the gods at death. The ba is comparable to the Western notion of the soul or personality ..."*
>
> *"At death, the ka separated from the body. In order for an individual to survive as a spirit in the afterlife, the ba had to be reunited with its ka, its life force: in the Pyramid Texts and elsewhere, the deceased are called 'those who have gone to their kas.'"*[5]

Allen explains that the function of the rituals described in the Pyramid Texts was to enable the reunion of the deceased's Ba and Ka to become an Akh. The Resurrection Ritual (Opening of the Mouth), and the repetition of invocations and magical words, served to release the Ba from the body to unite with the Ka to become "Akhified." Without the limitations of the physical body, the Akh was free to explore the cosmic plane and to live eternally in the domain of the gods. Contemplating the journey to arrive here, the Black Stone dreams, the Palermo Stone with its earliest mention of the Opening of the Mouth ritual, once again, I felt like a pawn on a chessboard, being moved by an invisible hand, glimpsed in mysterious dreams.

Above and framing the Perella retable was a colorful fresco depicting the parted curtains of a bridal tent. This image fit perfectly with the meaning of the old spelling of the site, which was *Parella*, meaning "a couple or pair." The *chuppah*, as this tent is called in Hebrew, is the canopy under which the bride stands for her marriage, symbolizing the house of the bride, and perhaps, her womb. In the Bible's Joel (2:16) it says:

"Let the bridegroom emerge from his chamber (chedro), and the bride from her chuppah."

A beautiful example of the chuppah can be seen in the sixth tapestry of the extraordinary Lady and the Unicorn series of Flemish weavings, created circa 1500, currently in the Cluny Museum in Paris. Synchronicity was at work once again, as the Cluny Museum is also located on the Paris Meridian. Each of the tapestries shows Our Lady with the Unicorn, which during the era of their weaving represented the bride with the anointed horned one, the Messiah, as bridegroom. Many believe that the Unicorn Tapestries were a veiled portrayal of the love story of Jesus and Magdalena, and others see them as representing the Biblical Song of Songs, the erotic love poems of Solomon and Sheba, a love story as old as time. All six tapestries depict fruits, fauna, and flora symbolic of fertility, sexuality, and marriage. Each of the tapestries

Unicorn and Our Lady tapestry 6, Cluny Museum, Paris.

represents one of the six senses of sight, hearing, smell, taste, touch, and the sixth sense of the seer, the initiate.

In the sixth tapestry the bride stands before the doorway of her chuppah, and she and her attendant are both wearing turbaned headdresses with a stylized feather shaped as an *uraeus*. The uraeus is a well-known image from Egypt in the form of an upright cobra depicted on the crown of the kings and queens as strong protection, signifying an initiate. It can represent the awakened third eye of one who has accomplished the internal alchemical marriage, the union of the male and female principles within, and with the divine. Meditation and breathing techniques to achieve this union are described in chapter 20. This is the true treasure in developing the state beyond separation and duality, and an additional meaning of *A mon seul desir* ("To my only desire" in French), which is written above the bridal tent in the tapestry.

"He that hath the bride is the bridegroom: ... thus my joy therefore is fulfilled."

JOHN 3:29.

The Gospel of Philip speaks of the Bridal Chamber as being the holiest of the chambers of the Jerusalem Temple, a place of light and of the heart, *true intelligence of the heart*. The Bridal Chamber, of course, also relates to physical marriage, when traditionally the bridegroom was brought to the place where the bride awaited beneath the chuppah, and, in this case at Perella, she was Magdalena. As the Gnostic Gospel of Philip says:

"The companion [koinonos] of the Son is Miriam of Magdala. The Teacher loved her more than all the disciples; he often kissed her on the mouth ..."[6]

The text continues later with:

"This is how it is with those united in marriage. The mystery which unites two beings is great; without it, the world would not exist."[7]

Another telling image in the sixth tapestry is Our Lady showing the treasury of her jewelry box. Perhaps she is removing them from the golden chest to signify that there is a deeper treasure to be found in the ability to know the space of oneness and divine union beyond separation and the distraction of all that glitters. The jewels appear to be connected, as in a necklace. In The Song of Songs, it says:

"How lovely are your cheeks; your earrings set them afire! How lovely is your neck, enhanced by a string of jewels."[8]

An interesting correlation can be found in the Egyptian funerary rites, in which female deities present a *menat* (collar, necklace) to the deceased to endow them with "The persistence of life, durability, ever-renewed youth."[9] Lucie Lamy describes the scene of the offering of divine fragrance to protect the king, after which Isis shakes her sistrum and presents the menat necklace for his regeneration in the Afterlife. This ritual offering of the necklace also fits with the theme in the tapestries, as the unicorn represents the beloved Messiah, (and Osiris) as the dying and rising God. And the uraeus headpieces worn by Our Lady and her attendant certainly hint at Egyptian mystery traditions.

In pondering the mysterious bridal tent fresco of Perella, I wondered if it was connected somehow with the Kabbalists in nearby Girona. The views of these mystical Jewish teachers on the holiness of the bridal chamber were profoundly reverent and revealing. Girona was the bishop's seat for Perella, located 30.8 miles (49.6 kilometers) to the southeast. During the time the chapel of Magdalena at Perella was in active use, Nachmanides was one of the greatest Kabbalah scholars and teachers in Girona. Born Moses ben Nachman, (1194–1270 CE), he lived most of his life in Girona and was instrumental in rebuilding the Jewish community in Jerusalem after its destruction in 1099 during the Crusades. In his mystical writings we find some of the most telling insights into the bridal chamber mysteries. He writes in his "Letter on Holiness":

"The sexual relationship is in reality a thing of great elevation when it is appropriate and harmonious ...In the moment when a man unites with his wife in holiness, the shekhina *is present between them."*[10]

The Shekinah is the Holy Spirit, the sacred feminine principle, and completes the trinity in the union of the beloveds, infusing their love with light from the higher realms. (If we have wondered where the feminine exists in "Father, Son, and Holy Ghost," she is the third principle, the Holy Spirit that unites and permeates all.) Nachmanides explains that when the lovers are focused on the divine, the Shekinah, they anchor this illumination, which enters the seed of life of the semen and the egg to consecrate a new life.

He speaks of the strength of mind able to focus sufficiently to attract the higher light and integrate this into the life fluids, which is only possible with a mind that is clear through disciplined practice. This included controlled breathing, meditation, a focus on holy scriptures, humility, and the repetition of purifying sacred names. The Hebrew sacred names are comprised of seed syllables, with each of the twenty-two letters of the Hebrew alphabet containing creative principles, which are especially potent in the vowels. The letter *Yod* is shaped like a drop of liquid light, or semen, and the letter can be used as either a vowel or consonant, and is part of the holy name of God, *Yod He Vav He*. We find these secret mysteries in every major world tradition, often displayed in temples, in plain sight.

Yod He Vav He. Yod is the letter in the upper right within the triangle of fire.

In the Temple of Luxor, engraved on the inside of the western wall, are images of the collection of the pharaoh's semen in a cup, the life-producing fluid that was essential for the continuation of the royal lineage. Interestingly, one of the Egyptian hieroglyphs symbolizing "mother" is the cup shape, the womb, the receptive container. This seed of life shaped like the letter Yod is also found carved in the cornerstone at Rosslyn Chapel, near Edinburgh, Scotland. The 15th century edifice, which featured in Dan Brown's *Da Vinci Code*, is an alchemical book in stone recording key scenes from the Bible, the Knights Templar, and the Grail mysteries. The design was the brainchild of Sir William Sinclair, a prince of Orkney, who was a Knight of the Golden Fleece and of the Coquille Saint Jacques (the cockle shell of Santiago de Compostela). The Knights of Saint Jacques alludes to the 12th century Knights of Santiago that had strong Templar connections.[11] It is not surprising that we find unusual, coded messages engraved in Rosslyn Chapel's walls.

The Yod cornerstone was pointed out to me by the late Robert Brydon, past curator of the chapel. As we stood in front of the stone in the near the southwest corner of the chapel, he said, "Is the Yod God?" Most likely, yes. The creative principles are embedded in pure original sound, the syllables and symbols of life, and in a drop of liquid light of the beloved. Bob also pointed to the opposite corner in the Mary Chapel, where golden honey once dripped down the inside walls from a beehive in the niche of the spire above, another reference to fertility and royalty. In Egyptian sacred marriage tradition, it is Hathor, as the feminine power, who bestows the masculine force of fecundity on the god Amun.[12] Schwaller De Lubicz refers to this same principle enacted between Sekhmet and Ptah:

"Ptah ... cannot exercise his power until he has been untied by Sekhmet, his female principle ... it is she who will unbolt the lock, dissolve the obstacle and free his fire."[13]

She, who will unbolt the lock, dissolve the obstacle, and free his fire. Let's just sit with that for a moment or more. This echoes traditions in sacred Tantra, containing keys to liberation, whether practiced with a partner or alone. Jesus could not be all that he was destined to be without embracing both his masculine and inner feminine Shekinah nature. And he was able to experience the dissolving of obstacles and the alchemy of freeing his fire with his beloved companion, *koinōnos*.

The Bridal Chamber fresco at the humble chapel of Santa Magdalena de Perella shines quietly, deep in the Pyrenees, and the messages in the symbolism of her sites was continually calling for the unifying of the duality within our natures, a coming to meet in the center, between the thoughts of us and another, Earth and Spirit, resting in the still point, wherein the two become one. As my dear friend Henry Lincoln often said in his later years, "One plus one equals one."

The X in Mystery Traditions

There is more revealing symbology at Santa Magdalena de Perella in a series of unusually large engraved X's in the floor tiles. The X's are so prominent, that we cannot miss them. They are not uniform, preprinted tile designs, as they have slight variations, and one can see that were carved by hand. In the hundreds of chapels that I have visited across Europe and Britain, these are entirely unique. The X is the Nordic rune symbol for unity, marriage, and partnership, and Margaret Starbird says in *The Woman with the Alabaster Jar*:

> *"...the archaic meaning of the X, the union of the male and female in holy and equal partnership, is inherent in its very structure: a combining ... of the ancient and archetypal V, the feminine chalice, and Λ, the masculine blade."*[14]

Santa Magdalena de Perella Xs.

Starbird explains that the X is a favorite symbol for heretical groups, and symbolized enlightenment and truth.[15] During the medieval era, the X symbolized the underground stream, which included groups that were being persecuted by the Roman Catholic Church. "By this sign you shall know us," was the unspoken message of both the X and the red cross.[16] This underground network would have included groups of Cathars, Templars, or other Christians who honored Gnostic ideals. In other words, the X also represented the unity and direct line between Earth and spirit and the unity of the bride and bridegroom. The

French alchemist Fulcanelli writes in *Le Mystere des Cathedrales*:

"And this sign has been called ...the Seal of Hermes, Seal of the Wise, the Mark and the Imprint of the Almighty, his Signature..."[17]

We can also see the X in the foundation design of the Perella chapel, with a winter solstice sunset alignment perfectly dividing the building diagonally from the bell-tower at the northeastern corner to the statue of Magdalena and the offering niche in the southwest corner. According to my geomancer friend Juan Saez, this southwestern point marks the point of the soul's transcendence over death, forming the intentional alignment of her sanctuary. And it is in this southwest corner of Perella that Magdalena holds the skull, symbolizing death, resurrection, and rebirth. It was Magdalena who was present at each stage of Jesus' transition, the cycles of the dying and rising god, the same stages of the solar cycle, and like the Sun at winter solstice moving from the longest night (death) to the increase of light, longer days, and the ultimate return of new life. We would discover this same X pattern in the foundation design of a fourth century CE Magdalena Temple in Catalonia, which will be revealed in future chapters.

X is also an old symbol for crossroads, and I would soon discover that Perella marks the center of the crossing of two ancient pilgrimage routes, including *Cruce de Caminos*, and *Ruta de les Quatre Ermites* ("Route of the Four Hermitages"). This tiny chapel holds the center point of the landscape cross, north, south, east, and west, the Omphalos at the heart the Dragon Path. She is the sacred bride, the one who anointed Jesus, and the Pearl of Perella, her remote hill surrounded with bees and roses. The following extract from the 19th century poet and priest Jacint Verdaguer captures much of the essence of this outwardly humble Magdalena chapel, a lighthouse of love at the ancient crossroads of Catalonia:

"Come out, precious Pearl, from your shell,
All Catalonia would adorn herself
With you—take here, thornless rose, for vase,
And fill with fragrance of Spain and all the world ...

This mount where cenobites and hermits thrive
Will be a hive that brims with mystic honey,
Honey that the saints of earth collect,
Circling round like bees the Rose of Heaven."

JACINT VERDAGUER, *CANTO XI*, "DISCOVERY OF THE VIRGIN"[18]

Resonance in the Name Perella

Catalonia's "Pearl of Perella" was unraveling more threads in the endless mystery of the Magdalena sites in the Pyrenean landscape. We discovered the pearl of wisdom guarded by a dragon at Coves del Drach (Caves of the Dragon) near the southern end of the Magdalena Meridian, Dragon Path at Majorca, and the uncanny connection with Majorca's dragons in the Gnostic allegory *The Hymn of the Pearl* in chapter 4. As mentioned, the dragon traditionally guards the precious pearl and other treasures of great value, including the priceless treasure of sacred knowledge. The phrase "Here be dragons" also means "Here be hidden knowledge."

Old sign to Perella.

Additional mysteries were revealed when I asked Jordi about the source of the name Perella. He explained that the first recorded owner of the hilltop was the Parella family, as listed in a medieval Catalan document. They were originally Sicilian, from the area of Palermo, which is fascinating, given that this is the location of the museum with the Egyptian Palermo Stone, that guided me to Perella. But there was an even more interesting connection. Just 50 miles (80 kilometers) north of Perella there were two villages in the French Pyrenees with the name *Perelhe*, sometimes written as *Perella,* three miles apart near Montségur, named for their lord Ramon de Perelhe (also appearing in documents of the time as Perilla or Perella). Perelhe happened to be one of the closest knights in the service of the "Grand Dame of the Cathars," Esclarmonde, sister of Ramon Roger, Count of Foix, the family at the heart of the Cathar heresy.[19]

Under Esclarmonde's direction, Ramon de Perelhe oversaw the fortification of Montségur during the early 13th century and was a key figure in the Cathar network of the region. Legends tell us that the Grail was carried into the mountains following the fall of Montségur and the horrific burning by the Inquisition army of more than two hundred Cathars. Did the holy chalice that represented sacred knowledge held by the Grail families and the Cathars, find its way across the Pyrenees? We will discover that both found refuge in Catalonia. Was this the missing link in my dream of the medieval monastery and the image of the Grail and the footprint of Magdalena? The following account is from Parisian author Coincy-Saint Palais, who specialized in the Grail history of France and Spain:

> *"... [Ramon de Perelhe] is descended from three centuries of Sovereign Princes of the region, and a legend affirmed by their ancestors said that the "Perilha," [were] oriental kings who had brought and kept the Holy Grail! in the region."*[20]

In *Le Saint Graal et le Précieux Sang* ("The Holy Grail and the Precious Blood"), Coincy Saint-Palais mentions a medieval legend of Prince Pérille, said to be the guardian of the Holy Grail. Although she questions the source of the legend, it most likely arose out of a combination of medieval Grail romances and the actual history of Montségur. The legend describes Prince Pérille as the head of his family, which arrived from the East to settle in Gaul, and Palais compares him with the character Titurel in Wagner's 1882 opera *Parsifal*. Titurel was leader of the Knights of the Holy Grail and guardian of the sacred chalice that the angels brought from heaven to the Pyrenees: the "mysterious and ineffable cup that the eye could not grasp, and the tongue could not describe."[21] Interestingly, the mystic Rudolf Steiner also believed that the Grail was in the Pyrenees in a subtle dimension, illuminating the region.

During the 1100s and 1200s, several poets and authors were composing Grail romances, weaving the stories of the Grail knights, the Cathars, and the Holy Chalice into symbolic tales, which the Inquisition considered heretical. Following the French poet Chrétien de Troyes' Arthurian Grail tales, including the well-known *Perceval ou le Conte du Grael* ("Perceval or the Tale of the Grail," circa 1181). Two German authors also wrote their versions, focused more on the Pyrenees region: Wolfram von Eschenbach (c. 1195–1225) wrote *Parzival* (in which the Grail is a stone that fell from heaven), and Albrecht von Scharfenberg wrote *Der Jüngere Titurel* (1272). Both authors mention the Grail knight Perilla, whose castle is somewhere in the Pyrenees, normally thought to be Montségur, and sometimes Montréal de Sos. But just to the southeast is another, unknown, and unmentioned site at Santa Magdalena de Perella. René Nelli even states that in the medieval documents, Ramon Perelha's name is written with the Spanish spelling Perilla.[22] The name Perella provides us with an obvious clue and missing link to a secret held by Cathars and Grail families. But what is the Grail, but the eternal quest for truth, love, beauty, renewal, illumination, and the re-enchantment and regeneration of the Earth.

Author at Santa Magdalena de Perella.

The story of Santa Magdalena de Perella and its associations with the Grail stories, and its key position marking the center of ancient pilgrimage routes and the intersection with the Dragon Path does not end here. But for now, it was time to continue the quest to her other sites further south along the Magdalena Meridian. I had brought two candles that were recent gifts from a dear friend from sacred sites in Israel. One was from Magdala, on the Sea of Galilee, and the other from the Holy Sepulcher in Jerusalem. I asked Jordi if I could light the candles and offer a song to Our Lady. He responded, "Ciertamente, con muchas gracias por nuestra Magdalena." (Certainly, thank you on behalf of our Magdalena). I sang "Nuestra Doña de Catalonia" ("Our Lady of Catalonia"),[23] a song inspired by the flaming Grail images found in medieval chapels deep in the Pyrenees. Jordi climbed the bell tower and pulled the long rope that sent her resonance ringing across the valley and into the river Ter. The first visit was complete, but I would return many times, and with each visit more would be revealed.

CHAPTER 18

The Magdalena Meridian

We have visited several of the sanctuaries dedicated to Santa Magdalena located on the eastern arm of the Great Cross, "The Magdalena Path," and now we will explore her sites along the Paris Meridian from the Pyrenees to Majorca. As we have discovered, Perella is located at the center crossing point of both axes of the Great Cross. The following is a list of monasteries, hermitages, churches, and mountains dedicated to Santa Magdalena on the north-south meridian, which I am calling "The Magdalena Meridian." In illustrations 5 and 6, Magdalena Meridians North and South, you can see how her sites are carving a serpent path in and out of the Paris Zero Meridian. Additionally, the river Ter weaves in and out of her sites from the Pyrenees to Santa Magdalena de Conangle, which is described in the next section.

Looking at the symbology of numbers, it is no accident that this meridian has "shifted" since becoming France's Zero Meridian in the 17th century to its current longitude of 2°20' degrees east of Greenwich (the current global zero meridian). Once again, we find her number 22, relating to her feast day on the 22nd of July. As I studied the Magdalena chapels located on or near the Dragon Path, it seemed that every time I searched, more of her hidden hermitages appeared. But at some point, I had to stop looking, and get this book completed, and I will leave the additional sites for future questers to discover. Here is the work in progress for her sanctuaries on the "Magdalena Meridian" from the Pyrenees to Majorca:

- Santa Magdalena, Palais Rois de Majorca (Palace of the Kings of Majorca), Perpignan (28.38 miles/45.68 kilometers east of the meridian)
- Port de Madeleine, the Magdalena Gate in the medieval city wall at Mosset (on the meridian)
- Santa Magdalena de Conat (1 mile/1.6 kilometers East of the meridian)

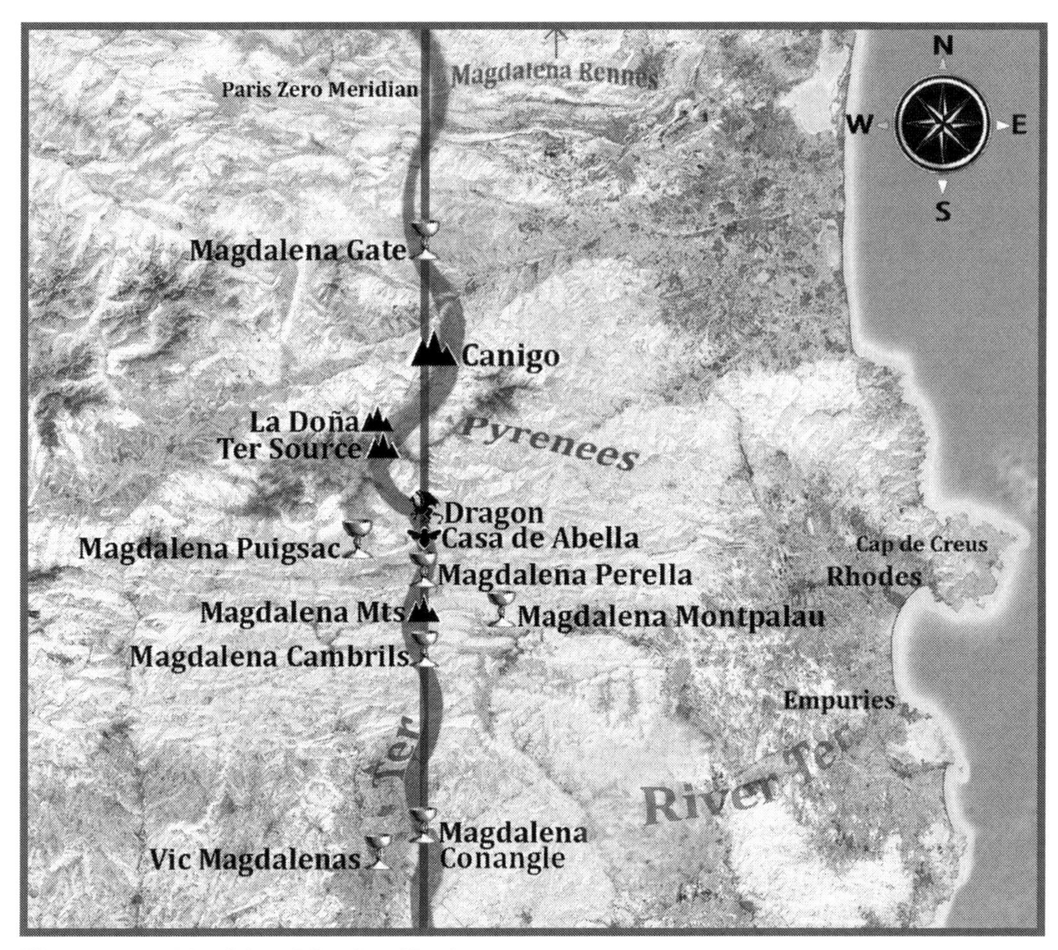

Illustration 5: Magdalena Meridian North

- Santa Magdalena de Puigsac (5.08 miles/8.18 kilometers west of the meridian)
- Santa Magdalena del Coll (4.6 miles/7.4 kilometers east of the meridian)
- Santa Magdalena de Perella (on the meridian)
- Santa Magdalena de Solanllong (14 miles/22.5 kilometers west of the meridian)
- Santa Magdalena San Joan des Fonts (9 miles/14.4 kilometers east of the meridian)
- Santa Magdalena de Olot (8.06 miles/13 kilometers east of the meridian)
- Santa Magdalena de Montpalau (13.9 miles/22.4 kilometers east of the meridian)
- Santa Magdalena de Cambrils (on the meridian)
- Serre Santa Magdalena (mountain range on the meridian)
- Santa Magdalena del Mont (3 miles/4.82 kilometers east of the meridian)
- Santa Magdalena de Guardiolans (Guardians) (19.43 miles/31.28 kilometers west of the meridian)

- Santa Magdalena de Conangle (0.67 miles/1.07 kilometers west of meridian)
- Santa Magdalena de Mosqueroles (5.2 miles/8.37 kilometers east of the meridian)
- Santa Magdalena Hermitage at the top of Montserrat (26 miles/42 kilometers west of the meridian)
- Santa Magdalena de Barcelona (9.61 miles/15.47 kilometers west of the meridian)
- Hermitage Santa Magdalena, Puig Magdalena, Majorca (33 miles/53.1 kilometers east of the meridian)
- Monastery of Santa María Magdalena, Palma (16.66 miles/26.81 kilometers east of the meridian)

The Dragon Path That Became a River

Or perhaps it is the river that became a Dragon Path, as the Ter passes numerous sites dedicated to Santa Magdalena on her southward journey, weaving in and out of the Paris Zero Meridian. The Ter is the longest river in Catalonia, and its source is in the heart of the Pyrenees at a site called Ull de Ter, meaning "Eye of the Earth," with the high peak La Doña ("The Woman" in Spanish) guarding the crucial life-giving waters. Catalan author Ramon Hervas in *Historia Secreta del Grial* (*"Secret History of the Grail"*) says that the older name of the Ter was *Thergerones* or *Tergemino*, a legendary "river of fire and gold" in the underworld.[1] Perhaps the name was derived from the river's path through Gerona, hence *Thergerones*. The Ter continues to carve her way past numerous Magdalena sites like a great serpent mama before merging with the Mediterranean next to one of her earliest chapels in all of Spain.

Trail to Ull de Ter.

Over the last seventeen years of exploring the Pyrenees and the valleys that stretch out below, it seemed as if I was having a love affair with this magical river Ter. This image of the river is from the high Pyrenees near her source, before she grows into a wide, powerful mama as she absorbs other rivers on her way down into the valleys. I sensed an uncanny magnetism between the Magdalena sites and the Ter that flowed past her sanctuaries on the long journey from the Pyrenees to the sea. I could imagine

Meeting wild Pyrenean horses on the trail.

all the stories and memories of her monasteries, hermitages, and chapels embedded in the crystalline minerals in the stone that flow in the lifeblood of the Ter's abundant waters.

Below the river's source at Ull de Ter, following the Vall de Ter ("Valley of the Ter") southward, a bronze fire-breathing dragon monument called Drac stands as guardian above the village of Vilallonga de Ter ("Long Village of the Ter"). In fact, the entire mountain above the village is shaped like a great dragon with white stone spires at its head looking much like horns. Drac is just 5.7 miles (9.17 kilometers) north of Perella as the crow flies. This impressive dragon bellows and breathes fiery smoke twice a day (created mechanically for visiting tourists) and one can clearly hear Drac echoing throughout the valley below. There is an annual festival "Fira del Drac" (A Dragon Fair) on August 14th, when dragons parade in the village square and show off to the children. I marveled at the perfection that this dragon is positioned as a guardian of the Dragon Path as it crosses the Pyrenees into Catalonia. The Catalan people have a great love for dragons, giants, fairies, and all things magical, which dwell in a dimension next to ours, yet invisible to most modern eyes.

Dragon of Vilallonga de Ter.

As related in the introduction, a creation story told by the Basque people of the western Pyrenees features a mother dragon named Benzozia, who they believe created this great mountain range, and who still sleeps in the caves and tunnels beneath the mountains. Martin Locker tells the following legend, recorded in 1879, relating to a time when the Earth was new, and the Iberian lands were flat and icy cold, perhaps during the last ice age, which occurred between 115,000 and 11,700 years ago:

> *"Benzozia slept in a cavern deep within the earth, and in her slumbers, she turned and rasped the cavern roof with her scales. She twisted and writhed in her restless sleep, causing the earth to groan and split. This great force pushed the ground above her up, creating the first mountains, the Pyrenees. From her seven jaws ... fire poured forth, and rose up through the cracks in the earth, scorching the soil and the air.*

Clouds formed, and the rains that they created reacted with the fire causing more clouds to form. The rain created by these clouds forced the fire back down to Benzozia's cavern, and formed the lakes we see today, allowing the first green shoots of trees and bushes to emerge from the burnt soil. As the fire retreated, from its embers and gases the first people came, the Basque people."[2]

Benzozia's seven jaws pouring forth fire is reminiscent of the seven creation dragons of the Tibetan Dyzan Texts and the seven cobras of Egypt issuing forth the seven tones of life described in the introduction. Legends of Pyrenean fire dragons who create the tremendous thunder and lightning storms abound, with one seven-headed dragon called Herensuge, who is most likely related to another dragon spirit of the mountains named Sugaar, who was the husband of the Basque goddess Mari. These dragons, as well as the goddess Mari, are associated with Pyrenean weather control, and are said to live in the subterranean caves and tunnels of the mountains, where rivers of milk flow. Is this the milk pouring forth from La Doña, the mountain peak of the "The Woman" above Ull de Ter, rising in the spring of the "Eye of the Earth," to become the great river of Catalonia? Or is this the milk flowing into the Earth from the breasts of the Egyptian goddess Nut of the Milky Way as she arches over the Pyrenees? (See Illustration 4, page 262.) These nature spirits and deities are guardians related to both the fiery star field and the terrestrial fertility of the Pyrenean region.

"The 'Dracs' are common features of [Catalan] street processions and festivities, snapping at the townsfolk and rushing them. In Tarragona one finds the unique 'Vibria', a female 'dragon' complete with human breasts and a womb, that totters around festivals and processions. This addition of highly specific human anatomical aspects is intriguing, and may suggest a more archaic origin that referenced fertility, before the Christian symbolism of the dragon (ie. evil) took root."[3]

Also, located along the Ter just 4.44 miles (7.14 kilometers) to the north of Perella is a village called Casa de Abella ("House of the Bee"). As we saw earlier, bees have a long association with fertility in cultures worldwide and can be seen carved in stone on Mayan pyramids and in Egyptian temple inscriptions. This Dragon Path across the Pyrenees is alive with hidden mysteries, with La Doña, a mountain mama guardian, a fire-breathing dragon, the House of Bees, and the source of a powerful river, named for the Eye of the Earth.

The Ter winds in and out of the Paris Meridian, passing a surprising number of Magdalena sites as she makes her way south, with Perella as the first Magdalena chapel that she meets on her long journey. The Ter continues down into the lower elevations from the heart of the cross at Perella, passing the western end of the Santa Magdalena mountain range. Then 19 miles (30.5 kilometers) to the south, the river turns eastward around Roda de Ter and circles the medieval hermitage of Magdalena de Conangle before she opens to form the expansive *pantas*, lake-like reservoirs, as the river spreads out between high red rock cliffs.

Winding eastward, the Ter passes through Girona, the medieval center of mystics and Kabbalists, absorbing more stories and mysteries, and finally, she reaches her destination at the Mediterranean. In ancient times, the Ter merged with the sea next to the Santa Magdalena de Empúries chapel and the temple of Isis at the Greek city of Empúries, and true to her pattern, always flowing near temples of the guardians. (The Ter now meets the sea further south near l'Estartit). (See illustration 8, Flower of Life.)

Santa Magdalena de Conangle, Crown of the Wheel of the Ter

I checked in to the small pension in Roda de Ter ("Wheel of the Ter"). I love Catalan hospitality, and since I had arrived late and shops were closed, the owner brought a bottle of good local wine to the room. Relaxing with a *copa de vi negre* (glass of red wine) on the balcony, I could feel a strong pulse of energy moving through the building, which was not surprising, since both the Ter and the Paris Meridian pass by the town. I could sense an ancient route and the passage of many footsteps over the millennia, following the river, perhaps in the ancient tradition of transhumance (herders moving livestock), trading, or on pilgrimage.

There are numerous megalithic sites surrounding Roda de Ter, established by Neolithic people between 6000 and 2000 BCE. Iberian *oppida* (hilltop villages, plural of oppidium) were discovered at Roda de Ter and nearby Vic, from circa 1000–800 BCE. The Iberians are an indigenous culture influenced by Phoenician, Carthaginian, Greek, Celtic, and most likely Egyptian and other traditions that came west in search of metal and fertile lands.

The following morning, I departed Roda de Ter, following the map and GPS toward Santa Magdalena de Conangle. The site is extremely remote, and these directional guides were not enough. At the first unmarked crossroads, the GPS was confused, but there were two men planting white lilies, symbolic of Magdalena. An auspicious sign, I thought. The men kindly directed me down a narrow country lane which wound through the countryside. The road passed various secondary tracks along the way, and there was no knowing if it was truly the correct route. Further on, the road was blocked by a farmer herding his cows, and I took the opportunity to inquire again. Luckily, most people here also speak Spanish, while still preferring their native Catalan. The herder directed me down another narrow track through the lush green fields, which ended at a large gate. Finally, there was a small wooden sign, *Ermite* (Hermitage) *Santa Magdalena.*

The gate was locked, preventing taking the car, and it would be a long walk up the winding road to the top, so I decided to explore the base of the hill first. The birdsong that flooded the woodland surrounding the river Ter permeated the air to the degree that it sounded surreal. The plants and trees appeared greener and lusher than normal, and the rock formations along the riverbank took on the anthropomorphic shapes of giant guardians. It seemed that I had entered an alternate reality. There was an enchantment surrounding the hill of Conangle, a magic that seemed to be related to this magnificent river and its affinity for Magdalena sanctuaries. This is echoed in the way the Ter curves around Santa Magdalena de Perella, then snakes past the Magdalena range, and here, as the river serves as a serpent guardian encircling Conangle. Remembering the name of her source, Ull de Ter, "Eye of Earth," what did she see on her long journey, woven of stories and prayers remembered in stone?

It was a long winding walk up the hill, which had become a familiar theme with Magdalena's sites, true to the Hebrew root of her name, meaning "High Tower." Approaching the hermitage, the fields were covered with wild sweet peas, fennel, and red poppies, where the members of the medieval community once had fields of edible crops, fruit and nut trees, and areas for livestock. We will discover that fennel has an ancient association with Magdalena, and it is often found growing at her sites. The path was paved with wild thyme, and the fragrance scented the air as I walked.

Santa Magdalena de Conangle, Mestre de Fonollosa, V.E.M.

I would discover later that above the monastery were more ancient remains of the people who inhabited this strategic hill, perfect for navigation, as it is surrounded by the Ter. At the top there was an Iberian village dated to circa 900 BCE, and surrounding this oppidium were numerous Neolithic engraved stones dated to circa 3000–1500 BCE. One called "Pedra de les Bruixis" ("Stone of the Witches") is engraved with more than two dozen crosses, and another called "Roc de l'Home" ("Rock of the Man") is engraved with a Neolithic human form. This could most likely indicate one of their gods, perhaps a god or goddess of the serpentine river below, as the Ter is the presence and force that dominates in the region. There were numerous stones with carved cup marks, perhaps marking astronomical alignments, and various stone tools have been found at the site.

Santa Magdalena de Conangle has a long and colorful history, including medieval hermit healers, fertility cults, witches, and bandits. The hermitage was founded in 1231 CE, as preserved in the Vic Episcopal Library Archives, and a document from 1239 refers to Santa Magdalena de Conangle as being adjacent to a defensive castle of great value founded in 1067, called "Fortress of Ter," built on the sheer rocky cliffs at the highest point above the Monastery. I would discover that numerous Magdalena sanctuaries were located next to castles, hinting at a special adoration and protection of her by the noble families.

Two of the original paintings of Magdalena from the hermitage are now displayed at the nearby Vic Episcopal Museum. One is a large piece depicting her in a red robe and jewel-studded golden crown, looking more like a queen, as she stands regally in front of her throne. In her left hand she is holding a golden vase for anointing and in her right a golden cross over her heart and a rosary. The second piece is an eight-paneled retable and in one scene she is being lifted by the angels above her grotto at La Sainte-Baume, wearing only her hair as a garment, referring to her ascent to hear the heavenly choirs, the "Music of the Spheres." Sound is always at the heart of mystery traditions. In the center of the retable, she is again wearing a golden crown, as our "Queen of Catalonia."

The hermitage was originally under the jurisdiction of the monastery of Sant Pere de Rodes at Cap de Creus, on the Mediterranean eastern end of the "Way of the Stars." We will discover that this great monastery was built over an earlier temple of Venus-Aphrodite. Conangle experienced a changing of the guard in 1304, when the founding monks departed and a community of Augustinian nuns arrived, who remained at the site until 1450. Interestingly, most of the Magdalena sites on this section of the Dragon Path were Augustinian, following their founder's proclamation of Magdalena as the Apostle to the Apostles. After a period of economic decline, accelerated by plague and famine, Conangle had become too difficult to survive as a small female order in a remote hilltop hermitage, and in 1450 the nuns relocated to the larger Santa Magdalena monastery in Barcelona.

Following their departure, a group of hermits arrived, one being a healer with a reputation for performing miraculous cures. The legend of "Santcrist (Saint Christ) de Santa Magdalena" tells of a fertility cult connected with the chapel's wooden image of Jesus, and women would arrive from all over the region to receive a blessing for the bearing of healthy children. Santcrist's fertility powers included the surrounding landscape and, apparently, control of the weather, bringing rain when it was needed.[4] The hermitage's well is said to be haunted by the souls of children, who still watch over the site, and there are numerous legends of witches and wizards living in the surrounding woods. It is no wonder that the hill felt enchanted.

A church document from 1610 CE says that after the departure of the hermits, bandits used Conangle as a hideout. Apparently, the famous brigand Perot Rocaguinarda and his band of two hundred men sheltered in the forest and controlled the hilltop site, which they used as a command center. Perot was from a well-to-do family, he but chose to lead a faction that was fighting political injustice, which had divided bishops and noblemen in Catalonia against each other. Perot was famous as a Catalan "Robin Hood" character, who defended both farmers and noble families. Magdalena de Conangle's storybook past was now quiet and peaceful, as if she was waiting to be remembered. These days, her church is a favorite place for weddings, evidenced in the confetti that had showered the small cloister, continuing the legacy of Magdalena's Bridal Chamber tradition. In the monastery's traditional goig, it speaks of her noble lineage from Bethany:

"*... From Bethany in the Old Town,*
Not far from Jerusalem,
You were born, as we all know,
From clear and noble descent;
With Lazarus and serene Martha
You are united in brother and sisterhood.

...to you come
All those who are moved
In the hermitage of Salou [Conangle]
To search for the lost goodness,
Glorious Magdalena ..."[5]

Santa Magdalena de Mosqueroles

The Monastery of Santa Magdalena de Mosqueroles was one more of her sanctuaries that featured a castle and is just 5.2 miles east of the Paris Meridian, and 24 miles (38.62 kilometers) northeast of Barcelona. It was established in the 11th century and is in the heart of a beautiful nature reserve surrounded by ancient oaks, sacred to the Druids. The

Castell Montclús by Sergi Boixander.

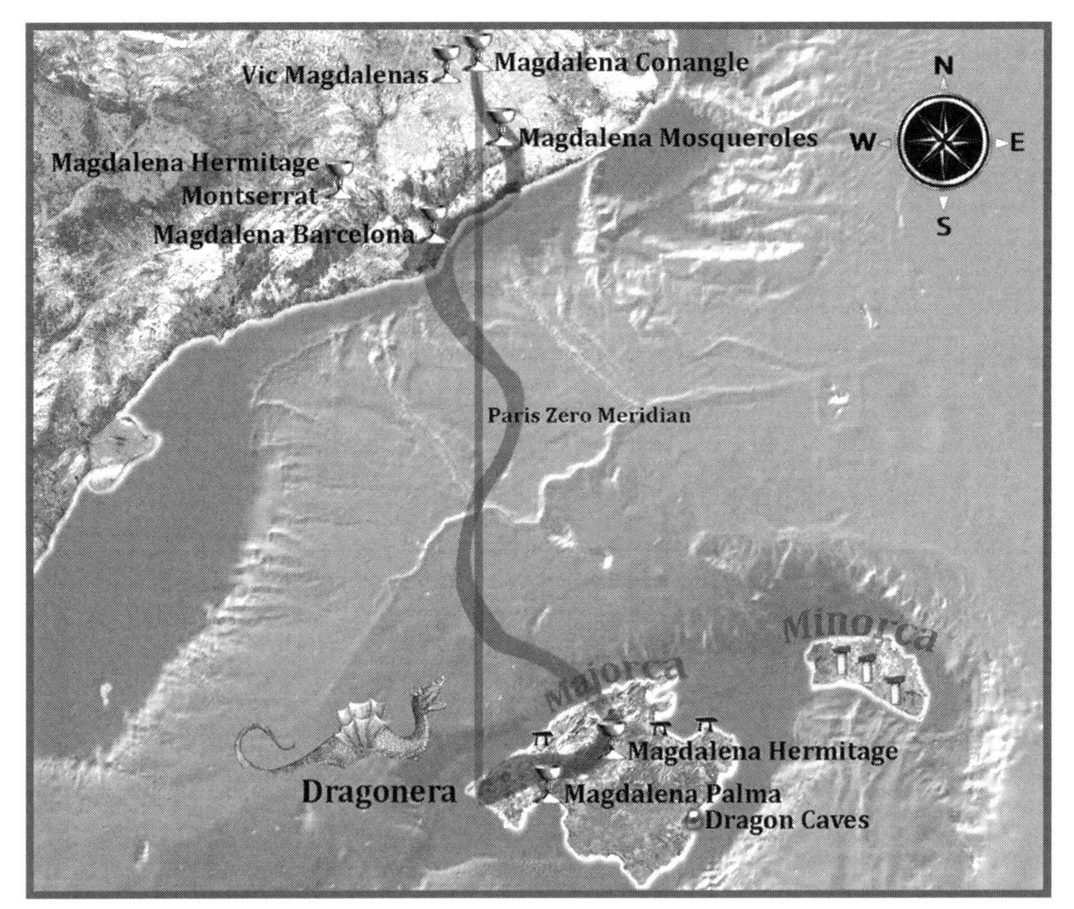

Illustration 6: Magdalena Meridian South

medieval castle of Montclús was established in the 10th century, and a second castle, Mateu (Saint Matthew), was established more recently nearby, with the monastery and castles all within walking distance, a popular hiking and cycling circuit.

The church has an oculus similar to the Paris Observatory's Cassini Room, which would have been used for marking the passage of the Sun across the chapel's interior. I have not visited the site, but it must have been a thriving spiritual center throughout the medieval era, being next to Montclús castle and close to Barcelona. I kept feeling that the Templars were involved with this monastery, and indeed, we will discover that both the Monastery of Santa Magdalena and the Knights Templar of Barcelona were important power players in the Mosqueroles—Barcelona region.

Barcelona's Knights Templar

The Knights Templar founded a commandery in 1134 in Barcelona at the *Palau Reial Menor* (Minor Royal Palace), utilizing old Roman walls, with an adjoining convent and castle. The Templars were engaged in active commerce and the defense of the region from the Moors and most certainly accompanied King James I to reconquer Majorca as described in chapter 4. Entering the palace through the Templar Gate there was a chapel decorated with an enigmatic "M" over the entrance. This gate leading to the "M Chapel" was also known as the Amoun Gate, which many believe relates to the Egyptian Theban god. Many have puzzled over the meaning of the "M Chapel," but my sense is that it must have referred to Magdalena, as the Templars were dedicated to defending her honor and memory. This dedication still endures today in numerous sites in Catalonia and France, including the Templar Commandery of Marie Madeleine at Rennes-le-Château. My late friend Joseph Tobias Dobler, who founded this commandery along with his wife Gerda Maria Francesca, always affirmed that the Mary honored by their order throughout the centuries was Maria Magdalena.

Les Magdalenes Monastery of Barcelona

According to Catalonia's official monastic history, Les Magdalenes Monastery was established in 1358 as a convent for penitent prostitutes, a refuge where women of a so-called "licentious life" could be housed.[6] The monastery was located on Carrer de les Magdalenes in the heart of Barcelona, within a few blocks of the current cathedral, where Templar ceremonies continue to be held to this day.

Sadly, Les Magdalenes suffered two huge fires in 1690 and 1909, which destroyed most of the buildings and archives, perhaps burning the old records retaining the image of Magdalena as a penitent sinner. But it wouldn't be until 1969 that the Vatican removed her prostitute designation from its official calendar. We have come a long way on the road to reclaiming the identity of Maria Magdalena, as we have seen in Pope Francis' 2017 declaration of her being "an apostle of the new and greatest hope." Barcelona's current monastery dedicated to Maria Magdalena was built following the second fire, in a different location, and continues today as an active monastic house. Since its founding, the monastery has been run by Augustinian nuns, the same order that we find at Santa Magdalena de Conangle, and Santa Magdalena de Palma, Majorca. This is important when we look at the proclamation of the theologian Saint Augustine (354–430 CE), who recognized Magdalena as the "Apostle to the Apostles."[7]

Augustine came from a North African Berber family and had a liberal education and background. According to the writings of Saint Jerome, early in Augustine's career he was fascinated by both Manichean and Neoplatonic traditions, which is extremely interesting, given the Manichean tradition was influential in the foundation of the Cathar faith and Neoplatonism incorporated the Hermetic sciences taught in Alexandria, Egypt.[8] Although Saint Augustine was "transformed" in his Christian awakening, these early influences formed his inclusive, visionary ideas, which he incorporated into his Order and Rule, and later adopted by the important monasteries of Santa Magdalena in Catalonia.

Another interesting connection with the Augustinian order is its purported presence in Jerusalem during the early foundation years of the Templars. According to *Holy Blood, Holy Grail* authors Baigent, Leigh, and Lincoln, to the south of Jerusalem on

Mount Sion there was a fourth century CE ruined basilica, upon which an abbey was constructed circa 1099, under the direction of Godfroi de Bouillon, crusader and newly appointed ruler of Jerusalem. It was called Notre Dame du Mont Sion, and a group of Augustinians were installed to run the abbey. The same authors proposed that this abbey provided a center of operations for the shadow group that would become known as the Priory of Sion, working secretly in concert with the Templars who occupied the Church of the Holy Sepulchre in Jerusalem.[9] This continuing connection with the Order of Saint Augustine, the Templars, and the monasteries of Maria Magdalena in Catalonia reveals the enduring guardianship of mysteries lying just beneath the surface, while still appearing "acceptable" to the masses.

In Barcelona there was a second house within the original Les Magdalenes Monastery, dedicated to Saint Mary the Egyptian, which became known as the Monastery of the Egyptians.[10] As we can see, with the purported nickname of the Amoun Templar Gate and this monastery, the Egyptian threads appear again and again in Catalonia's story. As described earlier, this Mary from fourth century CE Egypt was known for her early life as a prostitute, although she became a Jordan desert mystic with healing powers, and later "sainted." Throughout the following centuries she continued to be conflated with Magdalena, with the latter's images portrayed as Mary the Egyptian, wearing "nothing but her hair." Given Saint Augustine's proclamation of Magdalena as Apostle to the Apostles in the fifth century, it can be assumed that the sisters in Catalonia were able to discern between the two Marys and honored Magdalena as the Apostle, and not the prostitute.

The following song "Stella Maris" was inspired by the "Thunder Perfect Mind" text from the Nag Hammadi codices, which says, "I am the honored one and the scorned, I am the holy bride, and the whore,"[11] which I altered slightly to "not the whore." After all, we live in a time of great changes, and true to the chorus of the song our Mary is rising from two thousand years of being suppressed and misrepresented:

"I am the honored one and the scorned,
I am the holy bride, and not the whore,
I am the first and the last,
I am the one whom they call Life.

I was sent forth from the power of One,
Look upon me now and banish me no more,
You who have waited see and hear me now,
See the beauty hear my song within.

Chorus: Mary is rising, she is rising, she is rising up,
From the mountains, from the rivers, she is rising from the sea,
Stella Maris, Stella Maris, Star of the Sea.

I am the substance of all natures,
I am the Law of life, and the Lawless One,
I am She whom you have scattered,
And now you gather me together.

I am she who cried out, and I was cast forth
Upon the face of the Earth in the darkest hours,
Now I come shining on the Sea,
From my hidden cave I am awakening!"[12]

Hermitage of Santa Magdalena of Montserrat

Montserrat Ermita Santa Magdalena by Pere Pau Montanya 1790.

Listed as *Ermite de Santa Magdalena*, the stone ruin is nestled between the white limestone spires of the serrated ridge of Montserrat, known as the "Holy Mountain." As mentioned earlier, *mont* means "mountain" and *serrat* "serrated" in Catalan. Santa Magdalena sits high above the current monastery of the Black Madonna and is reached via dozens of ancient stone steps known as "Jacob's Ladder" that depart from a lower hermitage of Sant Jeroni (Saint Jerome). One of the highest needles of the Montserrat range called "Magdalena Superior" rises above her hermitage, and true to the pattern of Magdalena sites across Catalonia, she is truly a guardian at the high white stone tower of the sacred mountain visible from afar.

There were several hermitages that once formed an ancient pilgrimage route across the top of the Montserrat ridge, and these sites were supported by the nobility of the region. And again, we find the possible existence of a castle at the Hermitage of Santa Magdalena according to a chronicle from the Montserrat Scriptorium written by Father Gregorio de Argaiz.[13] It is recorded that the hermitages existed for hundreds of years before the Benedictine monks arrived in 1025 to establish the monastery of

Our Lady of Montserrat. The sanctuaries that housed the earliest anchorites (hermits) of the mountain, perhaps established in the fourth century, are all now in ruins, a testimony in stone to the longevity of Montserrat's history as a holy site, reaching back to the temple of Venus and earlier cave altars within the mountain dedicated to the ancient Mother Goddess.

Magdalenas of Majorca

Monastery of Santa Magdalena de Majorca retable center, V.E.M.

The Hermitage of Santa Magdalena is on the top of Puig (hill or mountain) de Magdalena, and the small chapel was founded in the 13th century by a group of hermits. It lies northeast of Palma and commands a 360-degree view of Majorca, true to the watchtower locations of her sites located on high points across Catalonia. The mountain is rich in iron, giving the earth a strong crimson hue and a magnetic energy, part of the attraction for the throngs of pilgrims who walk up the mountain each year for *Diumenge de l'Angel* (Angel Sunday, one week after Easter Sunday).

But by far the more intriguing story is at the Monastery of Sant Maria Magdalena of Palma, Majorca. It was founded at the beginning of the 1300s by a member of one of the most well-known Grail families of the Pyrenees, Esclaramunda (Catalan spelling of Esclarmonde) of Foix, Queen of Majorca,[14] married to King James (Jayme) II. She was called the "Princess of the Pyrenees" and was the grandniece of the famous Esclarmonde of Foix and Montségur, "Grand Dame of the Cathars," who was often called the "Guardian of the Grail." We have already discussed the connection between the Grail, Esclarmonde, and the Perella-Perelhe family as it appears to relate to Santa Magdalena de Perella, the Cathars and knowledge guarded by royal Grail families in Spain.

Another Cather connection for Majorca's Queen Esclaramunda was her grandmother Ermissende of Castelbon, a center of Cathar activity in southern Andorra. Ermissende's ancestral castle became a refuge for those fleeing the Inquisition launched across the Pyrenees in the Languedoc, and Ermissende was most likely a member of the Cathars.[15] Esclaramunda's brother Roger-Bernat III was the count of Foix, viscount of Castelbon, and the two sites are only 41.6 miles (67 kilometers) apart, located on the northern and southern flanks the Pyrenees, respectively, both sites friendly to Cathars. Their sister Sibila's husband Aimeric IV was the viscount of Narbonne and a Languedoc hero of the Albigensian crusades who helped defend the Cathar castle of Queribus.[16] Esclaramunda was raised in the heart of the land of heresies in Foix and we can easily see how she would have been influenced by the legacy of her two powerful Cathar matriarchs.

Additionally, the eldest son of Esclaramunda and James II, named for his father, was a Franciscan monk and founded a large Franciscan monastery in Palma. James II founded the Franciscan Monastery of Miramar on Majorca's spectacular western coast with the famed mystic, priest, "doctor illuminatus" Ramon Llull. (See image of Miramar in chapter 4.) It is well accepted that the royal family of the Kingdom of Majorca embraced the mystical Franciscan traditions, and this added another Cathar piece to the story. Saint Francis' mother Pica de Bourlemont was a French Cathar and raised him with Cathar virtues common to the "Way of Love." My friend and author Kathleen McGowan writes about this little-known Cathar connection with Saint Francis in her book *The Boleyn Heresy: Part I—The Time Will Come,*[17] and it is historically known that Pica came from a family and region supportive of the Cathars and that she influenced "Francesco" in the gentle ways of love and compassion.

Our Majorcan King and Queen founded the chapel dedicated to Maria Magdalena at their Perpignan royal palace, Palais Rois de Majorca, within the city's ancient citadel. The walled city was designed as a six-pointed star, the same "Seal of Solomon" that we discovered earlier, featuring Magdalena de Montpalau at the center of this star on the Way of the Stars. The two chapels were built on two levels, with the upper chapel of *Sainte Croix* (Holy Cross) featuring our equal-armed cross, and the lower chapel dedicated to La Madeleine. She is "Notre Dame de Souterrain," the subterranean force holding up the universal cross of harmony, the shape of the Cathar, Templar, and landscape crosses of the region. Interestingly, this Magdalena chapel at the royal palace of Perpignan is only 29 miles (47 kilometers) north of the eastern arm of the Great Cross and the Mediterranean departure of the Camino.

Grail of Castelbon, 14th c. section of altarpiece, anonymous artist, V.E.M.

In the families of Esclarmunda of Majorca, we can see a clear pattern of spiritual loyalties to Saint Francis, Magdalena, and the Cathars. And it is significant that the eternal parent flame for lighting the summer solstice fires of John the Baptist in the Pyrenees is kept at the Perpignan royal palace. With Esclaramunda we have a link between the Grail families, and two of the important Magdalena Meridian sites at Perella and Majorca. And the Kingdom of

Majorca was not limited to one Balearic Island, but included Catalonia, Roussillon (current France), Cerdanya, Montpellier, and beyond. We can see how this thread of sacred knowledge is woven in the traditions located along the Dragon Path.

We will go into more of the intricacies and mysteries of these Grail families in Book Two of this series, but for now it is enough to know that most of the families of the Counts of Foix, Andorra, and Barcelona, the Kings of Aragon, and Majorca, were all deeply involved with Grail traditions, and were for the most part, strong supporters of the Cathars. These ruling families on both sides of the Pyrenees were interwoven for hundreds of years through intermarriages and the shared knowledge they guarded. They embraced the traditions of the "Courts of Love," and many were troubadours and heroic knights of the Crusades in the Holy Land.

Following the crusade against the Cathars by the Church of Rome and the King of France, the remaining Cathars went underground, with many noblewomen who had either been active members or supporters establishing hospitals where they could continue to heal and be of service. Interestingly, Palma's Hospital of Santa Magdalena and the monastery in her name were located next to each other. The Cathar faithful continued under different guises, with the same noble families that had supported the Cathars founding and supporting hospitals, convents, and monasteries, similar to some Knights Templar becoming Hospitallers and continuing under a different name. These noble women were never penitents, and they continued their ministry in honor of their patron saint, the Apostle to the Apostles, Maria Magdalena.

We have completed our journey south along the Magdalena Meridian and I hope that some of the readers will continue the quest and find even more of her sites in Catalonia, hidden, mostly forgotten. One of Catalonia's favorite poets, Jacint Verdaguer, adored this land and wrote the following extracted from his homage to Mary, the Star of Montserrat. Keep in mind the earlier hermitage of Magdalena at Montserrat and several of the highest pinnacles are named for her. Which Mary is always the question:

"Into my homeland's heart pour down,
Mystical Fount, your waters of life;
Let grace and virtue be its blossoms;
Make of it your paradise.

Happy the eyes that see you, Mary,
Happy the heart that your light bathes;
Rose of Heaven that seraphim circle,
Enrich my prayer with your bouquet.

Rose of April, Morena of the mountain,
Star of Montserrat:
Light up the Catalan homeland ..."[18]

Cruce de Caminos—The Crossroads

*"...she is **MAGDALENE**, of the celebrated vase filled with healing balm. The initiated know her true name: **NOTRE DAME DES CROSS**."*

Le Serpent Rouge[19]

The initiated know her true name, *Notre Dame des Cross*, "Our Lady of the Cross." Normally the word in French would be *croix*, however *Le Serpent Rouge* is not a normal text, but, is embedded with strangely coded associations. The phrase fits perfectly, though, with my discoveries of Magdalena sites in the Pyrenean landscape temple. Our Lady is the guardian at the intersection of ancient paths at Santa Magdalena de Perella, the center point at the heart of the Great Cross, and it was all beginning to make sense. On the French side of the Pyrenees, at the northern arm of the cross, are two villages named Rennes, the old French word meaning "Queen": Rennes-le-Château (Queen of the Castle) and Rennes-les-Bains (Queen of the Baths) in what used to be called Val Crux (Valley of the Cross). The significance of the cross symbol continued to appear at important sites marking the four arms of the cross, revealing its symbolic importance (see illustration 2, Great Cross, p. xvi).

Pyrenees Cross, Madre de Deu, Catalonia.

Since my dream many years ago instructing me to light four sacred fires, three of the sites had been identified, and three fires had been lit, with each marking the end of an arm of the Great Cross. All three locations had concentrations of significant megalithic monuments, including dolmens and menhirs constructed between four and six thousand years ago, and all sites exhibited ancient engraved equal-armed crosses. I would soon be traveling to light the Fourth Fire at the western arm of the cross and would discover yet another megalithic route of dolmens engraved with the same crosses.

To review the foundation pattern of the Great Cross so far, the Paris Meridian forms the north-south axis Dragon Path at 2°20' E longitude and the east-west axis follows the southern slopes of the Pyrenees at 42°15' N latitude. Santa Magdalena de Perella sits at the intersection of not only the Great Cross, but also two ancient pilgrimage routes, called *Cruce de Caminos* (meaning "Crossroads") and *Ruta de les Quatre Ermites*, "Route of the Four Hermitages." The first is the crossroads of the Via Romana Capsacosta built more than 2000 years ago that intersects with a north-south branch of the Via Romana that leads past Santa Magdalena de Perella and Camprodon, to cross the Pyrenees into Gaul at Col de Ares. (Via Romana is overlaid on part of a route established at least six thousand years ago according to research that will be revealed.)

Via Romana is a short portion of the ruta Transpirenaica, marked GR 11 on maps, and runs from the Mediterranean at Cap de Creus to Basque country at the western end of the Pyrenees. *Transpirenaica* means "Across the Pyrenees," and this route is a network of old paths traversing the southern flanks of the mountains and still walked today. These ancient roads served travelers between eastern Iberia at the Mediterranean and connected with routes to the west toward Santiago de Compostela and Finisterre (Land's End) at the Atlantic, and to the north into Gaul.

Santa Magdalena de Perella's other old pilgrimage Route of the Four Hermitages is a seven-hour journey through the mountains that is still walked today. The pilgrimage begins at the Abbey of Sant Joan de les Abadesses and includes the sites of Sant Antoni de Padua, Santa Llucia de Puigmal, Sant Ponc d'Aulina, with the fourth at Perella, which completes the ancient path. There must have been a pilgrims' refuge set up along the way in ancient times. I know the importance of these pilgrimage stations from experience, after long climbs in the Pyrenees, where a welcome warm drink and food and sometimes a bed are offered.

We see a definite pattern occurring at Perella, sitting at the crossroads and nexus point of the four directions and the pilgrimage Route of the Four Hermits. The number four normally represents foundation, indicating that the cross pattern was providing an ancient equilibrium and stability to the region. In the final chapters we will discover the mysterious grid formed by Magdalena's fingers in several depictions of her in the region, forming multiple crosses. For the Druids, the equal-armed cross was a key to understanding the science of the Earth and cosmos, which included the alchemical interplay between the four elements, the celestial movements of the four directions, the great wheel of time and the wheel as a symbol of growth and consciousness. In the indigenous tradition of marking medicine wheels on the Earth, the equal-armed cross forms the foundation and mirror between heaven and Earth, and harmony is maintained by regularly activating and honoring the four points, the center, the above and below in the wheel of time and space.

As Godfrey Higgins describes in *Anacalypsis*, where the line of a north-south meridian crosses the east-west line intersection, a cross would have symbolized this important crossroads, which is exactly where we find Santa Magdalena holding this nexus point. And Higgins even mentions the mysterious X, such as those engraved across the floor of Perella's chapel:

"It [the X] was in each district the centre, the heart, of all their operations ... From this point of intersection two roads always branched off, which is the reason why we have a cross or merestone in the centre of every village, which arose by houses collecting round the sacred X: for this was ... declared most sacred and holy, and in suitable places the temples arose around or over these crosses."[20]

Part IV

The Fourth Fire and the Great Cross

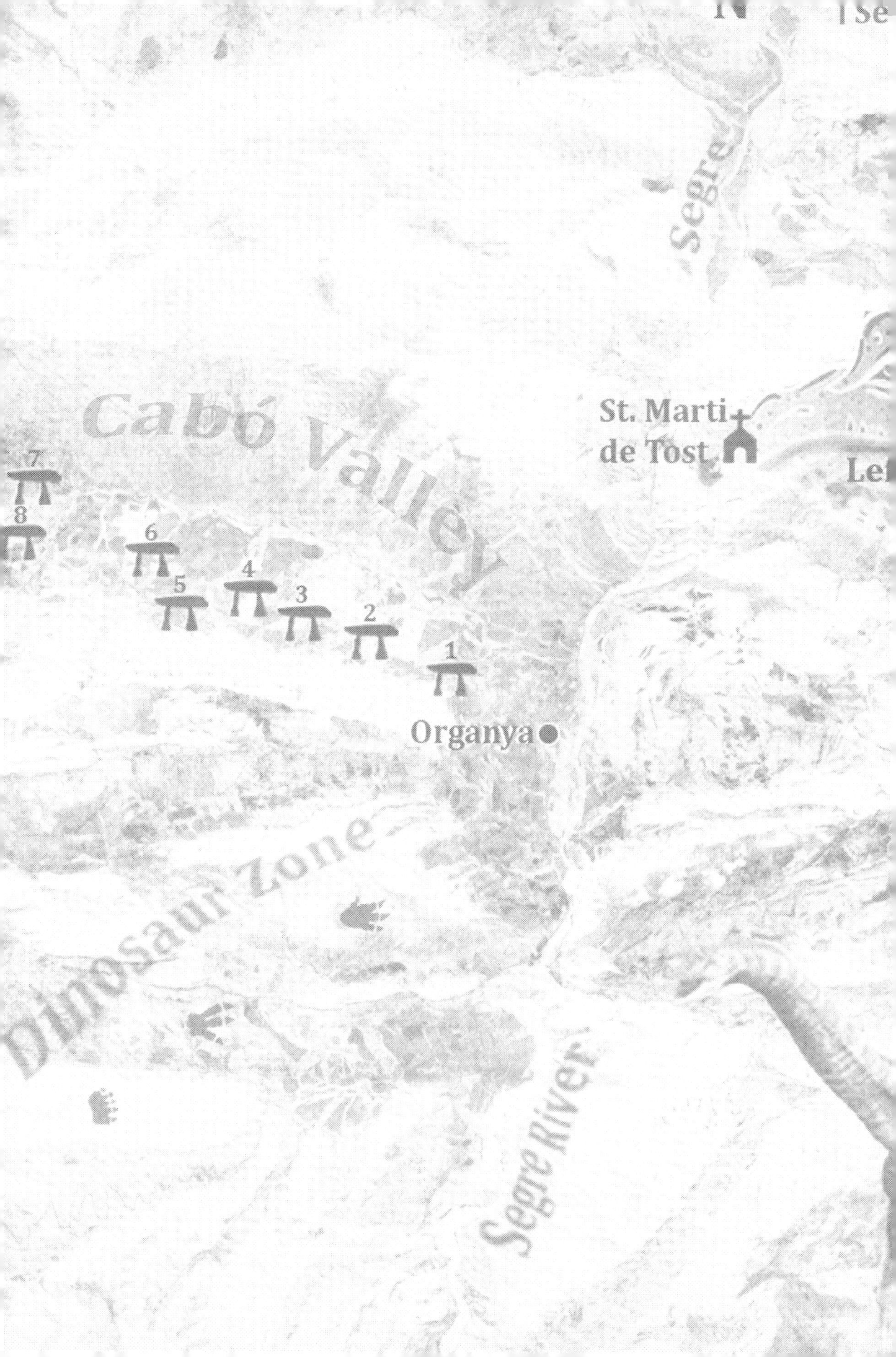

Segre

Cabó Valley

St. Marti
de Tost

7
8
6
5
4
3
2
1

Organya

Dinosaur Zone

Segre River

CHAPTER 19

Dolmens, Dragons, and Dinosaurs

"Igne Natura Renovatur Integra"
(By Fire Nature is Renewed Whole)

Elizabeth Van Buren,
Refuge of the Apocalypse: Doorway Into Other Dimensions[1]

I was on a quest to finally discover the site for lighting the Fourth Fire, and the quote above, "By Fire Nature is Renewed Whole," certainly fit the moment. Just three months earlier, I had taken a bad fall while riding a bicycle and had broken my femur in three places. Strangely, this occurred at the southern end of the Great Cross near Barcelona, and I felt like "a girl interrupted." The break was so severe that the doctors weren't sure if I would walk again. The night before the accident, I had a dream in which I was shown an ancient hinge. Since I was staying at a hotel close to the Paris Meridian, I assumed the symbol related to the hinges of the north-south axis and the guardian Goddess Cardea at her northern starry castle sending a warning.

During the eight days in the hospital, additional strong signs appeared. The first was the burning of Notre Dame Cathedral in Paris on April 15th, 2019, also on the meridian. The Catalan women in our shared room were weeping, and so was I. Something very strange was occurring and it was related to the Dragon Path axis. Still in the hospital, waiting for a surgeon who was on vacation for *Semana Santa* (Easter Week), I had another significant dream. The scene was an extraordinary garden with larger than normal sized trees dripping with ripe fruit and huge vegetables that were luminous. The gardener appeared, and I asked how he was able to achieve such impressive results. He said that the gardeners all work with the ninth harmonic realm, and that those higher dimensional subtle frequencies have a stronger effect on the density of matter. Before departing, he turned to me and said, "And you should work with these frequencies for your healing." I followed his advice and called forth the ninth harmonic dimension frequencies for healing, whatever they were. It worked. A strong intention and belief in the process is a powerful combination. In researching the ninth dimension, the physicist Michio Kaku provided a good explanation of our eleven-dimensional, harmonic universe in a fascinating short video.[2]

Miraculously, three months later I was driving a manual shift over the Pyrenees, with crutches, harp, and camera, ready to resume the quest. The magnificent views from the high peaks between France and Andorra are breathtaking, with the expansive valleys of the Cerdanya, and the sheer towering heights daunting in their wildness. The road through Andorra and further south through Seu de Urgell is another north-south meridian of sorts, marked with numerous castles, significant early medieval churches, and megalithic monuments. This route runs parallel to and west of the Paris Meridian and the road follows along the river Segre, a word from the Proto-Celtic language meaning "Sacred," according to my friend Juan Saez. Giant dinosaurs wandered along the Segre long ago, the ancient manifestations of dragons, and even the outcrops of cliffs overlooking the sacred river look like dragons guarding the way.

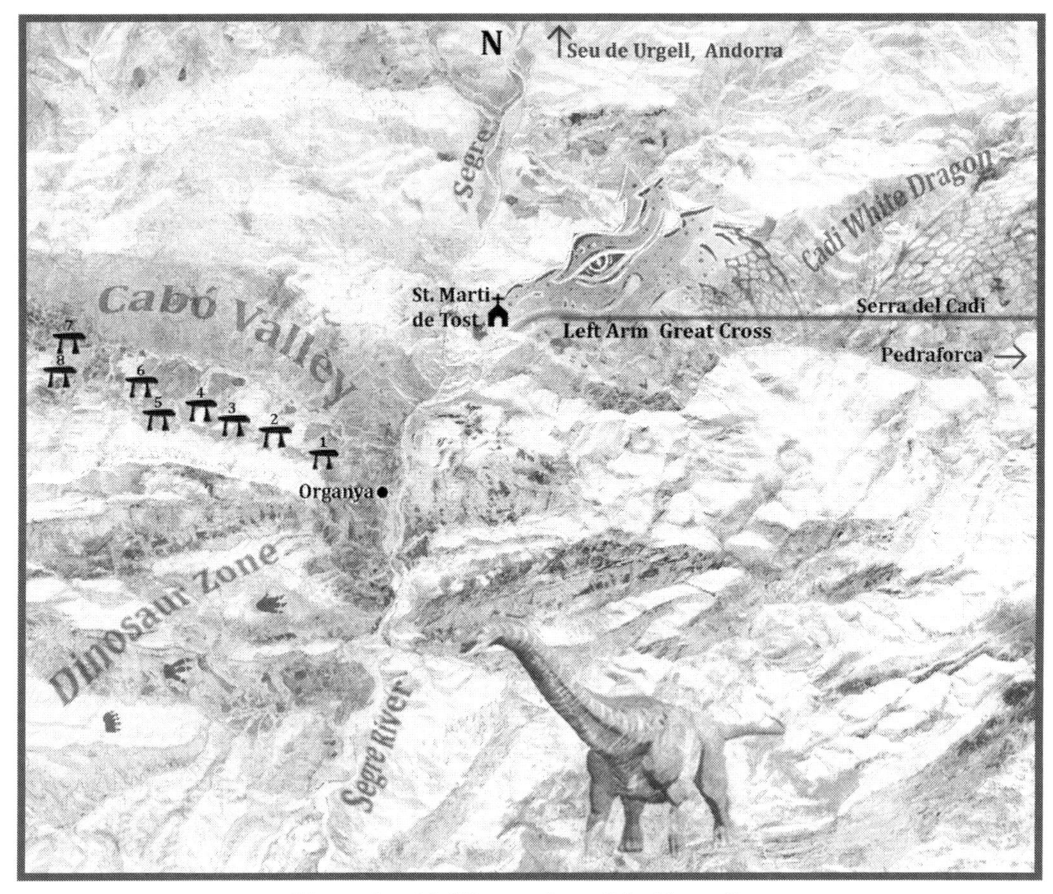

Illustration 16: Western Arm of the Great Cross

Dolmen Legend

1. Cobertrades
2. Colomera
3. Malpas
4. Tosal de Capella
5. l'Oliva
6. Pedra Cabana
7. Clots de les Canyes
8. Can Boixadera

The city of Seu de Urgell marks the border between Andorra and Spain, just inside Catalonia. I arrived at Castell de Ciutat, a hotel within a medieval fortified castle overlooking the city and the surrounding Pyrenees. The castle was built over an Iberian settlement, which would have existed circa 1000 to 200 BCE. Seu de Urgell has long served as a gateway to the Pyrenees and was an extremely influential bishopric, the Church's seat of power in the region from about 500 CE. *Seu* means "principal seat" or "center" and *Urgell* is a pre-Roman name, perhaps Celto-Iberian, indicating the presence of water. Two great rivers converge here, the Segre and the Valira, creating a powerful biofield with the confluence of two water dragon currents.

Surveying the maps and Google Earth for a site marking the western arm of the landscape cross equidistant from the center at Santa Magdalena de Perella, I noticed a high ridge of mountains called Serra del Cadi forming the natural western arm. The limestone ridge was strikingly white and seen from the air it looked very much like the spine of a white dragon, 14 miles (22.6 kilometers) long. The highest peak of the range is 8,688 feet (2,648 meters) high and called Vulturo (Vulture): Perhaps a winged white dragon?

The western end of the dragon ridge was 44 miles from Perella and the Paris Meridian axis and this point was marked by a site called Cornellana. (The eastern arm of the cross is 44.31 miles long, creating good symmetry.) The meaning of the name is most likely a "female horn" since *corn* means horn in Catalan and many Latin Romance languages, as in unicorn, "one horn." We could say that at the end of the western arm, we find a major landscape feature of a horned white dragon. And her horned head was pointing to the Segre, a sacred river in a region filled with imprints of ancient dragons, or dinosaurs. So far, so good.

Just three miles further west along the east-west axis was the only group of significant sites, named for the Tost Valley: Tora de Tost (Tora meaning "tower"), Sant Marti de Tost, a medieval church, and Castell de Tost, all marking the high ridges on both sides of the valley. The earth below is rich in iron, creating a deep vermillion hue, contrasting with the white limestone ridges, once again creating the classic alchemy of red and white that keeps appearing at the ends of the four arms of the Great Cross. At the northern arm we find red earth, similar serrated white ridges, and red and white springs.[3] The patterns of similarity were stunning, but where exactly was the location for the Fourth Fire? The horn of the white dragoness was extremely remote and there were no roads connecting directly with that site, so I decided to leave the white dragon for a future journey.

Exploring the Val de Tost sites was the next step. Driving south from Seu de Urgell, I followed the serpent path of the Segre through the sparsely populated open country. The first small town south of Urgell was Montferrer, meaning "Iron Smithy of the Mountain," which was interesting, as the town at the end of the northern arm of the landscape cross is called Montferrand ("Mountain of Iron"), both sites of iron-rich red earth, where the metal was mined for thousands of years. I have always believed that magnetic iron resonates with the iron in our blood, creating a subtle attraction to places of red earth, often considered sacred by ancient people. And we have seen that regions with high magnetism can promote altered states and unusual experiences.

The Tost region also has an abundance of salt, which is present at the other three arms of the cross. Val de Tost was once an ancient saline seabed and l'Aigua Salada (The Salted Water) runs just to the southeast of Tost. Thus, we find alchemical, purifying salt occurring at the ends of all four arms of the Great Cross. Salt is considered an essential ingredient in rituals and prayers by many cultures. Natrum (salt) is in the embryo's amniotic fluids and was used in pharaonic embalming as well as in the Opening of the Mouth ritual, thus life, death, and rebirth are all associated with this noble mineral. The 16th century Swiss physician Paracelsus called salt one of the three primary elements used in traditional alchemy, with the other two being mercury and sulfur, all used in the process of transforming lead into gold. On an esoteric level, this is the transformation of dense material existence into illuminating life energy, or awakening consciousness. Magnetic red earth and salt: good pre-requisites for the Fourth Fire.

Castell de Mur, photo by Einhoa.

At the end of the northern arm of the Great Cross, the Source de Sals (Salt Spring) flows into the Sals (Salt) river at the base of Mount Cardou and Cugulhou Levant's stone circles. At the southern and eastern ends of the cross, it is the salty Mediterranean where we find salt flats, where salt has been dried since ancient times. It sounds as if salt is everywhere in this region, but it happens to be highly concentrated at the four ends of the landscape cross, and as we will discover, salt has an intimate connection with Sophia, wisdom, and Maria Magdalena.

On the east side of the highway was a small old wooden sign for Castellar de Tost and Tora de Tost. The road to the castle was the righthand fork and the tower was to the left. I took the road to the right toward what I imagined would be the remains of the grand castle of Arnau Mir de Tost. This knight from the 11th century was called the "El Cid" of this region and became legendary for his miraculous conquests in reclaiming important strongholds from the Moors for Aragon and Catalonia during the *Reconquista*.

There is one amusing account of the brave and clever knight when he reclaimed the fortified Castell de Mur, which was held by a powerful Muslim king. This castle was not far to the southwest of Tost and was considered impregnable by all those who tried in vain to regain the fortification for the Christian counts. Here is the legend of "The Forest That Walks," told to me by a friend who grew up in the region:

> *The King of the Moors felt safe in his well-fortified castle, where he lived with his family and servants. The brave Spanish knight Arnau Mir de Tost had conquered other key holdings of the Moors and even though many others before him had failed, he decided to give Castell de Mur a go. He and his troops camouflaged themselves with small trees, bushes, and other greenery and proceeded at a snail's pace from the forest toward the castle. The king's young daughter happened to look out from her window and was surprised to see the trees marching. She ran excitedly to ask her father how this could be, but he assumed it was just a child's imagination, or perhaps the trees were moving in the wind and paid no attention. Arnau's men approached the castle walls and launched a successful attack to regain the strategic site for the region of Urgell and Lleida.*

I drove up the long road hugging the southern walls of the valley toward Castell de Tost. Two white hawks circled and drew my attention across the valley to a chapel perched high on the opposite ridge. I stopped and photographed the chapel, which included a ruined tower and fallen walls. After I finally arrived at the top, my visions of a romantic ruined medieval castle crumbled like the stones of the hamlet. There was no sign of a castle, not even partial walls, just a few houses and a farm with an overwhelming odor of pungent cow manure.

My Spanish was fluent enough to chat with one of the farm workers who confirmed that there was no sign of the old castle. Most likely the stones had been reused to build the hamlet's homes and barns. This is an efficient practice found throughout the world, and many a grand edifice forfeited its remains to the sheltering of future generations. I left the intense pervading cow dung aroma, feeling a bit duped. My research of the site online said nothing of what I discovered.

The next obvious step was to check the far side of the valley and the tiny chapel perched on the cliff that kept drawing my intention. I wound my way back down and then up the northern side of the valley, weaving around rockslides, to the chapel and ruins of a monastic settlement. The chapel of Sant Marti (Saint Martin) de Tost was founded by Arnau Mir de Tost and his wife Arsenda in 1030, according to the historical marker at the church. Saint Martin is known for his great compassion when, in winter, he cut and gave half of his cloak to a wandering beggar whom he met along the road. The beggar turned out to be Jesus in disguise, thus Martin won his sainthood, half a cloak, and immortality.

The chapel door was locked, but I found a spot at the entry porch, which looked out over the rugged Val de Tost and monastery ruins below. This felt perfect for the lighting of the Fourth Fire. I arranged the offerings and candle, and honored the four directions, the above and below, and gave thanks to the site's guardians. I added a prayer, to walk in balance, to always remember the fire in the heart, the flame of the eternal spirit, and never give up the quest for truth. This was the completion of lighting the Four Fires, but the journey was far from over: It was just beginning again.

Sant Marti de Tost, 1220, Museo Nat. Artes Catalunya.

I would discover on my return home that a Romanesque mural from inside this chapel is one that I had viewed and photographed several times in the Museu Nacional d'Arte de Catalunya (National Art Museum of Catalonia, or MNAC) in Barcelona. I had been immediately impressed by the unusual equal-armed cross within the circle depicting the halo crowning Jesus. Additionally, at each of the quadrants of the cross is one of the symbols of the Four Evangelists, the Eagle representing John; the Bull for Luke; the Lion for Mark; and the Man for Matthew. These symbols originated far earlier than our Four Evangelists and their gospels in the Bible, and represent the four zodiac signs, respectively: Scorpio, Taurus, Leo, and Aquarius. And beyond the four fixed sign constellations of the solar year, the symbols represent the four greater cycles of 6500 years each of a Great Year of approximately 26,000 years. We can see that there are numerous levels of knowledge embedded in medieval art. I marveled at the perfection of one more equal-armed cross reaffirming the repeating pattern at the end each arm of the Great Cross.

Val de Tost was now a desolate, largely deserted valley, but was once the site of castles, strongholds, and valiant medieval knights. And millions of years before, great dragons as dinosaurs walked the valley, and those with wings soared over the region, with some leaving their footprints embedded in clay that became memories in stone after millions of years. Perhaps the long white dragon spine of Serra del Cadi is a memory of the time when dinosaurs roamed here.

Just 1.5 miles (2.45 kilometers) south of the axis of the western arm and the Cadi range is a strange mountain named *Pedra Forca*, meaning "Forked Stone," that was known as a popular meeting place of the many witches and wizards of the region. Local legends say that on the winter solstice and on Sant Joan's night (Saint John the Baptist, summer solstice eve), witches would gather at the high gap between the forks of Pedra Forca and sing and dance in a circle, stirring up magic. It was said that they were endowed with supernatural powers, known for their medicinal cures, and often sang over their remedies imbuing them with magical incantations. This sounds more like the practices of a traditional medicine woman who knows the herbs, springs, and natural healing of her region. Unfortunately, in the early 17th century, hundreds of Catalan women were executed for being witches, and nearly seven thousand men and women in the Basque Pyrenees were accused of witchcraft.[4]

It seemed the entire western arm of the Great Cross was enchanted with the memory of dragons, dinosaurs, and witches. I headed south from Val de Tost toward Lleida, curious to see the area surrounding the western arm of the cross. A short distance south of Tost is a town called Organya, where I noticed a sign to "Ruta de Dolmens," indicating another grouping of megaliths marking the western arm! But after driving through the hills, there were no further signs indicating the dolmens' locations, and since it was getting late it would necessitate a return visit.

Back at the hotel I looked for any other megalithic sites in the region, and discovered at least forty dolmens between Seu de Urgell and Organya. There was a cluster of nine dolmens in the Tost region and one more at the base of the white dragon of Serra del Cadi, called l'Espluga de la Buixa, Catalan for "The Witch's Plug." I had no more information on this dolmen and its strange name, but there was certainly a major concentration of megalithic sites surrounding the western arm.

I later contacted Juan Saez and asked him to calculate the exact location of the Cabó Valley dolmens and was excited to discover that its eight dolmens were the only ones in the region to form an east-west line, a continuation of the western arm of the Great Cross, just southwest of Val de Tost and the Serra de Cadi. These dolmens are offset several miles from the nearly perfect symmetry so far, but I would discover that there had been a disruption of the western portion of the landscape cross, long ago. I would return to explore this megalithic route, but not before a very strange dream occurred.

Bringing Heaven to Earth, Placing of the Great Cross

"As humans, we have the ability to awaken the Earth energies through bringing cosmic energies into them. In the tradition of the Master Builders, this is called 'turning the telluric waters of the body into the cosmic waters.' Or, simply, 'bringing Heaven to Earth and Earth to Heaven.'"

Ferran Blasco and Elyn Aviva, *Where Heaven and Earth Unite*[5]

The dream was like an epic film, à la *Star Wars*. I was with a group who had arrived on Earth from a far galaxy for a special mission to prepare the planet before a cycle of great upheaval and change. We clearly knew what we needed to do, and all the members of the group worked with one focus, with a unified field of consciousness, and words were not necessary. We prepared the ground to receive a harmonious grid in the shape of an enormous equal-armed cross, made of a glowing, translucent material that seemed not to be solid, and infused with intentions for wellbeing and the stability of the region.

We placed the "Invisible Cross" in the ground, knowing it would expand in size and influence over time, imprinting the heavenly perfection and balance to emanate throughout the land. This would support evolving humanity during a time of Earth's great changes, after which migrating tribes would arrive to seed new civilizations. The location was on the southern edge of great mountains joining two bodies of water, now known as the Pyrenees. With our mission complete we returned to our home in the stars. The next morning, I wrote the dream in my journal and thought of the words of the prophet Edgar Cayce, who spoke of the arrivals of people in the Pyrenees following the deluge and destruction of Atlantis.

A few weeks later there was a second dream. In this segment, a few members of the galactic team had returned to Earth thousands of years later to ensure that the cross was in place and serving the telluric grid. We discovered an anomaly at the western arm, and found that the position had been altered, disrupting and weakening the energy of the Urgell, Segre region. It was not clear who had done this or why, but we did the repairs that we could.

When I awakened, it seemed an obvious message that the western arm of the cross needed support, and I sensed the disruption was in the electromagnetic currents in the region of the megalithic route of dolmens near Organya. Had the dolmens been moved? Ancient temple builders chose specific places of power for their sanctuaries, locations where the dragon force was concentrated, and the stones grounded and enhanced this vital force.

"...the earth was a living creature and its body, like that of every other creature, had a nervous system within and relating to its magnetic field. The nerve centers of the earth, corresponding on the human body to the acupuncture points of Chinese medicine, were guarded and sanctified by sacred buildings, themselves laid out as microcosms of the cosmic order of the universal body of god."

John Michell, The View Over Atlantis[6]

I contacted Juan Saez again, as I needed his skills in sensing Earth energies (geomancy) and asked him to join me at the site. But first we would need the exact locations, accessibility, and history of the dolmens. Juan mapped the coordinates and said they were in a remote valley called Cabó just outside the town of Organya. In his research, he discovered that at least two of the dolmens had been moved from their original locations. This would have upset the original grid network established at the sites at least five thousand years ago. Additionally, major electric towers had been erected directly next to several of the dolmens in the group, which would also affect the electromagnetic grid. Juan's discoveries matched my dreams and intuitive hunch.

I assumed that the megalithic groupings of stone temples at the ends of each of the four arms corresponded to the placement of the "Invisible Cross" in the dream. And the western arm was the only anomaly in an otherwise nearly perfect symmetry. Was it possible that the original grid was placed by beings from the stars, who had humanity's best interests at heart? Indigenous people around the world have a long history of contact with beings from other dimensions and locations beyond the Earth. I knew from years of experience with Hopi, Zuni, and Navajo elders that this contact is quite normal. My late friend, Hopi Grandmother Carolyn Tawangyama, spoke many times of visitors from space who were observed on a regular basis by the people on the Hopi Mesas and in other villages of the American Southwest. In fact, each tribe has a legacy of star knowledge they say was given to them long ago by beings who traveled from the stars. Another Hopi friend, the late White Bear Fredericks said that their deities, called Kachinas, are teachers or angels who come from the stars.

The Zuni elder Clifford Mahooty, a retired civil engineer from New Mexico, taught that his people descended from the Star People, who gave the Zuni a protocol, which included knowledge of a grid system and patterns to maintain balance on the Earth. Much of the Zuni ritual cycle incorporates communication with the stars so that they don't forget this galactic source connection. Clifford mentioned that ancient monuments maintained these grid patterns in certain places across the planet, and that the stones were receptors for star communication.[7] Their ceremonies today continue this tradition of giving thanks to the Star People.

Ancient people were aware of the subtle forces and effects of the cosmos on the anatomy of the Earth, not only because of their finely tuned sensibilities, but also because they were likely guided in this technology by their deities and visitors from the stars. Megalithic temple builders sensed and worked with the magnetic solar currents of a grid called the "Peyre net," and according to geomancer Ferran Blasco, this system of pathways on the Earth is fed by the Sun and stars and runs both north-south and east-west. Building their temples along these telluric lines would strengthen, renew, and increase the flow of energy. This in turn would have benefited the people and the wildlife, provided abundant food sources, and increased a feeling of well-being. Ferran says these grids:

> *"... seem to organize the energy of the Sun—or the wisdom of the Sun—in a way that carries information through specific pathways ... The ancients long ago already knew about something like 'optic fiber', but they were so sophisticated they didn't need cables. They used 'true wireless'!"*[8]

I felt a pressing need to revisit the western arm of the Great Cross and megalithic sites at Cabó, although it was winter, and we were in a complete lockdown in Europe due to the Covid epidemic. All travel within the EU, especially across the borders between countries, was heavily restricted. Juan, who lives in Catalonia, felt it was possible for me to cross from France, so we planned four days to visit the sites in mid-January of 2021. My friends questioned my ability and sanity in attempting the journey, but I was determined. I contacted the Catalan government and received an official travel pass to do archeological research for the book. I ended up with a stack of paperwork with special permissions, letters, and descriptions of the research for both countries, hopefully ensuring I could return home to France. Restaurants were closed, so I packed enough food for a week.

To add to the challenges, on the day before the trip, Spain had a "hundred-year storm" and all of Catalonia was covered with ice and snow. These combined abnormal conditions indicated something auspicious was afoot. I have found that a component of a powerful pilgrimage can sometimes be extra obstacles on the path that challenge our resolve to hold strong to our vision to continue against all odds.

Dolmens in Ice and Snow

Crossing the border was easy, and no one was even present at the guard station to question me or ask for my carefully prepared stack of papers. An otherworldly atmosphere pervaded the entire week with the roads strangely empty, as most sensible people had stayed home. I picked up Juan at his village near l'Escala on the Mediterranean and we headed toward Montserrat, where the highway turns west and then north toward Organya. We had to drive a longer circuitous southern route, as the northern direct route to Seu de Urgell was totally closed with snow and Covid restrictions. As we passed Montserrat, the serrated mountain looked surreal like a floating white island, snow covering the peaks, and fog blanketing the lower half of the mountain. The road became icy, so we drove slowly northward toward the higher elevations along the Segre River.

There were medieval castles on both sides of the river as watchtowers on the route leading north to Tost, Seu de Urgell, Andorra, and over the Pyrenees. As we drew closer to Organya, we saw the same dragon formations that I had discovered on the previous journey. One was formed by red-spiked stone ridges, and on the opposite side of the river, a long, white-spiked mountain, the two creating perfect alchemy with the red and white dragons guarding the passage along the sacred river. We laughed when the next sign said, "Dinosaur footprint next left," and we both sensed strong dragon currents running through the region. With his extensive training in Chinese geomancy, Juan was very familiar with dragon currents reflected in landscape features. (See illustration 14, Western Arm of the Great Cross, page 232.)

Author contemplating the trek after the storm.

We set out from Organya the next morning on more icy roads, winding up through the Cabó Valley, passing *Vilas Barranc de Bonica,* "Ravine of the beautiful Maiden," to reach our first destination. We parked near the unmarked forest track leading to our first site, the Dolmen del Serrat de Malpàs, at least based on Juan's maps and GPS readings. (*Serrat* meaning "serrated" in Catalan, must refer to the nearby dragon-looking mountains and *Malpàs* can mean "bad or dangerous pass.") The winds from the retreating stormfront were at hurricane force, and walking was slow over the snow and ice-covered path. We noticed tracks of several species of animals on the path, the only others braving the freezing conditions. Eventually, we saw a small wooden sign indicating that we were on *Cami Reial*, the "Royal Road." This was indeed interesting, as there is another road of the same name near the center of the Great Cross and on the same ancient Way of the Stars Camino route.

After forty minutes of trekking through the fierce wind and snow, we arrived at the dolmen Malpàs, well hidden in a pine forest. Several of the dolmen's stones had collapsed, but it still emanated strong energy. I took a baseline measurement with copper dowsing rods of the current energy field, which I marked at 6.5 feet (2 meters) out from the stone. After playing a song to the stones on a small dragon-shaped ocarina (clay flute), the energy field measured about 20 feet (6 meters). Juan calculated the orientation of the dolmen. The entry faces due east, marking the sunrise on the equinoxes, and a stone slab on the right of the doorway aligns to the winter solstice sunrise. Some unknown factor of the site had maintained a strong field of energy, perhaps its remoteness from disturbances and electric lines.

The next dolmen on the itinerary was Pedra Cabana ("Stone Hut"), another thirty-minute walk down snowy tracks, and luckily the wind had calmed down. This dolmen was again hidden within a forest, off the main track, but the site was next to a major power line. Dowsing the baseline energy of the dolmen detected no measurable energy. Juan confirmed this with his inner dowsing abilities. He had been trained to sense subtle energy by French and Chinese energy medicine masters, and he didn't need the copper L-rods that I used. I sat near the entrance of the dolmen and played the dragon flute with the intention to recall the connection between the stones and the stars, and to strengthen whatever was the original intention of the temple builders. Following the

Measure and notations, Pedra Cabana.

song, dowsing showed an energy field emanating 13 feet (4 meters) in diameter out from the dolmen, a sizeable increase from zero.

Juan calculated the orientation of Pedra Cabana to due east and the sunrise at the equinoxes, which would be the same alignment pattern in the other Cabó monuments we visited. This told us that the dolmens marking the western arm of the Great Cross were aligned toward the eastern arm of the Great Cross and the rising stars. Juan called Pedra Cabana a "Time Machine," as it was aligned to the four cardinal directions, north, south, east, and west, which also matched the landscape cross. A long, chiseled line on the top of the roof stone marked a perfect orientation to the north star axis, which would have been Thuban in the dragon constellation Draco when the dolmen was constructed.

Juan found an area near the dolmen's door that he felt had substantial force and played his flute for the guardians. He then suggested I align my spine with the stone and sense the energy. As I connected my breathing and presence with the stone, my heart expanded to the point that I was overwhelmed and quite emotional. I saw a scene of a pre-sunrise ritual in which the star Regulus in the heart of the lion constellation was rising in the east. In addition to the cardinal direction orientation, perhaps this dolmen was used ritually with this alignment to Regulus. When I researched the cycles of Regulus (Alpha Leonis), I discovered that its heliacal rising (pre-sunrise appearance) occurs during the first week of September for the Northern Hemisphere. And every eight years, Venus forms a conjunction with the star just two days before the heliacal rising event. This must have been observed by ancient people as an auspicious occurrence worthy of marking with stones. The importance of Venus in the Camino and the cycles of time and resonance will become evident in future chapters.

Juan Saez enchanting the stones of Pedra Cabana.

Juan and I lit a candle and Palo Santo incense for reigniting the sacred fire at the western arm of the cross, the second lighting to anchor the Fourth Fire in the west.

Following the dream, it felt important to reaffirm the harmonious grid pattern in the region where the grid had been altered and disturbed. The main interruption of energy at this site appeared to be the overhead electric lines, but we would discover a dolmen that had been totally relocated.

I handed Juan the replica of the drachma coin shaped as a wheel that I had brought from the Rhodes Museum in Roses, located at the eastern arm of the Great Cross. As he held the coin up to the Sun, we affirmed the stabilized grid honoring the wheel of the year, the four directions and the four arms of the landscape cross. I buried the drachma aligned to the four directions, reaffirming the original intention of the ancient pattern that the Earth's galactic guardians may have placed here eons in the past. I dowsed the energy field of the "Time Machine" dolmen once again and it had increased to 31 feet (9.5 meters)! Hopefully our offerings, songs, and intentions would be fixed and maintained in the crystalline memory of the stones.

Dolmen Clot de les Canyes.

There were at least eight dolmens in this megalithic group, but we couldn't access all of them given the winter conditions of the roads and paths. I will briefly mention the last two sites that we were able to reach. Dolmen Clot de les Canyes (*Clot* meaning cavity or hollow, and *Canyes* meaning reeds, hence, "Dolmen of the Hollow of Reeds") was a beautiful, snow-covered feminine-feeling monument in an even more secluded forest. She felt wild and magical, and had a dragon ally next to her, formed by the obvious shape of an old fallen oak. A single pine marked due east in front of the dolmen's entry, and a circle of nine oaks stood beyond, also marking the eastern Equinox sunrise gate.

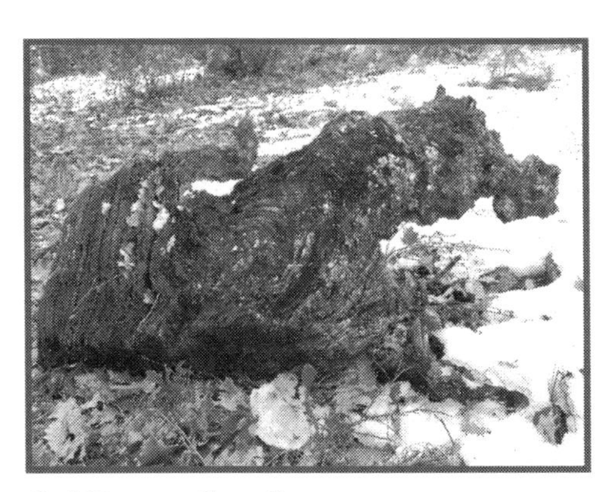
Oak Dragon Guardian.

The nine oaks reminded me of the Nine Maidens in Druid traditions. Nine Maidens tended the magical cauldron of the Welsh goddess Cerridwen; there were Nine Morgans (Sorceress-Sisters) of Avalon; and traditionally nine Druidess-healers were guardians of ancient sanctuaries, oak groves, springs, and caves, often marked with nine stones or trees. And, of course, they sang and knew the power of magical incantations. In Greek myth, the nymph Mnemosyne gave birth to nine daughters, who became the heavenly choir of the Nine Muses. Author Stuart McHardy quotes British folklorist Eleanor Hull in his *The Quest for the Nine Maidens:*

"... there is no break between the ancient magical formulae chanted by the Druids and the later incantations of the wizard and the wise woman. They both arose in the Veda-like sacred hymns ... of Druidical teachers and diviners and taught orally by the Druidic schools."[9]

Before working with the dolmen, I dowsed the baseline energy which measured 8 feet (2.5 meters) out from the dolmen. Juan noted narrow spaces between the stones at the four corners of the dolmen, which allowed the light of all four of the solstice Sun rising and setting points to enter. After singing a spontaneous vowel chant for the site, the energy field expanded to 38 feet (11.5 meters). The power of vowels to alter reality and realign energy was well known by every ancient tradition, including Druidic and Gnostic. In sound science, each vowel emanates a different harmonic wave form, creating unique effects on both matter and the etheric. As mentioned earlier, Jesus taught the disciples these principles, saying, "Nothing more excellent is there ... save only the mystery of the seven Voices [vowels] and their nine-and-forty powers and their ciphers."[10]

Dolmen Can Boixedera.

The final dolmen that we were able to reach was Can Boixedera, a Catalan term meaning "Crazy-making Place." It had a wild assortment of brightly colored orbs when we viewed the photos we took at the site. Orbs are plasma forms that sometimes appear in photos at sites with high or concentrated energy and may be interacting with the subtle electromagnetic energies and people present. Orbs can appear in brilliant colors, sometimes with distinct geometric patterns or images. This dolmen had been relocated and emanated a chaotic, confused, but lively energy.

Juan used the technique of knocking on the stone three times with a small stone to activate the dolmen, like turning on an electrical switch. Following this, we could both sense increased energy flowing through the site. Juan explained that the three strikes with a stone is like knocking on the door of a friend before entering their home. The entry currently opens to the winter solstice sunrise, but there was no way of knowing the original orientation. At least the dolmen was reawakened to resonate with the other seven monuments in the megalithic group. Hopefully this combined work will support the western arm of the great cross, to maintain a more coherent state and beneficial harmony in the region.

Although challenging, our journey to Cabó was successful. Juan's skill in finding the exact coordinates and alignments of each remote site, as well as sensing the telluric currents, was invaluable. Music was an important part of our work at the dolmens, with Juan's flute, my dragon ocarina, and vocal offerings. Our good intentions, music, and meditations, all combined to increase the energy field at each site, which we hoped would contribute to a stronger, more coherent forcefield in the matrix of the Great Cross. Departing Cabó, we headed south to the southern arm of the landscape cross. I wanted to return to Roca del Vallès on the Paris Meridian to visit a dolmen that forms a more perfect symmetry for the southern arm of the Great Cross. Our destination was Dolmen Can Planes, which I had discovered is exactly 44.57 miles from the center at Santa Magdalena de Perella, exactly matching the length of the northern arm. Roca del Vallès is the megalithic route marking the southern arm mentioned in chapter 7 on lighting the Second Fire.

Thuban
Eltanin
Ve
Deneb

CHAPTER 20

Harp Harmonics, Stones, and Stars

"The geomancer's vision interprets the earth in terms of the heavens. They saw the mountains as stars, the ocean and wide rivers as the Milky Way. From the great mountain ridges which conduct the main lines of the dragon power ... Each of these lines has its particular astrological character, its own harmony and color."

John Michell, *The View Over Atlantis*[1]

As the late brilliant British visionary John Michell said, each of the dragon paths has their unique star connections and frequencies. I have found over and over that the stone monuments along these dragon lines grow stronger with certain sounds, increasing their fields of measurable energy. Dolmen Can Planes (Dolmen of the Level Plains) is one of seven megalithic structures located on the Paris Meridian at Roca del Vallès near Barcelona, with another seventeen dolmens within a six-mile radius, creating a major megalithic route. As the reader may recall, this megalithic complex was described earlier with the lighting of the Second Fire at Dolmen de Céllecs. However, I had since discovered that a more perfect symmetry is formed by Dolmen Can Planes for the southern marker in the Great Cross. The weather was warm and sunny, a relief after braving the snow, ice, and winds in the north.

The dolmen sits on a slight rise, within an otherwise flat terrain, hence the name Planes, meaning level fields. It is surrounded by thick woodland, and close to an easy walking trail. Juan and I began with a baseline dowsing of the dolmen's energy field, which measured 6.5 feet (2 meters) out from the entrance. It was warm enough to bring out the small troubadour harp, and I asked the stones and guardians for

Dolmen Can Planes harp harmonics.

the tuning that would best serve the purpose of the site. I tuned to a G Major Middle Eastern scale and began to play as I circled the stone. (The scale for musicians is G A-flat B C D E-flat F.) As I continued the spontaneous piece, the wind picked up noticeably and the harp began ringing in enchanting harmonics, creating an aeolian harp effect, a mystical soundscape created by the wind moving through the strings.

Juan and I offered prayers for the beneficial flow of the dragon currents through the megalithic route and the Paris Meridian. We stood on either side of the meridian and reaffirmed the balance of male-female energies as they wind and spiral along the Dragon Path. We buried another silver drachma wheel aligned to the cardinal directions, anchoring the southern end of the Great Cross. Dowsing a second time showed the energy field had expanded from 6.5 feet to 29.5 feet (9 meters), a significant increase.

Before leaving the site, I noticed a forked tree marking the southern dowsed boundary of the dolmen, which was shaped like a Y with the central line extended, forming the three-pronged Nordic Rune oracle symbol Algiz. Earlier, I had picked up a small branch in the same perfect shape next to the dolmen, and whenever a particular symbol shows up two or more times, I pay attention. The meaning of Algiz in the Runic system is protection, guardianship, awakening, connection with the gods, and group effort.

This sign provided a sign that we had done our best in our mission to support, reawaken, and repair the damaged grid to benefit the entire region. The meaning of Algiz also matched the message received in the "Placing the Cross" dream: A group effort, guardianship, connection with the heavens, and a grid placed in the Earth long ago by visitors from an unknown region of the universe.

Ancient House of the Covered Cross

The long journey with Juan was complete, and it was time to continue north on my own. I booked a couple of days near Roses to rest and walk the coastal cliff paths above the turquoise waters of the Mediterranean. I also wanted to revisit an old friend, Creu d'en Cobertella, the largest dolmen in all of Catalonia, its name, as mentioned previously, meaning "Covered Cross." Again, this is the site of the lighting of the First Fire, and I had recently completed lighting all Four Fires, and an unexpected Fifth Fire at the center of the Great Cross at Santa Magdalena de Perella.

The Covered Cross dolmen marks the end of the eastern arm of the Great Cross. The view from the dolmen of the Mediterranean Sea and the Pyrenean peak of Canigó perfectly combines the elemental alchemy of water and fire. To review, the dolmen is located on the southern portion of Cap de Creus, meaning "Head or Cape of the Cross" in Catalan. As we will discover, an older name for this cape is Promontory of Aphrodite, named for the ancient Venus-Aphrodite temple that once stood as guardian on the high cliffs. One legend says that Hercules hurled giant stones to create this cape jetting into the sea. Strange anthropomorphically shaped stones decorate the dramatic cliffs that descend abruptly into the Mediterranean, forming the easternmost tip of Spain.

Illustration 10: Dolmen Creu d'en Cobertella aligned with constellation Draco

As mentioned in chapter 6, Cobertella has impressive "Sun Daggers" that form on the inside eastern and northern walls of the dolmen at winter solstice sunset. Cobertella was also constructed to align with the pole star indicated by a deep engraved hole, or umbilical indent, on the north-facing outer slab of the dolmen. This navel marks the pathway to what would have been the constellation Draco in 3500 BCE when the site was constructed, its stars stretching like a serpent between Ursa Major and Ursa Minor. These constellations at the northern axis appear to revolve in a circle with the seasons, and I wrote the song "Draco's Turning" with this in mind.[2] These northern stars were the destiny and celestial home of the soul in the afterlife journey of Egyptian pharaohs. One of my purposes in revisiting this dolmen was to not only anchor the eastern end of the Great Cross, but also to explore one of the dolmen's key functions, its alignment with the northern axis, the stones serving as a line of communication with the stars at the northern gate.

"The ancient shamanic cultures saw the north celestial pole as a point of exit and entry into the sky world from the physical world."

Andrew Collins[3]

As I approached the dolmen for perhaps the seventh time, I marveled again at its size. It seemed larger than the last time I visited, which was just three months earlier, most likely because I had just been visiting much smaller dolmens. Measuring 17 feet (5.2 meters) in length, it is hard to imagine the process of moving the enormous stone slabs into place. It is likely that rituals and specific sounds would have been used to *lighten* and *soften* the stones before moving them into place. Science has discovered *phonons*, which are quasiparticles created by acoustical waves, which have antigravity properties. This may be the key used by ancient temple builders. (See video "Archaeoacoustics in Stonehenge."[4]) Like many other dolmens in the region, the stone is granite that contains large amounts of silica, which has a piezoelectric effect, like a computer chip transmitting information. Various geological studies have measured both high and low-frequency acoustical emissions as well as increased electromagnetic energy produced by granite.

The dolmen is located at the eastern end of the major fault line caused by the meeting of the European and Iberian plates that pushed together to create the Pyrenees. As Paul Devereux has discovered over many decades of research with his "Dragon Project," many ancient sanctuaries have been constructed over these faults, including Tibetan temples and megalithic dolmens, and standing stones. He says:

"These fractures in the Earth's crust caused by seismic action not only can be sites of radiation and magnetic anomalies, but around these geological discontinuities are also various other phenomena, such as ... electrical effects associated with mineral enrichment around faulting, and the occasional occurrence of strange lights ... such locations could hold significance for ancient cultures."[5]

St. Benedict medallion in northern axis umbilical marker.

I began with the compass, reconfirming the rear stone wall and umbilical hole orientation to due north. Establishing the orientation of a site is essential in understanding its purpose and meaning. During the recent days with Juan Saez, he had commented, "The direction, orientation of a site is the key. This key opens the site and opens a path of knowledge, revealing its purpose." After returning to Cobertella numerous times, this ancient temple was slowly revealing its secrets.

At the entry at the southern end of the dolmen, I held the copper dowsing rods and asked permission to measure the dolmen's baseline energy field. Slowly walking southward, the rods indicated the dolmen's field to be about 5 feet (1.52 meters) beyond the entry, and I marked the measurement. I placed the Saint Benedict medallion with the cross in the umbilical hole facing north, which fit perfectly. Entering the dolmen, I lit a candle and offered a prayer to the four directions, the above and below, and to the guardians of the site. Before playing the harp, I took some time to attune to the stones and asked for the tone that would make a connection between the dolmen and the northern stars, a "song of the stones."

After receiving a clear impression, I began by plucking a single low E tone repeatedly to entrain with the site. A melody grew out of the meditation on the one tone, based on the perfect fifth interval of E and B. The fifth is the musical interval between the first and fifth notes, often used in sacred music, such as Gregorian chant, in which the listener can more easily enter an altered state of consciousness. Hearing perfect harmonics, such as the fifth, the brain state, body, and subtle energies of the listener become coherent, harmonious, and the person can experience "magnetoreception," or becoming one with magnetism and subtle energies. As the song developed, I noticed more birds flying close and singing around the doorway. I recorded the song and when I clicked save, the length was 2:22 minutes. A good omen. Here are the lyrics of the song "Always Remember You":

"I will always remember you
As long as stars will shine,
Your ancient promise to guard the light,
Until the end of time.

Song of stars and ringing stones,
On Earth as it is on High
Music in these stones shall remain
As memory through time.

Song of stones and singing star
Responding from afar,
A monument to bear the light
From Earth to Northern Star."[6]

Remeasuring the energy field of the dolmen following the meditation and music, the field had expanded to 23 feet (7 meters), reaching the outer boundary wall enclosure. That was a substantial increase, compared with other similar measurements. Returning to the back side of the dolmen and the north-facing stone, I reaffirmed the alignment of the dolmen to the northern axis and rededicated this work to benefit all sentient beings. I buried another silver cross-shaped drachma coin to symbolically ground the stability at the eastern arm of the great landscape cross and the dolmen's alignment with the polestar.

Before leaving the dolmen, I noticed an abundance of *Llombrigol de Venus*, meaning "Umbilical of Venus," growing in the stone wall at the southern end of the enclosure. The round leaves have a deep indent in the center, like a navel, and the plants were growing in an exact north-south alignment with the dolmen's umbilical carving. The plants also marked the outer ring of the dowsed expanded energy field at 7 meters, another example of nature's perfection.

The dolmen's engraved umbilical hole is an ancient tradition that can be found in megalithic temples and churches around the world, and Saez reported finding these carvings in numerous dolmens and on the northern face of Armenian churches. These umbilical marks confirm a site's key orientation with the northern stars. This invisible cord to our home in the stars can be compared with the human umbilical cord that connects us with our mother and the symbolic cord of the pathway to the circumpolar, Imperishable Stars taken by the soul in the afterlife journey home.

As Below, So Above—A Harmonic Response

"There is some kind of connection between the primal tone of the universe itself and the creation of form and structure in the physical world. Geometrical construction somehow contains this music, this hum, and it is found in the landscape in musical intervals."

ANDREW COLLINS[7]

The temple is a manifestation in form of the musical code of the universe. I recalled the German mystic poet Goethe's words, "Sacred architecture is frozen music." One can imagine the entire matrix of ancient temples across the Earth singing or emitting a symphony of resonant patterns, and this music communicating with the stars. As John Michell writes in his classic *The New View Over Atlantis*:

> *"... every building, every stone and wood, was placed in the landscape in accordance with a magic system by which the laws of mathematics and music were expressed in the geometry of the earth's surface... The main paths of planetary influence, determined by thousands of years of astronomy, were discovered in the landscape ..."*[8]

When I returned home a few days later, the following announcement was in my email inbox from Space Weather website: "At the Polar Light Center high above the Arctic Circle, a rare musical note was recorded from the earth's magnetosphere." The article continued that, during the late afternoon of January 18, 2021, on the same day that I was doing the North Star ritual and music in the Creu d'en Cobertella dolmen, a nearly pure sine wave musical tone was recorded at the Polar Light Center monitoring station. The scientist who received the signal, Rob Stammes, said that these pure musical tones are very rare. He explained that the resonance is caused by the solar wind blowing on the Earth's magnetic field, the breath of the Sun creating a hum. Stammes said that on this occasion, the rare sine wave pattern that emanated from the Sun entered the North Pole of the Earth and was replicated through the ground, lasting for more than two hours. He said the duration of the hum, resonating in the Earth as well as the atmosphere, was highly unusual.

The synchronicity of the timing was extraordinary, and of course, I was curious what tone was measured. I contacted Stammes and asked him for the exact frequency of the musical hum. He kindly responded and sent the very low infrasound measurement containing about twenty digits, and I needed to mathematically bring the frequency into a higher octave within the audible range to determine which musical tone the Sun was humming to the Earth.

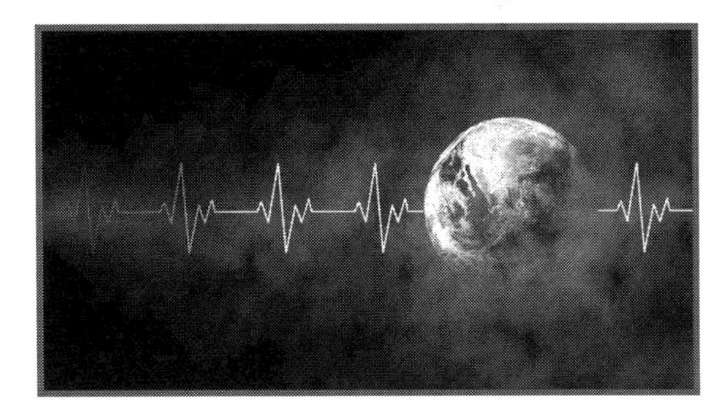

Earth Song.

The result was an F tone, which made no sense with what I had experienced in the dolmen. I contacted Stammes again and asked if he was sure that the figure that he had given me was correct. He responded that he had rounded off the number, assuming an approximation would suffice. He gave me the more exact number, which was about forty digits long. I repeated the calculations, raising the tone many more octaves, and found the tone was a B at 7.639072 Hertz (cycles per second). This fit perfectly, as B is the first primary harmonic of an E tone, and I was playing the E B chord in the dolmen. Amazingly, the tone created by the breath of the Sun entering the Earth at the northern axis perfectly matched the musical chord in the ancient stone temple.

The important research that Stammes is doing is evidence that the frequencies of the stars and Sun are bathing the Earth in cosmic music. This resonance is transmitted through the atmosphere, the Earth, and through our bodies, and is magnified by the silica and crystalline structure of our bones, and in the stones. Scientific models of the magnetic energy and resonance from the cosmos entering the Earth's northern pole, show that this normally travels southward down the magnetic meridians, or Dragon Lines, toward the South Pole. R.A. Schwaller de Lubicz writes in *The Temples of Karnak* that the North Pole is the direction for incoming celestial energies that inspire terrestrial life:

> *"The course of the starry sky and its luminaries imposes upon natural life its becoming and maintenance... the magnetic north pole attracts the electronic effects of solar emission ..."*[9]

Science has been able to identify these cosmic rays that are also entering into the Galactic Core. The research from astronomer Farhad Yusef-Zadeh of Northwestern University discovered harmonically organized magnetic filaments at the center of the Milky Way. These filaments containing cosmic rays create a magnetic field moving close to the speed of light, described as looking "like the strings of a harp."[10]

On that January day in the dolmen, the subtle frequencies of the "Song of the Sun" kissed the northern axis of the Earth, traveling through the silica-rich, conductive terrestrial crust southward down the magnetic meridians and entered the stone temple. And the song and intention coming from an ancient dolmen at the eastern end of the Pyrenees circled back to the stars in response. Ancient people the world over believed that the stars thrive on our songs and our receptivity to their radiance. After reporting my findings to the Arctic monitoring station, I asked Robb Stammes if he thought the pure sine wave from the Sun being simultaneously played in the dolmen was a coincidence or a cocreation? He said he preferred to think of it as a wonderful cocreation.

An Umbilical Cord from Earth to the Stars

> *"... [the King] rises up to heaven, traverses the firmament ... He ascends to the sky; the tips of his wings are like those of a great bird ... He climbs to the sky among the Imperishable Stars."*
>
> PYRAMID TEXTS, UTTERANCE 509[11]

Temple relief Kom Ombo.

The ancient temple builders always had an eye on the sky, and the alignments of their temples reflected the pattern in the heavens on Earth. For these "Sky Watchers," the temples provided a sanctuary to remember and re-enact the cosmic drama on Earth, thereby maintaining harmony in the above and below. This basic Hermetic principle, *to make that which is below, like that which is above*, has guided ancient cultures far beyond Egypt. We often forget that not only are the stellar realms constantly interacting with us, but our thoughts, feelings, and actions are heard by the universe.

Egypt was created in the image of heaven, as were the megalithic stone temples, and many cathedrals and chapels across the world. The invisible umbilical cord from dolmen Creu d'en Cobertella to the stars can be compared to the umbilical cord connecting us with our Earthly mothers, providing nourishment during the fetus' development. As it is at birth, so it is in the afterlife for the ancient people, who believed that they would use this invisible umbilical cord to return to their Creator and the Great Mother in the sky.

"The Pyramid Texts make it clear also that on achieving rebirth in the afterlife, the king's [or queen's] spirit as Osiris receives the warm embrace of his mother, Nut, who in her celestial form exists in the northern part of the sky."

ANDREW COLLINS, *THE CYGNUS KEY*[12]

2nd tomb Tutankhamun.

The umbilical carving facing north from the dolmen is a perfect example of this cross-cultural belief in humanity's home in the stars. The Egyptians believed that this long sky journey required extensive preparations during one's lifetime, and that the preparation for the afterlife was even more important than our lifetime of activities on Earth. The mind needed to be trained in the ability to focus and navigate in this life to be prepared for the journey to the stars. For the initiate, meditation and receiving the illumination and knowledge from the stars was a daily practice and learning the science of sound and the sacred names formed an integral part of this training.

An Egyptian pharaoh traveling through the afterlife needed to know the names of the seven gates, the seven realms, and their guardians before he could pass through to the next. There were words of protection to ensure safe passage. Of course, this process will change according to our traditions and beliefs. Perhaps a Christian might repeat the Lord's Prayer, or a Tibetan, a set of mantras for passage through the Bardos. But the principle is the same. The preparation and discipline for the afterlife journey would not only aid the initiate to navigate to the right place in the stars, but with the discipline and skills, he or she would also be able to live life to the fullest potential to benefit their community during their life on Earth. In the following from the Pyramid Texts, Isis and her sister Nephthys are waiting to greet the king on his arrival in the stars:

> *"'How lovely to see!' says she, namely Isis; 'How pleasing to behold!' says she, namely Nephthys to ... the King, when he ascends to the sky among the stars ... his magic is at his feet, and he goes thereby to his mother Nut, he ascends upon her in this her name of 'Ladder'."*[13]

Djed Pillar Horns, Edfu temple relief.

"The Ladder of Nut" was also known as the Djed Pillar of Osiris, or Ladder of Horus. This bridge connecting Earth and Sky and the road to ascension can be compared to the human spinal column. When the initiate activates his or her inner temple, the vital force begins to circulate through the channels up the spine, and the doorway to the universe at the crown is nudged open. It is indeed strange that we are born with the crown open and with at least some of the memories of our origins intact. Normally, during the second year of life, the sutures begin to close, and then as adults who are on a spiritual path, we must work with such diligence to reawaken our connection.

In the shamanic traditions of the Americas, travel between the dimensions was on what they saw as either a ladder, stairway, or rope connecting Heaven and Earth. This also enabled communication with the spirit world, and in a deep trance or meditation, a "soul is believed to leave the body and ascend to the sky or descend to the underworld."[14] On these journeys, the shaman could access cures for a sick person, see clearly into the past or future, and bring back messages for the tribe. These shamanic travelers, not limited by time and space, were what Romanian-born scholar of mysticism and religious historian Mircea Eliade termed "technicians of ecstasy."[15]

However, one does not need to be a shaman to be a "technician of ecstasy." There are various methods that can be used to achieve altered states in which visions, clear guidance, or ecstatic states can occur. Practices like the "Microcosmic Orbit," or the Taoist "Secret of the Golden Flower," and various yogic breathing meditations are available. I received the following basic meditation from one of my dearest teachers, the late Venerable Khenpo Karthar Rinpoche (February 6, 1924–October 6, 2019), a senior lama in the Karma Kagyu school of Tibetan Buddhism. This technique is very easy and effective, and I often use it with my Voice Analysis clients to help them relax and connect with their authentic self and true voice.[16]

The process is simply sitting in a meditation posture that is comfortable and following the breath with our awareness as it rises and falls. Rinpoche suggested having the eyes almost closed and looking down the ridge of the nose. Placing the tongue on the roof of the mouth helps to complete the circuit through the subtle centers in the brain. A practice that I have added is to follow the movement of the breath on the inhale up the spine to the crown, and on the exhale back down to the base of the spine. Just as the sap rises in a tree to feed its leaves and branches, a subtle nourishment arises within the internal spinal meridians to circulate throughout the body and etheric field with this simple exercise. One can visualize the movement of the breath as a serpent winding up and down, similar to the Kundalini tradition of awakening the sleeping coiled serpent at the base of the spine. You can also see this as a golden cobra, which for the Egyptian initiate resulted in the cobra uraeus being raised to the third eye.

Many years ago, I discovered another interesting meditation tradition from the ancient Nahuatl (Aztec) culture. During the 1990s, I spent several years working in Mexico doing concert tours and sound trainings and attended the annual *Primavera* (spring equinox) gatherings with Aztec and Mayan elders. The week-long celebration was held in an archeological park near the Cuicuilco temple ruins in the southern part of Mexico City (called Tenochtitlan in the Nahuatl language). *Cuicuilco*, most likely meaning "place where songs and dances are made," is one of Mexico's oldest pyramids and may date to the time of the mysterious Olmec people. And true to ancient tradition, music and dance were an integral part of the Primavera gathering, including a good friend, Mazatl Galindo, and myself presenting traditional music with harp, flute, drum, and vocal harmonies in the old languages. Circles of dancers with feathered headdresses performed the traditional dances to the Sun with the beat of large drums. Classes on healing plants, astronomy, Mayan and Aztec calendars, and other traditions were held under the old trees of the park in the ancient way of classrooms without walls.

Uraeus Abydos temple relief.

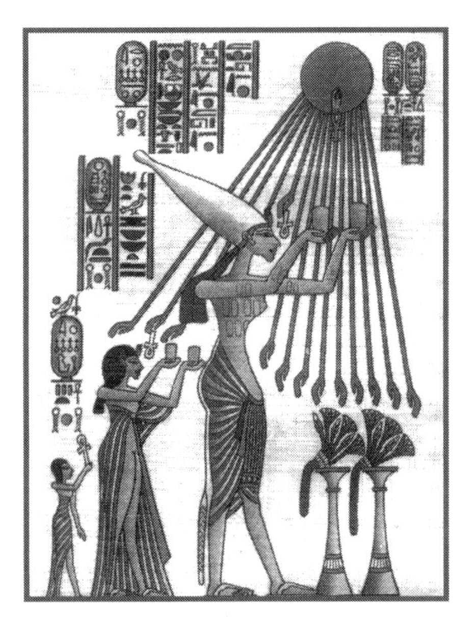

Akhenaten receiving Re.

One of the classes was in Nahua Yoga, basically meaning "yoga of clear sound." To begin, the Nahuatl instructor had us sit in a lotus position, or if needed, in a chair, with back straight but relaxed, facing the rising Sun. He explained the importance of the solar plexus, the third chakra, located between the diaphragm and the navel, as a network of radiating nerves, sending information and energy to all parts of the body, like the illuminating rays of our Sun. In the Vedic system of ancient India, this energy center is called *Manipura*, meaning "lustrous city of jewels," or "shining gem." The yoga instructor guided us to draw the light of the rising Sun into the solar plexus with the breath for quite some time before circulating the vital force. I normally do this exercise drawing the rays of the rising Sun into the *Ajna* ("sixth chakra, or Third Eye") rather than the solar plexus, and on the exhale, sending gratitude for the Sun's warmth and life-giving radiance. One can also draw the illumination of the solar vital force into the entire body, receiving the full spectrum of frequencies as a refined form of nutrition. After all, the Sun provides much of the energy for all of nature's growth.

Special note: Doing these practices with the eyes open, called "Sun gazing," is only done briefly, in the moments when the is Sun rising and only when viewed from a flat horizon. In other words, if the horizon is blocked by a hill, and it rises after the official sunrise, don't stare at the Sun. Normally, the solar exercises are done safely with the eyes closed and drawing in the radiance with focused intention, although, I did once meet a Sun gazer from India who did not eat and lived only on the natural frequencies of the Sun. An adept at photosynthesis?

The Hindu practices include adoration of the Sun as *Savitr*, "protector and giver of life." The *Rig Veda* texts from circa 1500 BCE, contain chants and musical notation for rituals and prayers, and the mantra given for Savitr is the "Gayatri." (Savitr is the illumination at sunrise, and Surya at sunset.) The "Gayatri" is considered the "Mother of all mantras," and can be recited or sung at sunrise, drawing in the solar particles as suggested above, flooding the seven internal centers with illumination, receiving, and sending gratitude back to the Sun. I recorded the "Gayatri" mantra in a medieval church with expansive acoustics in Bugarach, southern France, for the album '*Song of Sophia.*'[17] The following commentary on the role of Savitr from the *Rig Veda,* sounds similar to the role of Egyptian gods in the pharaoh's journey through the Afterlife. According to 19th century scholar H.H. Wilson:

"Savitr acts as a protector of all beings ... as well as guard [of] the world of spirits. He is prayed [to] in order to convey the departed spirit to where the virtuous dwell. He confers immortality on the gods as well as length of life on man ... He has a major role in creation."[18]

One can do the suggested solar meditations with other stars, such as Sirius, Antares, or the star of your choice. Drawing in the illumination and knowledge of the celestial luminaries contains subtle frequencies and light particles that can result in the direct transmission of knowledge and energy, as well as experiencing the ecstatic states mentioned by Mircea Eliade. And remember, the stars are still emanating their light particles during the day when all but the Sun disappear from our sight. Stars emit a myriad of frequencies and particles, including neutrinos, which science calls the most mysterious particle of the universe. In fact, there are trillions of them passing through you right now! Research is currently underway to harvest the cosmic neutrino radiation and convert it into usable energy, including electricity.[19] The ancient people knew about the subtle benefits of receiving the full spectrum of frequencies of the stars, and when we also make this intimate connection, we may ultimately begin to hear their songs, the music of the spheres.[20]

Part V

An Ancient Camino

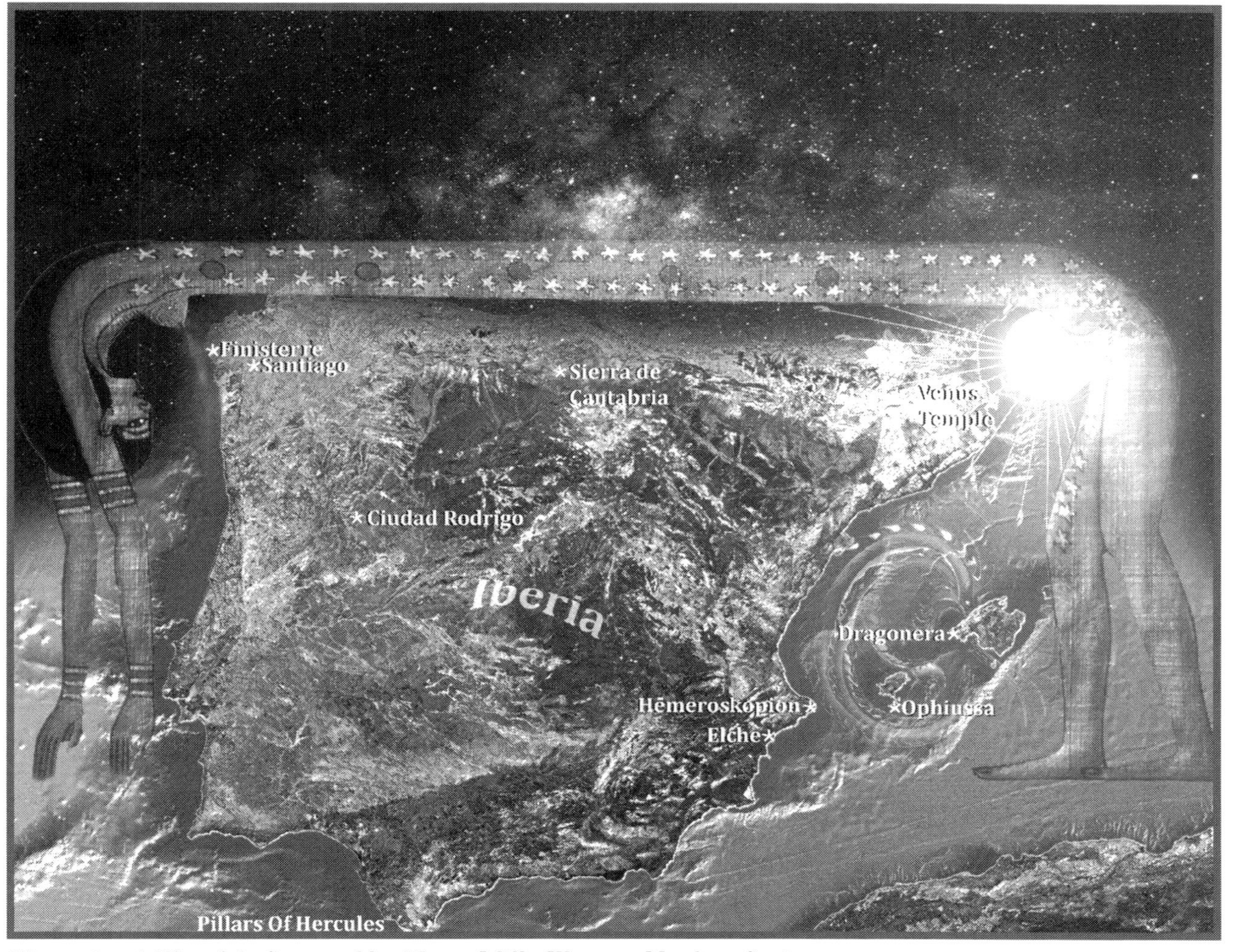

Illustration 4: Way of the Stars, goddess Nut as Milky Way over Northern Spain

CHAPTER 21

Way of the Field of Stars

"The sky and its stars make music to you
The sun and the moon praise you
The neteru [gods] exalt you
The neteru sing to you."

Hymn to Het-Heru (Hathor), Dendera Temple inscription[1]

Nearly every culture has a story about their origins from the stars, and most knew of the song of the stars before modern science finally rediscovered this musicality of the heavens.[2] Ancient people of the Pyrenees navigated by observing the heavens, and they followed the path of the Sun, Moon, and stars from their birthplace in the east. These divine lights appeared to rise out of the waters of the Mediterranean, continuing their daily and nightly progress into the west, to be swallowed by the great Atlantic, only to be born again. One account described the Sun sizzling as it plunged into the western waters.

In illustration 4, Way of the Stars, we can see the Egyptian sky goddess Nut giving birth to the Sun and the stars of the Milky Way with her body arching over Northern Spain. She is the bridge between the east and west, the places of birth and death, light and dark, day and night, and she is overseeing the initiation path of the Way of the Stars across the Pyrenees and the Cantabrian Mountains. The mountain ranges are at the 42nd degree north latitude and lie at a bit of an angle, with the eastern end at about 42°N16' and the western end at about 42°N57'. (In the next segment, it will be explained that although the Milky Way appears to rise in the southeast and set in the southwest, the rotation of the Earth makes it appear to turn with the seasons and hours.)

Megalithic monuments established by Neolithic people circa 4000–3500 BCE, trace this star route along the base of the mountains from Cap de Creus at the easternmost landmass of Spain, to the westernmost point at Finisterre, meaning "End of the Earth." These stone monuments seem to be concentrated at the eastern and western ends of the star route. This ancient path predates the Christian way of the Camino de Santiago de Compostela, meaning "Way of Saint James of the Field (or Land) of Stars," by thousands of years.

German astronomer Heinz Kaminsky has gathered invaluable research on ancient star pilgrimage routes and has added much to what has often been considered legend and folklore, especially regarding the antiquity of the prehistoric star route in Northern Spain. In his *Sternstrassen der Vorzeit: Von Stonehenge nach Atlantis* ("*Star Routes of Antiquity: from Stonehenge to Atlantis*"), he documented numerous megalithic tracks mirroring the heavens around the world, and reaffirms Spain's claim to be the world's oldest, and that people from across Europe traveled this same path long before the era of the Camino of Saint James.

> *"It can be demonstrated that, at least 4000 years before Christ, all inter-regional cultic centres in Megalithic times were joined in a network. There are three great star routes. The first leads through northern Spain ..."*[3]

Although the Way of the Stars predates the Christian tradition by about five thousand years, the Camino pilgrimage is much more famous, having a revival in modern culture with Shirley MacLaine's book *The Camino*, Paolo Coelho's *The Pilgrimage*, and the film *The Way*, starring Martin Sheen. The popularity of the Camino tradition grows stronger every year, as the search for meaning in life gains momentum and the awakening of humanity makes its slow but steady progress.

The better-known routes of the later Christian Camino begin in Northern Spain and various sites in France and Portugal. But the six-thousand-year-old path, the Way of the Stars, began at the place of the rising Sun, where the Pyrenees range meets the sea, and where we find a network of more than thirty-four megalithic monuments at Cap de Creus, each site marking celestial alignments. Later, during the first millennium BCE, the departure would likely have been from the Greek temple of Venus-Aphrodite[4] located on the same cape, which was known in ancient times as the Promontory of Aphrodite. Then, during the medieval era, this same location remained a popular eastern departure point from the monastery of Sant Pere de Rodes.

If we review some of the myths and traditions at the eastern end of the Way of the Stars, some interesting themes emerge that give fresh insights to the old initiation path. This region has long had a strong Greek presence, and with their arrival came their gods, goddesses, traditions, and magical tales. Their legends are still retold and include stories of the giants and gods that walked the coastal cliffs and across the

Siren of Roses Bay.

Pyrenees, the same gods that ultimately became known in the constellations in the heavens. We shall see that these heroes and their deeds can be seen reflected in the formation of the land, and even the cape's metamorphic rocks took the shapes of the legendary characters. Songs of the sirens can still be heard soaring over the bewitched stones of Dolmen Encantats ("Enchanted"), and in honey-voiced seductions whispered to fishermen on the lonely sea at night. And sighs of the sirens rise out of the crashing waves below the enchanted caves, Les Coves de les Encantades.

These caves are located on the southern side of Cap de Creus, at Cap de Norfeu, (Cape of Orfeu, or Orpheus), a narrow finger of land that extends into the sea with cliffs more than 300 feet (90 meters) in height. First-century BCE Greek historian Diodorus said that Orpheus accompanied Jason and the Argonauts on their expeditions across the Mediterranean,[5] and local Catalan legend says that Orpheus was shipwrecked on the rugged shoals of Norfeu. As he was precariously clinging to a large rock surrounded by the sea, Orpheus was so struck with the beauty of the coastline that he forgot his dire situation and began to play a new verse on his lyre. The land and the Pyrenean peaks were completely enchanted and began to move closer to hear

Illustration 20: Orpheus and Cap de Creus

Legend

1. Ciutadella, Rhodes-Roses 5-pointed star
2. Trinitat Hapsburg Castle 4-pointed star
3. Visigothic Castle
4. Dolmen Creu d'en Cobertella
5. Megalithic Route 1
6. Megalithic Route 2
7. Megalithic Route 3
8. Torre de Norfeu, Tower of Orpheus
9. Cap de Norfeu, Cape of Orpheus

his song, which built a bridge of stones that saved the soulful singer's life. My local guide said there are ruins of two temples to this god of music on the highest ridge of Norfeu, and in illustration 20, the Tower of Orpheus is a visible testimonial to the god. Greek legend tells us that Orpheus received his seven-stringed lyre from Apollo, which was crafted by the wise Hermes, indicating that the instrument incorporated Egyptian principles of sound knowledge. Regarding Orpheus' Egyptian studies, Diodorus says:

"And after he had devoted his entire time to his education and had learned whatever the myths had to say about the gods, he journeyed to Egypt, where he further increased his knowledge and so became the greatest man among the Greeks both for his knowledge of the gods and for their rites, as well as for his poems and songs."[6]

Hermes, inventor of the lyre, was the Greek name for Egyptian god Thoth, or Djehuty, whose precious texts included the mystical knowledge of the stars and the power of music. Orpheus, with his lyre embedded with Hermetic song-knowledge, became the legendary master of the science of music, known for opening gateways and re-enchanting nature, the gods, and the underworld. And more importantly, this is the science of the transmutation of the soul. This knowledge was spread through the Orphic cults, the Pythagorean mystery schools, and other Gnostic traditions that arrived with Greek settlers along the coasts of Gaul and Iberia. As Marsilio Ficino wrote to Cosimo de' Medici in 1462:

"Orpheus, in his book of hymns, asserts that Apollo, by his vital rays, bestows health and life on all and drives away disease. Furthermore, by the sounding strings ... he regulates everything ..."[7]

In Greek myth, Orpheus charmed and tamed the fierce Cerberus, guardian dog of the underworld, during his journey to retrieve his beloved Eurydice. And it is telling that just to the north of Cap de Norfeu is the ancient coastal city Cap de Cerberus, now called Cerbere, which even features the legendary three-headed dog on its coat of arms. Orpheus, as a guardian of the eastern end of the Way of the Stars, is a perfect metaphor for this ancient path of initiation, for music and transformation have always been an integral part of this journey.

The legends tell us that when Orpheus died and arrived in the underworld for the second time, Hades threatened to keep him. The great muse cried out and Apollo took pity on him and turned Orpheus into a swan, placing him in the heavens as the constellation

Image of Orpheus and Cerberus, Boijmans Museum, Netherlands.

Cygnus next to his beloved lyre in the stars of Lyra. The imprint of Orpheus opens the gates of the Camino and the Milky Way path with enchanting music, unlocking the dimensional doors for the initiation journey of the soul. And we can imagine that pilgrims departing from the Cape of Orpheus would have commenced with prayers at his temple, greeting and singing praises to the rising Sun. British musician, scholar, and author Angela Voss comments in her *Father Time and Orpheus*:

> *"Orpheus's music will be resurrected at sunrise, which can be seen as not only the dawn of a new day, but the dawn of a new era."*[8]

Did the pilgrims on the Way of the Stars use the celestial Northern Cross formed by Cygnus as a stellar guide on the long road to Finisterre? Or perhaps they were guided by the Summer Triangle formed by Cygnus' tail star Deneb, Lyra's bright Vega, and Altair in the Aguila ("Eagle") constellations?

Cap de Creus is associated with another Greek (and Egyptian) hero, Hercules, who according to Pyrenean legends, may have accomplished his twelfth and most difficult labor here, that of conquering Cerberus. This makes sense given the ancient towns of Cerberus and Pyrene are both located just north of Cap de Creus. Remember, the Celtic Princess Pyrene was the legendary lover of Hercules. Greek myth describes the fierce guardian Cerberus as part dog and part dragon, or serpent, and his mother as half woman and half dragon, or serpent. Again, this speaks of the strong dragon traditions of the region, and the dragon-serpent is also associated with Pyrene, who in Pyrenean tradition gave birth to a serpent, symbolizing wisdom traditions, guardianship, and regeneration.

With the likely eastern departure of the pre-Christian pilgrimage route at the temple of Venus-Aphrodite we find a source of two of the themes of the Camino, the scallop shells, and the swan. In addition to the numerous Camino myths explaining the meaning of the seashells prized by pilgrims and displayed on the hat of Saint James, they must certainly relate to the Greek myth of our goddess emerging out of the brine of the Mediterranean and riding a scallop shell to shore. For those on the long walk to Santiago, this shell is worn to identify them as pilgrims on the journey and is also the symbol of completion of the Camino. The signs marking the various routes display yellow shell symbols, and the multiple rays from the center of the shell represent the many pathways leading to the same destination. Are pilgrims with their scallop shells of Saint James aware that they are also paying homage to the ancient goddess?

Venus-Aphrodite was said to have arrived ashore gliding in a celestial chariot pulled by swans, and the attributes of grace, beauty, and love were applied to both the goddess and her mounts. We will discover in the last chapters that the initiation path of the Way of the Stars is related to Venus, the planet associated with the goddess and the transformation of the soul into the purity and elegance of a swan.

Piecing together the legends, place names, and archaeological discoveries, a magical, layered history emerges at the eastern end of the Way of the Stars, a portal both to the underworld and to the heavens. This is a place of elemental alchemy, with the Pyrenees named for fire, meeting the salty sea, where the initiate enters the path of evolution of the soul. Quite amazingly, even the profile of the southern portion of Cap de Creus takes the form of Cerberus, the dog tamed by Orpheus.[9] The perfection of the image is uncanny and is a good example of a simulacrum, a Latin term meaning "likeness, similarity" to a person or thing. And the imprint of Cerberus remaining at Cap de Creus and Cap de Norfeu's rocky coastline is a testimonial throughout the ages to the legendary Orpheus, who enchanted the fierce guardian with his music.

The Milky Way

"We are the stars which sing,
We sing with our light,
We are the birds of fire,
We fly across the heavens,
Our light is a star which sings."[10]

For the Mayans, the center of the Milky Way has a unique sound, represented by a spiral glyph shaped like our letter "G."[11] This design is featured on temple walls and in their weavings, as a constant reminder of their origins. They see the center of our galaxy as the zero point, the seed of beginnings, where modern science has discovered a black hole that it says is holding together the entire galaxy. The Mayans call this center "Hunab K'u, the Only Giver of Movement and Measure ...,"[12] where the seeds of all life arise. (We can also see this zero-point of origins in the Mayan numbering system, which begins with zero, represented as a seashell with its natural spiral shape.)

Indeed, our bones are composed of the minerals of stardust, and from our point of origin we ultimately return. "Every atom of oxygen in our lungs, of carbon in our muscles, of calcium in our bones, of iron in our blood—was created inside a star before Earth

"Bugarach" by Dani Valdés.

was born."[13] Many tribes of North America see the Milky Way as an eternal "Path of Souls," where the departed spirits walk. Ethnoastronomer George E. Lankford found that the Manitou people of Ontario, Canada, are greeted in their afterlife journey to the stars by a Great Mother figure called "Our Grandmother,"[14] perhaps similar in principle to the Egyptian sky mother Nut, who welcomes the pharaoh on his journey to the stars.

My friend Dani Valdés captured a magical moment with the Milky Way over Mount Bugarach, aligned perfectly with the north-south Dragon Path, exhibiting the perfection of "As Above, So Below.[15] Ancient people saw the Milky Way as mirroring the prominent features in their landscape, such as the Egyptian view of the star path aligned north-south with the river Nile and the placement of their temples. The Pyrenean cultures saw the Milky Way as a reflection of their mountain range and ancient stone monuments, aligned east-west. The small portion of the Milky Way that we see is aligned at a 63-degree tilt, and because of the motion of the Earth and the Sun around the galaxy, the river of stars appears to turn according to the seasons and the hours. For example, if you were to spend a summer night under the stars, you could observe the Milky Way rising in the southeast and appearing to turn very slowly, like the spoke of a great wheel. At midnight it appears to be aligned north-south, but by early morning, it shifts to east-west.

For a Pyrenean shepherd moving his herds in the predawn cool hours in July, the path of stars is aligned basically east-west. And similarly, for Camino pilgrims when

Hunab K'u, Mayan glyph.

they wake up early before the heat of a Spanish summer, they could use the orientation of the Milky Way for their path westward. For most people today, this is very confusing, but for ancient people, understanding the orientation of the stars could mean the difference between life and death. Suffice it to say, the Egyptians and the Pyreneans were both correct!

The oldest Camino routes formed more of a network of paths, with the older, more rugged routes passing higher in the mountains and the later routes following easier paths across the lower-elevation valleys. The mountain route is marked by megalithic monuments, such as stone circles, dolmens, menhirs, and engraved stones, which formed an initiation path maintained by Neolithic people from at least 3500 BCE. At the eastern end of the Way of the Stars at Cap de Creus, the dolmen Creu d'en Cobertella is the largest monument of its kind in all of Catalonia and would have been a likely Camino departure point.

These same pathways were also used by people who arrived in the region thousands of years earlier. Located just 0.33 miles (0.53 kilometers) to the northwest of dolmen Cobertella is a site named in Catalan *Cau de les Guilles*, meaning "Den of the Foxes," inhabited 17,000 years ago. According to Catalan archeologist Enriqueta Pons I Brun, the Magdalenian era hunter-gatherer cultures inhabited Cap de Creus and the surrounding valleys from about 15,000 BCE.[16]

When I first observed the maps showing locations of megalithic structures at the Eastern Pyrenees on the Mediterranean, I was struck by the alignment of the dolmens and menhirs forming a serpentine path that begins at the sea and follows the hills to the Pyrenees and westward. These megalithic sites were used as tombs and temples of ritual and prayer to mark the turning points of solar, lunar, and stellar alignments, each temple like a cog in the great wheels of time, each site indicating the ritual timing to maintain the rhythms on Earth and in the cosmos. Ancient people viewed the perpetual daily birth, death, and rebirth of the light as corresponding with the stars rising in the east, and their descent into the dark underworld in the west.

"Great and mighty is the river of the sky, flowing across the heavens and through the Duat, the world of night and of thick darkness, and on that river floats the Boat of Ra. Boat of Millions of Years is its name."[17]

They viewed the Earth and Sky as populated by their deities who were playing out this perpetual drama of the cycles of movement of light and time. In Egyptian cosmology, the stories of their gods and goddesses were enacted in the movements of the stars. In the story of Isis searching for the dismembered parts of her beloved Osiris, she is following his trail, and we can see her chasing him across the sky in the Milky Way. The rising of Osiris as Orion (called Sah by the Egyptians) is always followed by the rising of Isis as Sirius (Sopdet/Sothis) as she tracks him through the night sky. What stories were the megalithic builders seeing in the constellations? As we have seen, their monuments were aligned to specific stars, especially the pole star at the northern end of the Milky Way, and we will soon discover a series of dolmens in Cantabria, Spain, placed to perfectly mirror the northern constellation Cassiopeia.

The Pyrenean Paleolithic and Neolithic cultures had their own gods and goddesses, rooted in the natural world, and they actively communicated with this living matrix, believing it had consciousness. How did they view the Milky Way? Perhaps like the indigenous people of the Americas, who saw this silver stream of stars as a Path of Souls and the way of the dead. Or did they view the Milky Way as the Egyptians did, as a Sky Mother stretched across the heavens, giving birth each day to the Sun, and offering us her nourishing milk, as in illustration 4?

The old star route across northern Spain that followed the Pyrenean 42nd parallel was used throughout the ages by Paleolithic and Neolithic people, as well as Celts, Iberians, and later Greek arrivals circa 700–500 BCE, and hundreds of years later by the Romans and Visigoths. These ancient roads were multi-purposed and served both practical and spiritual functions for the various cultures. The route was later marked by Knights Templar commanderies, churches, castles, and Maria Magdalena monasteries and chapels, as we have seen.

Ancient cultures used these same routes for their survival in the practice of transhumance, moving groups of people and their herds for grazing to lower and higher elevations according to the seasons. Spanish archeologists have confirmed the use of these routes also by hunter-gatherer cultures for at least 17,000 years, based on discoveries of old roads and stone and bone artifacts found at Cau de les Guilles (Cave of the Foxes) near Dolmen Creu d'en Cobertella.[18] These same tracks were used by migrating mammals for millions of years, footprint after footprint. The people using these routes also used the stars to navigate their paths that reached from the Mediterranean westward to the Ter River valleys below Santa Magdalena de Perella at the ancient crossroads, and beyond to Seu de Urgell and the Segre River. Amazingly, this route spans the entire eastern and western arms of the Great Cross, which indicates this same east-west axis has been in use for at least seventeen millennia!

"We know the existence of livestock routes that during the winter went from the high valleys of Freser and Llierca to the Alberes and the Serra of Rodes, and that the previous winter pastures of the high valleys of Ter [Magdalena de Perella, center of the cross], Llobregat, Freser and Segre [western arm of the cross] went to the plains of the Emporda [eastern arm at Rhodes]."[19]

"We suspect that these regions were the ideal paradise during a good time of the year ... Up and down, and every year passing through the same places ... footprint after footprint ..."[20]

We have established the antiquity of the Way of the Stars traversing northern Spain as one of our world's oldest continuously used pathways. The Camino de Santiago de Compostela overlays the older Way of the Stars, beginning at the Mediterranean, also aligning with the east-west axis of the Great Cross, and the Magdalena Path. In later chapters, we will discover that the number of sites dedicated to Magdalena at the western end of the Camino is almost beyond belief. The 20th-century mystic teacher Rudolf Steiner related that the essential nature of the entire Camino was experienced as an initiation path of the stars mirrored in nature and the four elements. He also said it is a path of the "goddess Natura" and is experienced through Mary Magdalene and Saint James (Santiago).[21] Steiner stresses that the Grail is to be found in northern Spain along the Camino in a hidden place in the Pyrenees, most likely in the invisible realms.[22]

Steiner's overview of the Camino as being experienced through Magdalena is a theme that kept appearing, and related to something I was told by a friend when he completed the road to Santiago. Luiz Pontual had been walking for many days and was tired but elated as he entered the northern entrance of the great Cathedral of Santiago, and his keen intuition guided him to an apse to the left. There, he discovered a beautiful statue of what he described as Maria Magdalena dressed in red and an old man gazing reverently at her image. Luiz began speaking with the older pilgrim, who told him his story. He was 87 years young, and after losing his wife several years before, he began walking the Path to Santiago and had just completed his fourteenth Camino. He told Luiz that this apse with Magdalena was by far the most potent section of the cathedral, and was part of the older, original structure.

This chapel was the original Marian temple in Santiago, called La Antigua, "The Old One," where resident monks maintained the Cult of the Apostle. The chapel has been incorporated into the great Cathedral of Santiago and is now called Santa Maria de la Corticela. The statue of Maria appears like numerous images of the Virgin Mary, except for her red dress, and I recalled her image in the chapel of Santa Magdalena at Montcal looking very similar, in red, but with her signature vase for anointing oils. Whoever this Santiago Santa Maria is, she is crowned, enthroned, and adored as the feminine face of God, which is more to the point. The more I researched and heard numerous accounts of the prominence of Magdalena on the various Caminos, I was convinced that she was and still is a guiding light on the Way of the Stars.

Each of the sanctuaries along the Magdalena Path would have been a stopping point for prayers, songs, and offerings, strengthening and renewing the vital energy of the pilgrim as well as the surrounding region. Through the principle of sympathetic resonance and the wisdom of Orphic tradition, what occurs in one stone structure affects the related sites in the network. The chants and hymns offered by pilgrims would have also served to open the gateways between Earth and spirit, and in this way, the old sites remained active, communicating with the cosmos, and the initiatic path of the Way of the Stars endured. The essence of the path mirroring the Milky Way across the Pyrenees is remembered in the names of its mountains, such as Mont de Estrella, "Mountain of the Star," or the similar Puig Estella, "Star Hill," and temples dedicated to the sacred feminine. The song "Field of Stars," from the album "Calling Pyrene," is dedicated to this timeless Camino that mirrors the heavens on Earth.[23]

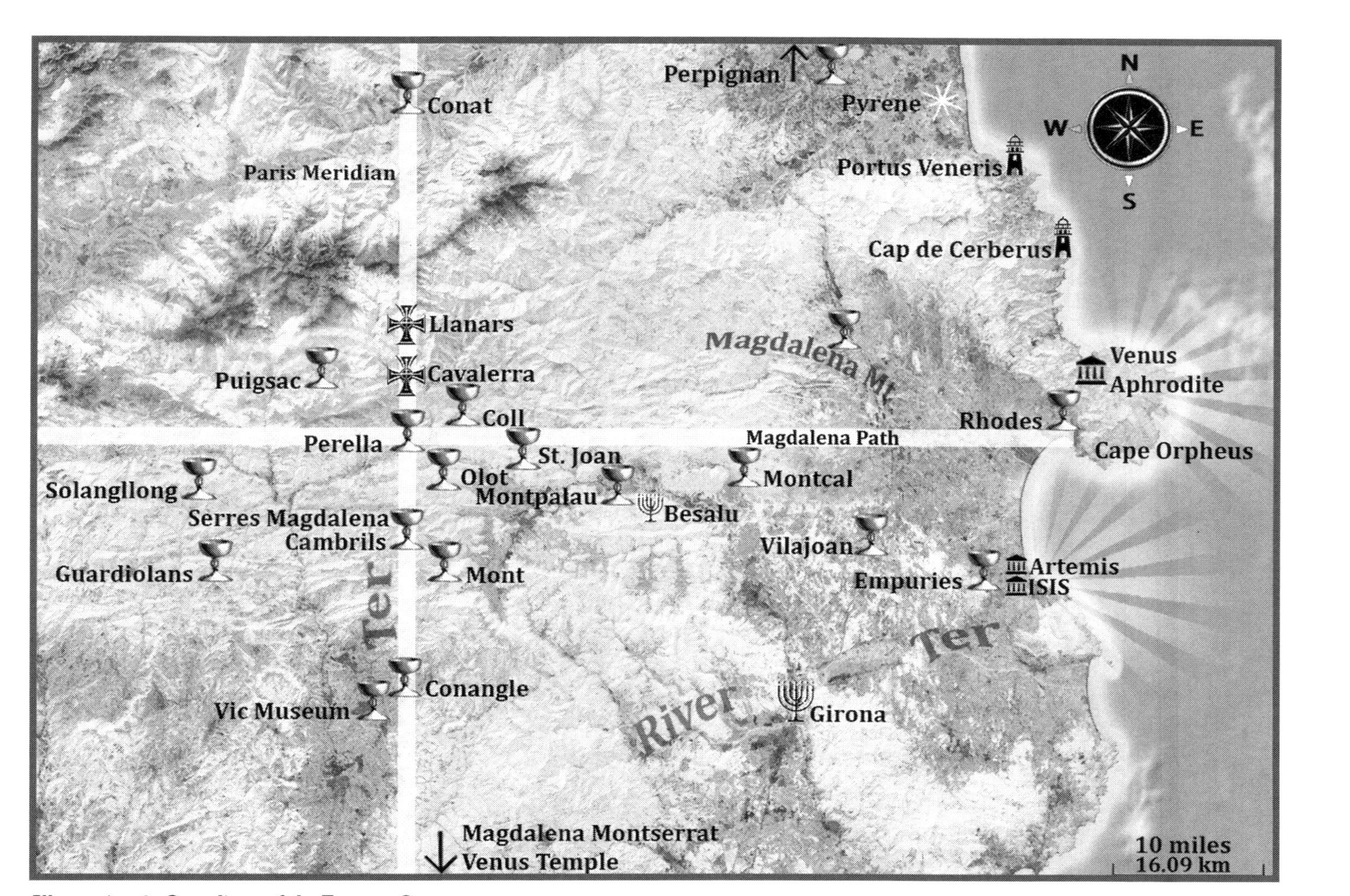

Illustration 3: Guardians of the Eastern Gate

CHAPTER 22

Goddess Guardians of the Eastern Gate

"The Rhodians, masters of the mountain, raised a temple to Venus on the north face and at the foot of the main peak. The navigator recognized it, like a lighthouse, long before rounding the promontory, and the guardians of the temple were the first to point out ships on the sea in the distance ..."

Francesc Jaubert de Paça[1]

The French archeologist Francesc Jaubert de Paça (1785–1856) paints an extraordinary image in the quote above of the early temple built on what he calls the Promontory of Aphrodite. The temple of Venus-Aphrodite was built high on the cliffs that tower above the Mediterranean, on the easternmost landmass of Spain, now known as Cap de Creus. During Neolithic times, the eastern departure for the Way of the Stars was from the megalithic temples at the Mediterranean, with later pilgrims likely departing from the temple of Venus-Aphrodite. The temple also served as a lighthouse for mariners arriving from afar. We are reminded of the ancient Magdala lighthouses with their signal fires, watchers from the high places across the entire Mediterranean. In this case, the watchers were the priestesses and attendants of the temple guarding the eastern gate to Iberia.

Claudius Ptolemy was a Greek astronomer and geographer living in Alexandria, Egypt, in the second century CE, and lists this site as the Pyrenean Temple of Venus on his maps of the Iberian coast. As mentioned previously, Ptolemy used this temple as a starting point for mapping the entire Mediterranean coast of Iberia from the Pyrenees to the Pillars of Hercules, using precise measurements of the stars. Many archeologists date the temple to the time of the first arrivals of Greek traders in the eighth and seventh centuries BCE. However, Jaubert de Paça says that Catalan historians from his sources date their arrival as early as 910 BCE,[2] the same time as the Phoenician presence in Iberia (not to be confused with the later Ionian Greek arrivals from Phocaea, current Turkey).

The Venus-Aphrodite temple gave up its remaining foundation stones and walls for building the Benedictine Monastery of Sant Pere de Rodes (945 CE) and according to Luiz Pontuel, when archeologists were excavating the monastery the remains of three

Venus Temple, now Monastery Sant Pere de Rodes with Camino sign: "Galicia 1250 kilometers."

pillars in the crypt were identified as being from the ancient temple. Another Venus temple that existed at the sacred mountain of Montserrat gave its stones to the earliest Christian structure at the site of the current cathedral of the Black Madonna, still considered the guardian mother of Catalonia. Paça says that in the year 253 CE, the Spanish Emperor Felipe converted the Montserrat Venus temple into one of Spain's earliest Christian edifices, retaining some of the original structure.[3]

Located 13.6 miles (22 kilometers) to the north of the Venus-Aphrodite temple, at the current Monastery of Sant Pere de Rodes, was Portus Veneris ("Port of Venus"), today's coastal town of Port Vendres. Juan Saez told me of significant connections from ancient times between Venus, Pyrene, and Melusine as *La Sirena*, The Siren, as she was honored in the region. Melusine is a beloved serpent-tailed goddess of Scythian origin who was popular throughout Celtic and medieval Europe. She is often depicted as a mermaid a with split fish tail, a guardian of ancient springs and waterways, and considered to be the partner of the solar god Lug. Juan added that these sirens forged a link between pagan traditions and the Benedictine cloisters and cathedrals where she can be found, and her placement often marks the seasonal point of entry of light in the temples. He discovered that a siren in the cloister at Sant Pere de Galligants in Girona marks the master X point of the temple with the first rays of light at equinox and solstice, forming axes of light.[4]

Medieval carvings of sirens are also found at Sant Pere de Rodes (site of the Venus-Aphrodite temple), the cloister at Elne (ancient city of Pyrene), and numerous other sites in the region. And serpent tailed Melusine reminds us of Pyrene giving birth to a serpent, and the Egyptian serpent goddess Renenutet, both symbols of wisdom, fertility, and regeneration (see image of Renenutet-Isis on page 10).

On some old maps the site of Portus Veneris is listed as Venus-Pyrene, and Otto Rahn, the German officer of the SS, who arrived in the 1930s in his quest for the Pyrenean Grail, claimed that the port was founded by the Phoenicians, who came for the region's gold. He also proposed that Jason and the Argonauts landed at the Port of Venus, in search of the Golden Fleece, said to be guarded by a great dragon, perhaps the guardian of the Pyrenees?[5] We don't know if Jason found the Golden Fleece, but he did encounter the fierce Celtic warrior King Berbyx, none other than the legendary father of Pyrene. Rahn's suggestion regarding the Argonauts matches the Catalan legends of Orpheus arriving with the Argonauts on this same coast and that his music protected Jason's ships from the seduction of the siren songs.

Just 9 miles (14.5 kilometers) northwest of Portus Veneris was the ancient Iberian city of Pyrene. The hilltop city was a short distance from the sea in view of Mount Canigó, and surely had a Magdaluma watchtower, common to all cities located on major Mediterranean trade routes. The city was later called *Illiberis* ("Island of the Iberians") and may have been surrounded with water when the level of the Mediterranean was higher. In the fourth century CE, the name changed again to Helena, named for Emperor Constantine's extraordinary mother, who may have stopped along this coast on her several journeys to Jerusalem, even when well into her eighties. She was an extraordinary visionary who dreamed of the correct locations of the Holy Sepulcher and the "True Cross." The name of the city was shortened over the centuries to become Elne.

Siren Sant Pere de Galligants cloister, Girona.

An Imaginary Journey from Egypt to the Iberian Temples

To the south of the Promontory of Venus-Aphrodite, the temples at Rhodes (Roses) and Empúries each had their watchtowers, and then near Barcelona, the light of the temple of Venus-Aphrodite radiated from the white spires of Montserrat. Continuing southward beyond Valencia, we will discover yet another temple of Artemis that stood at the cape of Hēmeroskopeion at Dénia. The evidence gathered from numerous archeological studies has shown that from at least the seventh–sixth centuries BCE, perhaps earlier, the entire northeastern coast of the Iberian Peninsula was dominated by temples dedicated to numerous goddesses, whose eternal fires stood as Magdaluma watchtowers, long before Hannibal, Caesar, and other well-known historical figures set foot on these shores. What would our present world look like if the invaders from North Africa and Rome (circa 218–206 BCE) had not conquered these lands? And what might it have been like to approach this land as a Mediterranean trader in 300 BCE? Join me in a hypothetical journey from Egypt to Iberia:

Your name is Hermodorus, a Greek trader living in Memphis, Egypt, and you are one of the respected owners of a large fleet of ships. You are ready to sail to Empúries on the Iberian coast, and your ships are manned with sailors from Egypt, Phoenicia, and Greece, and you will be transporting hundreds of amphoras (large clay jars) filled with wine, olive oil, perfumes, and resins from the East. Your trade arrangement made with Empúries the year before, and inscribed on a lead tablet, was to trade for pure Iberian silver, grain, and linen textiles woven by the excellent Iberian weavers. Before beginning the voyage, you will perform a ritual and make offerings to Isis, "Mistress of the Sea" and protector of all sailors. An inscription from your home at Memphis reads:

"... I [Isis] invented fishing and seafaring... I am Mistress of rivers, winds, and sea ... I am Mistress of the thunderbolt. I calm and agitate the sea... I am the Mistress of seamanship. I make the navigable unnavigable whenever I decide."[6]

Your ritual and supplications to the goddess include invocations and offerings at the temples at Memphis, and again at Sais on the Nile Delta, before departing for the open sea. Stops are made along the way for replenishing fresh water, food, and additional trade at Cyprus and Sicily. In Syracuse, you take onboard a group of traveling performers to entertain your sailors, and later, your friends at Empúries.

After many days, favorable winds, and enough clear skies that allow for navigation by the stars, you pass the shores of Gaul and see the great peaks of the Pyrenees rising to the west. Your chief navigator has identified the shoals and landmarks of the coast with the trusty "periplus," a sailing book made in Iberia sometime before 530 BCE, listing every harbor and cape. Your ships pass the Promontory of Aphrodite with its temple and lighthouse, warning you to steer clear of the dangerous rocky cliffs.

Finally, your fleet arrives safely in the harbor of the thriving market city of Empúries, protected by the Greek jetties. The glistening white marble of the temple honoring Artemis of Ephesus shines like a beacon on the small island one kilometer to the north, and the walled city of Empúries is adorned with lighted towers that surround the city. Before celebrating with your men at the agora, the main public marketplace, you head straight to the temples of Isis and Serapis with your chief navigators and assistants to make offerings and give thanks to the gods for their protection and your safe passage. The temple sector is at the southern end of the city, and outside the door of the shrine to Isis, you each make ablutions with the spring water provided in the large, decorated stone basin. The image encircling the rim is Agathos Daimon, the noble serpent guardian of good luck and health, the guardian of the city.

Entering the temple, a grand white marble image of Isis greets you, her sistrum in one hand and a vase of offerings in the other. You pay homage and proceed to the altar, where urns of pungent, purifying resins are infusing the air with heady perfume. You leave your offerings at the altar of Lady Isis, images of her cast in precious gold, and jewelry of lapis and turquoise from Egypt. You make your way to the adjoining temple dedicated to Serapis, who combines your great god Osiris with attributes of the Apis Bull. You, Hermodorus, regularly pay homage to your deity at the Serapeum of Alexandria, and wish to make offerings to your god, who along with Isis, is a protector of sailors. With one more passage across the great sea completed, you are ready to join your men for music, wine, and relaxation at the symposium, a Greek term meaning "drinking together."

"... they had poured out the libation, and had sung the hymn. To promote the revelry, there entered now a Syracusan, with a trio of assistants: the first, a flute-girl, perfect in her art; and next, a dancing-girl, skilled to perform all kinds of wonders; lastly, in the bloom of beauty, a boy, who played the harp and danced with infinite grace."

XENOPHON, THE SYMPOSIUM[7]

Our Greek trader might have also visited one of the nearby temples of Artemis or Aphrodite to pay homage to the other Mediterranean goddesses that his ship was not one of the many shipwrecks filled with cargo lying at the bottom of the sea, broken open by the rugged rocky shores of Iberia. He may have stopped briefly at the temple of Venus-Aphrodite at Cap de Creus, where one is impressed by the high cliffs of this promontory that provide a dramatic and stunning location overlooking the sea of the goddess' legendary birth. Before entering the current monastery of Sant Pere de Rodes, to the left is a stone enclosure with an ancient healing spring that has a spectacular coastal view, part of the original Venus temple, where our pilgrimage groups have often paused to pay homage to the goddess.

Venus Temple spring, now the Monastery of Sant Pere de Rodes.

The Greek myths say that Aphrodite was born of the salty seafoam, and came riding on a scallop shell, wearing nothing but the foam of the sea and her hair. Wearing nothing but her hair reminds us of the associations with Mary the Egyptian and Maria Magdalena, and her scallop shells are worn by pilgrims on the Camino. Aphrodite is now remembered as a goddess of sexuality and love and her name is the root of our word for sexual stimulants, *aphrodisiacs*. However, Aphrodite is much, much more. She is an ancient Mother Goddess of life's abundance and wherever she traveled, it is said that beauty sprang forth along her path.

The early Greek arrivals who built this temple at the promontory of Venus-Aphrodite would have brought their well-known oracular tradition that was founded at Delphi. The Rhodians who arrived here circa eighth-seventh centuries BCE had the Delphic tradition of oracles on their Aegean isle. These prophetesses were integral to decisions of state, religion, and for the common people, guiding nearly every aspect of life. Some say the Oracle of Delphi was founded by the Great Mother Goddess Gaia, and others say it was Themis, who we shall soon meet again at Empúries. The oracles were priestesses of Pythia (the Pythoness), who was related to Drakaina, a she-serpent guardian. Again, we find the serpent-dragon associations with the guardians of the ancient Pyrenean sites.

Watchtower of the Morning

The temple of Artemis at Hēmeroskopeion, Dénia, was about 290 miles (466 kilometers) south of the Cap de Creus temple of Venus-Aphrodite, on another great promontory reaching into the sea. (See illustration 3, Way of the Stars.) Hēmeroskopeion is a Greek term meaning "Watchtower of the Morning,"[8] which fits perfectly with the Guardians of the Eastern Gate. The lighthouse at Hēmeroskopeion looked across to the Island of Ibiza, and, as we know, the Balearic Islands of Majorca, Minorca, Ibiza, and Formentera were important landmarks for ships arriving from across the Mediterranean. Interestingly, the old name for Formentera was Ophiussa, evidence of the Ophite serpent wisdom healing sects that arrived in the West. We can also recall the theory proposed in chapter 4, "Is the Ca Ka?" regarding the Balearics and its serpent guardian of the island of Ka, based on Egyptian legends of Atlantis. The distance by sea between Ibiza and Hēmeroskopeion was only about 55 miles (88 kilometers).

Just 59 miles (95 kilometers) southwest of Hēmeroskopeion is the ancient Iberian settlement at La Alcudia, where the extraordinary Mother Goddess Lady of Elche was discovered, the Iberian priestess-queen whose image is on the cover. (We covered much of the history of the Lady of Elche in chapter 8.) This city was known as Ilice and was one the largest and most important sites on the coast, inhabited since Neolithic times. The Lady of Elche would have had an honored position in the Iberian temple as a guardian of the eastern coastline, and as some archeologists have mentioned, she may be related to the goddess Tanit. Tanit was known as "Queen of the Stars," and her priestesses were famous astrologers, known for their prophecies throughout the later Roman Empire.[9] As we discovered in chapter 8, Tanit was an aspect of Aphrodite and Astarte for the Carthaginians, and she may even be related to the Egyptian goddess Neith. This connection with Egypt is strengthened in the ancient annual mystery plays at Elche.

In *Egyptian Romany: The Essence of Hispania*, Moustafa Gadalla[10] tells of an annual ritual at Elche that joins the Egyptian and Christian mystery traditions. He says that on August 15th, Ascension Day of Mary, a musical theater is held at the cathedral of Elche, which he claims is based on an old Egyptian festival called "Bride of the Nile" that was held at the same time. The timing of the Christian Ascension Day marks the end of the annual "Lamentations of Isis" festival cycle, in which Isis and Nephthys have been mourning Osiris and their tears have filled the Nile, ensuring fertility of the realm. Of course, we can relate the tears of the Egyptian goddesses to the tears of Magdalena and Mother Mary for Jesus, another dying and rising god.

Gadalla says the "Elche Mystery" ritual goes back at least to medieval times when local tradition says an ark drifted ashore carrying an image of Mary and the texts and songs for a liturgical drama. Interestingly, the liturgy honors three Marias, the "Virgin" and her two companions. Gadalla says the Elche Mystery plays merged the goddess sisters Isis and Nephthys with two Marias, and he firmly believes that many traditions, including the musical styles and culture, were highly influenced by early Egyptian visitors. Which Mary is the question, since we will discover in future chapters, the strong Spanish traditions for the presence of four Marias: The Virgin, Maria Magdalena, Maria Jacobus, and Maria Salome, although it is very doubtful that the Virgin Mary ever came into the West. Her presence is more of an archetypal blending with Isis.

The Elche tradition of the ark and three Maries coming ashore is a repeating pattern that we have seen in the three Maries arriving in Gaul near another temple of Artemis at Marseilles. (Not far from Elche was the Artemis temple at Hēmeroskopeion.) The name Mary may have its origins in the Egyptian Mery and Meryt, meaning "Beloved," and it becomes clear how Isis, as the "Beloved Bride and Virgin of the Nile," would have been equated with Mary the mother, or Maria Magdalena, as the bride. The Egyptian lamentation rituals of Isis and Nephthys inspired my song "Tears of Isis," referenced in "Isis Sails to Phoenicia," chapter 5. Elche is in the heart of the region of flamenco tradition, and you can hear the flavors of Egypt and Spain featured in the song and music video linked in the footnote.[11] Interestingly, the French philosopher and historian Voltaire (1694-1778) described Spanish music and ritual customs as being descended from the Egyptian priests and priestesses of Isis.[12]

Elche and Hēmeroskopeion are only two of the impressive number of temples of the goddess that stood as guardians of Iberia's eastern gate, greeting the rising Sun, Moon, and stars, as well as weary travelers navigating from the far reaches of the Mediterranean and beyond. These temples anchored the sacred feminine traditions of the eastern Mediterranean in this new land in the west. And watching from above was the Egyptian Sky Mother Nut as the Milky Way, her feet at the Mediterranean and her breasts pouring light from distant star nebulas over Finisterre ("End of the Earth") at the western end of the Way of the Stars pilgrimage route. (See illustration 4, Way of the Stars.) According to Andrew Collins in *The Cygnus Key*:

"...she is depicted arching naked over the earth, her feet on one horizon and her fingers touching the other...Nut's body is festooned with stars...Clearly this is meant to imply that her body is itself a stream of stars—a reference to the Milky Way as it arches across the sky...the Milky Way becomes a shining arch stretching from horizon to horizon..."[13]

Nut, also spelled Nwt, Nuit, meaning "Sky," is seen arching over the Pyrenees, depending on the season and hour of the night. And this river of stars is not only an awesome visible phenomenon of our heavens, but science has also discovered a heavenly chorus emanating from the Milky Way. As mentioned earlier, fascinating research has discovered harmonically organized magnetic filaments at the center of the Milky Way. Astronomers have described these strands as being like the strings of a harp, so we can now imagine the Milky Way is not just filled with magnificent shining lights that mark the starry path, but also with a myriad of harmonic chords ringing across the sky. The Dendera temple inscription quoted at the beginning of the "Way of the Field of Stars" chapter begins to make more sense: "The sky and its stars make music in you."

CHAPTER 23
Pyrenean Star Gates

"... the dolmens located on that route [Way of the Stars], as well as the oldest temples, were located on the great fault caused by the impact of the plate of the Iberian Peninsula with the South of the European plate and the Cantabrian Sea."

Juan Saez, ***Lugares de poder***[1]

Magnetic anomalies along fault lines in the Pyrenees are well known to geologists, as discussed in chapter 2. It is likely that by placing dolmens and menhirs along the highly magnetic fault line, ancient temple builders would have utilized the sites as portals for rituals and interactions with their deities. Ancient people considered their sanctuaries as magical, places of the gods. Juan Saez mentioned on one of our journeys that the energy generated by the pressure of the tectonic plates is concentrated in megalithic and other sanctuaries along this route, generating intense sensations of wellbeing and enhancing altered states of consciousness.

In Paul Devereux's Dragon Project, its members measured ancient sites for decades and found a consistent presence of increased radiation that was being emitted from megalithic sites by radioactive elements such as uranium and radon. Their measurements registered magnetic anomalies, and increased magnetism readings that often coincided with sightings of plasma forms and unusual lights over the sites. These sites were located over fault lines and geological discontinuities, all of which were associated with stories of interdimensional activity.[2]

The megalithic structures built along the Pyrenean range interact with human consciousness, as well as the stars, as we have seen in the dolmen Creu d'en Cobertella. I have organized numerous pilgrimages in this region, and my guests have often commented that they feel closer to their origins and the spiritual realms at certain sites, and many have life-changing experiences. I spoke to a friend living in my village, a retired electrical engineer, and he commented that the Pyrenees fault is still active, and the Iberian plate is still slowly shifting north-eastward toward the European plate. He explained that the crystal and silica content compresses from the pressure created by the meeting of the plates, and several types of energy are released, including electromagnetic and infrared radiation. Discussing this with my friend Andrew Collins, he added, "This highly ionized environment is ripe for the creation of plasma and light phenomena and has subtle effects on the human brain and the body."

In addition to the terrestrial effects that are occurring, the stars are constantly interacting with the elements in the Earth and cracks in the crust at fault lines may be places where more galactic energy can access the inner Earth. English retired geological engineer and author Rory Duff believes that powerful cosmic energies from the center of the Milky Way and other galaxies are interacting with the elements deep inside the Earth. Duff says cosmic neutrinos enter the inner core of the Earth and then emanate out to the surface as energy lines. These are what he calls the "Emperor Dragon" lines mentioned in the introduction, some of the rarest measured fields of energy that traverse our planet. And to repeat, Duff says the greatest number of these Dragon lines are present across Spain and have been measured to emit the lowest infrasound frequency of any telluric current that he is aware of.

Duff explains that it is believed that the iron and nickel elements in the Earth's core attract the galactic energies such as neutrinos, one of the most abundant particles in the universe. As subatomic particles, they act similarly to an electron, but have very little mass, so are not affected, or scattered by matter, and freely move through it. If we can imagine being a neutrino, we could walk through walls, pass through human bodies, or fly freely through the stars. Neutrinos were discovered when they were detected up to eight kilometers deep within the Earth in gold and salt mines. Neutrinos have been measured from monitoring observatories deep within the Mediterranean Sea and within the ice sheets at the South Pole. The Antarctic observatory called "IceCube" announced in 2018 that they were able to trace the long journey of a high-energy neutrino that hit their station back to its source located 3.7 billion light-years away in the direction of the constellation Orion. The announcement appeared in the *New York Times* and was entitled, "It Came from a Black Hole and Landed in Antarctica."[3]

The stars are constantly interacting with the Earth and the complex energies created by our planet's orbit, gravity, and elements. (Previously I mentioned various practices to "imbibe" the light and knowledge from the stars, including the high energy neutrinos.) If we imagine the neutrinos that are entering the earth from far distant galaxies, what other cosmic energies from the stars are being absorbed by the Earth and all living things? And are the interactions between neutrinos and the Earth, as Rory Duff proposes, somehow connected with Dragon lines? Are the sites along the Dragon Path across the Pyrenees and the east-west path of the Camino communicating with the stars, and is this why people often have transcendent experiences at these sites? The answer is certainly yes, and as the frontiers of science expand and come to meet the interdimensional realms normally known only by mystics and shamans, we will continue to discover more about our magical and mysterious world. The ancient pilgrimage path reaching back more than six thousand years called The Way of the Stars is well-named. Not only is it mirroring the Milky Way, but it is also receiving particles and music from the stars.

Following the Star Path Westward to Cassiopeia

"Glory to Re in the east, when he rises in beauty eternal,
Shining like gold as he crosses the heights of the heavens.
Glory to Re in the west, when he passes to night and thick darkness ...
Grant that my path, like thine, may lead through the stars never wearied ...
Grant me to be renewed by the sight of thy beauty eternal."

Egyptian Book of the Dead[4]

The Way of the Stars departed from the Mediterranean, following the southern slopes of the Pyrenees westward along the 42° North latitude. As we have seen, the eastern end of the star route is marked with numerous megalithic stone monuments

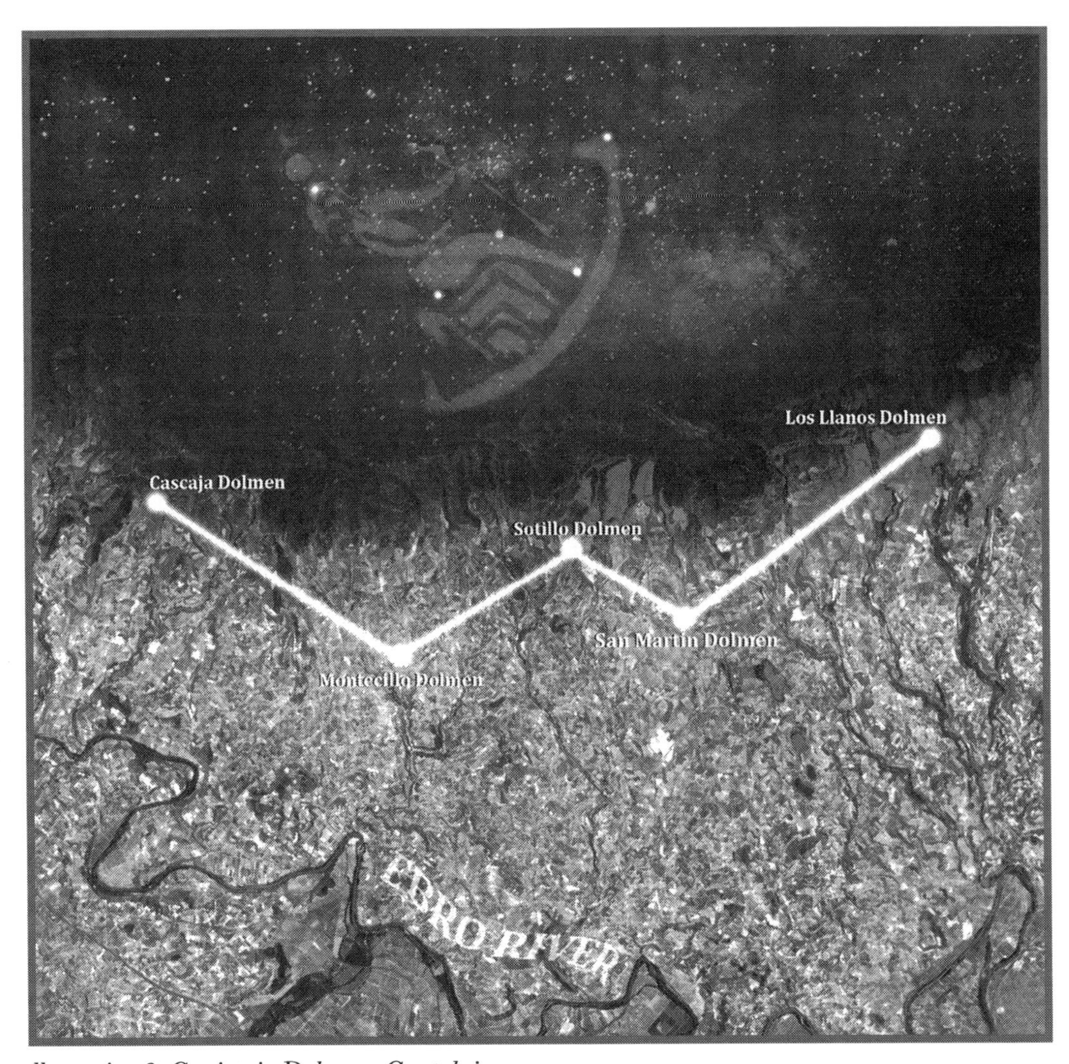

llustration 9: Cassiopeia Dolmens, Cantabria

and temples of the goddesses Aphrodite, Artemis, and Isis, as watchtowers of the eastern gate. And this eastern gateway to Iberia also forms the end of the eastern arm of the Great Cross. Additionally, there are no less than fourteen sanctuaries and mountains dedicated to Santa Magdalena located along this eastern arm of the cross, further confirming the importance of the Pyrenean cross alignment, perhaps placed in the Earth eons in the past.

Moving further west along the Way of the Stars into the Rioja region, we arrive at the halfway point of the journey between the Mediterranean and the Atlantic. It is here that we find nine dolmens, that were laid out in a pattern to mirror the constellation Cassiopeia. The dolmens are found along the base of the Sierra de Cantabria, a mountain range located at 42°58'N, 2°35' E, midway between the Cap de Creus and the cape of Finisterre. (See Milky Way illustration 4.) When Juan Saez was researching the megaliths of the Cantabria region, he noticed that nine dolmens were placed to mark the halfway point in the Camino, indicating that there was a master plan, a blueprint in the stars that guided the placement of ancient megalithic sites along the entire east-west route following the base of the mountains across Northern Spain.[5]

Juan discovered that the nine dolmens are laid out in a wide stretched "W" pattern mirroring Cassiopeia in what he calls a "dolmen cathedral," and that the stones are communicating with each other to create a unified force field. He reminds us that if we are receptive when we enter this energetic field, it can regulate and revitalize our body-mind, inspire feelings of lightness, happiness, and cause altered states of consciousness. Juan adds that this effect can even be experienced by consuming products grown in the region, as the coherent energy produced by the megalithic network affects the surrounding bio-fields. Perhaps this is why Rioja wine is so wonderful! Juan believes that a masterplan marked by stone structures in remote times marks the entire route of the "Megalithic Camino," the Way of the Stars.

Dendera Zodiac papyrus, Ursa Major as the bull's thigh, Draco as the hippopotamus Neith, Osiris as Cassiopeia.

The Cassiopeia constellation is at the northern end of the Milky Way, one of the circumpolar star groups, which slowly circles around the northern axis. This constellation is seen in various interesting ways by different cultures. Beginning with the Egyptians, in the zodiac pictured on the ceiling at the temple of Dendera, Cassiopeia was illustrated as Osiris seated on his iron throne, riding his sky boat, and is mentioned in Utterances 506 and 509 of the Pyramid Texts:

"O men and gods, your arms under me! Lift me up, raise me to the sky ... To the sky! To the sky! To the great throne among the gods!"[6]

"I ascend to the sky among the Imperishable Stars, my sister is Sothis [Sirius], my guide is the Morning Star, and they grasp my hand at the Field of Offerings. I sit on this iron throne of mine ..."[7]

The throne association for Cassiopeia is also found in Greek mythology, however, it is not Osiris but an extraordinarily beautiful Ethiopian queen who sits on her royal seat in the sky. Cassiopeia got into heaps of trouble when she boasted of her superior beauty and angered the sea nymphs. The siren-nymphs immediately appealed to Poseidon, the god of the sea, who sent a great water dragon to ravage the Ethiopian coasts. Cassiopeia's husband, King Cepheus, was desperate to save his land and immediately sought the advice of the Oracle of Ammon of Libya. Perhaps this was the well-known oracle at the temple of the Egyptian god Amun at Thebes, especially as all of North Africa was referred to as Libya in ancient times.

The temple oracle told Cepheus that if he wanted to save his kingdom, he must sacrifice his beautiful daughter Andromeda to the dragon. With great sadness, the king had young Andromeda tied to a cliff on the Ethiopian coast, but fate intervened in the form of the handsome and clever Perseus, who arrived riding his winged horse Pegasus. Perseus repelled and conquered the sea dragon with the powerful serpent-entwined head of Medusa, winning the day and the heart of the beautiful princess Andromeda.

Greek myth says that Andromeda's mother Cassiopeia was placed in the heavens upside down to humble her pride, but her position is one of the most notable constellations at the northern end of the Milky Way. Her tipped and extended W shape does indeed look like a throne, and Cassiopeia is surrounded by her family in the heavens in the constellations Andromeda, Cepheus, and Perseus.

The stars of Cassiopeia have been important for scientists in calculating the Paris Meridian and the measurement of the Earth's diameter. And astrophysicists discovered an interesting frequency emanating from Cassiopeia, broadcasting the strongest sound ever measured from outside of our solar system. The radio signal from Cassiopeia A, a supernova remnant, was the first to be measured in 1947, called the brightest astronomical radio source in the sky. It turns out that Cassiopeia is singing from her sky throne, and NASA has translated the frequency of the elements from the same exploded star to produce a short symphony![8]

Or is this music from the stars of Cassiopeia the god Osiris shouting at Earth, telling us of his long sky journey, and how he met up with Isis at Sothis and was guided by the goddess Neith, the mama Hippopotamus of Draco?

> *"I traverse the sky ... a third to Sothis [Sirius-Isis], pure of thrones. I have bathed in the pools of the morning, and the Cow [Hippo of Draco] who traverses the waters prepares my fair roads and guides me to the Great Throne which the gods made, which Horus made and which Thoth brought into being. Isis conceives me, Nephthys begets me, and I sit on the Great Throne [Cassiopeia] which the gods have made."*
>
> PYRAMID TEXTS, UTTERANCE 511[9]

In the North American indigenous legend of Star Woman, who also rides in a sky boat, we find a story most likely related to the constellation Cassiopeia. Several researchers in the field of ethnoastronomy have identified the constellation of Star Woman as being in the northern sky and the circumpolar stars. American ethnoastronomy researcher George Lankford relates an interesting story from the Shawnee people of the Southeastern United States called "The Celestial Skiff" in his book *Reachable Stars*.[10] The story says that Star Woman descended from the sky riding in a canoe, singing and laughing. During one of her visits to Earth, she was captured by a man who became enchanted by her beauty and her song. She must have enjoyed his adoration, as they married and had children, who learned their mother's songs for traveling to the stars.

After many years on Earth, Star Woman loaded her children in a canoe, leaving her husband behind, and they began to sing the songs of the stars as they lifted higher and higher to her home in the sky. The story says that after some time, and missing his family, her husband remembered lyrical patterns, and sang the star songs to rejoin his family. This familiar tradition of knowing the songs and singing, found in most indigenous cultures, is a prerequisite for the movement between the Earthly world and the Sky world, similar to the shamanic traditions of singing and drumming to open a portal between the dimensions. And in Egyptian cosmology, when Ra makes his nightly journey in a sky boat, there were magical incantations to recite for the opening of each of the gates, as described in the *Egyptian Book of the Dead*:

> *"Open the gates of Heaven, raise the gates of sky! ...*
> *Open, O Heaven! Open, O Earth! Open, O West! Open, O East! ...*

Illustration 21: Magdalena in Cassiopeia, in midheaven 22nd July at Perella

Let the doors be flung wide and the Nether World be opened ...
Open for him the gates, Oh Boat of the Evening;
fling wide for him the Nether World ..."[11]

We can't leave Cassiopeia without mentioning that none other than Maria Magdalena once occupied this sky throne. In the 17th century, an effort was made to convert the celestial constellations into a Christian pantheon, although the new system didn't find enough public support and faded from popular memory. A German mapmaker, amateur astronomer, and devout Catholic named Julius Schiller published *Coelum Stellatum Christianum*, *"Christian Starry Heaven"* (1627), which was effectively his swan song, as he died the same year. As Gretchen Cornwall points out in *The Secret Dossier of a Knight Templar of the Sangreal*,[12] putting Magdalena on the throne moves her into the position of "Queen of Heaven," and strangely, Schiller did not place Mother Mary in his heavenly array. This is indeed curious, as he was a prominent man of the Church. What was his motive? Was he inspired by the writings of Rabanus Maurus on the life of Maria Magdalena? To repeat the earlier quote, Rabanus describes Magdalena's death scene when Jesus appeared before her:

"... Come my beloved, and I shall place you on my throne, for the king desires your beauty, more lovely than any of the sons of men ... Rejoice and exult forever amidst the heavenly choirs."[13]

We don't know Schiller's reasons, other than his having a special devotion to Magdalena. However, placing her in Cassiopeia is not arbitrary, and we find interesting parallels in the Rennes-le-Château mysteries. Kaj Lilliendal found a telling alignment that occurs at sunrise on Magdalena's feast day, the 22nd of July. The line runs from her church in Rennes-le-Château through a menhir called Roc Blanc (White Rock), continuing northeast to a hilltop called Cazopie (Cassiopeia).[14] This provides a wonderful link between Magdalena and Cassiopeia, with the addition of a megalith marking the rising Sun on her feast day. Additionally, Kaj states that this date is when Cassiopeia is closest to the zenith (midheaven), another celestial time-marker linking Magdalena to this constellation and her feast day.

As I gazed at the night sky from a position on the Paris Meridian in the Pyrenean foothills during the third week of July, Cassiopeia was indeed directly overhead, aligned north/south. This means that at the time of her Feast Day, her chapels located along the Magdalena Meridian are aligned and resonating with this constellation of the enthroned Queen of the Northern Sky. We can imagine that Cassiopeia is singing above the Magdalena chapels and ringing in the dolmens of Cantabria. Symphonies of frequencies and light particles are raining down from the starry path of the Milky Way, onto the countless stone sanctuaries along the Way of the Stars and along the Dragon Path. And this timeless miracle of the universe is enacted in the ancient tradition of the pilgrims who sang as they walked this long path.

Camino de Canciones

"It is unique in human history that thousands of miles in this area [Camino de Compostela] were suffused with singing ... this singing lasted for centuries, and, naturally, it lives on in the ether realm."

VIRGINIA SEASE AND MANFRED SCHMIDT-BRABANT,
PATHS OF THE CHRISTIAN MYSTERIES[15]

The ancient pilgrimage of the Camino de Santiago de Compostela has always been a *Camino de Canciones*, a Spanish phrase meaning a "Way of Songs." And before that, for at least six thousand years, Neolithic people and transhumance travelers using the ancient Pyrenean star route sang as they walked. *Andando y cantando* ("Walking and singing" in Spanish) is a tradition that is inseparable from the land, and the people who walked across France, Spain, Catalonia, and Portugal. The songs were a way of connecting with the Earthly and Divine, weaving a unity between the people and the places, and singing gave strength and courage for the long road.

The quote above speaks of the longevity of the songs sung along the Camino and how they endure in the subtle realms. Perhaps you have had the experience of being somewhere and hearing a distant sound, perhaps in an old monastery, and hearing the echo of choirs chanting and wondering if it was only in your imagination. This subtle "hearing" has guided much of my quest as well as musical compositions received over the last decades, and there are numerous examples that may one day become another book. A few brief memories come to mind. One was in Edinburgh, Scotland, at a home in which I was a guest. I kept hearing a soft chanting that seemed to infuse the air, and when I asked my hostess if she heard it, she said she didn't, but mentioned that her home was once a medieval monastery.

Another occasion was during a week in Dartmoor, Devon, England when a friend and I were staying in an old farmhouse alongside an ancient trackway once used by the Celts and in modern times by the wild Dartmoor ponies. One night about midnight, a white stallion was whinnying as he waited on the track, just below my window. Earlier that day at sunset, I had run with his herd for a short distance, inspired by the sense of freedom and strength of their stride, although, of course, I couldn't keep up with their pace. I greeted the proud stallion, who was obviously trying to draw my attention outside, and then I heard it, a haunting melody coming from across the moor. I sensed it was the memory of the ancient ones who had chanted at the nearby Scorhill Stone Circle, and immediately found the melody on the harp, which became the song "Voices of the Moor."[16]

Another time at West Kennet Long Barrow in Wiltshire, England, on a summer solstice, I heard a song emanating from the stones of the burial chamber constructed about six thousand years ago. The words were in an unfamiliar tongue, and I immediately repeated the melody and words with the frame drum I had, and it was recorded as the song "Earth Mother."[17] Interestingly, when we played the song in concert in Glastonbury years later, a woman in the audience claimed she heard the same exact melody emanating from the stones at West Kennet. When we stop our busy minds and listen, the subtle realms of sound sometimes become audible.

Along the various routes of the Camino de Santiago de Compostela, chapels, monasteries, and hermitages dedicated to the saints, including Santa Magdalena, were places to rest and pray. As we saw in the Magdalene Path chapter, every Magdalena site has its own *goig*, a devotional song not only honoring her various attributes, but often describing the uniqueness of the site and its location. Songs to Mother Mary were also sung along the Camino and are preserved in several collections, such as the medieval *Las Cantigas de Santa Maria*. The courts of medieval Spain incorporated Christian, Jewish, and Arab musical styles, and these cultures lived together harmoniously for long periods.[18]

Walking for many days, often traversing arduous paths and mountains of spectacular beauty, praying, and singing, often produced visions and mystical experiences. Appearances perceived as Mary were most common, and there are hundreds of Marian visions documented by the Catholic Church in Spain from medieval times. Her appearances created additional Marian pilgrimages that emerged over the centuries in Spain and other countries. Sometimes she appeared as a young woman wearing a red or white cloak, whom they simply called Nuestra Dama, "Our Lady." For others, she was Sophia, the Mother of the World, and her identity surpassed the personages of Mother Mary or Magdalena. When she appeared, she was often singing, and her presence was preceded by heavenly sounds like multitudes of bells or polyphonic birdsong. Many experienced her surrounded with rainbow colors and the fragrance of flowers, and always radiating extraordinary light.[19]

Opening doorways of perception has always been an important function of music. In addition to serving as a dimensional bridge, music moves us beyond any perceived differences in culture, belief systems, and language. Medieval Spanish culture was a musical mélange, rooted in ancient Iberian, Egyptian, Phoenician, Greek, and Carthaginian influences. This music later added Judaic, Visigothic, and Arabic styles, and in regions where Christians were living with Moslem influence, the people were called *Mozárabes* and their musical blend was termed *Mozarabic*. Their music celebrated the divine feminine in a continuation of Spain's ancient goddess traditions:

"The Mozarabic rite is of considerable interest to scholars, by reason of its strange formulae and passionate Mariolatry; but it seemed very near heresy to the more orthodox Christians ..."[20]

J. B. Trend, *The Civilization of Spain*

The most popular surviving piece from the Mozarabic rite is *Ordo Prophetarum*, from the Latin meaning "Procession of the Prophets." It was originally derived from pagan ritual music dedicated to the goddess Sibyl and even included the Queen of Sheba as a character in the liturgical drama. This musical is still performed at Christmas at the Cathedral of Santiago de Compostela, with roles including the Biblical prophets, pagan goddesses, and the Messiah.[21] A variation called "The Song of Sibyl" is still performed for Midnight Mass at the Cathedral of Valencia (site of a Grail Chalice), on Majorca, and Sardinia.

One of the most important collections of liturgical music of Catalonia and Spain survives in the 14th-century *Llibre Vermell*, the "Red Book" of Montserrat, named for its crimson velvet protective cover. Sadly, the great fire at the monastery during the 1808 Napoleonic War destroyed most of the extraordinary library, and this was one of the only books to survive. The text was written by an unnamed monk, who gathered ten songs from the 12th and 13th centuries with songs in Latin, Occitan, Catalan, and including five dances. The monk writes in *Llibre Vermell*:

"Pilgrims wanted to sing and dance to stay alert at night in the Church of Blessed Mary of Montserrat, but also in daylight. Moreover, singing was only allowed in the church if they remained chaste and pious ... taking care not to upset those who were immersed in prayer or contemplative devotion."[22]

Having been to Montserrat many times, it is wonderful to imagine dancing and singing occurring day and night in the great cathedral. I had an opportunity to watch one of the dances that may have been performed during the medieval era in Montserrat, the Catalan round dance *Sardana*. Many authorities believe it may be a surviving remnant of Catalonia's early Greek and pre-Roman dances.[23]

It was on a summer solstice, June 23rd, during the fire lighting ritual of Saint John the Baptist at Vernet-les-Bains, located below Mount Canigó in the French Pyrenees. The solstice torch had been carried by runners in a serpentine procession from high on the mountain and arrived in a plaza near the Canigó route by late morning. The flame was celebrated with dozens of children singing and dancing, all wearing traditional red Phrygian caps. These conical hats originated in 14th century

BCE Anatolia, worn by Phrygian slaves, and evolved into a revered symbol of freedom and independence. It is a beloved symbol of the passionate, independent spirit of Catalan people that continues today.

Later that afternoon a great bonfire was lit from the same flame in the town's central plaza, and adults danced the Sardana with live musical accompaniment. The woman sitting next to me, who had driven up to Vernet from Prades for the day, joined the circle of dancers. I was hypnotized by the complex, fluid movements. She was a large woman, yet her feet nimbly traced the patterns on the ground, as light as air, and she appeared to be almost floating. My new friend explained that this beloved dance, as well as Catalan traditional music, was banned during the Franco regime as threatening to the national order. Perhaps Franco was right to feel threatened, as music and dance create coherence and unity, a force far more powerful than any dictatorship. I marveled at the longevity of cultural traditions that resurface over and over and can never be totally suppressed.

One important song shared on the Camino de Santiago de Compostela from the 12th century is *Canto de Ultreya* from the *Codice Calixtino,* also called the *Liber Sancti Jacobi* (*Book of Saint James*), a pilgrim's handbook of songs, legends, and travel information. *Canto de Ultreya* has been sung by pilgrims for a millennium as a greeting on the Camino and can still be heard being sung every day in the cathedral of Santiago. *Ultreya* meaning "go further, go beyond," is an old Latin greeting on the long road to Santiago. Here is an excerpt of the English translation of the lyrics, a message of hope, strength, and vision:

"Every morning we take to the Way,
Every morning we go further.

Further, Further, and Higher,
God, help us!

"The Way of the Earth and the Way of Faith,
Millenium Route of Europe,
The Milky Way of Charlemagne,
It is the Route of the Pilgrims to Santiago.

Further, Further, and Higher,
God, help us! ..."[24]

Singing as we navigate our life paths was nearly as essential as food and water to the ancient people. Basilius Valentinus, a 15th century CE German alchemist, Hermetic philosopher, and Benedictine monk said:

"The psalm drives the demons away and draws the help of the angels close. It is the work of the angels, the heavenly consecration, the spiritual incense..."[25]

The psalms of pilgrims on the Camino infused the land and all living things with this *spiritual incense*, transforming the dark places in themselves, the music maintaining their state of reverence. The songs emanated an enchantment all along the pilgrimage roads. Their singing gave them strength, courage, and connection and were offerings to the gods. And the memory of their songs and prayers inseminated the stones and mountain valleys for all time. The Way of the Stars is the most ancient and continually used pilgrimage route known on our planet and has left an indelible legacy of sacred tradition. It has kept alive the importance of pilgrimage and its gift of renewal, the return to the center of one's being, to what truly matters in our lives. Walking these paths today, our feet mirror the footprints of the ancients, who also followed the movement of the stars, from east to west. The old Spanish saying, *andando y cantando*, became a song, a tribute to all those who have walked the long road of the Way of the Field of Stars. (This song is included in the *Guardians of the Dragon Path* album, linked in the following footnote.)

Andamos y Cantamos (We are Walking and Singing).

"Andamos y cantamos
El camino de la vida
Andamos y cantamos
El camino a llegar
Andar cantar, andar cantar"[26]

Translation:
"We are walking, and we are singing along the road of life.
We are walking and we are singing along the road to arrive.
To walk, to sing, to walk, to sing."

Illustration 8: Flower of Life and temples of Empúries

CHAPTER 24

Five Keys and the Flower of Life

"Hafiz drops keys all night long for the self-imprisoned souls,
Keys to unbolt the door to mysteries known by gods and sages.
Rumi tells us, you are the key, become the key."

The author paraphrasing two great medieval Persian poets,
Rumi and Hafiz

It was time to return to Empúries and an extraordinary circle of five temples, all located within a short walk. The Way of the Stars that commenced at Cap de Creus (Temple of Venus-Aphrodite) had a southern branch that departed from the Artemesian temple at Sant Marti at Empúries, 13.7 miles (22 kilometers) to the south. This ancient road is labeled GR 1 on modern maps of the region, perhaps being the first numbered local road. Just to the west of Sant Marti, the GR 1 intersects with GR 92, which connects the northern sites of Roses (Rhodes), Cap de Creus, and the monastery Sant Pere de Rodes, built over a previous temple of Venus-Aphrodite. In other words, these roads connected ancient temple sites from at least 600 BCE.

Three roads intersect at a hamlet called Cinclaus, or *cinc claus*, meaning "five keys or clues" in Catalan. These roads included the GR 1, GR 92 and an unnamed track that connects to the temples at the Greek city of Empúries. We have already spoken about the importance and antiquity of three-way tracks that were normally marked with wayside stone crosses, and at Cinclaus, it was a Templar stone cross on the chapel dedicated to Saint John the Baptist. The chapel was built over earlier Roman ruins, perhaps a temple to one of their gods or goddesses, most likely over an earlier Greek or Iberian temple.

First documented in 958 CE, the village of Cinclaus had a castle owned by a family of knights, and the medieval bridge, entry gate, and tower are still visible. The village is now a tiny hamlet, but sits at the crossroads leading to the Via Augusta, the Via Romana, and the Compostela route to the north. What are the five keys of Cinclaus? My Catalan friend who lives near to the site said that there were five homes in this tiny hamlet. Okay, that is a logical, mundane reason for the name, but there must be an older meaning to the five keys, given that it sits at the crossroads leading to major temples and centers of trade for the Mediterranean. According to the tourist information posted next to the old castle, in the past there were at least a hundred buildings at Cinclaus.

Every time I have stopped at the hamlet's small chapel, I have sensed some ancient mystery, as if the stones held a secret, the same stones recycled throughout the ages. Within an arc of less than a mile (1.61 kilometers) from Cinclaus, there are five ancient temple sites, including the fourth century CE ruins of a Santa Magdalena church, an earlier necropolis, and the remains of much earlier temples of Artemis, Isis, Serapis, and Asclepius. Five temples, providing five keys? And almost unbelievably, these five sites surround a large mosaic "Flower of Life" design built during the first century BCE.

Flower of Life.

On a hill to the west of the Greek city of Empúries, the Romans built a separate city in about 100 BCE. The extraordinary Flower of Life mosaic is still visible today measuring approximately 4 feet (1.22 meters) in diameter, which decorated the floor of a Roman villa. If we mark the heart of the Flower of Life as the center point and then use the Egyptian method of stretching a cord to the furthest of the temples at Santa Magdalena, we have a radius of 0.44 miles (0.7 kilometers), and we can draw a circle enclosing all five key sites. Each site is within a five-minute walk from the center.

This concentration of five temples surrounding the Flower of Life is significant and unique, with sites dedicated to Maria Magdalena, Artemis, Isis, Serapis, and Asclepius-Hygeia, all within a radius of less than a mile, and it may be the only such example in the world. Additionally, there is a fourth century chapel to Santa Margarida, who we will meet shortly, as her story involves dragons. Five keys represented by five world wisdom teachers and their temples surrounding the Flower of Life, a pattern symbolizing beauty, harmony, and perfection. We find the Flower of Life designs around the world, two examples being at the Osirian complex at Abydos, Egypt, and at the Library of Celsus at Ephesus, Turkey, the location of the cult of Artemis.

Looking at the entire layout and development of Empúries, two adjoining Greek cities were established, Palaiapolis ("Old City") and Neapolis ("New City"), with a later Roman city established on the hill above. All three cities overlooked the gorgeous scenic coves of the Mediterranean, surrounded by two important rivers, the Fluviá and the Ter. (The courses of the two rivers have altered over the centuries, with the Fluviá now meeting the sea to the north, and the Ter to the south.) Remember, the Ter descends from the high Pyrenees from its source at Ull de Ter, "Eye of the Earth," and passes numerous Magdalena sites before it merged with the sea at Empúries, where we have one of the earliest known Santa Magdalena sites in Spain. The path of this river followed her fragrance, magnetized by the power concentrated at the sites of some of the most revered female archetypes.

Palaiapolis was established circa 575 BCE at what is now the modern-day village of Sant Marti, over an earlier Iberian settlement, inhabited since at least the end of the Bronze Age, 10th-8th centuries BCE. The Iberians must have been trading with the Phoenicians, as fragments of their pottery were found at Sant Marti dating to the seventh century BCE.[1] At that time, Palaiapolis was an island with a narrow isthmus, surrounded by the mouth of the Fluviá and the Mediterranean. It was here that the Phocaean settlers (from modern day Turkey) founded a temple dedicated to Artemis of Ephesus. The decorated foundation stones of the original temple can be seen under the present church which was built utilizing the stones and original foundation of the temple. White alabaster perfume jars were found at the site, and a white alabaster memorial stone set into the pavement at the church entry is inscribed in Greek letters with the name of Artemis of Ephesus.

Artemis of Ephesus site marker, Sant Marti.

The temple stood on a rocky eastern-facing promontory overlooking the aquamarine sea and must have been an incredibly elegant white-columned edifice with the expansive Mediterranean coastline backdrop. Discoveries were made at the site of two stone sphinxes that archeologists believe decorated a temple wall, and a capital in Ionian style from a temple column.[2] What additional treasures of her temple might be lying under the current church? But, unfortunately, excavations under the church are not allowed. Let us look at each of the five sites, and the five keys they provide.

The Coming of Artemis and the Lyre of Orpheus

"For thee [Artemis] ... in Ephesus beside the sea [was] established an image beneath an oak trunk, and Hippo [Queen of the Amazons] performed a holy rite for thee, and they ... around the image danced a war-dance—first in shields and armour, and again in a circle arraying a spacious choir. And the loud pipes thereto piped shrill accompaniment, that they might foot the dance together ..."

CALLIMACHUS OF CYRENE, *HYMN TO ARTEMIS,* 3RD CENTURY BCE[3]

The Greek geographer and historian Strabo described the Greek-Phocaeans being driven from their Ionian homeland by invasions from Persia and arriving as exiles in Gaul and Iberia, bringing their essential goddess tradition with them. His account tells of the dream of a woman from Ephesus named Aristarche, who was guided to board a ship heading for the western frontiers, taking with her a replica of the temple of Artemis. There were several temples established to the goddess in the west, at Marseilles, Empúries, and Hēmeroskopeion, with the last two sites being on the Iberian coast. When a new temple was established, a temple model or statue of the deity would traditionally be brought to the new location in a "transference" ritual. The tradition included receiving a dream or oracular guidance regarding how this transfer should be accomplished, preserving the integrity and resonance of the home temple, which in this case was overseen by Artemis. Here is Strabo's account:

> *"It has been said that when the Phocaeans were setting sail from their homeland, they heard a voice which told them to name as head of their expedition the man chosen by the Goddess Artemis of Ephesus. Having sailed towards Ephesus, they looked for a way to discover the chosen one. One day, Aristarche, one of the most respected women in the city, had dreams in which she saw the Goddess standing in front of her, telling her to embark with the Phocaeans and take with her a model of the sanctuary. The colonists carried out this command and when they reached the end of their expedition, they built the sanctuary and bestowed the highest honours on Aristarche by making her a priestess ..."*[4]

Thus, Artemis arrived in the West. In Greek myths, Artemis and Apollo were twins born to the Olympian gods Zeus and Leto, with Artemis representing the Moon, and Apollo, the Sun. The twins were both skilled with the bow and arrow and played the music of the spheres on their lyres. It may have been the design of the curved bow with a single string that gave rise to the idea of adding more strings to make the first lyre. Perhaps one day an Amazon idly plucked her bowstring out of boredom and noticed the tone. In the male way of the tale, is said that Thoth-Hermes invented the seven-stringed lyre and gave it to Apollo, who in turn gave a lyre to Orpheus. I'm sure Artemis had her lyre, however, we normally only hear about her bow.

About the time that I began visiting the sites at Empúries and writing about Artemis, she began to appear in dreams and meditations, instructing me in various things. One night, she came in a dream sequence, teaching me how to make a wooden bow—how to bend and string it properly. I assembled the materials from what I could find around the house (still in the dream) and was in the process of bending an old wooden rake handle and stringing it with clothesline. A man suddenly appeared, jeering at my progress, saying that I couldn't build a bow that way. But when I ignored him, he disappeared. Carl Jung comments on the importance of not allowing any interference with our visions and dreams. He recommends not allowing any intruder that does not belong, as the dream contains all that it needs. Anyway, it was a magical bow and perhaps the Cyclopes would refine my crude bow, as they did for Artemis. The following is from the beginning of the Hymn to Artemis by Callimachus, who was a poet and scholar at the Library of Alexandria during the third century BCE:

> *"And give me arrows and a bow—stay, Father,*
> *I ask thee not for quiver or for mighty bow:*
> *for me the Cyclopes will straightway fashion*
> *arrows and fashion for me a well-bent bow.*
> *But give me to be the Bringer of Light and give*
> *me ... a tunic with embroidered border reaching*
> *to the knee ...And give me sixty daughters of*
> *Oceanus for my choir..."*[5]

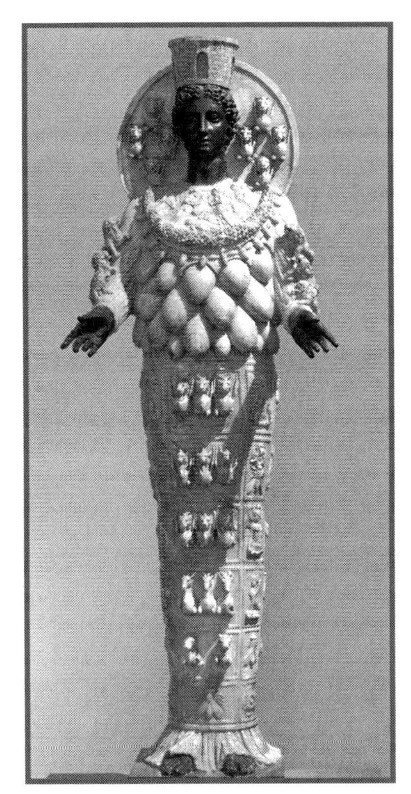

Artemis of Ephesus, 2nd c CE alabaster bronze, Naples Archaeo Museum, Marie-Lan Nguyen, 2011.

In this quote, Callimachus indicates that although Artemis was a famed huntress, she was more concerned about being a "Bringer of Light" and having her female choir of singers. She was a famed huntress and would deal swiftly with any who would threaten her domain, a fierce protectress of all that is wild in nature, and a guardian of childbirth. It is said that her earlier temples offered refuge to the Amazons who were fleeing the abuse of Dionysus and later Theseus. Or perhaps Artemis was their queen. Artemis is associated with the crescent or waxing Moon, and she is often portrayed as black, one of the earliest representations of the Black Madonna. Anne Baring and Jules Cashford in *The Myth of the Goddess* write that in her blackness, she is most likely related to Cybele, the Great Mother Goddess of Anatolia, and that through her, we can trace the various manifestations of the goddess from Neolithic times. We can find the bow also held by Inanna, the Sumerian Mother Goddess, and she is crowned by the star Sirius, which they called the "Bow Star,"[6] These patterns and archetypes continue through time, the names changing, but the essence remains.

It is indeed interesting that "The Song of Sibyl" (the later Latin spelling of Cybele) is a Mozarabic musical still performed today in Spain, a remnant of the ancient Mother Goddesses of Anatolia, whose memories seeded the entire Mediterranean cultures. And this ancient mother, portrayed as black as night, a creatress of life out of the void, gave her potency to Artemis as well as the matrix (matrice) of Black Madonnas throughout Europe.

In her image at Ephesus, Artemis has breasts in the form of numerous bee cocoons, and she wears a cape with the twelve constellations, signifying her as a goddess of fertility and a celestial guardian. Artemis was known as the Great She-Bear of Ursa Major at the northern axis of the sky:

> *"...ruler of the stars and protectress of the axis mundi,*
> *Pole of the World, marked in heaven by the Pole Star..."*[7]

We can understand this association of Artemis with Ursa Major by looking at the etymology of her name. *Ar* relates to the root syllable *ars, urs*, meaning "bear," as in King Arthur, relating him also to the Great Bear constellation. The second part of her name *temis* or *themis*, is a Greek word meaning "divine law, order, time," linking her with Themis, goddess of divine justice. Hence, Artemis is named for the cycles of time and the turning of the axis mundi, connecting the Earth with the northern stars. Themis, Cardea, and Artemis are all associated with the starry castle at the northern gate of the sky.

Artemis as the "She-Bear" of Ursa Major was traditionally celebrated with young girls dressed in bear skins in a dance called the "Arkteia." The girls would stomp their feet and chant, imitating the slow movements of a She-Bear, and turn in a circle as drums, double flutes, lyres, and voices guided the increasing intensity and rhythms.

Artemis continued to appear in my daily life and provide guidance and inspiration. One morning during a breathing meditation, she came as the sound of a thousand bees rising in my spine, creating a strong buzzing in my ears, most likely a kundalini experience. (In addition to the breasts of Artemis of Ephesus being shaped like bee cocoons, her oracular bee nymphs, called "Melissa," fed honey to the gods.) In her role as a guardian of the light and knowledge of the stars entering at the northern gate, she appeared in the middle of the night showing images of the turning of the hinge at the northern axis, and how it related to the north-south meridian of the Dragon Path across the Pyrenees in the great landscape cross that had begun to reveal itself.

These visions and dreams of Artemis during this period became the lyrics of a song entitled "Dance of Artemis," recorded on the album *Dragon & Pearl.* The melody and rhythm of the piece reflects the image of young women dancing as She-Bear Amazons, stamping their feet under a crescent moon. During one of the pilgrimages that I led to Empúries, one of the participants was a professional dancer and brought an Artemis deer antler mask that she sometimes used in ritual performance. The group gathered at the sea below the cliffs of the original Artemis temple, and we sang and danced for her, bringing her memory to life. "Finally," she must have whispered, "I am honored again at this site where thousands of tourists pass by and never remember me or call my name."

"Artemis lady of the wilds
Dance in us your wild heartedness
Artemis of the crescent Moon
Fearless Amazon, Mother Earth renewing,
Wild and free, O, dance in me. (repeat)

Artemis lady of the bees
Prophetess teaching us to see
Artemis golden nectar dripping
Honey-voiced siren, enchant the stars to sing
Wild and free, O, sing in me. (repeat)

Artemis Great Bear Mother turning
Ursa Major high above us turning
Artemis round the polestar humming
Spinning, spinning, round the center turning
Sing in me, your magical turning,
Dance in me, celestial turning. (repeat)"[8]

The New City and Temples of Isis and Serapis

"... in the prow of the Boat stands Isis, the great enchantress, whose magic none can withstand; Isis, the greatest of goddesses, she who can raise the dead, and to whom all mankind pay love and reverence. With arms outstretched, she recites the Words of Power; ..."

M. A. Murray, *Ancient Egyptian Legends*[9]

Neapolis was the second Greek city to be established in the sixth century BCE as an expansion of Palaiapolis when the trade and population at the small island city increased. Neapolis is now called Empúries, from the Roman Latin word for market or trade city. It rapidly became a distribution center for goods traded between the Levant and the Iberian coast, and was surrounded with watchtowers to notify the city of ships carrying visitors from afar. As mentioned, Isis was the goddess who controlled the sea, to whom all sailors prayed for safe passage. Upon their arrival in the harbor, paying homage and making an offering at her temple would be expected.

Neapolis featured a large temple district at the southern end of the city, which included separate healing shrines and porticos (columned structures) dedicated to Isis, Serapis, Asclepius, and earlier, to Hygeia. All overlooked the sea, each temple containing a series of columned sanctuaries that rivaled the beauty of the turquoise waters and the rocky shore below. The fourth-century CE Roman soldier and historian Ammianus Marcellinus writes a beautiful description of the Alexandrian Serapeum, and although the Empúries Serapeum would have been smaller, the Iberian sanctuary was nevertheless inspired by the design of the great temple next to the Library of Alexandria:

Isis and Serapis art by Giulio Ferrario, Africa Vol 1.

> *"... the Serapeum ... is so adorned with extensive columned halls, with almost breathing statues, and a great number of other works of art, that next to the Capitolium ... the whole world beholds nothing more magnificent."*[10]

During the fourth to third centuries BCE, Egypt underwent a great transition when it was conquered by Alexander the Great (332 BCE) and Ptolemaic Greek rule was established. In an attempt by Ptolemy I to unite the Egyptian and Greek people and their religions, Osiris was absorbed into Serapis, integrating the fertility and solar cult of the Apis bull as well as the sky god Zeus. Serapis became the transformed consort of Isis and was known in Egypt as Osiris-Apis, or Usar-Api. The new god was often depicted with his two allies, *kerberos kai drakōn* (Greek for "Cerberus the dog and the serpent-dragon"), companions he shares with Asclepius, the god of medicine. (We met Cerberus earlier as the guardian of the underworld, who was enchanted by Orpheus and conquered by Hercules, perhaps at the Iberian Cap de Creus, according to legend.) Serapis wore a *Kalathos*, an Egyptian crown symbolizing abundance, one of which was recovered at Empúries,[11] one of the many traditions from both Greece and Egypt that formed the cultural mélange in the West.

Two engraved stones were uncovered beneath a watchtower next to the temples of Isis and Serapis that state that a wealthy man named Noumas from Alexandria commissioned and paid for the building of the temple to Serapis and, most likely, Isis.[12] Another inscribed fragment of marble from the base of a statue of Harpocrates (the later Greek absorption of Horus) was dedicated to Isis: "*M. Opsio Navio Fannianus,*"[13] perhaps indicating Fannianus as another doner to her temple, or the owner of a ship that carried one of her statues from a Greek marble foundry, as *Navio* means "Ship." In the temple sector toward the sea from the main city entrance at the south end of Empúries, archeologists identified a temple to Isis reminiscent of her Egyptian sanctuaries.

"O Serpent! I am the flame which shineth upon the Opener of hundreds of thousands of years, and the standard of the god Tenpu [snake-headed protector] . . ."

THE BOOK OF THE DEAD[14]

As we can see from the illustration of Isis and Serapis, both are wrapped in an ascending serpent, signifying medicine, regeneration, and wisdom. The late cults of Isis in Greco-Roman culture outlived not only Osiris but also most of the old gods, continuing until the fourth century CE across the entire Mediterranean and enduring until the sixth century CE at Philae.[15] She has been represented as winged, identifying her as a sky goddess, "Lady of Heaven," seated and enthroned with the power of rulership, and with the serpent, her chthonic, underworld aspect. She danced freely between the realms of Heaven, Earth, and the underworld, and was called the one "Great in Magic."

Numerous images of Hermes, the Greek name for Thoth, Djehuty, the wise councilor of Egypt, were found in Empúries excavations and as funerary offerings in the adjoining necropolis. At least one bronze image of Hermes was found at Rhodes, the neighboring city to the north. The trade cities of Empúries and Rhodes stood at the southern and northern edges of the Gulf of Roses, only 9.5 miles (15 kilometers) apart, bringing the Alexandrian Hermetic mystery traditions and the Gnostic and Ophite schools of wisdom from the Isle of Rhodes into the west at the foot of the Pyrenees. The ancient wisdom of the *Corpus Hermeticum,* the wisdom of Thoth-Hermes, was called by some scholars the "bible" of the Egyptian Serapis mysteries.

Isis, 1st c. CE alabaster, Hadran's Villa, Palazzo Nuovo, Capitoline Museum, photo Carole Raddoto.

Both the Serapis and Isis cults were associated with the serpents of healing and renewal, and outside the entry of the *Isieon,* "Temple of Isis," at Neapolis, several small serpent offerings were uncovered. During this era, serpents were the signatures of guardianship and, as such, were the protectors of Neapolis. Similar to the tradition at Alexandria, these guardians were the male and female serpent deities *Agathos Daimon* (meaning "Good Spirit") and *Agathe Tyche* ("Good Fortune"), both providing protection, health, and all manner of guidance.[16] A coiled serpent in stone would have guarded the entrance to the Serapeum, and before entering the sanctuaries, a person would ritually wash their hands and feet with the holy water provided in a *perirrhanterion* (ablutions basin).

There would have been numerous statues of the gods and goddesses in the two temples, but little remains to their testimony. Two sculpted feet of a woman wearing sandals were recovered, identical to statues of Isis in Italy and Greece of the same period. Site archeologists assume that the feet belonged to a statue of Isis that stood at the entrance to her temple, similar to the illustration, in which Isis is holding in her right hand the sistrum, the magical rattle to accompany her invocations, and in her left, a vase of libations, the image also associated with Magdalena. The temple statues are believed to have been carved in the eastern Mediterranean and then shipped to Iberia. Isis, Lady of Enchantments, healing, and "Ruler of the Sea," had taken flight on the great ships across the Mediterranean, spreading her wings of protection over the new world.

In the time of the Roman Empire half of the sailors in the imperial fleet were recruited in Egypt and in the Hellenistic East. They traveled all over the "Old World" as soldiers and sailors of merchant ships. Egyptian cults, for example, spread from the seaports into the mainland through the major ports.

> *...Merchants were very movable and they brought over some new ideas and religious beliefs throughout the Roman Empire. Most of them were originally from Egypt and the East. In the places where they raised their families they often formed ... religious* collegiums *of Isis and Serapis."*[17]

Serapis and Isis shared many attributes, as healers, overseers of the elements, and protectors for sailors. Professor Mladen Tomorad of the University of Zagreb describes the goddess Isis as she was known by those establishing her temples in the West: "Mother of the Pharaoh, Mistress of Heaven, the goddess of Eternity and of Resurrection, the life giver and from the 3rd century BC as the Ruler of the Sea."[18] And in Egyptian poetry Isis is "... Mistress of the Gods, Mistress of Magic, she is the skilful Healer, in her mouth is the Breath of Life, by her words she destroys pain and by her power she awakes the dead."[19] Isis was all-pervading, and the first-century Greco-Roman authors Proclus and Plutarch claimed there was an inscription on a temple statue dedicated to her in Sais, in the Nile Delta, which read, "I am all that has been and is and shall be; and no mortal has ever lifted my mantle [unveiled me]." This phrase inspired the song "I Am All That Is," celebrating this goddess' all-encompassing domains of the Earth, the stars, and the elements.[20]

At Empúries, it is Isis who survives the Greek and Roman cultural mutations of the Egyptian trinity of Isis, Osiris, and Horus. Osiris became Serapis, Horus became Harpocrates, but Isis maintained her essence and her name. And as a guardian of the "Eastern Gate" of Iberia, a watchtower stood next to her temple, overlooking the turquoise waters and sandy beaches of the Mediterranean, contrasted with the rugged snowy peaks of the Pyrenees visible to the north. With Iberia's open fertile land, abundance of Pyrenean-fed rivers, and plentiful precious metals, it is no wonder that the Egyptians, Phoenicians, Carthaginians, Greeks, and early Christians found this region an idyllic site for temples to their most sacred saints, gods, and goddesses. We can imagine how it must have been to live in Empúries near the temples overlooking the sea, in a city of people with a shared belief in the power of healing.

As I sat writing this chapter on a balcony overlooking the Mediterranean, Isis' temple ruins were illuminated across the Bay of Roses by the early morning sunrise. Dozens of swallows circled and dove incredibly close, and a small feather spiraled down to land at my fingers resting on the keyboard. It was my birthday, and this tiny gift felt huge in its symbolism. There is a text in *The Egyptian Book of the Dead* called "The Chapter of Making the Transformation into a Swallow," in which Isis becomes a swallow in order to work her magic and reanimate Osiris. I counted 52 swallows sitting on the line in front of the balcony, emissaries and reminders of Beloved Lady Isis.

"The swallow was the harbinger of glad tidings, and was, and still is, welcomed everywhere in Egypt ... Isis took the form of a swallow, and raised up Osiris to life ... the form of a swallow is able to restore to life ..."[21]

During a pilgrimage to Egypt in 1987, I recorded the *Song of Isis* album with harp and voice in several temples, including Philae, Saqqara, and in the Queen's Chamber of the Great Pyramid. The songs were spontaneous offerings to the deities and their shrines and the link to the recording, which has become an underground classic, is in the notes.[22]

Asclepius-Hygeia Temple of Healing

"Do you not know, Asclepius, that Egypt is an image of Heaven, or, to speak more exactly, in Egypt all the operations of the powers which rule and work in heaven have been transferred to earth below? Nay, it should be said that the whole Kosmos dwells in this our land as its sanctuary."[23]

Hermetica, ascribed to Hermes Trismegistus

Asclepius, Empúries Museum.

Next to the temples of Isis and Serapis in the temple district at the southern end of Neapolis was the healing temple of Asclepius, dated to the beginning of the fourth century BCE, or perhaps earlier. According to Greek mythology, Asclepius was the son of Apollo (twin of Artemis), who inherited his father's magical solar abilities with music, prophecy, healing, and even raising the dead, reminding us of the healing power of Jesus. Chiron taught a young Asclepius astronomy and medicine, and how they worked in the human body and psyche.

And just as Serapis was not worshiped without Isis, Asclepius was always honored along with Hygeia. Archeologists have discovered earlier temple altars and foundations beneath the Asclepieion that were most likely dedicated to Hygeia. She was the daughter, or perhaps the sister-wife, of Asclepius and the pair appeared together in hundreds of temples across the Mediterranean. Only the impressive marble statue of Asclepius was uncovered, and can be seen in the onsite museum, with a replica standing guard in the temple ruins. The older temple remains below the statue tell us that the site was used as a sanctuary well before the fourth century BCE.

Asclepius was considered a Divine Physician with a focus on healing the body-mind, but especially the soul. The cause of sickness was considered a problem with one's disconnection from the divine, and was treated with a divine remedy, *similia similibus curantur*, a Latin phrase meaning "similar treated with likeness."[24] It is like an ancient form of homeopathy in which the divine sickness is cast out by the divine remedy. The Asclepieion complex included the sanctuary and many adjoining healing rooms and courtyards. The remaining broken stone walls and steps leading to double altars speak of a greater time, when robed priests and priestesses offered a wide spectrum of medicinal offerings for the supplicant. The Asclepieion philosophy of healing most often recommended treating the soul and psyche of the patient first, which then affected the physical, mental, and emotional symptoms and maladies.

Fragment of Serpent of Asclepius, Empúries Museum.

A person coming for healing would first be cleansed in a ritual bath and given a fresh linen robe. They would normally fast on herbs and spring water, and any medicines would be infused with invocations, using the Greek knowledge inherited from the Egyptians on the power of magical words and sound. Patients would enter a dream incubation in the *abaton*, "innermost sanctuary," and ask for guidance in which the god or goddess would appear and instruct them in the needed protocol. Lyre players strolled through the complex softly singing uplifting invocations, while the healing serpents representing Hygeia and Asclepius silently moved among the patients, sometimes touching them gently exactly where healing was needed. (The serpents were non-venomous, and were considered servants and messengers of the gods, not feared as they often are today.)

Hygeia, 3rd c BCE alabaster, Heritage Museum, St. Petersburg, photo Pushkar Ekbote.

Although no statue of Hygeia has been found at Empúries, those that decorated the Asclepieion temples across the Mediterranean depict her holding a large serpent, to which she offers a cup of medicine or milk. An image of the cup of Hygeia at the top of a serpent staff can still be seen on the signs of pharmacies across Europe, in memory of the healing prescriptions of the goddess. She is named for the Greek word meaning "health," from which we have our word *hygiene*. The serpent-carrying Hygeia also reflects earlier traditions of ancient goddess figures holding snakes, from Crete to Anatolia, symbolizing her power of healing, regeneration, and wisdom.

Asclepius was seen in the form of a great dragon at the healing temple of Cos in Greece, a tradition which was passed to the Isle of Rhodes and its healing temples and related to the Ophite serpent traditions of wisdom and healing. Asclepius was portrayed at Neapolis with a serpent wound around his staff, much like the staff of Egyptian-born and educated Moses. The serpent winding up the staff is also symbolic of the Tree of Life, and perhaps the most important meaning of this symbol is transformation, the raising of one's consciousness. Inherent in the symbol are some of the oldest Tantric traditions that are also found in the Vedas, Taoism, and Buddhism. In Numbers 21:8 of the Bible, God instructs Moses:

"Make thee a fiery serpent, and set it upon a pole: and it shall come to pass that every one that is bitten, when he looketh upon it, shall live."

As already mentioned, many researchers believe that Asclepius was conflated with the earlier Egyptian Imhotep from the Third Dynasty of the Old Kingdom (2686–2637 BCE). Imhotep was astrologer, scribe, architect, and physician to the pharaoh Djoser (Zoser) and was ultimately worshiped as the god of medicine. It is believed that he was the architect of the step pyramid of Djoser at Saqqara and perhaps the original author, or at least the inspiration for, the Edwin Smith Papyrus of circa 1600 BCE, the earliest known writing on medicine. According to a paper written by Kayley Boddy, of Hamilton College, New York, if Imhotep was the author of the Edwin Smith Papyrus, this would make him Egypt's first known physician:

"If Imhotep was the original author of this papyrus, he could also be credited with being the first physician in the ancient Mediterranean to extract medicine from plants, used in several of the papyrus' treatments. He is known to have discovered the diagnosis and treatment of over 200 medical issues, including tuberculosis, appendicitis, gout, gallstones, and arthritis. He is also recorded as the first physician to use honey to treat wounds, and is believed to have founded the first school of medicine in Memphis ..."[25]

If, as many believe, Asclepius absorbed the traditions of Imhotep, it is likely that the Egyptian study of the movements of the heavens and its effect on health and wellbeing would have been continued in the Asclepieion tradition. (This tradition of combining astrology and medicine was covered earlier in the work of Marcilio Ficino, and in my current work in sound medicine. Remember, Ficino was the first to translate the *Corpus Hermeticum* into Latin, and he incorporated these principles along with Egyptian healing traditions in his academy in Florence.) Both medicine and astronomy were included in the education of Asclepius by Chiron, a legacy continued by the fifth century BCE Hippocrates. He created the Hippocratic Oath circa 400 BCE, which has continued to be required before practicing medicine until today. In fact, astrology and astronomy were required courses before taking the Hippocratic Oath until the 18th century. For more than two thousand years, the Hippocratic Oath included a promise to honor the teachings of Asclepius and Hygeia, although after various revisions during the 20th

Author at Temple of Asclepius, Empúries, photo Dani Valdés.

century CE that portion is no longer in most modern versions. The following is an excerpt from the beginning of the classic oath:

"I swear by Apollo Physician and Asclepius and Hygieia and Panaceia and all the gods and goddesses, making them my witnesses, that I will fulfill according to my ability and judgment this oath and this covenant."[26]

The steps leading to the double altars in front of the statue of Asclepius at today's Empúries ruins are some of the few remaining structures of the once spectacular temples of healing and medicine of the soul. Often our pilgrimage groups would gather on the temple steps with lyre and our voices as Hygeia's choir, to pay homage to the ancient traditions of soul healing of Hygeia and Asclepius. The following song inspired by an Orphic Hymn to Hygeia, which is included in the *Guardians of the Dragon Path* album:

"O come now Blessed Goddess,
To the seekers of mystic healing;
O come now, O Hygeia,
To the temple of mystic healing.
Born from the heart of Asclepius
Your serpent's touch brings healing;
We drink from your cup of remembering,
Come to these seekers of soul dreaming,
Mystic healing, temple dreaming.
(Chorus invocation to Hygeia in Greek: Yγεία *'Eeyeeia')"*[27]

Themis Oracle for Justice

"If the gods are pleased,
by righteous prayers, and their wrath can be
appeased, then tell us, Themis, by what means
the ruin of our race can be redeemed;
and, kindest goddess, help this flooded world."[28]

Ovid, *Metamorphoses*

Ovid's call to Themis, written in the first century BCE, is even more poignant today. Indeed, Themis, by what means can the ruin of humanity be redeemed? And sadly, few

Themis inscription, alabaster, Empúries Museum.

have even heard of you, although you have been honored as a Mother Goddess since ancient times. Although Themis does not have an Empúrian temple per se, her shrine was either in the Court of Justice at the northern side of the Agora (the public plaza for meetings and markets) or in the southern temple sector. A marble inscription naming Themis as the Goddess of Divine Order and a white marble statue of her were uncovered and both are now in the site museum. An ancient path called *Cami Vel a les Corts,* "Old Path to the Courts," connects the Greek city with the Santa Magdalena church ruins to the west and to the watchtower *Torre de Corts,* "Tower of the Courts."

Themis was the goddess of truth, oracles, and justice, who ensured that divine law was carried out on Earth. She was called "The Inescapable One," the revealer of transgressions against truth, and like the Egyptian goddess Ma'at she carries the scales for weighing the true against the false. In Egypt, maintaining divine order included the cosmic harmony that regulates all of life, and Ma'at was often depicted on harps, as she guided the musician on correct tuning and performance to maintain that universal harmony, the *Harmonia Mundi.* I mention this connection with Ma'at, as many of the Greek gods and goddesses were absorbed from the Egyptian pantheon, and Themis may well represent the same cosmic harmony.

Themis as divine oracle was mentioned earlier in the chapter on the Greek Queen Pyrrha. In brief, according to Greek myth, after being blown westward for nine days on the sea, Pyrrha and her husband King Deucalion arrived in a new land following the great deluge. Hermes appeared and advised them to find the temple of Themis and consult with this mother of oracles, who instructed them on how to create a new civilization. In that chapter, I proposed that the new civilization to the west is Iberia, based on various clues in the myth.

Themis relief reproduction, author's collection.

Whether or not the western land that the king and queen founded was Iberia, Themis was their guiding voice of wisdom. As mentioned in the chapter on Artemis, Themis may be an older goddess that was absorbed into Artemis. Themis was thought to have founded the oracular shrine at Delphi with her priestesses, called *Themistes* oracles, the "Divine Voices." Hesiod mentions Themis as one of the six sons and daughters of Gaia and Uranus, rulers of the Earth and Sky. Themis is the voice of truth for Gaia, and I can imagine a better world with courts of law filled with judges listening to the guidance of Themis for divine justice on Earth.

Santa Magdalena—Temple of Transcendence

Just a few footsteps over the hill to the west of Neapolis, one finds the old path *Cami Vel a les Corts* leading to the fourth century CE ruined church of Santa Magdalena, although these days the Greek city is fenced for security so it's necessary to either drive to the site of the church or enjoy a roundabout walk. Many people on their way to the city of l'Escala or the ruins of Empúries pass Santa Magdalena without noticing it, and only the foundation and low walls remain. I discovered the site many years ago by simply chatting with a local woman and asking if there was an early site dedicated to Magdalena in the area. I have always found that having at least a basic understanding of the local language opens many unexpected doors.

Early Christian sepulchre, Santa Magdalena de Empúries.

The dating of the site is exciting, as it is the oldest known sanctuary of Santa Magdalena in the entire region. Visitors to the ruins will see an information board that says it was built in the fifth century CE, however more recent archeological excavations show the church was developed from a mausoleum and chapel that dates from circa 370 CE.[29] And there is a necropolis of earlier Christian burials at the site.

The fields surrounding the old chapel are always covered with flowers and herbs. Often wild alyssum, also called "Carpet of Mary," is blooming and scenting the air with sweet fragrance. As mentioned, in Spanish it is often called *mucha miel* ("abundant honey"), and in plant folklore, alyssum is related to prophecy and inner sight, recalling the Delphi oracular Melissae, bee priestess traditions. (*Melissa* is a Greek word meaning "bee"). It is extraordinary that flora has a natural affinity for growing in specific sacred sites, in a form of resonant entrainment between the attributes of the saint or the site and the plant's qualities.

I have noticed this pattern in many archeological sites, where for instance, maiden hair fern is prolific at ancient wells of the Mother Goddess. The graceful fronds look like her long hair as she is leaning over the spring like a watchful guardian. And the wild bush herb *yerba santa* ("holy herb") often grows like an aromatic guardian at megalithic stone sites and ancient ruins, both in Spain and the Americas. The sweet alyssum at Santa Magdalena, and its association with inner sight and prophecy, is joined by fennel, which carries similar associations, with these plants maintaining a biofield for "The Woman Who Saw the All."

Wild fennel dominates the site and covers the entire landscape all the way up the hill to the ruins of Empúries. Fennel is a multiuse plant, providing food from the roots, medicine, and flavoring from the seeds and greens. It was a favorite of the Greeks, so perhaps they cultivated it here. But even more interesting is the history of fennel as it relates to Magdalena's death. This seemed to be a theme in Catalonia, with the scene of her deathbed and the Opening of the Mouth Ritual at Perella, and the western alignments to winter solstice sunset of many of her key sanctuaries, the direction of death and rebirth.

There is a tradition at Saint-Maximin-la-Sainte-Baume in Provence that when the tomb of Magdalena was discovered they found her mouth was filled with fennel. I had often wondered what the connection was between the legend and the unusually prolific fennel at one of her earliest sites in Catalonia. I asked my friend Veronique Flayol, a French lecturer and guide to Magdalena sites in Provence, and the following is her response:

> *"In December 1279, King Charles II gave the order to make excavations at the Basilica of Saint-Maximin-la-Sainte-Baume and they found the sarcophagus in the crypt. It is mentioned in the records that immediately after opening the sarcophagus, a wonderful odor escaped. We can make the connection with the anointing of Jesus by Mary Magdalene at the Last Supper with the broken bottle and the aroma spreading throughout the house. [Bishops] Bernard Gui and Philippe de Cabassole confirmed that from her mouth came a root with a rather long branch of fennel. This root was divided into several pieces which were also considered as relics."*

> *Veronique continued: "On a symbolic level, here is my interpretation: According to Pliny, fennel has, among other things, the property of clearing the sight. Mary Magdalene had the privilege of being the first to see Jesus out of the tomb, risen. Fennel symbolizes not only the resurrection but also the gift of second sight. The story of this discovery is mentioned by Father Faillon in* Unpublished monuments on the apostolate of Saint Mary Magdalene in Provence.*"*[30]

It was extraordinary to hear that Magdalena's fennel became holy relics! To clarify the references that Veronique mentions in her enlightening response, the Roman herbalist

Pliny (23–79 CE) wrote a detailed summary on the use of herbs in *Naturalis Historie*. He said that fennel is generally thought to be a female plant. The association with sight and resurrection seems to come from his account that serpents ate and rubbed against fennel because it was able to improve their eyesight after shedding their skins. Pliny also recommends steeping fennel in wine to drink for the stings of serpents, and that the pith of fennel is good for the uterus. During medieval times fennel was hung over doorways as a protection from evil spirits.

Illuminated manuscript, sepulchre of Magdalena, Maître Boucicaut,1415 Paris.

The association of fennel with the miracle of second sight and serpents connects once again with serpent wisdom, medicine, and regeneration of the ancient Mother Goddess traditions in the region. There is yet more symbolism at the site in the thousands of tiny snail shells attached to the fennel stalks surrounding Magdalena. There must be dozens of white spirals attached to every stalk and I pondered the spiral labyrinth symbol and the constantly turning path of life connecting to our ancient origins. Large ammonite stones with their spirals formed millions of years ago traditionally marked the entrance to temples, in addition to spiral engravings at Neolithic sites such as those marking the entrance of New Grange, Ireland. At Santa Magdalena, the spirals, symbols of eternity, are multiplied by the thousands in a rare profusion.

Two large white thorn trees stand as sentinels at the top of the hill above her chapel; they bear bright red berries, hinting again at the alchemy of red and white, the male and female in the alchemical vessel of the hermaphrodite transmutation. In Catalan, white thorn is called *Espino albar* or *Maria del Espino* ("Mary of the Thorn"). Interestingly, white thorn is a multi-use healing tree, including its use as a cure for snake bite. White thorns, white flowers of the carpet of Mary, and a large stand of white flowering yucca was again in full bloom, all floral testaments to spiritual purity. And her fields are covered with the two plants associated with the gift of second sight. It seemed that all of her sanctuaries were surrounded with varieties of flora—wild, unplanned gardens with species that matched her essence. The song "Garden of Blue Roses" is an anthem to the mystical and enchanted gardens of Magdalena, inspired by the medieval Lady and Unicorn tapestries, woven in the tradition of *mille-fleurs* ("thousand flowers").[31]

I wanted to know more about the orientation of the original church and had invited my friend Juan Saez to meet me at Santa Magdalena for a day of field research. As mentioned in previous chapters, Juan is trained in earth energy dowsing (geomancy) and is an expert in measuring the structural and celestial orientations of ancient sites. As we shall see in the following, not only is this chapel related to Magdalena's gift of second sight, but also to the death and resurrection mysteries, the journey of the soul in the afterlife associated with the west, which Juan said identifies this church as a "Temple of Transcendence."

Juan began by walking the property inside and surrounding the ruins and taking measurements and compass readings. He found that the area at the church altar was very strong, grounded in the earth, and that the energy was still quite active. He found an underground water path connecting the Magdalena chapel with another chapel dedicated to Santa Margarida, just across the road to the north, which added to the power of the site. Recent excavations date both religious centers to circa 370 CE.[32] Margarida had a baptismal ritual pool large enough for full immersion, fed by a spring that once flowed at the site. This pool may also be related to Margarida's legend of being tortured, burned, and then put into a pool of water, which she proclaimed would be transformed from waters of pain and suffering into waters of everlasting life.

Santa Margarida and Saint Anthony, Lluis Borrassa 1360, Santa Maria de Rubio, VEM.

Santa Margarida, or Saint Margaret of Antioch, was born circa 280 CE, or some say earlier, in the Syrian city, which is now Antakya in southern Turkey. According to Jacobus de Voragine, she was the daughter of a noble patriarch and prince named Theodosius, who worshiped the old gods and goddesses.[33] During that era, Antioch was a thriving hub of trade and culture, with temples to Hygeia and Asclepius and numerous other Greek deities. Jews, Greeks, Romans, and Syrians comingled in a scene filled with luxury, academies of learning, and magicians, and the city's guardians that greeted arrivals were the Tyche serpent deities.[34] We can immediately see some similarities with Empúries in the temples, cultures, and guardian deities of Antioch.

Saint Margaret was tortured and martyred circa 304 for refusing to marry a Roman prefect—she claimed that she was already the bride of Christ. The interesting part of her story is that she was swallowed by a dragon and emerged alive and well from its belly. Hence, she became the patron saint of childbirth. The legend is most likely a metaphor indicating her being "on the inside" or initiated in dragon wisdom and healing, especially given her father's adoration of the old gods and goddesses. The name Margaret comes from the Greek word meaning "pearl," and when we remember that the dragon traditionally guards the pearl of great price—purity, wisdom, and illumination—Santa Margarida's legacy becomes clear. She is portrayed in Catalan paintings with dragon's feet and in several of these images Saint Anthony is holding a closed red book, symbolizing secrets, and hidden mysteries. He is pointing at her clawed feet, making sure that we notice her dragon lineage. More common images show her holding or standing next to her dragon, much like Saint Martha, the sister of Magdalena, and John the Evangelist are often depicted with a dragon.

The Church's story is always the same, with the dragon being a monster or devil, serpents and dragons categorically representing the worship of any god or goddess of the time, other than Jesus. But for the Gnostics and practitioners of the more ancient mystery traditions, the dragon symbolized knowledge and wisdom. It is interesting that Santa Margarida's church at Empúries was established soon after her martyring circa 304 CE, further confirming the strong communication lines carried via the trade ships arriving from the Levant at Empúries.

And it is no accident that the feast days of Santa Margarida (July 20th) and Santa Magdalena (July 22nd) in the Catholic calendar are so close. This was also the time of the annual heliacal rising of Sirius celebrated in Egypt, with temple rituals and music honoring two sisters, Isis and Nephthys, as Sirius was the star of Isis. The heliacal rising occurs after Sirius has been obscured by the Sun for some months, and one early morning, the star appears and briefly sparkles on the horizon just before the Sun rises. The heliacal rising occurred on July 22nd during the fourth century CE, when the two Christian churches were established in Empúries. The synchronicities are uncanny and reveal perfection in the cycles of time, mirroring events in Heaven on Earth.

Two towers originally stood close together on the hill to the west and equidistant from Santa Magdalena and Santa Margarida, forming a perfect triangle between the towers and the two churches. Called *Torres de Defensa de les Corts* ("Towers of Defense of the Courts" in Catalan), only one tower remains today. The second is now just a circle of stones marking the original foundation. Juan said the large size of the stones indicates it is an ancient construction, Greco-Roman.

Having two watchtowers above the Santa Magdalena church is significant and another example of the Migdol, Magdaluma tradition across the Mediterranean. Gerald Massey, the 19th century Egyptologist, writes in *A Book of the Beginnings*, comparing the Egyptian and Hebrew words for watchtower. He says that the Hebrew *migdol* comes from *gadal* (gdol) meaning "great." The Egyptian word for watchtower, *makatura*, is formed by *tura*, "tower," and *mak*, "the mage" and "watcher."

Massey states that both words, migdol and makatura, mean the same: "It was the tower of the Mag or mage, the starry watchman of the night. Mak, the mage and to watch, doubly identifies the Egyptian origin of the Migdol as the watch-tower."[35] Hence, we might say that Santa Magdalena's church with two watchtowers at Empúries represents the "Starry Watchwoman, Mage of the Night."

Measuring from the Magdalena church altar, the visible tower lies at the declination of 240° SW, which Juan said marks the 18.6-year lunar return. The general layout of the church is north-south, which he indicated is an older axis orientation used in pre-Christian and Neolithic temple construction. This might indicate that the fourth century church was built on an earlier sanctuary. There is an octagon-shaped chapel (or mausoleum) aligned at the corners to 95° (winter solstice sunset point) and 185° (summer solstice sunrise point). After completing his measurements, Juan said, "Maria Magdalena is the keeper of the tower of the Sun here." The church had a lunar orientation and a solar tower, as it marks winter solstice sunset. He called Santa Magdalena a "Church of Transcendence" because most of the church alignments focus on the west.

The west is the direction of death before rebirth. In death is liberation and resurrection, as we must die to be reborn. Jesus, Osiris, Dionysus, Hercules, Asclepius, and many other gods exemplified transcendence in the resurrection mysteries as dying and rising gods, witnessed and understood by Magdalena, as indicated by the skull that is part of her iconography. Her chapel at Empúries was surrounded by an older necropolis, which confirms the western orientation focus.

There was one more natural feature of Santa Magdalena that was equally stunning. Looking due south from the site there is another tower standing on the long ridge called *Montjuic,* meaning "Jew's Mountain" in Catalan, named for of the number of Jewish people who came and settled here long ago. Viewed from the Santa Magdalena chapel, the silhouette of Montjuic looks distinctly like a woman lying on her back, with the tower forming the nipple of her breast and her long flowing hair spreading over the hills. Some local people call this landscape formation *l'Extranjera*, meaning "the Foreign Woman" in Spanish. Was this a reference to Mary Magdalene coming to Iberia from the east?

At the northwestern end of Montjuic, which forms her long tresses, there is the ruined medieval castle of Bellcaire, which was said to be a refuge for Cathars. Spanish author Ramon Hervás Marcó writes that the Montjuic and Bellcaire sites held Grail secrets and a legend of Magdalena being in the region. In *Historia Secreta del Grial* (*Secret History of the Grail*) he claims that the Grail lineage came to the Pyrenees with Magdalena, who came to find refuge and to give birth to a royal son. He says she arrived at Port Vendres, "Port of Venus," which is just 26 miles (42 kilometers) north of Empúries on the coast of Gaul. Ramon continues that the Grail is "... the blood of that man Jesus who had descendants through his wife Magdalena and whose son came to be born in Occitan or Catalonia."[36]

He does not cite any references, and yet his suggestion is definitely possible, as Empúries is the site of perhaps the earliest western church dedicated to Magdalena and is next to a temple of Artemis. Various historians mention her taking shelter in a pagan temple when she arrived in Gaul, most often believed to be at the temple of Artemis at Marseilles. She may well have found a welcome refuge in the other Artemis and Venus-Aphrodite temples along the coast, located at ports where ships were regularly coming and going.

To summarize this long chapter on the Five Keys, at Empúries we have five temples that surround a large Flower of Life mosaic, five strands of ancient wisdom teachings, and the gods and goddesses who carried these key teachings into Iberia.

Part VI

IBERIA'S MAGDALENA LEGACY

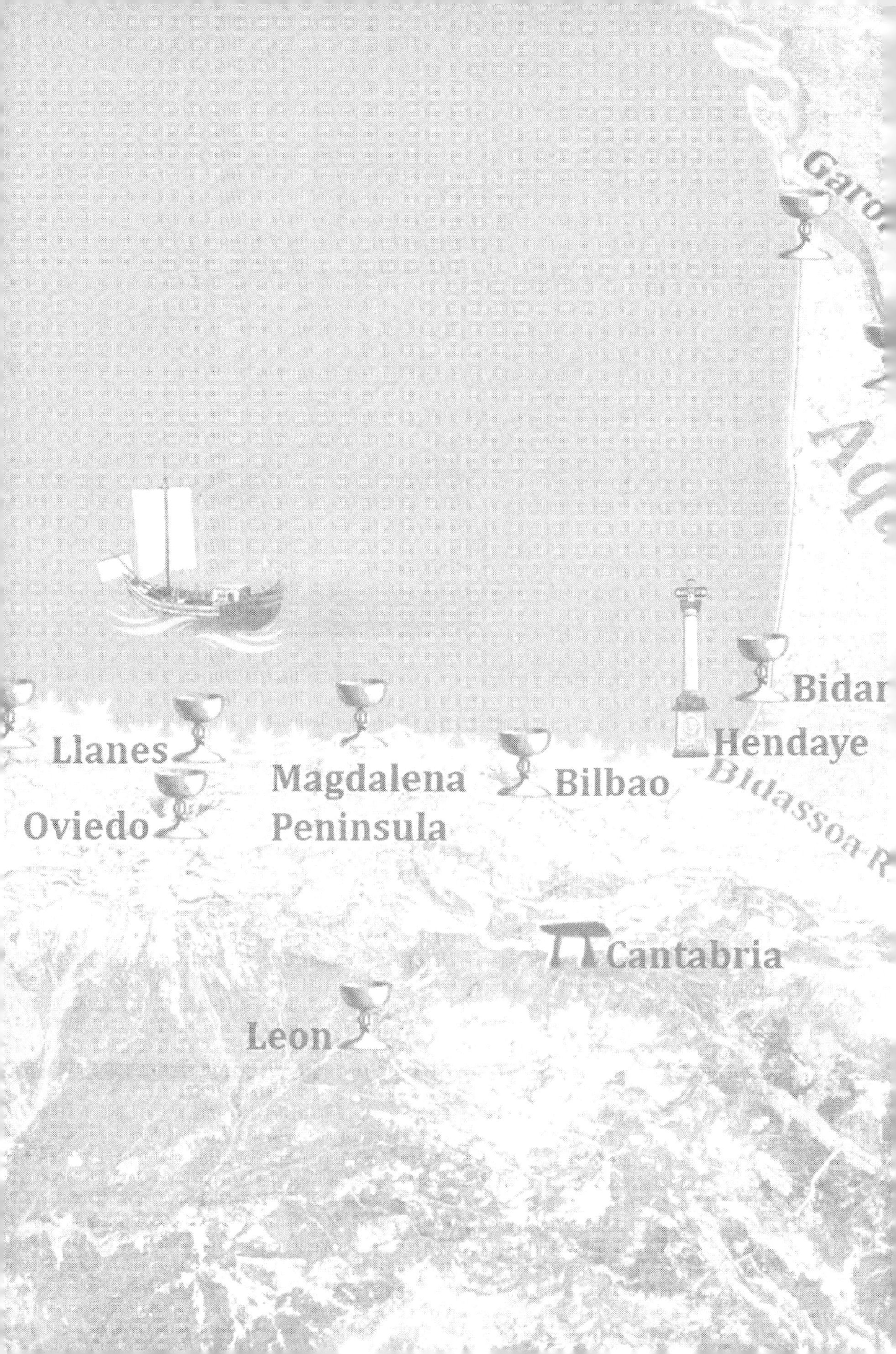

Bidar
Llanes
Hendaye
Magdalena
Peninsula
Bilbao
Bidassoa R
Oviedo
Cantabria
Leon

CHAPTER 25

From Judea to Provence

THE PYRENEES AND BEYOND

"Leaving the shores of Asia and favoured by an east wind, they went round about, down the Tyrrhenian Sea between Europe and Africa, ... they came near to the city of Marseilles, in the Viennoise province of the Gauls, where the river Rhone is received by the sea. There ... they parted: each company going to the province where the Holy Spirit had directed them; presently preaching everywhere ..."[1]

John William Taylor, in *The Coming of the Saints* (1907), writes of the Mediterranean journey taken by Magdalena and her companions and their arrival on the shores of Gaul. The romantic Provençal tradition says that the holy entourage set off in a boat without oars or sails and that, by the grace of God, they landed safely at Les Saintes-Maries-de-la-Mer. But it is much more likely that these important people of means had traveled in a large trade ship, a much more common sight on the Mediterranean. There may be a reason, though, for the humble boat version of the story. "A boat with no oars" is a metaphor for total surrender and infinite trust in a greater power to guide our way. Henry Lincoln also pointed out an old European tradition that a boat without oars indicated a person of royal lineage was aboard. Was the royal person Maria Magdalena, the Apostle to the Apostles, potentially, the "Bride of Christ," who inherited the mission to share the message of healing and love? Or was it the royal child Saint Sara, whose name means "princess" in Hebrew?

Magdalena arrives in Gaul, Sainte Baume convent church mural.

Taylor lists those on the ship as Magdalena's sister Martha, Maximin, Marcella, the follower of Martha, and numerous other disciples and leaders, and says that Lazarus was already Bishop of Cyprus.[2] However,

Saint Sara Kali in crypt of the Saintes Maries de la Mer Church.

the strong Provençal tradition lists three Marys: Magdalena, Mary Salome (mother of James the Elder), Mary Jacobi (mother of James the Younger), plus Martha, Lazarus, Maximin, and Sara the dark Egyptian, as all being on the ship. The story has numerous variations and accounts of the many disciples who dispersed in all directions as messengers of the new dispensation.

The gypsies who come to Les Saintes-Maries-de-la-Mer every May to celebrate their Black Madonna Saint Sara Kali, say there was once a temple of Isis, which is now submerged under the sea. The fourth-century Roman geographer Rufius Festus Avienius listed the site as *Ra* and it was later known as Notre-Dame-de-Ratis (Our Lady of the Boat). The annual festival draws many thousands, and the town fills with the sounds of gypsy music late into the night, and young girls as well as old women dance the familiar and intoxicating rhythms. A highlight is the ritual procession of the relics of the two Marys and Saint Sara to the sea, guarded by the gypsy men on their white Camargue horses, as they proudly hold staffs with the crescent Moon of the goddess. To the accompaniment of guitars, the throngs chant, "Viva la Santa Maria, viva la Sara Kali!" After attending the festival many times, I was inspired to write "Viva la Santa Maria," an anthem for the baptism of the bones of the wise women in the sea.[3]

I believe that following her arrival in Provence, Magdalena would have traveled extensively throughout the western lands. Popular French tradition says that after arriving on the shores of Gaul, she spent her remaining years living as a hermit in the grotto of La Sainte-Baume, but it just didn't ring true. I cannot imagine a passionate, young, wealthy woman from Palestine, who was ignited with love and a mission to share, spending all her days as a penitent in a remote cave. She had the means and would have traveled extensively to spread the message of the "True Church of Love." Most likely, it was convenient for the Church to diminish the extent of her travels and influence as the "First Apostle," in favor of Peter and Paul. In the Nag Hammadi text, the *Dialogue of the Savior*, Jesus indicates that Magdalena is the one who truly sees and understands his teachings, hence her popular designation of "She who sees the All." In the dialogue Jesus tells the disciples that the one who speaks also listens, and the one who can see also reveals. And later in response to a question from Magdalena, he tells her that she is the one who makes clear the message of the revealer.[4]

The Gnostic texts reveal Maria Magalena as an essential voice in Jesus' teachings and the one who is well prepared to spread his message. And yet, she and her entourage were not alone, and certainly not the first Judean immigrants to enter the western

Mediterranean. The entire region had been populated by Jewish arrivals long before the time of Jesus, as far as Spain. Greek geographer and historian Strabo reported: "It is not easy to find a place in the inhabited world that has not received these people."[5]

The Jewish ruler Archelaus, the son of Herod the Great and brother of Herod Antipas, was exiled to Europe in the year 6 CE. And thirty-three years later, Herod Antipas himself, along with his wife Herodias, was ordered into exile by Emperor Caligula. The evidence is that they went to Lugdunum Covenarum in the French Pyrenees, the town now known as Saint-Bertrand-de-Comminges,[6] within the region known in the first century as Gallus Aquitania (the later Aquitaine), the land of many Celtic tribes.

The name *Lugdunum* comes from the old language of Gaul, meaning a fortress of the Celtic solar god Lug, or Lugus. The site had been populated at least since 3000 BCE, and legend says that Hercules came here to rest after his labors in western Spain. This would have been after his legendary love affair with the Celtic Princess Pyrene, through which, I propose, they initiated a royal Egyptian and Celtic bloodline in the Pyrenees. The journey of Hercules on his twelve labors from the East to the West is an allegory of the sun's journey through the twelve signs of the zodiac during a solar year, and the names of the sites he visited often carry a solar designation.

Saint-Bertrand-de-Comminges is also on one of the Santiago de Compostela routes. The town is on the Garonne River and this route is often called Via Garona, which is very interesting, given what we will discover regarding Magdalena and her companions coming to the region. In the first century CE, Saint-Bertrand-de-Comminges was a thriving trade center with 10,000 inhabitants, and throughout its history, many interesting players had either lived here or passed through, including most likely, members of Jesus' inner circle. Now it is a sleepy hilltop village, sometimes called the "Mont-Saint-Michel" of the Pyrenees, nestled between mountain peaks, silently holding its secrets and stories.

But why is a crocodile from the Nile mounted on a high column in the town's church of Sainte Marie—another testimonial to the Pyrenean dragons? As mentioned earlier, for the Egyptians, the crocodile represented the god Sobek and was seen as the constellation Draco. Pyrenean legend says that Saint Bertrand fought a great dragon, becoming one of the many *sauroctones* (from the Greek "lizard killers"), the saints and knights who either tamed or slayed dragons throughout history. No one seems to remember who brought the dragon god Sobek to the Pyrenees or when.

Another amazing player in Saint-Bertrand-de-Comminges' past is the disciple Joanna, the wife of Chuza, the household manager for Herod Antipas. According to the Gospel of Luke, she was a loyal disciple of Jesus, who, along with Susanna and Maria Magdalena, helped fund his ministry. I would discover some strange legends regarding Salome, the proposed daughter of Herodias, step-daughter of Antipas, her famous "Dance of the Seven Veils," and Joanna knowing the location of the head of John the Baptist. But that story will wait for book two, as it's beyond the scope of this writing. Let's stay with Joanna and Magdalena for now, and in Luke, 8:1-3 it says (King James Version):

"And the twelve were with Him, and certain women which had been healed of evil spirits and infirmities, Mary called Magdalene, out of whom went seven devils, and Joanna the wife of Chuza, Herod's steward, and Susanna, and many others which ministered unto Him of their substance."

Again, Luke mentions Joanna coming with Magdalena and Mary Jacobus to the sepulcher with holy oils to anoint the body of Jesus but finding the tomb empty. Joanna is called "Saint Joanna the Myrrhbearer" in Eastern Orthodox tradition, and her purported presence with Magdalena at the sepulcher establishes her importance as a disciple and tells of the close relationship of the two women. Here is the passage in Luke 24:10:

"It was Mary Magdalene, and Joanna, and Mary the mother of James, and other women that were with them, which told these things unto the apostles."

Presumably, the exile of Herod and Herodias included their household members such as Chuza, who would have continued to manage Herod's affairs and he would not have left his wife Joanna behind. If Joanna was living in Lugdunum Covenarum, did Magdalena visit her? This is quite possible if Luke's account of the two women being together at the sepulcher is true. Sharing such poignant, life-changing moments together would have forged a strong bond between them. Being with someone at a birth or death is never forgotten.

Local traditions, as well as the following document, tell us that the holy entourage, including Magdalena, eventually came even further west into Aquitaine, which encompassed much of western Gaul and south to the Pyrenees. This region included Lugdunum, where Joanna and Chuza were likely living in exile. According to the *Acta Sanctorum Aprilis* (1675):

"Magdalene, the sister of Lazarus, came with Lazarus, Maximinus, Chelidonius, Marcellus, and Joseph of Arimathea, to Aquitainian Gaul ... as the histories of the Gauls clearly teach, and is a tradition well received everywhere in that region."[7]

There is an earlier 10th-century legend that Joseph of Arimathea was in Limoges[8] (the old Lemovices) in Aquitaine, perhaps on the same journey with Magdalena, Lazarus, and others. In the 11th-12th centuries, the cult of Santa Magdalena in this region was clearly linked with the Camino de Santiago, and the route passed through Limoges from the abbey at Sainte-Marie-Madeleine of Vézelay. Knowing nothing of this history, on the summer solstice of 2009, I was driving back home to the Aude after a performance in Troyes Cathedral. On a hunch, I left the main road just north of Limoges, drove down a country lane, and stumbled upon an extraordinary tiny chapel and hamlet dedicated to Magdalena, called La Bussiére Madeleine. The red door of the chapel was unlocked, and I entered to find a Black Madonna on the altar and one of the most beautiful, elegant images I've ever seen of Magdalena, about 7 feet (2.13 meters) high in white marble, holding a white skull and a cross. Was this in memory of Magdalena and her companions passing through this region?

Magdalena church at La Bussiére Madeleine, France.

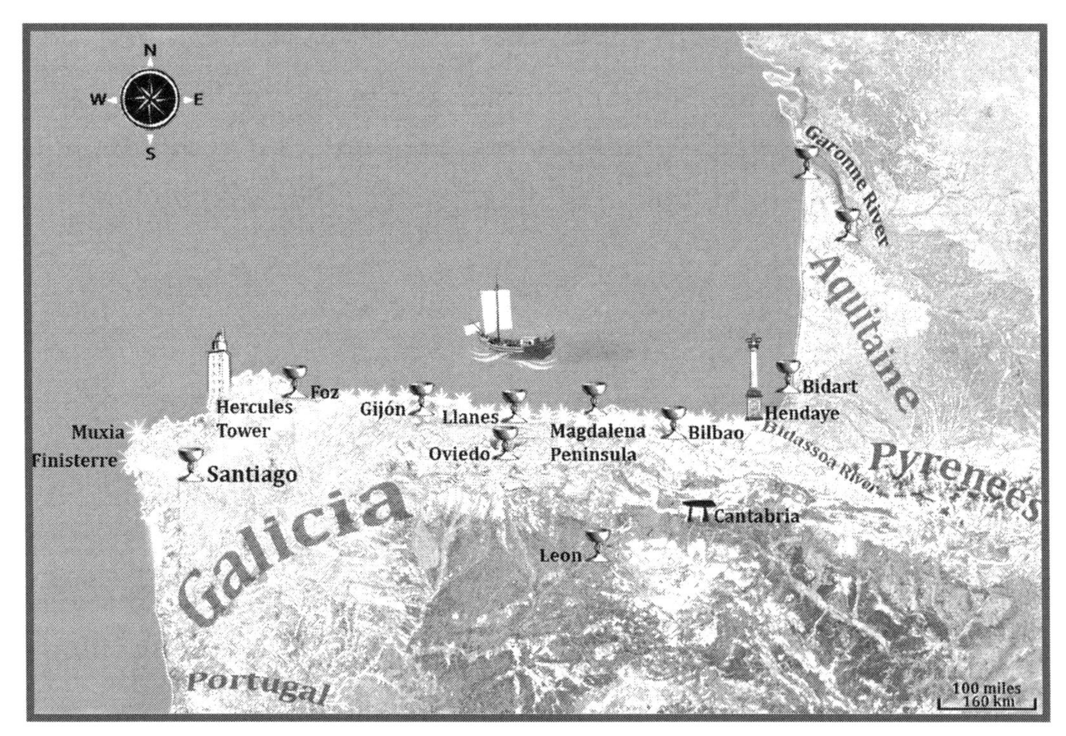

Illustration 18: Northern Camino

Aquitaine was the western region of Gaul, with natural borders formed by the Pyrenees and the Bay of Biscay, which also borders Galicia. The overland route from the Mediterranean would have been accessible via the largest river in Aquitaine, the Garonne. The river's source is in the high Pyrenees, and it flows through Toulouse, Agen, Bordeaux, and Gironde, and is fed by other large rivers of the region, including the Ariège, Tarn, Lot, and Dordogne. This matrix of rivers flowing through Aquitaine was commonly used in ancient times for trade and transport, hence the name Aquitaine, "Land of Waters."

Santa Magdalena, Joseph of Arimathea, and others in their group could have traveled, at least partially, by boat on the Garonne River, which flows approximately 360 miles (580 kilometers) through Aquitaine. Impressively, and with only a brief look, there are at least twenty-two churches of La Madeleine surrounding the Garonne at its western end near Bordeaux. The river's name is said to be from Garumna, the Latinized version of the old Aquitanian *kar ona,* meaning "stony river." However, I couldn't help but marvel at the phonetic similarities between the words Garonne and the Hebrew *garon,* which means "throat." The extensive delta formed at the mouth of the Garonne as it meets the Atlantic could have been seen as a throat, and so was it possible that the original term derived from early Jewish arrivals in the region?

I mention this possibility, as the function of *garon* was very important in Judaism, as it related to the throat as a channel for the voice in music and prophecy. It is important to know that during the era of Magdalena's lifetime, there existed the order of *Bath Kol*, meaning "Daughters of Voice," who were prophetesses for the voice of heavenly wisdom. The Hebrew *Soncino Zohar* defines *garon* as the vehicle for the creative word, infused with pure intention, and states that the glory of the holy passes through it: "... through which perennially flows the mystic force of the 'spirit of life'."[9]

A beautiful example of the Bath Kol by Gustave Doré, "Jephthah Met By His Daughter," 19th c.

The creative power of the word or song, as it manifested through their voices, was well known by the Bath Kol. These holy women were considered as aspects of the Shekinah, "Divine Presence," the *Ruach Ha Kodesh*, "Holy Spirit," and their prophetic state was precipitated by sacred music and singing the holy names. I will paraphrase this teaching from the *Zohar:*

> *"Like the voice of many waters, and like the voice of loud thunder, the Bath Kol, Daughters of Voice, sang a song descended from heaven. Their oracular messages served as guidance for the people and their wisdom was a mediation between the Holy Spirit and Earth."*

The tradition of singing the sacred names would have been maintained by the entire extended family of exiles from Palestine. And just as we have already seen in the Camino traditions of singing on the long journeys, we can assume that Magdalena and her companions maintained this tradition as Daughters of Voice, giving them strength and clarity on their long voyages. Maria Magdalena, as one of the likely practitioners of the Bath Kol tradition, inspired the song of the same title, and you can imagine them singing, their voices rising in harmony.[10] As Robert Powell states in *Meditation on the Tarot*, "Just as the Word became flesh is Jesus Christ, so did the Bath-Kol, the Daughter of the Voice, become flesh in Mary Sophia."

Did the Apostle to the Apostles Come to Spain?

> "*... straight from the open sepulchre with the very words of the Blessed Saviour on her lips, in the way that even no one else could do, St. Mary [Magdalene] would carry the great new message of Light and Life—'Christ and the Resurrection'—from the East to the West, from the Old World to the New.*"
>
> John William Taylor, *The Coming of the Saints*[11]

Like a star rising in the East, Magdalena carried the light and a new message of love and liberation to the western frontiers. How far west did she come? The question always arises from new visitors to the Pyrenees region: Did Maria Magdalena really come here? Although the Church did not want to reveal her extensive ministries and influence, there are too many legends and indications that say she did. When I first arrived in the area, my intuitive sense was that she had traveled from Provence through the Languedoc and Aquitaine regions of southern France several times, on her way further west, across the Pyrenees to Spain. On my long walks in the foothills and verdant valleys, I could sense her footsteps and feel the potent imprint that she left in the land.

There are records of other early missionaries that were sent to Spain, and the Benedictine Archbishop Rabanus Maurus lists seven, each to one of the seven

Iberian provinces: Torquatus, Thesiphon, Secundus, Indalecius, Caecilius, Esicius, and Euphrasius.[12] Saint Paul was also believed to have sown the seeds of the new doctrine in Catalonia, Aragon, Valencia, and Andalusia.[13] And according to tradition, sometime circa 32–42 CE, Saint James the Greater (or Elder) was in Spain. He is called the "first herald" of the new message in Spain: "... the apostle traversed the peninsula, from Lusitania and Galicia to the heart of Aragon."[14]

James the Greater was the brother of John, called the "Sons of Thunder," and both were part of the original twelve apostles of Jesus. James is Santiago el Mayor, Spain's patron saint, who became the inspiration for the Camino de Santiago de Compostela. (As we have discovered, the Christian Camino was established much later than the Way of the Stars.) After his extensive teaching in Spain, James returned to Jerusalem in 42 CE, where he was considered dangerously influential, and was beheaded by the Romans. Following James' unfortunate end, we find references from various sources of his body being brought to Spain by unnamed disciples:

> *"...after his martyrdom at Jerusalem his body was brought by his disciples from Syria to Iria Flavia (now El Padron), [in Galicia] and thence transferred to Compostela..."*[15]

Who were the unnamed disciples that brought James' body to Spain? Given the strong traditions in the region that Magdalena, Joseph of Arimathea, and other disciples came through Aquitaine, they are strong candidates. There were numerous Jewish communities already established on the Iberian Peninsula, and based on her popularity there, it is likely that she made more than one voyage. At the mouth of the Garonne, Magdalena and her companions could have boarded a ship that headed south along Aquitaine's Atlantic coast, and then sailed west along the Basque and Iberian coasts in a direct route to Santiago. (See Northern Camino Illustration 18.)

As travelers by ship do, they would have landed at various ports to refresh water and food supplies, and numerous locations on the Aquitaine and Iberian coasts are dedicated to Santa Magdalena. It is telling that Magdalena's popularity on this northern coastal route to Santiago has lasted throughout the centuries, with popular festivals on her feast day attended by thousands. The festivals include music, the lighting of sacred fires, liturgies, and processions simulating her arrival on the shores of ancient Iberia. The sheer number of Magdalena churches along the Atlantic northern coast of Spain is almost unbelievable, with her sites marking what would become known as the Camino del Norte (Way of the North), also known as Camino de la Costa (Coastal Way), to Santiago. (The "Camino Frances" route is further south through León.)

Voyages and Footprints

"In medieval times, ... the Camino de Santiago path became hermetic and was used as an initiation route by holy orders such as the Templars, who guarded and used these enclaves ... [dedicated] to Mary Magdalene, venerated by the Templars as the one who gives the initiation."[16]

This quote is from my correspondence with Carlos Martin la Moneda, a Zaragoza architect and dedicated researcher of the Camino path. As I had discovered at the eastern end of the Camino, the route from the eastern Pyrenees is marked with numerous sites of the Knights Templar and Maria Magdalena, and Carlos confirmed this continuity in the entire Way of the Stars. Magdalena was a woman burning with a passion to share the message of love as a direct dispensation from Jesus. This original, pure version of Christianity would continue to resurface in the movements of the Cathars, the Templars, in Grail traditions, and its flame has been kept alive by pilgrims on the ancient Way of the Stars.

We will sort through the clues in the place names, rituals, and legends of Spain's Northern Camino that indicate Maria Magdalena's presence. In the Basque country, on the French side of the Pyrenees, there was an ancient port called *Bide Artean*, meaning "Crossroads," now shortened to Bidart, where we find one of the more than ninety-four churches dedicated to Maria Magdalena that mark this coastal Camino. It sits on a high cliff with expansive views of the nearby Spanish coast, and suspended from the ceiling is a large model of a sailing ship. Was this in memory of her arrival during her voyages? The churchyard features standing stone memorials to the fierce Basque resistance and those who died protecting this beautiful land during World War II. The next site on the French side of the northern Camino is Saint-Jean-de-Luz, (John of the Light), featuring a cathedral of John the Baptist.

Further south on the Basque coast is the picturesque coastal settlement of Hendaye, located at the western end of the Pyrenees. The Bidassoa river runs through the town, and creates the natural border between France and Spain, with Hendaye on the eastern French side of the river. The port's wide and protected bay formed by the mouth of the river would have been another natural place to land. Irun, a tiny village three miles southwest of Hendaye, is another starting point of the Northern Camino, which passes through four regions: Basque country, Cantabria, Asturias, and Galicia.

In Hendaye's town square, there is an enigmatic stone cross erected in the 1600s that has captured the attention of alchemists and mystics for centuries. The square pedestal features eight symbols on its four faces: the Sun surrounded by four five-pointed stars, the Moon, an eight-pointed star, and the wheel, the "roda" symbol that we found at

Rhodes, at the eastern end of the Mediterranean Camino. The alchemist Fulcanelli calls the wheel symbol the "hieroglyph of the universe."[17] We can see the Sun and the Moon as the male and female principles in alchemical union, and the eight-pointed star as the star of Isis, or Sirius, guiding the pilgrims on the Way of the Stars as they progress from east to west, moving with the river of stars.

The equal-armed stone cross at the top of the column is inscribed with a coded message, "OCRUXAVES PESUNICA," which doesn't make sense, unless we move the position of the 'S' and add spaces, which reveals "O CRUX AVE, SPES UNICA" ("Hail o cross, the only hope"). And yet the cross that is honored in the inscription is not that of the crucifixion, but the more ancient and universal symbol of balance and harmony. This cross reappears at key sites in our story, placed as clues to a simple yet profound mystery, and we are reminded of the Great Cross at the eastern end of the Camino, the symbol that has been sacred to all cultures throughout time.

Additionally, the same Latin letters can be rearranged to form a secret message in French, indicating the site as a place of refuge. The Pyrenees have long been a place of safety for those in exile, and this included Maria Magdalena and the later Cathars. At the top arm of the cross is an engraved X, which we have discovered symbolizes crossroads and sacred union, which Fulcanelli calls the "Seal of Hermes," "Seal of the Wise."[18] The X was also a secret code used by medieval artists to represent Magdalena and the "Hidden Church." In *The Mysteries of the Great Cross of Hendaye*, Jay Weidner and Vincent Bridges say the symbols on the cross reveal the mysteries of the imperishable Light Body, the secrets of alchemical transmutation from base metal into gold, and our entry into a Golden Age. Whoever carved the symbols on the Hendaye cross wants us to know that a mystery was seeded in this place, along with a message of hope for a new era on Earth.

Santa Magdalena de Llanes.

Did that hope depend on the return of the wisdom of the sacred feminine, and the return to balance and harmony embedded in an ancient cross spanning the Pyrenees? It would seem so, and Maria Magdalena is an important archetype of our greatest hope, as Pope Francis has proclaimed. Continuing west along the northern coast there are more than ninety Magdalena chapels, cathedrals, and hermitages, perhaps the greatest concentration in all of Spain! (See appendix B.) From Hendaye, their ship would have passed the ports of Bilbao, Santander, Llanes, and Gijón. Santander's cape is called Magdalena Peninsula, where we find Magdalena Palace, Magdalena Beach, and two lighthouses, once again her "Migdal-Magdaluma" watchtowers.

There is an obvious passionate devotion to Magdalena along this Camino that has endured throughout the centuries. The ancient town of Puebla de Aquilar (Town of the Eagle), now known as Llanes, claims Santa Magdalena as its first patron saint. They celebrate her feast day on the 22nd of July every year with thousands in attendance, and her image is carried from the 12th-century church in a long procession to the sea, linked with the mariner tradition. The procession is guided by the music of "Banda El Magdaleno," with dozens of tambourine players, reminding us of the Bath Kol, Daughters of Sion musical tradition. As stated in the official city guide, Llanes is proud of its roots in La Magdalena and the northern Camino route since time immemorial.

Further west, we arrive at Gijón, known as Gigia in the first century, and one of Spain's most important ports for coastal trade since antiquity. Gigia is at the northern end of the *Via de la Plata*, the "Silver Route" from Seville in the south, an important route used since 2000 BCE and later by the Celts, Greeks, Egyptians, Carthaginians, and Phoenicians. Surrounding Gijón there are at least six chapels in Magdalena's name, and the more of her sites that were revealed, the more I became convinced that she must have traveled this ancient coastal route.

There is a strange Spanish rumor that says a Mary brought the remains of Saint James to Spain and then continued her journey south to Ciudad Rodrigo, on the Via de la Plata. The Church says this legend refers to Mary Salome, wife of Cleophas, and mother of James the Younger. The actual truth of who went where, and with whom is unknown, but we can see that Spain is no stranger to the presence and popularity of the earliest disciples and the Marys:

> *"St. Mary brought the martyred body of St. James into Spain and died at Civitatensum (Ciudad Rodrigo, Spain), a city in Lusitania, on April 10th."*[19]

Continuing west on her voyage, Magdalena may have landed at Foz, an ancient river port and site of a first-century Celtic hill fort, Castro de Fazouro. Here we find Hermida da Madalena de Foz (Hermitage of Magdalena of Foz), near where the current Coastal Camino turns south. If she landed here, she could have traveled overland, continuing south on the Camino Norte to Santiago, 77 miles (124 kilometers) away, with this route having at least eleven Magdalena chapels. Or if she continued to sail around the cape and Torre (Tower) Hercules, and landed at Muxia, the overland path to Santiago was shorter, only 39 miles (62.7 kilometers).

The ancient mariner's association on this Camino is also evident in the well-known pilgrimage and festival at Muxia, at the sanctuary known in Galician as *Virxe da Barca*, "Virgin of the Boat." The Virgin Mary is not known to have come into the West, and we can better understand the ancient tradition at Muxia as remembering when another Mary came ashore. The festival celebrating her arrival is recorded as having been held every September since at least the 14th century. However, the tradition may well be more ancient. Muxia is also the destination of a popular later pilgrimage route called *Camino dos Faros*, "The Lighthouse Way," another reference to the Magdaluma watchtower traditions. There are eight stages in this coastal route that begins to the northeast at Malpica, near the Tower of Hercules, a lighthouse built in the first century upon Phoenician foundations, which followed the plan of the famous lighthouse of Pharos, Alexandria.

Muxia's rocky coastal point was the site of a pre-Christian temple, and the strangely shaped stones are said to have healing powers, with miraculous cures being claimed after touching them. Belief is a powerful force. During the Middle Ages, the site was Christianized, as was much of the Camino, and history has been confused, and often altered. Galician tradition says that Muxia's stones represent parts of Mary's boat. Could that be a memory, lasting 2000 years, of when Maria Magdalena came ashore on her long voyage? Muxia has always been considered sacred because it sits at the westernmost end of Spain. It is the place of death before resurrection, where the Sun and stars disappear into the Atlantic, and it is considered the second Finisterre, or "End of the World," of the Camino.

In addition to the more than ninety-four sites dedicated to Magdalena in a narrow band along the Northern Camino route from Bidart to Santiago, there are a great number of megalithic dolmens along the same route, mainly concentrated around A Coruña (The Crown), Finisterre, and Muxia. This westernmost land of Spain had long been considered sacred and numerous Celtic ritual sites dot the landscape. The references to the unnamed disciples bringing the remains of Saint James to Santiago and "a Mary" doing much the same before continuing to Ciudad Rodrigo are isolated accounts, most likely created long after the first centuries. But the strong tradition of James having spent years in Galicia and the great number of Magdalena sites on the Northern Camino are enough to support the vision of her coming to this beautiful land.

The symmetry and mirroring that we find at the eastern and western ends of the Way of the Stars is striking. Marking the easternmost point of Spain at the Mediterranean, we find the beginning of the Camino, a temple of Venus, the legendary site of Hercules' Twelfth Labor, a high concentration of dolmens, and the beginning of the Magdalena Path in Catalonia. At the place of the setting Sun at the Atlantic and the completion of the Camino, we find a nearby Tower of Hercules, a high concentration of dolmens, the "Boat of Mary," and an ancient path dotted with even more Magdalena churches. This Camino could have been called *Camino de Magdalena de las Estrellas*, "Way of Magdalena of the Stars." At the two ends of the Way of the Stars where it meets the salty sea, *mar*, *mer*, Magdalena's sanctuaries and the footsteps of the earliest disciples mark the ancient pilgrimage paths.

CHAPTER 26

Sixty-Four Shrines to Magdalena in Catalonia

"... by measured steps and a sure eye, I can discover the sixty-four dispersed stones of the perfect cube ..."[1]

Le Serpent Rouge

Why are there sixty-four churches dedicated to Maria Magdalena in Catalonia, a relatively small region in northeastern Spain?[2] The number strikes a familiar chord, not only the phrase from the favorite Beatles tune "When I'm Sixty-Four." There are sixty-four codons or possible combinations for the amino acids that biological organisms use, the sixty-four codes in the human genetic blueprint for life.[3] Sixty-four possible hexagrams result from combinations of the yin and yang lines of the Chinese I Ching oracle, a mirror of life's choices and changes. There are sixty-four squares on the chess board, the game of life, which formed a portion of the Hermetic knowledge of Persia that the Knights Templar brought from the East.[4]

And it seems more than a coincidence that the Gnostic manuscript the *Pistis Sophia* (meaning "Faith Wisdom") contains sixty-four questions posed to Jesus, with most asked by Maria Magdalena. Written in the fourth–fifth centuries CE in the Upper Egyptian dialect, based on an earlier text called *The Questions of Mary,* it was acquired by the British Museum under the name Askew Codex in the 18th century.[5] In the text, Jesus has come to teach those closest to him eleven years after the crucifixion. Magdalena is joined by both the female and male disciples, including Mother Mary and Martha, but it is Magdalena who plays the dominant role, asking more insightful questions and making more intelligent comments regarding Jesus' teachings. The dialogue reveals Magdalena as the true Sophianic voice of wisdom, indicating that she understands the teachings as if they were made for her. Jesus speaks in the *Pistis Sophia*:

"Mary [Magdalena], thou blessed one, whom I will perfect in all mysteries of those of the height, discourse in openness, thou, whose heart is raised to the kingdom of heaven more than all thy brethren."[6]

In trying to further understand the underlying importance of sixty-four, I asked my local source, and he began with the symbology of the game of chess: "It is simple, life happens at intersections. The eight times eight pattern exhibits this concept of the intersection of roads, of destinies. The chess game is nothing less than a metaphor of this confrontation of crossings, choices, and the result is life itself." He casually added that in the game of chess, the Queen is more powerful as she can move in any direction, hence, she has more freedom, and the Knight has twenty-two moves, another connection with Magdalena, whose feast day is on the 22nd of July. And it is not by chance that the Rennes-le-Château priest Bérenger Saunière placed twenty-two steps up to the belvedere, twenty-two steps that spiral up her tower, and twenty-two crenelations crowning the rooftop. (There are twenty-two letters in the Hebrew alphabet, in the major arcana in the tarot, and the number of paths in the Tree of Life of Kabbalah.) The priest placed sixty-four floor tiles in his Tour Magdala, and apparently, an old visitor's guide from the village said that originally the church floor dedicated to Magdalena had sixty-four black and white tiles.[7] Manly Hall indicated that a site such as this contains hidden knowledge:

> *"The chessboard consists of 64 squares alternately black and white and symbolizes the floor of the House of the Mysteries."*[8]

My friend's statement regarding the game of chess involving intersections rang another bell. One of Catalonia's sixty-four churches, Santa Magdalena de Perella, sits at the intersection four ancient pilgrimage routes, called *Ruta de les Quatre Ermites,* "Route of the Four Hermitages" or *Cruce de Caminos,* meaning "Crossroads." The equilibrium and balance in the shape of the Great Cross spanning the Pyrenees emanates a radiant zone, stabilized, and magnified in the Earth's stone temples, radiating this harmony to the four directions. This Great Cross formed by the axes of the Dragon Path (the Paris and Magdalena Meridians) and the Way of the Stars (the Magdalena Path) exists in both the etheric planes and on Earth. We often view alignments on a map from a flat linear perspective, however, these dragon currents are alive, breathing, pulsing, and creating subtle sounds in their movements. Magdalena sits at the center of this foundation geometry, an archetype for our age, shining like an invisible Grail over the Pyrenees. The sixty-four churches of Magdalena can be seen as a giant chessboard of life covering Catalonia and we are the players, making our choices at the intersections of life's journey. Will we choose the path of wisdom and love?

Maria Magdalena altar relief, Rennes-le-Château.

In another conversation with my source, he elaborated regarding the chessboard symbology. The choices we make determine the quality of the fabric we are weaving for our lives. He explained that Magdalena represents these crossing points, represented by the black and white squares on the board, the interplay between shadows and light, the material and spiritual, the corporal and the etheric, and that during her life she was moving between these dimensions. He reminded me of the interwoven grill pattern of Magdalena's fingers in her imagery in the region, including at the altar of her church in Rennes-le-Château. Her hands form multiple crosses, or X's, representing nexus points, and we are reminded once again that she is "Our Lady of the Cross" from the Leo poem in *Le Serpent Rouge*. This indicates Magdalena is holding a key to knowledge. She is asking us to embrace the opposites in duality, for therein lies the power. He finished by saying, "It all goes back to Egypt, to the dance between the opposing natures of the two divine couples, the Sacred Four, the foundation of Egyptian cosmology: Set, Isis, Osiris, and Nephthys, the letters spelling Sion."

The strange connections continued. In a conversation with my friend Luiz Pontual, he pointed out that in the Way of the Stars there are sixty-four *etapes*, meaning "steps or stages." This was a revelation and another potential key in the Pyrenean mysteries! I asked Luiz for the source of this information, and he said it came from the teachings of Carlos Martin La Moneda, an architect in urban development and an educator in geometry living in Zaragoza. I immediately contacted Carlos, who was generous and willing to share his knowledge. In his extensive research of the Camino, Carlos deployed teams of explorers across the Pyrenean valleys, who confirmed the sixty-four stages or segments on the ancient route departing from the Mediterranean.

Juego de la Oca, 19th c. Juan Francisco Piferrer printing, Barcelona.

Carlos compares the Camino with an old popular board game, *Juego de la Oca*, "Game of the Goose," which incorporates the sixty-four stages of development and transformation of the soul, symbolized by the goose ultimately becoming a swan. Some sources believe that the Knights Templar developed the game based on the lessons of the Camino, but that its roots are found in more ancient games, such as Egyptian, Greek, or Minoan. Other researchers trace its origins to Renaissance Europe. The Game of the Goose is designed as a spiral path and is described by scholar Adrian Seville in his paper "*The Geographical Jeux de l'Oie of Europe*"[9] as the most important spiral game ever devised. But it may have its origins in the mysterious coded Phaistos Disk from Crete, dating from circa 2000 BCE. The Disk is a spiral design of hieroglyphic symbols, and archaeologist Gareth Owens has spent thirty years trying to decipher it and suspects that it is a Minoan hymn to Astarte, the goddess of love.[10] Astarte has been compared to Venus-Aphrodite, who has the swan as her emblem, so this is indeed interesting. And of course, we can think of all the "Mother Goose" children's stories. It always goes back to the Mother Goddess.

The Game of the Goose is a journey through the labyrinth of life's lessons and diversions, with only 63 stages illustrated on the playing board, the additional stage being at the beginning position outside of the spiral. The beginning is at zero point. This is an important clue, as many ancient numbering systems, such as the Mayan 20-count system, begin with zero as the first number, or, 0–19. Another example is the 22 Major Arcana of the tarot are numbered 0–21. Zero is not "nothing," but instead it defines a marker, a place of origins, such as the Zero Meridian Dragon Path. The ultimate goal in the Game of the Goose is to arrive at the center of the spiral, a return to our origins. I reflected on how there is no game without the player, and no Camino without the pilgrim.

The Game of the Goose has been played by families and royalty across Europe since at least 1480 CE. One version was given as a gift by the Medici family to King Philip II of Spain, and we can be certain that this Florentine family, who supported the translation of ancient texts and the neo-Platonic Academies, was well aware of the game's Hermetic symbolism. Interestingly, the timing of the popularity of the Game of the Goose corresponds to the formation of the Order of the Swan Knights in Germany in 1440. The members were from noble families, and the Order was dedicated to veneration of the Virgin Mary and doing acts of charity. It is believed that the Swan Knights were inspired by a medieval French tale from the *chansons de geste*, "songs of heroic deeds."

In the famous story a Swan Knight came riding in a boat drawn by a beautiful swan and arrived at a grove along a lonely road, just in time to rescue a lovely damsel in distress. But, before he could save the noble lady, she had to promise never to reveal his name, suggesting that the fair knight was a member of a secret order, perhaps a Grail knight? In his epic grail story *Parzival*, Wolfram von Eschenbach incorporates the Swan Knight into the character Lohengrin, who lives in the Grail castle and is the son of the hero Parzival. The Swan Knights were woven into the Grail legends and were depicted as its guardians as well as protectors of the sacred feminine, often under the name of Mary.

The legend of the Swan Knight, the Knights Templar, the Grail, Maria Magdalena, the chessboard, the Game of the Goose, and the Camino de Santiago de Compostela seemed to be interwoven into a mysterious web, which when understood, would provide the key to understanding the Pyrenean legacy. As we have seen, Egypt has made its indelible imprint on Spain throughout the ages, and there is another possible correlation with the goose in the Camino. The Egyptian primeval god of Earth was Geb, who was represented as a goose and associated with all manner of creation. And overarching him in the sky is his divine counterpart, sister, and wife, Nut in the Milky Way. Is this a far memory of the original symbol of the goose in the Way of the Stars and culminating in the union of Geb and Nut in the marriage of Earth and Sky?

Swan Knight Lohengrin, postcard c. 1900.

The Game of the Goose is a puzzle with many possible dimensions of understanding. Carlos Martin confirmed many of my findings over nearly twenty years of explorations and research, regarding the dragon currents across the Pyrenees and the importance of Maria Magdalena in the initiation path of the Way of the Stars. The following are extracts from his response to my question regarding the sixty-four stages of the Camino:

Geb, Daniel Toye.

"I have traveled and studied the layout of this path ... and in the north of Catalonia, each valley, its sacred mountains, and its temples have a very specific vibratory and evolutionary function, the learning of the soul based on 64, like the squares of the Game of the Goose, and the final square (64), when the goose becomes a swan."

"The orography [shape of the mountains] of the north of the peninsula is characterized by the collision of two tectonic plates, the Iberian with the Eurasian, which gives rise to an important east-west fault ... it is a telluric place, where the fire from the interior of the earth flourishes, and for this reason, it is a propitious place to be used ... for internal evolution."

"... Telluric faults are called 'dragon currents' and are associated with places of transformation, of change of state. These places were sought by the Druids and master builders to locate temples. The equinoctial route from east to west of the north of the peninsula links the path of birth and death, of sacred initiation ... the path leads us to the union of polarity, the union of the masculine and the feminine. In esoteric tradition, Jesus and Magdalena represent the principle of sacred union that transcends life."[11]

Venus Tablet of Ammisaduqa, British Museum, Fae 2010.

In our correspondence, Carlos also described the Camino as an initiation path for the Templars, who venerated Magdalena. His comments confirmed the themes and patterns of sites I had discovered, including the Bridal Chamber chapel of Santa Magdalena de Perella, and the Seal of Solomon formation of Templar sites guarding Santa Magdalena de Montpalau. Both landscape patterns, the Great Cross and the Six-Pointed Star, feature Magdalena holding the center point, and both Perella and Montpalau are located on the Way of the Stars.

I showed my research on the Camino and the number sixty-four to Andrew Collins, and he pointed out that both the Mayan and Babylonian calendars used sixty-four-year Venus cycles. The Mayans observed that over periods of 8, 16, 32, and 64 years, Venus repeatedly returns to the same extreme rising and setting points on the horizon. (Hear "Return of Venus" music by author at the same footnote.)[12] These cycles were related to rituals ensuring the fertility of the land, their gods, and maintaining harmony and wellbeing in the realm. Babylonian astronomers were also recording Venus cycles, according to the "Venus Tablet of Ammisaduqa," dating to circa the 16th century BCE.[13] Could the sixty-four stages of the Camino be a

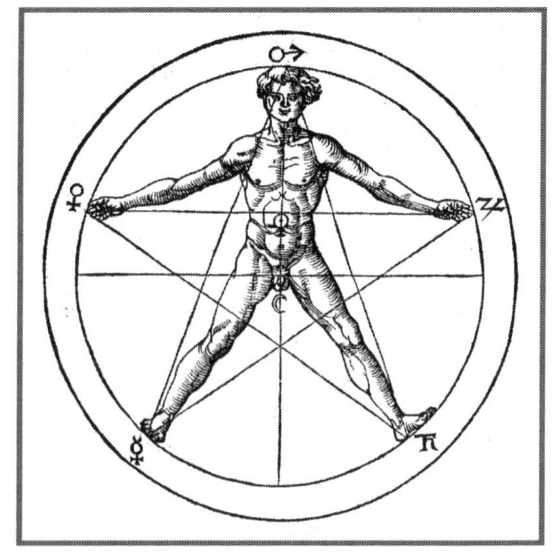

Heinrich Agrippa's Libri tres de occulta philosophia, 1486–1535.

fractal of time and space, tracing the greater Venus cycles in the heavens, and measured across the Earth in the steps of the initiate, culminating at the final stage and the transformation into a swan?

Aphrodite's Swan, 469 BCE Rhodes, British Museum.

I reflected on the importance of the multiple of eight as it relates to music. Eight tones form an octave, the word meaning "eighth." If we imagine plucking every eighth string of a harp, progressing up the scale, we ascend to higher and higher octaves. We could see the Camino as a harmonic progression, an evolutionary path, with each octave bringing a higher frequency, a lighter, more subtle dimension, thus purifying the initiate.

Remember that Venus is the only planet in our solar system to create a perfect geometric shape in her orbit. As viewed from the Earth, every eight years Venus makes thirteen orbits to form a perfect pentagram, a five-pointed star, comprised of golden mean angles, signifying perfection, harmony, and beauty. Rudolf Steiner called the pentagram the etheric human archetype. And the numbers five, eight, and thirteen are part of the Fibonacci sequence (attributed to the medieval Italian musician Leonardo Bonacci) and describe the Golden Ratio inherent in nature's growth patterns, such as pinecones, seashells, sunflowers, spiral galaxies, and the proportions of the human body. And most importantly here, is the musicality of the Fibonacci sequence, giving the harmonic patterns that produce beauty for our ears, and create coherence in mind, body, and spirit. (An octave on a piano has thirteen notes, eight white keys, and five black keys.) We can see how important Venus is in regulating harmony throughout our realm, and finding her perfection and beauty in the steps of the Camino is a revelation.

"The Ninth Table of the Spirits of Venus makes one beloved in all respects and makes known secrets through dreams."

THE SIXTH AND SEVENTH BOOKS OF MOSES:
FORMULAS OF THE MAGICAL KABALA,
TRANSLATED BY RABBI CHALEB.[14]

At the beginning of the Way of the Stars in the east, we have the sites dedicated to Venus-Aphrodite and Orpheus, both with strong associations with the swan. As

Saraswati's Swan, 1895, British Library.

mentioned, Aphrodite was carried to shore in her swan-drawn chariot and Orpheus ascended to heaven as the swan constellation of Cygnus. These ancient traditions at the eastern end of the Pyrenees set the tone for the initiation route and the final transformation into a swan, the bird of elegance, grace, and purity.

The association of the swan with liberation, rebirth, and the transformation of the soul is found in the Vedic texts dating from 1500–1200 BCE. This enormous body of early wisdom teachings describes the principle of Brahman as the ultimate reality and cause of the universe, the source of creation, which is symbolized as a "swan" (*hamsa* in Sanskrit). Brahma, the Hindu god of creation, is depicted riding this great white bird, as is Saraswati, the goddess of knowledge and the arts and music. In the Vedas, the flight of the swan symbolizes the liberation from suffering and from the cycles of birth, death, and rebirth.

This is a perfect metaphor for the Camino and the Way of the Stars, with the swan in the heavens as Orpheus, Brahma, Saraswati, Aphrodite, and the other multitudes of gods and goddesses related to this majestic winged one symbolizing the transformation of the pilgrim at the final stage. Orpheus, the god of harmony in the stars of Cygnus the swan, with his lyre of Lyra emanating celestial music, shines from above during the summer months guiding pilgrims by the Northern Cross and the Summer Triangle.[15] And does the great enchanter inspire songs in the travelers on the long road, the Camino de Canciones, the "Path of Songs?"

Many years ago, I composed a piece called "The Swan" for the wedding of a woman who had a special adoration for these mystical birds. But sadly, it became the song I played for her memorial following her sudden and unexpected death. I could imagine her soul flying free on the elegant harmonies and riding on its great white wings across the spacious skies.[16]

"And now, the swans, Apollo's future companions, most musical of birds, birds of the Muses ... flew in circles seven times around Delos (later the child god strung his lyre with seven strings, to match the seven songs they sang wheeling overhead)."

Callimachus (310–240 BCE), "Hymn 4: To Delos[17]

In Conclusion

"With these [magical] words Moses spake to the sorcerers in Egypt:

'The Lord appeared to his servant in the fire, to seal the earth in its four quarters, and the nether earth.'"

The Sixth and Seventh Books of Moses: Formulas of the Magical Kabala, translation by Rabbi Chaleb[1]

As a musician, I have always been fascinated by patterns of resonant similarities expressed in the shapes of things, geometry, number, music, patterns in the landscape, and the principles they represent, the language of mysticism. There is an uncanny perfection in the number sixty-four, the genetic codes of life, the number of Magdalena's churches in Catalonia, the foundation design and intersections of the cube and the Great Cross, and the Camino de Compostela. There is so much more to share regarding the patterns and synchronicities of this story, but I will save them for book two in this series, covering the meridian mysteries and guardians, from Paris to the Pyrenees.

Catalonia is magical, alive, alluring, inviting us to return again and again. It is the land I first discovered in dreams. In the first dream, I received the message to light four sacred fires, but exactly where was not made clear. Then in a vision, I saw an image of the Pyrenees shrouded in thick clouds, and as the fires were lit and the hidden places revealed, the clouds dissolved and the peaks became visible, shining, awakening ancient knowledge placed in this land long ago. Through the process of locating the sites for the fires, a Great Cross was revealed, perhaps placed by visitors from a far distant place in the stars.

Then in the dream of the Black Stone hieroglyphics the syllables Ka Ba were whispered, giving the crucial clue leading me to Magdalena de Perella, sitting at the center of the Great Cross and the intersection of the Dragon Path and the six-thousand-year-old pilgrimage route of the Way of the Stars. Following the path of the Paris Meridian across the Pyrenees and the Way of the Stars, I found they were both located on powerful terrestrial and celestial currents, and there were megalithic stone temples and sanctuaries of Magdalena with alignments marking the cycles of time, serving as guardians of the light.

The journey became a "Path of Songs," a *Camino de Canciones*. Music, poetry, and art have always been part of the creative fire and passion of Catalonia and all of Spain. Throughout the long process of nearly two decades, discovering the sites and lighting the sacred fires, a greater fire was lit in my heart, a "coming home" to forgotten aspects of myself. It was often consuming, overwhelming, always stimulating, and igniting deeper remembering.

Yet the journey has only just begun and countless discoveries await each initiate on the path, each step a portal to a new dimension of consciousness and possibilities. Who we truly are is unknown, but trusting in the dream, the imaginal realm, following our unique quest and the song within reveals the path. As in the journey of the initiate on the Camino of the Way of the Stars, we are all ultimately seeking true freedom, accessible when the outside noise dissolves in the stillness within. The present moment is pregnant with possibilities and the future is ours to create.

I shall close with a poem that poured forth in the wee hours of the morning when I began writing this book. Orpheus was already dropping hints, guiding my footsteps along the Way:

Orpheus mosaic, Antakya Archaeological Museum.

Sing O Orpheus,
Whisper through these lyre strings—
Enchant the rivers the springs and the stones,
And refine this fickle rascal wind.

Oh Orpheus, I see the colors of our flaming Sun,
Burning more radiant with your charming chant—
Even the ether cannot resist thy numinous golden tongue.

Play O Orpheus, move these bones to dance,
And send laughter shivering through the smallest cells,
Remembering an Earth more glorious, more possible.

Enchant us O Orpheus,
To enter the puissant power of your song,
Infusing, transforming the denser portions of this hour.

APPENDIX A

64 Maria Magdalena Sites in Catalonia

	SITE NAME	LOCATION
1.	Ermita de Santa Magdalena de Perella (Parella)	Sant Joan de les Abadesses
2.	Capilla de Santa Magdalena de Montpalau	Argelaguer (la Garrotxa)
3.	Santa Magdalena de Montcal	Maià de Montcal
4.	Ermita de Santa Magdalena	Terrades (Alt Empordà)
5.	Capella de Santa Magdalena	Olot
6.	Santa Magdalena de Vilajoan	Vilajoan (Garrigàs, Alt Empordà)
7.	Santa Magdalena de Puigsac Pardines,	Ripollès
8.	Santa Magdalena del Mont	Les Olletes
9.	Santa Magdalena del Coll	Vall del Bac (la Vall de Bianya)
10.	Santa Magdalena de Sant Joan les Fonts	Sant Joan les Fonts
11.	Santa Magdalena de Conangle	Les Masies de Roda
12.	Monestir de Santa Magdalena de Mosqueroles	Fogars de Montclús (Vallès Oriental)
13.	Santa Magdalena de Empuries	Sant Marti de Empuries
14.	Església de Santa Magdalena	La Seu d'Urgell
15.	Ermita de Santa Magdalena Hermitage Montserrat	Montserrat
16.	Convent de Santa Magdalena de Palma	Palma, Majorca
17.	Magdalena Hermitage	Puig Magdalena, Majorca

	SITE NAME	LOCATION
18.	Santa Magdalena de Cambrils	Vidrà, Girona
19.	Monestir de Santa Maria Magdalena	Barcelona
20.	Capilla de Santa Maria Magdalena de Solanllong	Gombrèn
21.	Iglesia de Santa Magdalena dels Arquells	Població d'Oliola, la Noguera Solsona
22.	Ermita de Santa Magdalena de Berrús	Riba-roja d'Ebre (Ribera d'Ebre)
23.	Santa Magdalena de Blancafort	Blancafort (Conca de Barberà)
24.	Santa Magdalena de Canyelles	Canyelles (Garraf)
25.	Església de Santa de Cervera	Cervera, a la comarca de la Segarra
26.	Santa Magdalena d'Esplugues	Esplugues de Llobregat (Baix Llobregat)
27.	Església de Santa Maria Magdalena	Pla del Penedès
28.	Església de Santa Magdalena	Pont d'Armentera (Alt Camp)
29.	Església de Santa Magdalena de Pontons	Pontons (Alt Penedès)
30.	Santa Maria Magdalena de Pradell	Pradell de la Teixeta (Priorat)
31.	Iglesia de Santa Magdalena de Puigbarral	Terrassa (Vallès Occidental)
32.	Santa Magdalena de Sanaüja	Sanaüja (Segarra)
33.	Ermita Santa Magdalena de Serramitja	Moià (Moianès)
34.	Esglesia Santa Maria Magdalena de Vergós Guerrejat	Municipi d'Estaràs, la Segarra
35.	Església de l'Hospital de Santa Magdalena	Montblanc, Conca de Barberà
36.	Església de Santa Magdalena de l'Astor	Pujalt
37.	Església de Santa Magdalena de l'Espelt	Òdena
38.	Santa Magdalena de l'Estela	Piera (Anoia)
39.	Capella de Santa Magdalena de la Vall (o del Soler)	Calonge de Segarra
40.	Capella de Santa Magdalena (Sant Feliu Sasserra)	Sant Feliu Sasserra
41.	Santa Magdalena de Castelladral	Navàs
42.	Capella de Santa Magdalena del Pla	Pont de Vilomara i Rocafort
43.	Ermita de Santa Magdalena de Talamanca	Talamanca

	SITE NAME	LOCATION
44.	Santa Magdalena de Cuberes	Baix Pallars, del Pallars Sobirà
45.	Santa Magdalena de la Pobla de Segur	Pallars Jussà
46.	Santa Magdalena de Ribalera o de Farrera	Pallars Sobirà
47.	Santa Magdalena de Cal Setó	Pinell de Solsonès
48.	Santa Magdalena del Collell	Guixers
49.	Ermita de Santa Magdalena de les Planes	Navès
50.	Iglesia de Santa Magdalena del Sàlzer	Sàlzer, al municipi d'Odèn
51.	Iglesia de Santa Magdalena de Tragines	Coma i la Pedra
52.	Santa Magdalena del mas Vilaprinyó :	Iglesia Castellar de la Ribera
53.	Església de Santa Magdalena de Vilaprinyó	Ruïnes Castellar de la Ribera
54.	Ermita De Santa Magdalena del Boixader	Vallcebre
55.	Santa Magdalena de la Cortada dels Llucs	Santa Maria de Merlès
56.	Santa Magdalena de Fígols	Montmajor
57.	Capella de Santa Magdalena	Torre De Faia, Gisclareny
58.	Església de Santa Magdalena de Guardiolans	Vilada, al Berguedà
59.	Convent de la Magdalena	Vinaròs
60.	Iglesia de la Santa Magdalena de la Tria	Prats de Lluçanès, Barcelona
61.	Capella de Santa Magdalena de Còdol-Rodon	Barcelona
62.	Ermita Santa Magdalena d'Ulldemolins	Ulldemolins (Priorat)
63.	Santa Magdalena de Bell-lloc	Sallent (Bages) vora el mas Martorell
64.	Parròquia Santa Maria Magdalena	Arnes, Tarragona

APPENDIX B

94 Maria Magdalena Sites in Northwestern Spain

(COASTAL AND NORTHERN CAMINOS)

Sites are named in Spanish and Galician, hence the variations in spelling.

	SITE NAME	LOCATION
1.	Capilla de Santa Maria de la Magdalena	Llanes
2.	Parroquia católica Santa María Magdalena	Doiras La Foz
3.	Church of St. Mary Magdalene	Carretera Ruedes (Gijon)
4.	Estanque secreto de la Magdalena	Santander (Nature sanctuary)
5.	Santuario da Virxe da Barca (Virgin of the Boat)	Muxia
6.	Capela da Magdalena	Ames (Santagio)
7.	Santa Maria Magdalena	La Penilla
8.	Iglesia de Santa Maria Magdalena	Población de Arriba
9.	Iglesia de la Magdalena	Cantabria
10.	Church of the Magdalena	Monasterio, Cantabria
11.	Iglesia de Santa María Magdalena	Rucandio
12.	Iglesia Santa María Magdalena	Póo de Cabrales
13.	Parroquia Santa María Magdalena	Quintana de Toranzo
14.	Humilladero Santa María Magdalena	Quintana de Toranzo
15.	Iglesia de Santa Maria Magdalena de Cáraves	Caraves
16.	Iglesia parroquial de Santa María Magdalena	Parres-Llanes
17.	Ermita de la Magdalena	Rases
18.	Ermita de Santa Magdalena near Cangas de Oris	Asturias
19.	Iglesia de Santa María Magdalena	Valle
20.	Capilla Santa María Magdalena	Villanueva, Asturias

	SITE NAME	LOCATION
21.	Iglesia de Santa María Magdalena de Los Pandos	La Magdalena, Asturias
22.	Parroquia católica de Santa María Magdalena	Doiras
23.	Iglesia Parroquial de Santa María Magdalena de Cayarga	Fuentes
24.	Iglesia Santa María Magdalena	Ribadesella
25.	Ermita de la Magdalena	Vega
26.	Iglesia de Santa María de Lugás	Cajide
27.	Parroquia católica de Santa María Magdalena	Isoba
28.	Santa Maria Magdalena Church	Marentes
29.	Colegiata de Santa María Magdalena	Cangas del Narcea
30.	Iglesia de Santa María Magdalena	Valle de Lago
31.	Iglesia de Santa María Magdalena de los Corros	Aviles
32.	Iglesia de Santa Maria Magdalena	Mieres del Camino
33.	Parroquia católica Santa María Magdalena	Peñafuente
34.	Parroquia católica de Santa María Magdalena	Doiras
35.	Capilla de Santa Maria Magdalena De Cabruñana	Loreda
36.	Iglesia de Santa María Magdalena de Linares	Linares
37.	Parroquia católica Santa María Magdalena	Linares del Acebo
38.	Parish of St. Mary Magdalene	Villafría
39.	Capilla de la Magdalena	Lugar Villanueva de Pria
40.	Iglesia de Santa María Magdalena de Barros	Langreo
41.	Igrexa de Santa María Magdalena de Fonfría	Fonfria
42.	Iglesia de Santa María Magdalena de Judán	A Pontenova
43.	Iglesia de Santa María Magdalena	Urria
44.	Iglesia de Santa María Madanela	A Proba de Burón
45.	Ilesia de la Madalena de Veigal.lagar	Cangas del Narcea
46.	Parroquia de Santa María Magdalena	Piedrafita de Babia
47.	Igrexa de Santa María Magdalena de Moscán	Castro
48.	Igrexa Santa Maria Magdalena	Baralla
49.	Igrexa de Santa María Magdalena de Matela	Outeiro de Rei
50.	Parroquia católica Santa María Magdalena	Escoureda
51.	Parroquia católica Santa María Magdalena	Castroverde
52.	Igrexa de Santa María Madanela de Pena	Pena

	SITE NAME	LOCATION
53.	Parroquia católica Santa María Magdalena	Manán de Santa María
54.	Parroquia católica Santa María Magdalena	Neira
55.	Parroquia católica Santa María Magdalena	Sabarei
56.	Igrexa de Santa Maria Madanela de As Nogais	As Nogais
57.	Ermida da Magdalena	Guntín
58.	Igrexa parroquial de Santa María Madalena de Coeses	Trasfontao
59.	Igrexa de Santa María Madalena de Mougán	Mougán
60.	Convento da Mercé	Portomarín
61.	Church of Saint Mary Magdalene of Montemaior	A Laracha
62.	Iglesia de Santa María Magdalena	Vedra
63.	Antiga Capela da Madalena	Betanzos
64.	Igrexa de Santa María Madalena de Aldemunde	A Coruña
65.	Capela da Madalena	Betanzos
66.	Capela de San Blas e da Magdalena	Cangas
67.	Capela da Madalena	Arzúa
68.	Cruceiro da Capela da Madalena	Vilarrel
69.	Capela de Santa Maria Madalena de Remourelle	Barreiros
70.	Capela da Madanela	Meira
71.	Capela da Magdalena	Ventas de Narón
72.	Capela da Madalena, Cruceiro e Fonte Santa	Dubra
73.	Ermida da Madalena A Coruña	A Coruña
74.	Igrexa de Santa María Madalena de Cedofeita	Ribadeo
75.	Ermita de María Magdalena	A Pontenova
76.	Capela da Madalena	Ribadeo
77.	Igrexa de Santa María Madalena de Sobrada de Aguiar	Outeiro de Rei
78.	Igrexa de Santa María Madalena de Neira de Cabaleiros	Láncara
79.	Igrexa de Santa Maria Madalena de Adai	Lugo
80.	Igrexa de Santa María Madalena de A Couboeira	Lugo
81.	Igrexa de Santa María Madalena de Vilarente	Lugo
82.	Capela da Madalena	Vilalba

	SITE NAME	LOCATION
83.	Parroquia De Santa María Magdalena	Plentzia
84.	Magdalena Baseliza	Mungia
85.	Ermita Santa María Magdalena de Nocedal	Nocedal
86.	Iglesia Santa Maria Magdalena	Zugaztieta
87.	Ermita de Santa María Magdalena de Arantzai	Bizkaia
88.	Ermita Santa María Magdalena	Durango
89.	Madalena baseliza	Azpeitia
90.	Parroquia Santa María Magdalena	Arrigorriaga
91.	Parroquia Santa María Magdalena / Albiz ondo gernika	Albiz
92.	Ermita de Santa María Magdalena	Ubidea
93.	Ermita de Santa María Magdalena de Zeinka-Zearregi	Ziortza-Bolibar
94.	Igrexa de Santa María Salomé	Santiago (one of the three Maries who arrived together from Palestine: Maria Salome, Jacobi, and Magdalena)

Endnotes

Introduction and Chapter 1

1 Martin Locker, "The Dragon in the Pyrenees" Perennial Pyrenees Project website, April 24, 2017: https://perrenialpyrenees.com/2017/04/24/weekly-article-6-the-dragon-in-the-pyrenees/.

2 Using information from ESA's Swarm satellite constellation, scientists have made a discovery about how energy generated by electrically-charged particles in the solar wind flows into Earth's atmosphere—surprisingly, more of it heads towards the magnetic North Pole than towards the magnetic South Pole... the electromagnetic energy transported by space weather clearly prefers the north." "Energy from solar wind favors the north" by European Space Agency, January 12, 2021, https://phys.org/news/2021-01-energy-solar-favors-north.html.

3 R.A. Schwaller de Lubicz, *The Temples of Karnak,* Inner Traditions, Rochester, VT, 1999. P 71.

4 Rory Duff, *A Guide to Leylines, Earth Energies, Nodes, & Large Vortexes,* 2021, 2nd edition, self-published Amazon print, p. 42.

5 Mega meaning large, and lithic meaning stone.

6 See Appendix A, "Sixty-Four Santa Magdalena Churches in Catalonia."

7 H. P. Blavatsky, abridged & annotated by Michael Gomes, *The Secret Doctrine,* Jeremy P. Tarcher/Penguin, New York, 2009, p. 172. Originally published 1888.

8 *Ibid.,* p. 169.

9 Philip Gardner with Gary Osborn, *The Serpent Grail: The Truth Behind the Holy Grail, the Philosopher's Stone and the Elixir of Life,* Watkins Publishing, London, 2007, p. 130.

10 Paul Broadhurst and Hamish Miller, Dance of the Dragon, Pendragon Partnership, Launcestion, 2000.

11 John Michell, The New View Over Atlantis, Thames and Hudson Ltd, London, 1983, p. 62.

12 Ibid., p. 37.

13 *The Homeric Hymns,* translated by Hugh G. Evelyn-White, 1914, II, lines 299–300, Sacred Texts online (www.sacred-texts.com).

14 Buffy Johnson, *Lady of the Beasts: The Goddess and Her Sacred Animals,* Inner Traditions, Rochester Vermont, 1994, p. 169.

15 Ani Williams, "Mag-Ma of the Deeps," *Guardians of the Dragon Path and Return of the Shining Ones* albums, Songaia Sound Productions, 2023 and 2021: https://aniwilliams.com/product/guardians-of-the-dragon-path-mp3/and https://aniwilliams.com/product/return-of-the-shining-ones-mp3/.

16 Throughout this book I will use the Catalan spelling *Canigó,* rather than the French *Canigóu,* as most of the story transpires in Catalonia.

17 Ani Williams, "Dragon's Serenade," *Guardians of the Dragon Path and Return of the Shining Ones* albums, Songaia Sound Productions, 2023 and 2021: https://aniwilliams.com/product/guardians-of-the-dragon-path-mp3/and https://aniwilliams.com/product/return-of-the-shining-ones-mp3/.

18 Eusebius, *Praeparatio Evangelica V,* xiv, 1, cited by Joscelyn Godwin, *The Mystery of the Seven Vowels: In Theory and Practice,* Phanes Press, Grand Rapids, MI, 1991, p. 22.

19 Blavatsky, p. 174.

20 Ibid.

21 Ibid., p. 175

22 *Pistis Sophia* translated by G.R.S. Mead, Mockingbird Press, 2016, p. 236. Originally published 1921.

23 Ibid., p. 234

24 Ibid., p. 232.

25 Ani Williams, "Treasury of Light," filmed September 2021, Puivert Château, by Paul Vlaicu for Earthling Project, *Ancient Harmony to the Moon:* https://www.youtube.com/watch?v=bcIsMb7nW-8.

26 Richard H. Wilkinson, *The Complete Gods and Goddesses of Ancient Egypt,* Thames and Hudson, London, 2020, p. 185. One example of the astronomical painting mentioned is on the ceiling of the tomb of Sethos I in the Valley of the Kings.

27 Andrew Collins, The First Female Pharaoh: *Sobeknereru, Goddess of the Seven Stars,* Bear & Company, Rochester, VT, 2023, p. 303, citing Coffin Texts Spell 612.

28 Description of Sound Alchemy—Bio-Acoustic trainings: https://aniwilliams.com/songaia-sound-training/.

29 Cynthia Bourgeault, *Introducing the Imaginal,* Part 1 of a three-part blog, Nov. 13, 2018: https://www.cynthiabourgeault.org

30 Paul Murdin, *Full Meridian of Glory: Perilous Adventures in the Competition to Measure the Earth,* Springer Science and Business Media, New York, 2009, p. 12.

31 Murdin, p. xiv. (The first experiments by the Academy of Sciences carried out by Cassini I, Huygens, Picard, and Romer produced the result that sound passes at a speed of 180 toises, or 1080 Parisian feet per second).

[32] On March 30, 1791, the French Academy of Sciences defined the measure of one meter as one ten-millionth of the distance from the Equator to the North Pole. They established the relationship between the meter and the speed of light as the distance traveled by light in a void in 1/299,792,458 of a second.

[33] Camille Flammarion, *L'Atmosphère.* Paris, Hachette, 1888, pp. 362–3.

[34] Graham Hancock and Robert Bauval, *Talisman: Sacred Cities, Secret Faith,* Penguin Group, London, 2004, pp. 366–7

Chapter 2

[1] Quoted in Malcolm Godwin, The Holy Grail: Its Origins, Secrets & Meaning Revealed, Viking Studio Books, New York, 1994, p 242.

[2] Ani Williams, *A Troubadour's Journey in Cathar Country,* 2012, Part I, p. 1: https://aniwilliams.com/a-troubadours-journey-in-cathar-country-part-1/. Also see parts 2 and 3.

[3] Quoted in Sabine Baring Gould, A Book of the Pyrenees, Methuen & Co., London, 1907, p. 5.

[4] Jean Abélanet, L'homme et le cerf, préhistoire d'un mythe, Editions Trabucaire, Canet, 2017, pp. 33–4.

[5] René Char, "Black Stags," reproduced in ibid., p. 34. Translated from the French by the author.

[6] *The Life of Teresa of Jesus: The Autobiography of Teresa of Ávila,* trans. and ed. by E. Allison Peers, from the critical edition of P. Silverio de Santa Teresa, Crown Publishing, 1960, p. 191.

[7] Erich von Däniken's Chariots of the Gods Podcast, Episode 3, guest Andrew Collins with von Däniken discussing Collins' 2022 book Origins of the Gods: https://youtu.be/7nxxh3MmJWk.

[8] Robert Graves, *Mammon and the Black Goddess,* Cassel & Company, London, 1965, p.164.

[9] E. W. Gifford, *Northeastern and Western Yavapai,* University of California Press, Berkeley, CA,1936, p. 313.

[10] Francesc Jaubert de Paça, Històriques i Geogràfiques Sobre La Muntanya de Roses I el Cap de Creus, Roses Publicacions Municipals, Roses, p. 112. First published Paris 1824. Translation from Catalan by author.

[11] Godwin, p. 211.

[12] Ean Begg, *The Cult of the Black Virgin,* Penguin Books, London, 1996, p. 197.

[13] Ani Williams, *Regina de Montserrat,* live video, Montserrat: https://www.youtube.com/watch?v=YcExHBARhoE. Studio-recorded version on *Guardians of the Dragon Path* and Calling *Pyrene* albums, 2023 and 2017: https://aniwilliams.com/product/guardians-of-the-dragon-path-mp3/ and https://aniwilliams.com/product/calling-pyrene-mp3/.

Chapter 3

1 Marija Gimbutas, *The Language of the Goddess,* Thames and Hudson, 1989, p. 319.

2 Ani Williams, "Quest for Invisible Treasure," 2023, Le Poulpiquet Films, Rennes-les-Bains, https://youtu.be/Lf-BIgdD1dc Henry Lincoln's books include *Holy Blood, Holy Grail* (co-authored with Michael Baigent and Richard Leigh) *The Holy Place,* and *Key to the Sacred Pattern.*

3 Manfred Clynes, *Sentics: The Touch of the Emotions,* Anchor Press, New York, NY,1977. For more information on the human voice and healing: http://aniwilliams.com/voice-spectrum-analysis/

4 Ehime Ora, Twitter, October 17, 2021: https://twitter.com/ehimeora/status/1449598870791630850

5 *Vajra Guru Mantra* by Ani Williams, *"Medicine Song I"* CD, Songaia Sound Productions, Sedona, AZ, 2000: https://aniwilliams.com/product/medicine-song-i-mp3/. Ani Williams, *Archaeoacoustics in Stonehenge,* Zoom presentation "Sound and Sacred Places" for Linea University, 2022, https://youtu.be/3pODY2wQg-4.

6 Ferran Blasco and Elyn Aviva, *Where Heaven and Earth Unite: Powerful Places, Sacred Sites, and You,* Pilgrims Process Inc., Santa Fe, NM, 2014, p. 33.

7 John Michell, *The New View Over Atlantis,* pp 65–6

8 Gerald Massey, *A Book of the Beginnings Vol II: Egyptian Origines in the Hebrew, Akkado-Assyrian and Maori,* Williams and Norgate, London, 1881, p. 13

9 We can find the same wave form used for the symbol of the zodiac sign of Aquarius, the era which we are currently on the cusp of entering. Aquarius, the "Water Bearer," is illustrated as two parallel wave forms. This same symbol can also be seen as electromagnetic currents, sound waves, and as depicting serpent and dragon currents. The Age of Aquarius is certainly bringing an era of electrical connections, instant global connectivity, acoustical research, and wave-form technology, used in communication networks, and non-invasive forms of sound medicine, all varying forms of *nadi,* subtle currents of energy.

10 This principle of sound and subtle energy imprinting matter is called "cymatics," a term created by Hans Jenny (1904–1972), a Swiss physician and scientist. His cymatics experiments showed how the effect of sound waves create visible shapes, which he called a "dynamic ordered pattern."

11 Ani Williams, Songaia Sound Medicine research on brain states with the late Dr. Juan Acosta, University of Washington, Seattle, 1997. https://aniwilliams.com/songaia-sound-medicine/

12 Ajit Mookerjee,: *Kundalini The Arousal of the Inner Energy,* Destiny Books, Rochester, VT, 1986, p. 29.

13 Michio Kaku, *The Universe Is a Symphony of Vibrating Strings,* Big Think video series, May 31, 2011: https://youtu.be/fW6JFKgbAF4.

Chapter 4

1 Quoted in Shannon Grimes, Ph.D., *Becoming Gold: Zosimos of Panopolis and the Alchemical Arts in Roman Egypt*, Rubedo Press, Auckland, 2018, p. 109.

2 *One Hundred Syllable Mantra,* Ani Williams, Tibetan mantra, "Medicine Song I and Lyric Book" CD, 2000: https://aniwilliams.com/product/medicine-song-i-mp3/.

3 Quoted in Azriel Reshel, "Science Finally Proves Meridians Exist," https://uplift.love/science-finally-proves-meridians-exist/.

4 Oscar Herradón, "Jaime I el Conquistador, el rey cruzado," *Historia de Iberia Vieja: revista de historia de España*). 2008, no. 39, p. 15.

5 Ani Williams, "Ode to Ramon Lull," Calling Pyrene CD, 2017, https://aniwilliams.com/product/calling-pyrene-mp3/. Lyrics in Hebrew: HA BAHIR, MALAKIM, BERACHAH (Brilliant, illuminating blessings of the Angels). Lyrics in Arabic: YA SALAAM ALLAHU (Oh peace of God).

6 George Sand, *Les Sept Cordes de la Lyre,* Michel Lèvy Frères Editeurs, Paris, 1869, translation from French for the author by Henry Lincoln. (Henry and I performed an extended version of this Hermetic play as an interactive theater event at a French castle in 2012).

7 Translation by Bart D. Ehrman, *Lost Scriptures: Books That Did Not Make It into the New Testament,* Oxford University Press, New York, 2003, p. 326.

8 Ibid., p. 325.

9 Ibid., pp. 325–6.

10 Swami Muktanda, *Does Death Really Exist?,* SYDA Foundation, New York, 1981, p. 36.

11 Ehrman, p. 326.

12 Ibid.

13 Choa Kok Sui, *Om Mani Padme Hum: The Blue Pearl in the Golden Lotus,* Institute for Inner Studies, Manila, p. 55.

14 Ani Williams, "Dragon & Pearl," *Guardians of the Dragon Path* and *Dragon & Pearl* albums, 2023 and 2020: https://aniwilliams.com/product/dragon-pearl-mp3/ and https://aniwilliams.com/product/guardians-of-the-dragon-path-mp3/

15 Henry Smith Williams, "Colossus," *The Biography of Mother Earth,* National Travel Club,. New York, NY, 1931, p. xxvi. (Williams was the great grand uncle of the author).

16 Sir Clements R. Markham, The Story of Majorca and Minorca, Smith, Elder & Co., London, 1908, p. 225.

17 For more information see: Andrew Collins, *Göbekli Tepe: Genesis of the Gods,* Bear & Co., Rochester, VT, 2014, and his upcoming book on Karahan Tepe.

18 Mallorca's official website: https://yosoymallorca.com/en/history-of-mallorca/

19 Francesc Sàbat, Bernadí Gelabert Ferrer, Antonio Rodríguez Perea, "Minorca, an Exotic

Balearic Island (Western Mediterranean)," *Geologica Acta:* an international earth science journal, vol. 16, special no. 4, 2018, p. 413.

20 Ibid, p. 422.

21 Strabo, *Geography,* translated and edited by H.C. Hamilton and W. Falconer, George Bell & Sons, London, 1892, vol I, p. 252 (Book III, chapter V).

22 Video example of Minorca's taulas: https://youtu.be/7nm9Di0rdtY and history https://youtu.be/bGqVjPTPUCI

23 With appreciation for research provided by Andrew Collins, from *Hűrriyet Daily News* June 28, 2022.

24 Hunbatz Men, *Secrets of Mayan Science/Religion,* Bear & Company, Rochester, VT, 1989, p. 58.

25 James Maffie, *Aztec Philosophy: Understanding a world in Motion,* University Press of Colorado, Boulder, CO, 2015, p. 137.

26 Ani Williams, *Stones and Stars That Sing,* 2022 article on archeoacoustics: https://aniwilliams.com/stones-and-stars-that-sing/.

27 Michael Hoskin, "The Talayotic Culture of Menorca: A First Reconnaisance," *Archaeoastronomy* supplement to *Journal for the History of Astronomy,* vol. 16, no. 9, 1985, p.142. http://adsabs.harvard.edu/full/1985JHAS...16..133H

28 Antoni Ferrer, Irene Riuvadets, Gerard Remolins and Cristina Bravo, "What meaning do the taula venues have in Menorca?," talk at the Menorca Museum, February 25, 2021.

29 Andrew Collins, *The Cygnus Key: The Denisovan Legacy, Göbekli Tepi, and the Birth of Egypt,* Bear & Company, Rochester, VT., 2018, p. 18.

30 Margaret Murray, *Egyptian Religious Poetry,* John Murray, London, 1949, p. 17.

31 Quoted in Joscelyn Godwin, pp. 72–4.

32 Sir Alan Gardiner, Egypt of the Pharaohs, Clarendon Press, Oxford, 1961, p. 73.

33 Dietrich Wildung, *Egyptian Saints: Deification in pharaonic Egypt,* New York University Press, 1977, p. 34.

34 Margaret Murray, *Egyptian Religious Poetry,* p.103.

35 Graham Hancock, *Magicians of the Gods: The Forgotten Wisdom of Earth's Lost Civilisation,* Hodder & Stoughton Ltd, 2016, p 170, drawing from E.A.E. Reymond, The Mythical Origin of the Egyptian Temple, Manchester University Press, Manchester, 1969.

36 Ibid, pp. 174–5. The papyrus containing the *Tale of the Shipwrecked Sailor,* dating from circa 2000–1700 BCE of Egypt's Middle Kingdom, was in the *Imperial Museum of St. Petersburg* and is now in Moscow, identified as P. Leningrad 1115.

37 Ibid, referencing Miriam Lichtheim, *Ancient Egyptian Literature: A Book of Readings, Vol. I: the Old and Middle Kingdoms,* University of California Press, Berkeley, 1991, pp. 212–3.

38 Philip A. Harland, "Egyptian wisdom: Plato on Solon, the Egyptian priest, and Atlantis," Ethnic Relations and Migrations in the Ancient World website, October 15, 2022, http://philipharland.com/Blog/?p=7109.

Chapter 5

1 Henry Smith Williams, *The Historian's History of the World, Volume X—Spain and Portugal,* Hooper & Jackson Ltd. London, 1909, p 3.

2 Moustafa Gadalla, *Egyptian Romany—The Essence of Hispania,* expanded edition, Tehuti Research Foundation, Greensboro, NC, 2018, p. 129.

3 Herodotus, *The Histories,* translation A.D. Godley, Harvard University Press, Cambridge, MA, 1920, vol. I, p. 414.

4 Ibid., vol. II, pp. 239–41.

5 Henry Smith Williams, *The Historian's History of the World, Volume 2,* Hooper & Jackson Ltd. London, 1908, p 247. Note: 1500 BCE is the date listed for the Phoenician expansion and settlements in Cyprus, and other eastern Mediterranean sites. Following the departure of the Egyptians from Phoenicia in 12th century BCE, the Phoenicians founded settlements in Iberia.

6 Benjamin Collado Hinarejos, Los fenicios en la peninsula Iberica, Ediciones Akal, 2017, p. 11.

7 Ibid.

8 R. O. Faulkner, *Egyptian Seagoing Ships, The Journal of Egyptian Archaeology,* vol. 26, 1941.

9 Diodorus Siculus, translated by C.H. Oldfather, *Library of History: Books III-VIII,* Harvard University Press, Cambridge, MA, 1935, p. 193.

10 From the Berlin Papyrus, 1425, in James Teackle Dennis, *The Burden of Isis: Being the Laments of Isis and Nephthys,* E. P. Dutton and Company, New York, 1910, p. 21.

11 Ibid.

12 E. A. Wallis Budge, *Egyptian Book of the Dead: The Hieroglyphic Transcript and English Translation of the Papyrus of Ani,* Gramercy Books, Random House, Avenel, New Jersey, 1995, p. 524.

13 Ani Williams, "Tears of Isis," *Guardians of the Dragon Path* album, 2023. lyrics inspired by Egyptian text *The Burden of Isis:* https://aniwilliams.com/product/guardians-of-the-dragon-path-mp3/. Music video at Dendera, Egypt, 2022, with Floriana Rubino on frame drum. Thank you to Kathleen McGowan's temple team: https://www.youtube.com/watch?v=KfkQUxB5gu4

14 Henry Smith Williams, Vol II, p. 251.

15 Ibid., pp. 309–9.

16 Barbara G. Walker, *The Woman's Encyclopedia of Myths and Secrets,* HarperCollins, New York, NY, 1983, p. 70.

17 Ibid.

18 Franck Goddio, "Thonis-Heracleion: From Legend to Reality," Frank Goddio: Underwater Archaeologist website, November 16, 2022, https://www.franckgoddio.org/projects/sunken-civilizations/heracleion/

19 Gadalla, *Egyptian Romany,* p. 120, quoting Herodotus, *Histories, Book II*

[20] William Smith, *Dictionary of Greek and Roman Biography and Mythology,* Taylor & Walton, London, 1846, vol II, p. 401.

[21] *The Archaeologist—Ancient Civilizations of the World* website, December 22, 2021, on the findings of Ricardo Belizón, Seville University: https://www.thearchaeologist.org/blog/spain-researchers-believe-they-found-fabled-temple-of-hercules-gaditanus.

[22] Quoted in Andrew Collins and Chris Ogilvie-Herald, *Tutankhamun—The Exodus Conspiracy,* Virgin Books, London, 2002, p. 172.

[23] Ralph Ellis, *Scota—Egyptian Queen of the Scots,* Adventures Unlimited Press, Kempton, IL, 2007, p. xiv.

[24] Ibid., pp. 69–73.

[25] Luisa Bonadies, "Cultural Exchange in the Stone Vessels Production of the First Millennium BCE," in E. Foietta *et al, Cultural & Material Contacts in the Ancient New East: Proceedings of the International Workshop, 1–2 December,2014 Torino,* Apice Libri, Florence: https://shs.hal.science/halshs-03176353/document

[26] *Avant les Celtes—l'Europe a l'Age du Bronze—2500–800 J-C,* l'Association Abbaye de Doualas, 1988, p. 102.

[27] Joan Muñoz, Oscar Ross, Patricia Bassa editors, *L'enigma iber: Arqueologia d'una civilització,* Museu d'Arqueologia de Catalunya, Barcelona, 2022, p. 174.

[28] Gadalla, *Egyptian Romany,* pp. 234–5.

[29] Collins and Ogilvie-Herald, p. 172.

[30] *History and Antiquities of Tara Hill,* MS in Trinity College Dublin, quoted in Michael Slavin, *The Book of Tara,* Merlin Publishing, Dublin, 1998, p. 21.

Chapter 6

[1] Ani Williams, "Fire on the Mountain," *Guardians of the Dragon Path* and *Calling Pyrene* albums, Songaia Sound Productions, 2023 and 2017: https://aniwilliams.com/product/calling-pyrene-mp3/.

[2] Juan Saez, *Lugares de poder: Los guardianes de la Luz,* Ediciones EcoHabitar, Navarre, 2017, p. 46, translation by the author.

[3] David Cowan and Chris Arnold, *Ley Lines and Earth Energies: A Groundbreaking Exploration of the Earth's Natural Energy and How It Affects Our Health,* Adventures Unlimited Press, Kempton, IL, 2003 pp. 28.

[4] *Ibid.,* p. 29.

[5] Ronald W. B. Morris, *The prehistoric rock art of Galloway and the Isle of Man,* Blandford Press, 1979.

[6] Pope Gregory, *Dialogues, Book 2: Life of Benedict,* chapters 1, 5, 11, https://www.osb.org/gen/greg/tocalt.html

[7] H. P. Blavatsky, *Isis Unveiled: A Master-Key to the Mysteries of Ancient and Modern Science and Theology,* Vol. 1, J. W. Bouton, New York, 1877, p. 35.

Chapter 7

1 Robert Graves, *The White Goddess: A Historical Grammar of Poetic Myth,* revised edition edited by Grevel Lindop, Farrar, Straus and Giroux, New York, 2013, p. 426.

2 E. W. Gifford, "Northeastern and Western Yavapai," *American Archaeology and Ethnology,* Volume 34, No.4, 1936, p. 313.

3 Gimbutas, p. 71.

4 *Ibid.,* p. 218.

5 Dea Madre discovered Senorbi, Sardinia, Museo archeologico nazionale di Cagliari. Image wikicommons.

6 John Michell, *The Sacred Center: The Ancient Art of Locating Sanctuaries,* Inner Traditions, Rochester, VT, 2009, p. 26.

7 It is best to leave the site clean, without melted wax, so using tealights and removing them when you leave is important. "Honor the place but leave to trace" is my motto.

8 Anne MacKaye Chapman,"The Moon-Woman in Selk'nam Society," The Reed Foundation, https://www.thereedfoundation.org/rism/chapman/moon-woman.htm

Chapter 8

1 Walker, p. 972.

2 *The Ancient Egyptian Pyramid Texts,* translation by R.O. Faulkner, Clarendon Press, Oxford, 1969, p 137.

3 Gerald Massey, *A Book of the Beginnings: Volume I—Egyptian Origines in the British Isles,* Williams and Norgate, London, 1881, pp. 13–14.

4 See James Cameron's 2017 TV film *'Atlantis Rising'.*

5 Von Del Chamberlain, "Navajo Constellations in Literature, Art, Artifact and a New Mexico Rock Art Site," *Archaeoastronomy* Vol VI, Numbers 1–4, January-December 1983.

6 "Sunken Civilizations," Franck Goddio, Underwater Archaeologist website, https://www.frankgoddio.org/projects/sunken-civilizations/heracleion

7 Joan B. López, Assumpció Malgosa, Josep Gallart, and Núria Rafel, "Cova de Montanissell (Salent-Coll de Nargó, Alt Urgell). Operació 'Senyora de les Muntanyes'," Cota Zero, no. 20, 2005.

8 Robert Graves, *The Greek Myths,* Penguin Books, London, 1992, p. 497.

9 Silius Italicus, *Punica (The Second Carthaginian War),* Book III, translated by A. S. Kline, 2018: https://archive.org/details/punicasi01siliuoft/page/144/mode/2up

10 Faulkner, *Pyramid Texts,* p.272, PT Utterance 662, line 1875.

11 Herodotus, p. 329.

12 Barry Cunliffe, *The Ancient Celts* Penguin Books 1999, p. 109.

13 Ani Williams, "Calling Pyrene," *Guardians of the Dragon Path* and *Calling Pyrene* albums, 2023 and 2017, https://aniwilliams.com/product/guardians-of-the-dragon-path-mp3/ and https://aniwilliams.com/product/calling-pyrene-mp3/.

14 Walker, p. 832.

15 Graves, *The Greek Myths,* p. 148.

16 Anne Baring and Jules Cashford, *The Myth of the Goddess: Evolution of an Image,* Penguin Books Ltd. London, 1993, p. 518.

17 Walker, p. 991.

18 Manly P. Hall, *The Secret Teachings of All Ages: An Encyclopedic Outline of Masonic, Hermetic, Qabbalistic, and Rosicrucian Symbolicall Philosophy,* Wilder Publications, 2007. (Originally published 1928.)

Chapter 9

1 Ibid., p. 442.

2 Just below the solar plexus is another cauldron of fire, the Dan T'ien, the navel center often called the Hara, which can be translated as the "Elixir Field" the qi/chi center. The Dan T'ien is another source of inner fire and a center point of equilibrium.

3 Jacint Verdaguer. *Canigó, Cant II : Glordeneu,* Fundacio Jacint Verdaguer i Edicions 62, Barcelona, 1980, p. 27. Translation by the author.

Chapter 10

1 John Michell, *The View Over Atlantis,* Ballentine Books, New York, 1973, p. 160.

2 Abbé H. Boudet, *The True Celtic Language and The Stone Circle of Rennes-les-Bains* English edition, Les Editions de l'Oeil du Sphinx, Paris, 2008, p. 245. (Original French edition, *La Vraie Langue Celtique et le cromleck de Rennes-les-Bains,* Carcassonne, 1886.)

3 Quoted in Jean-Yves Leloup, *The Gospel of Philip: Jesus, Mary Magdalene, and the Gnosis of Sacred Union,* Inner Traditions, Rochester, VT, 2003, p. 67.

4 Ani Williams, "Salt of Earth," *Guardians of the Dragon Path* and *Song of Sophia* albums, 2023 and 2012: https://aniwilliams.com/product/guardians-of-the-dragon-path-mp3/ and https://aniwilliams.com/product/song-of-sophia-mp3/. Music video: https://aniwilliams.com/salt-of-the-earth/.

5 Michell, *The Sacred Center,* p. 69.

6 *The Fountain of the Lovers of the Science* by John Fountain of Valencienn, County of Hainault, Lyons 1590, third edition. A 17th-century manuscript English translation is in MS Sloane 3637 in the British Library.

7 Boudet, p. 247.

8 Dolmen Can Planes would be the third fire lit at the southern end of the Great Cross, adding precision to the length of the northern and southern arms.

9 Boudet p. 233. On Boudet's map there are two Cugulhou sites in the Cromlech of Rennes-les-Bains, Cugulhou Levant and another which is located on a hill at the opposite northwestern edge of the village. The Cassini map established during the measuring of the Paris Meridian only lists the northwestern worked stone labeled *Cuguillou.*

10 Hildegard of Bingen, "Hymn to the Holy Spirit": http://www.hildegard-society.org/2015/01/o-ignee-spiritus-hymn.html

11 Ani Williams, "Earth Mother," *Children of the Sun and Earth Rising* albums, 1990 and 2020, Songaia Sound Productions. https://aniwilliams.com/product/earth-rising-mp3/ and https://aniwilliams.com/product/children-of-the-sun-mp3/

12 Chang Sok Suh, *Acupuncture Anatomy: Regional Micro-Anatomy and Systematic Acupuncture Networks,* Taylor & Francis, Abingdon, 2015, p. 3.

13 Boudet, p. 233.

14 Sus Krassel and Kaj Lilliendal, *Rennes-le-Château, Maria Magdalena and the Master Builders,* Blanche-Negre, Rennes-les-Bains, 2017, p. 100.

15 Earthling Project "Ancient Harmony to the Moon" music videos filmed at Cugulhou Levant with Lauren Pederson, Sara Grabow and the author under the film direction of Paul Vlaicu: 13th century runic chant for dreaming, "Drømde mik en drøm I" https://youtu.be/xlGlV_71JVs, longer version: https://youtu.be/xlGlV_71JVs ; Nahuatl traditional song, "Santa Maria Guadalupe," https://www.youtube.com/watch?v=j-YJqfQi0a4. Navajo Beauty-Way song, "Shinaasha," https://www.youtube.com/watch?v=BPtZ9J5VnWs.

16 A note regarding the site Cugulhou Levant. It is very difficult to find, as I have tried on my own and have gotten lost each time. There is no marked trail, and it is in rough terrain. My sense is that the site is better left that way. Some places need to be protected to maintain their natural peace and sanctity, protected by the guardians, and continually renewed by the elements that surround the stones.

17 René Guénon, "The Language of the Birds," reprinted in Martin Lings and Clinton Minnaar, *The Underlying Religion: An Introduction to the Perennial Philosophy,* World Wisdom, Inc., Bloomington, IL, 2007, p. 172.

18 Margaret A. Murray, *Ancient Egyptian Legends,* John Murray, London, 1913, p. 30.

Chapter 11

1 Elizabeth Van Buren, *The Sign of the Dove,* Neville Spearman, London, 1983, p. 106.

2 Ian Heron, "The Roerichs' Stone: A Summary of Research Findings," Nicholas Roerich and the Chintamani Stone blog, March 13, 2012: https://roerichandchintamani.wordpress.com/.

3 Ken Zoll, "Archaeoastronomy in the Verde Valley," lecture attended by author in Sedona, Arizona in 2019.

4 Esther Harding, *Women's Mysteries,* Harper Colophon, New York, 1976, p. 41.

5 Marie Parsons, "The Opening of the Mouth Ritual," Tour Egypt website, no date: http://www.touregypt.net/featurestories/open.htm.

6 Gadalla, *Egyptian Romany*, p. 27.

7 Parsons.

8 E.A. Wallis Budge, *The Pyramid Texts,* Kindle edition by Patricia Spencer on CreateSpace Independent Publishing Platform, 2016, p. 8.

9 Lucie Lamy, *New Light on Ancient Knowledge: Egyptian Mysteries,* Thames and Hudson, London, 1989, p.59.

10 Budge, *The Pyramid Texts*, p. 13. (Added text by Budge.)

Chapter 12

1 Marta Crispí and Míriam Montraveta, *A Guide to the Monastery and Museum of Sant Joan de les Abadesses*, Junta de Monestir de Sant Joan de les Abadesses, 2006, p.5.

2 Marsilio Ficino, translation and critical notes by Carol V. Kaske and John R. Clark, *Three Books on Life,* Arizona Center for Medieval and Renaissance Studies (ACMRS) Press, Tempe, AZ, 2019, p. 45.

3 Ibid., pp. 249, 355.

4 Ani Williams, *Voice Spectrum Analysis*, Songaia Sound Bio-Acoustic Medicine: https://aniwilliams.com/voice-spectrum-analysis/.

5 *The Gospel of Mary Magdalene*, translation by Jean-Yves Leloup, Inner Traditions, Rochester, Vermont, 2002, p. 115.

6 Ibid.

7 Rabanus Maurus, translated by David Mycoff, *The Life of Saint Mary Magdalene and of her Sister Saint Martha: A Medieval Biography*, Cistercian Publications, Athens, Ohio, 1989, pp. 55–56.

8 Ibid, p. 56.

9 Ani Williams, "Fragrance of Fire," from the album *Garden of the Magdalene: Banish Me No More*, 2007: https://aniwilliams.com/product/garden-of-the-magdalene-mp3/; https://youtu.be/zKSUyMKdJ-c.

10 Michel Tardieu, *Écrits gnostiques : Berlin Codex,* Éditions du Cerf, Paris, 1984, p. 518.

11 Jacobus de Voragine, William Caxton translation (1483), *The Golden Legend: Lives of the Saints,* Aeterna Press, 2015, p. 620.

12 Jean Houston, *The Passion of Isis and Osiris: A Gateway to Transcendent Love*, Ballantine Books, 1995, p. 359.

13 Rabanus Maurus, p. 107.

14 See appendix, "A Sixty-four Maria Magdalena Churches in Catalonia."

15 Ani Williams, "Nefer Ka Ra," lyrics adapted from Margaret Murray, *Egyptian Religious Poetry, Song of Sophia* album, 2013, recorded live in Sainte Salvayre Chapel, Southern France and featured on Guardians of the Dragon Path album, 2023: https://aniwilliams.com/product/guardians-of-the-dragon-path-mp3/ and https://aniwilliams.com/product/song-of-sophia-mp3/

Chapter 13

1 Morton Smith, *Jesus the Magician: A Renowned Historian Reveals How Jesus was Viewed by People of His Time,* Red Wheel/Weiser, San Francisco, California, 2014, p. 111.

2 Ibid., p. 116.

3 Ibid., p. 117.

4 Jacobus de Voragine, p. 614.

5 Gregory I, Homilia XXXIII, *Homiliarum in evangelia,* Lib. II, *Patrologia Latina* vol. 76, col. 1239A.

6 Jacobus de Voragine, p. 421.

7 Ibid.

8 Ibid., p. 423.

9 Cynthia Bourgeault, *The Meaning of Mary Magdalene: Discovering the Woman at the Heart of Christianity,* Shambhala Publications, Boston, Massachusetts, 2020, p. 227.

Chapter 14

1 Aaron A. Burke, "*Magdalūma, Migdālîm, Magdoloi,* and *Majdāīl*: The Historical Geography and Archaeology of the *Magdalu* (*Migdal*)," *Bulletin of the American Schools of Oriental Research,* Vol. 346, no. 1, 2007, Appendix 1.

2 See ibid. for a detailed study of these sites.

3 Ibid., pp. 30–1.

4 https://www.vatican.va/content/francesco/en/audiences/2017/documents/papa-francesco_20170517_udienza-generale.html, https://www.vatican.va/roman_curia/congregations/ccdds/documents/articolo-roche-maddalena_po.pdf

5 Ani Williams, "Apostola Apostolorum," *Garden of Blue Roses: Banish Me No More* CD, 2007: https://aniwilliams.com/product/garden-of-the-magdalene-mp3/

Chapter 15

1 Quoted in Xavier Aquilue, *Iberia Graeca,* Centro Iberia Graeca, Girona, Spain, 2012, p. 180.

2 Rhodes-Roses is located less than a mile south of the site of lighting the First Fire at dolmen Creu d'en Cobertella. This dolmen in the megalithic route marking the eastern arm of the Great Cross is on the same latitude as Santa Magdalena de Perella, 42°15' N. This latitude of the east-west axis would become more important as new discoveries were revealed.

3 *Quoted in Elizabeth Silverthorne and Geneva Fulgham, Women Pioneers in Texas Medicine, Texas A&M University Press, College Station, TX, 1997, pp. xvii.*

4 Godfrey Higgins, *Anacalypsis, an Attempt to Draw Aside the Veil of the Saitic Isis,* Longman, Rees, Orme, Brown, Green and Longman, London, 1836, Vol I, p. 218

5 The Hapsburg castles and fortifications were situated at strategic Mediterranean sites in addition to Rhodes, at Barcelona, Majorca, and Ibiza, all sites in Catalonia and close to the northern, southern, and eastern arms of the landscape cross. Another Hapsburg castle to the west, overlooking the city of Camprodon ("Camp of the Wheel," *rodon*) is near the Paris Meridian and the center of the landscape cross, a short distance north of Santa Magdalena de Perella. The castle guarded the pass leading to France through the Pyrenees via the Col de Ares (Catalan for "Neck of Ares," the Greek god). This route was on a branch of the old Roman Road, Via Romana, where it turns north near Perella.

6 Olivier Defaux, *The Iberian Peninsula in Ptolemy's Geography: Origins of the Coordinates and Textual History*, Berlin Studies of the Ancient World No. 51, Edition Topoi, Berlin, 2017: https://edition-topoi.org/download_pdf/bsa_051_00.pdf.

7 Kenneth Heuer, *City of the Stargazers*, Charles Scribner's Sons, New York, 1972, p. 97.

8 Defaux.

9 Lluís Buscató I Somoza, *La colònia grega de Rhode*, BRAU edicions, Figueres, 1999, pp. 145–155.

10 Walker, p. 218.

11 Ibid., p. 972.

12 Somoza, p. 148.

13 Manuel Forcano & Victor Hurtado, *Atles d'Història dels Jueus de Catalunya*, Barcelona Department de Cultura, 2019. p. 10.

14 John William Taylor, *The Coming of the Saints: Imaginations and Studies in Early Church History and Tradition,* E.P. Dutton and Company, New York, 1907, p. 2.

15 Mycoff, Introduction to Rabanus Maurus, p. 3.

16 Josep Burch and Lluis Palahi editors, *The Monastery of Santa Maria de Roses*, Documenta Universitaria, Girona, Spain, 2019, p. 24.

17 Francesc Jaubert de Paça, *Recerques Històriques i Geogràfiques Sobre La Muntanya de Roses I el Cap de Creus*, Roses Publicacions Municipals, Roses, 2008, pp. 72, 144. (Catalan translation from French original, translation from Catalan by the author).

18 Strabo, *Geography* Book III, Chapter, 4,8–9, quoted in *Empúries: Guia Didàctica*, Museu d'Arqueologia de Catalunya-Empúries, Empúries, 2013, p. 36.

19 Ani Williams, "Mariam Maria," *Guardians of the Dragon Path*, 2023, and *Chalice of Holy Fire*, 2015: https://aniwilliams.com/product/guardians-of-the-dragon-path-mp3/ **https://aniwilliams.com/product/chalice-of-holy-fire-mp3/ Music video recorded in Serres Church, France:** https://www.youtube.com/watch?v=g80lmbYC0lM&t=24s

Chapter 16

1 Josep Maria, "Santa Magdalena de Montcal," associate priest of Opus Dei, Girona, Catalonia, https://algunsgoigs.blogspot.com/2016/06/goigs-santa-magdalena-esglesia-de-santa.html

2 *Oxford Dictionary of Languages:* https://www.oed.com/search/dictionary/?scope=Entries&q=Palladion

3 Santa Magdalena de Montpalau, *Goigs I devocations populars*: https://algunsgoigs.blogspot.com/2016/03/goigs-santa-magdalena-argelaguer.html

4 Luiz Pontual Marx, "Essencias de Magdalena": https://esenciasdemagdalena.com

5 Gimbutas, p. 145.

6 Ani Williams, "Guardianes," *Guardians of the Dragon Path* album, 2023: https://aniwilliams.com/product/guardians-of-the-dragon-path-mp3/

7 https://algunsgoigs.blogspot.com/2018/04/goigs-santa-magdalena-vallfogona-de.html

8 *Goigs a llaor de la Gloriosa Santa Magdalena* de la Parroguia de Sant Esteve de Pardines. https://bd.centrelectura.cat/items/show/17848

Chapter 17

1 *Goigs a Llaor de Santa Maria Magdalena*, (Joyful songs at the House of Saint Mary Magdalene), song sheet given to the author at Perella chapel on Magdalena's feast day celebration.

2 Manal B. Hammad, "Bees and Beekeeping in Ancient Egypt" (A Historical Study)," *Journal of Association of Arab Universities for Tourism and Hospitality*, Vol. 15, Issue 1, 2018, p. 2: https://jaauth.journals.ekb.eg/article_47990_882687660670d76346cdfda54f7b3e20.pdf

3 R. A. Schwaller de Lubicz *The Egyptian Miracle: An Introduction to the Wisdom of the Temple,* Inner Traditions, Rochester, Vermont, 1985, p. 40.

4 Dante Alighieri, translated by Charles Eliot Norton, *The Divine Comedy of Dante Alighieri, Vol III: Paradise*, Houghton, Mifflin & Co., Boston, 1892, p. 198.

5 James P. Allen, *The Ancient Egyptian Pyramid Texts*, second edition, SBL Press, Atlanta, Georgia, 2015, p. 7.

6 Leloup, p. 83.

7 Ibid., p. 87.

8 Song of Solomon 1:10, New Living Translation: https://biblehub.com/songs/1-10.htm.

9 Lamy p. 82.

10 Leloup, pp. 29, 30.

11 Robert Brydon, *The Guilds the Masons and the Rosy Cross*, Rosslyn Chapel Trust, Roslin, 1994, p.8.

12 Maria Rosa Valdesogo, *Hair and Death in Ancient Egypt: Mourning Rites in the Pharaonic Period*, BLKVLD Publishers, Zandvoort, 2019, p. 29.

13 R. A. Schwaller de Lubitz, *The Temple of Man*, Inner Traditions, Rochester, Vermont, 1981, p. 42.

14 Margaret Starbird, *The Woman with the Alabaster Jar: Mary Magdalen and the Holy Grail*, Bear & Co, Rochester, VT, 1993. p. 131.

15 Ibid., p. 91

16 Ibid., p. 95

17 *Fulcanelli: Master Alchemist. Le Mystère des Cathédrales*, 1964 Paris, C.W. Daniel, Essex, England, 1991, p. 148.

18 Jacint Verdaguer, *Selected Poems of Jacint Verdaguer*, edited and translated by Ronald Puppo, University of Chicago Press, Chicago, Illinois, 2007, p. 137.

19 Christian Bernadac, *Le Mystere Otto Rahn (Le Graal e Montségur) du catharisme au nazisme*, Éditions France-Empire, Paris, 1978, p. 79.

20 Coincy-Saint Palais, *Esclarmonde de Foix: princesse cathare*, Éditions des Deux Rennes, Rennes-le-Château, 2021, p. 67. First published Collection Belisane, Paris, 1954, Translations by author.

21 Coincy-Saint Palais, *Le Saint Graal et le Précieux Sang,* self-published, 1972. (Wagner's work was inspired by Wolfram von Eschenbach's *Titurel* and *Parzival* Grail romances, written circa 1220 CE.)

22 René Nelli, *Dictionaire des heresies meridionale,* Toulouse, 1968, p. 216, quoted by Michael Baigent, Richard Leigh, and Henry Lincoln, *Holy Blood, Holy Grail*, Delacort Press, Random House, New York, NY, 2004, p. 62.

23 Ani Williams, "Nuestra Doña de Catalonia," *Guardians of the Dragon Path*, 2023 and *Calling Pyrene* albums, 2020: https://aniwilliams.com/product/guardians-of-the-dragon-path-mp3/ and https://aniwilliams.com/product/calling-pyrene-mp3/

Chapter 18

1 Ramon Hervás Marcó, Historia Secreta del Grial, Ediciones Royland, Barcelona, Spain, 1998, p. 248, translation by author.

2 Martin Locker, "The Dragon in the Pyrenees," Perennial Pyrenees website, April 24, 2017, https://perrennialpyrenees.com/2017/04/24/weekly-article-6-the-dragon-in-the-pyrenees/.

3 Ibid.

4 Xavier Roviró i Alemany, *100 Llegendes de la Plana de Vic*, Farell Editors, Barcelona, 2000, p. 99.

5 Alguns Goig blog: https://algunsgoigs.blogspot.com/2018/08/goigs-santa-magdalena-ermita-de-santa.html

6 www.monestirs.cat/monst/bcn/cbn02magd.htm

7 Ken Doyle, *Apostle to the Apostles: The Story of Mary Magdalene*, Catholic Times, September 11, 2011.

8 Eugene TeSelle, *Augustine the Theologian*, Wipf and Stock Publishers, Eugene, Oregon, 2002, p. 343.

9 Baigent, Leigh, and Lincoln, p. 112.

10 "Monasterio de las Egipcíaques," Monasterios de Calalunya website: www.monestirs.cat/monst/bcn/cbn02egip.htm

11 "The Thunder Perfect Mind," translated by George W. MacRae, The Gnosis Archive website: http://gnosis.org/naghamm/thunder.html.

12 Ani Williams, "Stella Maris," *Garden of the Magdalene: Banish Me No More* album, Songaia Sound Productions, 2007. https://aniwilliams.com/product/garden-of-the-magdalene-mp3/

13 "Ermita de Santa Magdalena," Tot Montserrat website: https://totmontserrat.cat/religio/vida-eremitica/les-ermites-de-la-muntanya-de-montserrat/ermita-de-santa-magdalena/

14 Albert Cassanyes Roig, "Monges i Patromoni del Monestir de Santa Magdalena de la Ciutat de Mallorca a Mitjans del Segle XIV," *Bolletí di la Societat Arqueològica Lul·liana*, vol. 70, 2014, p. 103.

15 Coincy-Saint Palais, *Esclarmonde de Foix: Princess Cathare,* Editions des Deux Rennes, Rennes-le-Château, 2021, based on first edition, p. 13.

16 Jean Reynal, Jean-Philippe Alazet, *Le Palais des Rois de Mallorca: Lixique Illustré,* Editions Trabucaire, Perpignan, 2010, pp. 64–65.

17 Kathleen McGowen, *Boleyn Heresy: Part I—The Time Will Come,* Flower of Life Press, Lyme, CT, 2022, pp. 270–271.

18 Verdaguer, "Virolai to Montserrat," Selected Poems of Jacint Verdaguer, p. 153.

19 *Le Serpent Rouge,* attributed to Pierre Feugère, Louis Saint-Maxent, and Gaston de Koker, quoted in Baigent, Leigh and Lincoln, *Holy Blood, Holy Grail,* p. 102.

20 Higgins, vol. II, p. 413.

Chapter 19

1 Elizabeth Van Buren, *Refuge of the Apocalypse: Doorway Into Other Dimensions,* C.W. Daniel, Ashingdon, 1986, p. 10.

2 Michio Kaku, *The Multiverse Has 11 Dimensions*, Big Think Series, September 29, 2010, https://bigthink.com/videos/the-multiverse-has-11-dimensions-2/#

3 The traditional alchemical vessel is often illustrated containing the White Queen and the Red King, representing the alchemical marriage and the process of transmutation into the Hermaphrodite (the union of Hermes and Aphrodite), gaining potency through the unification of female and male qualities. Symbolically, this produces a being capable of parthenogenesis, or "virgin births" similar to procreation in species such as bees and some serpents.

4 Pere, "Witches in Pyrenees," Barcelona website, April 16, 2020: https://www.barcelonawalking.net/witches-in-pyrenees/

5 Blasco and Aviva, p. 46.

6 John Michell, *The View Over Atlantis*, Ballantine Books, New York, NY, 1973, p. 159.

7 Clifford Mahooty, interviewed in "Honoring Clifford Mahooty—Star People," directed by Mikey Leisner, The Strange Road YouTube channel, January 27, 2022, https://www.youtube.com/watch?v=BQur3Af5SLA

8 Ibid Blasco and Aviva, p. 41.

9 Eleanor Hull, *Folklore of the British Isles,* 1928, quoted in Stuart McHardy, *The Quest for the Nine Maidens*, Cromwell Press, Trowbridge, 2003, p. 145

10 *Pistis Sophia*, p. 236.

Chapter 20

1 Michell, *The View Over Atlantis,* p. 49.

2 Ani Williams, "Draco's Turning," on album *Dragon & Pearl*, 2020: https://aniwilliams.com/product/dragon-pearl-mp3/

3 In "Interstellar Links to Gobekli Tepe," *Ancient Civilizations*, TV series, Gaia, 2017.

4 See "Archaeoacoustics in Stonehenge: The Effects of Mantras and Aeolian Harp," presentation by the author to Linea University Archeology Department's "Sound and Sacred Places" program, 2022, https://youtu.be/3pODY2wQg-4.

5 Paul Devereux, *The Powers of Ancient and Sacred Places*, Daily Grail Publishing, Brisbane, 2022, p. 105.

6 Ani Williams, "Always Remember You," *Guardians of the Dragon Path*, and *Return of the Shining Ones* albums, 2023 and 2021: https://aniwilliams.com/product/guardians-of-the-dragon-path-mp3/ https://aniwilliams.com/product/return-of-the-shining-ones-mp3/

7 In "Energy Secrets of the Great Pyramid," episode in *Ancient Civilizations,* Gaia.

8 John Michell, *The New View Over Atlantis,* Thames and Hudson, London, 1983, p. 62.

9 R. A. Schwaller de Lubicz, *The Temples of Karnak*, Inner Traditions, Rochester, Vermont, 1999, p. 71.

10 Amanda Morris, "Nearly 1,000 mysterious strands revealed in Milky Way's center," Northwestern Now website, January 26, 2022: https://news.northwestern.edu/stories/2022/01/nearly-1000-mysterious-strands-revealed-in-milky-ways-center

11 Pyramid Texts, Utterance 509, lines 1120–23, quoted in Lucie Lamy, *Egyptian Mysteries: New Light on Ancient Knowledge,* Thames and Hudson, London, 1989, p. 28

12 Andrew Collins, *The Cygnus Key: The Denisovan Legacy, Göbekli Tepe, and the Birth of Egypt,* Bear & Company, Rochester, Vermont, 2018, p. 132.

13 Utterance 474, lines 939–941, R.O. Faulkner, *The Ancient Egyptian Pyramid Texts*, Oxford University Press, London, 1969, p. 162

14 Mircea Eliade, *Shamanism: Archaic Techniques of Ecstasy*, quoted in Jeremy Narby, *The Cosmic Serpent, DNA and the Origins of Knowledge*, Jeremy P. Tarcher/Putnam, New York, 1999, p. 17

15 Ibid., p. 16.

16 Voice Spectrum Analysis, https://aniwilliams.com/voice-spectrum-analysis/

17 Ani Williams, "Gayatri Mantra," *'Song of Sophia'* CD, Songaia Sound Productions, 2012: https://aniwilliams.com/product/song-of-sophia-mp3/. Mantra: AUM BHOOR BHUWAH SWAHA TAT SAVITUR VARENYAM, BHARGO DEVASAYA DHEEMAHI DHIYO YO NAHA PRACHODAYAT.

18 H. H. Wilson and Bhasya of Sayancarya, RGVEDA SAMHITA: Rig Veda in 4 Volumes, Parimal Publication PVT. Ltd. 2022, from the 1866 text no. 3.62.

19 See: https://power.nridigital.com/power_technology_jan19/events

20 Ani Williams, *Stones and Stars that Sing,* article 2022, https://aniwilliams.com/stones-and-stars-that-sing/.

Chapter 21

1 Quoted in Moustafa Gadalla, "Music and Entertainment in Ancient Egypt: Excerpt from *Historical Deception: The Untold Story of Ancient Egypt*," p. 2: https://studylib.net/doc/7610992/music-and-entertainment

2 "NASA Voyager Space Sounds—Jupiter," Ambispheric YouTube channel: https://youtu.be/N10ySpqc9r4

3 Quoted in Virginia Sease and Manfred Schmidt-Brabant, *Paths of the Christian Mysteries: From Compostela to the New World*, Temple Lodge Publishing, Forest Row, 2003, p. 89.

4 Francesc Jaubert de Paça, p. 104, Translation from Catalan by author. ("Aphrodite's Sea" is a movement in the song by Ani Williams, "Calling Hygeia," *Dragon & Pearl* album, 2020: https://aniwilliams.com/product/dragon-pearl-mp3/.)

5 Diodorus of Sicily, translation C.H. Oldfather, *Diodorus of Sicily in Twelve Volumes*, William Heinemann, London, 1935, Vol. II, p. 425.

6 Ibid.

7 Quoted in Angela Voss, *Father Time and Orpheus*, Abzu Press, Oxford, 2003, p 5.

8 Ibid., p 4.

9 Turn the image 20 to the right 90 degrees to see Cerberus clearly.

10 Algonkian traditional song "We Are the Stars Which Sing," (Nilun Pesēsmuk Elintakwik) recorded by Ani Williams, Lauren Pedersen, Sara Grabow, at Château Ducs de Joyeuse, Couiza, France, September, 2020, as part of Earthling Project's Ancient Harmony to the Moon series: https://www.youtube.com/watch?v=8pDVjRqTMWE

11 Hunbatz Men, p. 30. The Mayan pronunciation is *Ge*, with a breathy soft "G" and short "eh" sound. An interesting correlation is found in the frequency of G#, related to the Galactic Center in the direction of the constellation of Sagittarius, as illustrated in the "Zodiac Tone Wheel" of Songaia Sound Medicine: https://aniwilliams.com/songaia-sound-medicine/.

12 Ibid., p. 34.

13 American Museum of Natural History website: https://www.amnh.org/exhibitions/permanent/the-universe/stars/a-spectacular-stellar-finale/we-are-stardust

14 George E. Lankford, *Reachable Stars: Patterns in the Ethnoastronomy of Eastern North America*, University of Alabama Press, 2007, Tuscaloosa, Alabama, p. 206.

15 Dani Valdéz, see more of his amazing videos and photography at https://danivaldes.com.

16 Enriqueta Pons I Brun, *Pobles de Muntanya, Pobles d'Aigua al Pirineu Oriental (110–650 aC)*, Brau Edicions, Girona, 2000, p. 38. (translation from Catalan by author)

17 Murray, *Ancient Egyptian Legends*, p. 86.

18 Pons, p. 38.

19 Ibid., p. 38.

20 Ibid., p. 39.

21 Sease and Schmidt-Brabant, pp. 91–92.

22 Ibid., p. 52.

23 Ani Williams, "Field of Stars," *Calling Pyrene* CD, 2017: https://aniwilliams.com/product/calling-pyrene-mp3/

Chapter 22

1 Jaubert de Paça, p. 110.

2 Ibid., p. 71, citing Jerónimo Pujades, *Crónica de Catalunya.*

3 Ibid., p. 112.

4 Juan Saez, "Light and Alchemy: The Secret of Sant Pere Galligants": http://artezahori.blogspot.com/2018/01/light-and-alchemy-secret-of-sant-pere.html

5 Otto Rahn, *Lucifer's Court: A Heretic's Journey in Search of the Light Bringers*, Inner Traditions, Rochester, Vermont, 2008, p. 56.

6 Mladen Tomorad, *Egyptian Cults of Isis and Serapis in Roman Fleets: The diffusion of Egyptian cults in the Greek and Roman World*, University of Zagreb, Croatia, 2003, p. 5.

7 Xenophon, *The Symposium*, from the Project Gutenberg website: https://www.gutenberg.org/files/1181/1181-h/1181-h.htm

8 J. B. Trend, *The Civilization of Spain* by Oxford University Press, London, 1958, p. 9.

9 Walker, p. 972.

10 Gadalla, *Egyptian Romany*, p. 22.

11 Ani Williams, "Tears of Isis," *Guardians of the Dragon Path* album, 2023. lyrics inspired by the Egyptian text *The Burden of Isis:* https://aniwilliams.com/product/guardians-of-the-dragon-path-mp3/. Music video at Dendera, Egypt, 2022, and later studio recording: https://youtu.be/ZedBgaCeEew

12 Gadalla, p. 115.

13 Collins, *The Cygnus Key*, p. 132.

Chapter 23

1 Saez, p. 111.

2 Devereux, p. 105.

3 Dennis Overbye, "It Came From a Black Hole and Landed in Antarctica," *New York Times*, July 12, 2018.

4 Murray, *Egyptian Religious Poetry*, p. 60.

5 Saez, p. 98.

6 Faulkner, p. 182.

7 Ibid., p. 184.

8 Chandra X-ray Center, translated images of four elements from Cassiopeia A in a sonification process to produce this music: https://youtu.be/X3SJo9BZ7o4

[9] Faulkner, p. 187.

[10] Lankford, pp. 185–6, The Star Woman myth was originally told by Tenskwatawa, a Shawnee prophet.

[11] Murray, *Egyptian Religious Poetry*, p. 57.

[12] Gretchen Cornwall, *The Secret Dossier of a Knight Templar of the Sangreal*, Grapevine Press Ltd., Ramsgate, 2018, p. 321.

[13] Rabanus Maurus, quoted in Mycoff, p. 107.

[14] Lilliendal, p. 82.

[15] Sease and Schmidt-Brabant, p. 125.

[16] Ani Williams, "Voices of the Moor" *Earth Rising* CD, Songaia Sound Productions, 2021: https://aniwilliams.com/product/earth-rising-mp3/

[17] Ani Williams, "Earth Mother," ibid.

[18] Sease and Schmidt-Brabant, p. 128.

[19] William A. Christian, Jr., *Apparitions in Late Medieval and Renaissance Spain*, Princeton University Press, Princeton, New Jersey, 1989, pp. 29, 52.

[20] Trend, p. 56.

[21] Francisco Luengo, conductor, "*Ordo Prophetarum,*" http://franciscoluengo.com

[22] "El Llibre Vermell of Monserrat": https://www.musicologie.org/sites/l/livre_vermeil_de_montserrat.html

[23] "Sardana: Music and identity in the most popular Catalan dance," Patrimoni Cultural de Catalunya website: https://patrimoni.gencat.cat/en/collection/sardana

[24] This link of *Canto de Ultreya* is performed by the choral group Antorei de Pozuelo and the instrumental group La Tricotea. https://youtu.be/6ncUg54EsDk

[25] Sease and Schmidt-Brabant, p. 122.

[26] Ani Williams, "Andamos y Cantamos," *Guardians of the Dragon Path* and *Return of the Shining Ones* albums, 2023 and 2020: https://aniwilliams.com/product/guardians-of-the-dragon-path-mp3/, https://aniwilliams.com/product/return-of-the-shining-ones-mp3/

Chapter 24

[1] Xavier Aquilué, "Las Colonias Griegas en Iberia,"in *Iberia Graeca: El legado arqueológico griego en la península Iberica*, Centro Iberia Graeca, Girona, 2012, p. 50.

[2] Ibid.

[3] Callimachus of Cyrene, *Hymn III. to Artemis*, translated by Mair in A.W. Mair and G. R. Mair, *Callimachus, Lycophron, Aratus,* Loeb Classical Library edition, William Heinemann, London, 1921, p. 81.

[4] Strabo, *Geographika*, IV, 1, 4, posted in Museum of Empúries special exhibition, 2017.

[5] Callimachus, *Hymn III to Artemis*, in Mair & Mair, p. 61.

6 Baring and Cashford, p. 202.

7 Walker, p. 59.

8 Ani Williams, "Dance of Artemis," *Guardians of the Dragon Path* and *Dragon & Pearl* albums, 2023 and 2020: https://aniwilliams.com/product/guardians-of-the-dragon-path-mp3/ and
https://aniwilliams.com/product/dragon-pearl-mp3/

9 M. A. Murray, *Ancient Egyptian Legends*, John Murray, London, 1920, p. 96.10.

10 Ammianus Marcellinus, *History, Volume II: Books 20–26,* (Book XXII.16.12), translated by John C. Rolfe, Loeb Classical Library edition, Harvard University Press, Cambridge, MA, 1940, p. 303

11 Joaquín Ruiz de Arbulo and David Vivó, "Dubtes sobro un déu: Ascelpiu o Serapis?," in *L'Esculapi: El Retorn del Déu*, Museu d'Arqueologia de Catalunya, Barcelona, 2008, p. 170.

12 Ibid., p. 176.

13 Ibid., p. 172.

14 Quoted in E.A. Wallis Budge, *Egyptian Magic*, Cosimo Classics, New York, New York, 2005, p. 59.

15 Richard Wilkinson, The Complete Gods and Goddesses of Ancient Egypt, Thames and Hudson, Ltd, London, 2020, p. 149.

16 Ibid., p. 173.

17 Tomorad, p. 242.

18 Ibid., p 245.

19 Murray, *Ancient Egyptian Legends*, p. 85.

20 Ani Williams, "I Am All That Is," *Guardians of the Dragon Path* and *Song of Sophia* albums, 2023 and 2013: https://aniwilliams.com/product/guardians-of-the-dragon-path-mp3/ and https://aniwilliams.com/product/song-of-sophia-mp3/

21 Budge, *Egyptian Book of the Dead*, p. 305.

22 Ani Williams, *Song of Isis*, 1987 album recorded live in the temples of Egypt: https://aniwilliams.com/product/song-of-isis-mp3/

23 *Hermetica: The Ancient Greek and Latin Writings which contain Religious or Philosophical Teachings ascribed to Hermes Trismegistus*, translated by Walter Scott, Clarendon Press, Oxford, 1924, Vol I, p. 341.

24 C.A. Meier, *Healing Dream and Ritual: Ancient Incubation and Modern Psychotherapy,* Daimon Verlag, 2009, Einsiedeln, p. 3.

25 Kayley Body, "Imhotep and Asclepius: How Egyptian Medical Culture Influenced the Greeks," *Haley Classical Journal* Vol. I Issue II, July, 2020, p. 16: https://issuu.com/haleyclassicaljournal/docs/the_haley__issue_ii_final/s/10730817

26 Ludwig Edelstein, *The Hippocratic Oath,* Johns Hopkins Press, Baltimore, MD, 1943.

27 Ani Williams, "Calling Hygeia," *Guardians of the Dragon Path* and *Dragon & Pearl* albums,

2023 and 2020: https://aniwilliams.com/product/guardians-of-the-dragon-path-mp3/ and https://aniwilliams.com/product/dragon-pearl-mp3/

28 Ovid, *Metamorphoses*, Book 1, translation by Allan Mandelbaum: http://www.webwinds.com/thalassa/themis.htm

29 Père Castanyer, Marta Santos, Joaquim Tremoleda, Roger Sala, Helena Ortiz, Ramon Julià, Jordi Montaner and Santiago Riera, "New information about the Santa Margarida sector in Empúries based on archaeological excavation, geophysical prospection and the sedimentary register," *Méditerranée: Revue géographique des pays méditerranéens*, Issue 133, 2021, p. 47.

30 Veronique Flayol www.magdalenesacredjourneys.com in conversation with the author. Father Faillon is Etienne Michel Faillon and the full account of the discovery of Magdalena's sarcophagus can be found in his book *Monuments inédits sur l'apostolat de Sainte Marie-Madeleine en Provence,* published in Paris, 1865. Philippe de Cabassole was a cardinal who was elected bishop of Cavaillon, France, in 1334 CE. Bernard Gui was a Dominican friar, Bishop of Lodeve, France, and an official Inquisitor during the Albigensian Crusade against the Cathars and other rebellious factions in the region. Gui became a key character in Umberto Eco's novel *The Name of the Rose.*

31 Ani Williams, "Garden of Blue Roses," *Garden of the Magdalene: Banish Me No More*, 2007: https://aniwilliams.com/product/garden-of-the-magdalene-mp3/

32 Castanyer, *et al.*

33 Jacobus de Voragine, p. 609.

34 Janet Tassel, "Antioch Revealed: Treasures from an ancient city dazzle in a new exhibit," *Harvard Magazine,* November 1, 2000, p. 1: https://www.harvardmagazine.com/2000/11/antioch-revealed.html

35 Gerald Massey, *A Book of the Beginnings, Volume II: Egyptian Origines in the Hebrew, Akado-Assyrian and Maori,* Williams and Norgate, London, 1881, p. 27.

36 Marcó, p. 269.

Chapter 25

1 Taylor, p. 106.

2 Ibid., p. 105.

3 Ani Williams, "Viva la Santa Maria," *Guardians of the Dragon Path* and *Song of Sophia* albums, 2023 and 2013: https://aniwilliams.com/product/guardians-of-the-dragon-path-mp3/ and https://aniwilliams.com/product/song-of-sophia-mp3/

4 *The Dialogue of the Savior,* Nag Hammadi Library, translation by Stephen Emmel, The Gnostic Society Library: http://gnosis.org/naghamm/dialog.html.

5 Quoted in Manuel Forcano and Victor Hurtado, Atles de la historia dels Jueus de Catalunya, TGA, Barcelona, 2019, p. 10.

6 Ibid., p. 11.

7 Godefrido Henschenio and Daniele Papebrochio, *Acta Sanctorum Aprilis,* Michaelem Cnobarum, Antwerp, 1675, vol. I, p. 817.

8 Taylor, p. 174.

9 Miriam Jaskierowicz Arman, *Revealed: The Secret Codes of the Voice in the Zohar,* quoting "Soncino Zohar, Bereshith, 74a," Hadassa Word Press, Beau Bassin, Mauritius, 2019, p. 171.

10 Ani Williams, "Bath Kol," *Guardians of the Dragon Path* and *Medicine Song II* albums, 2023 and 2001: https://aniwilliams.com/product/guardians-of-the-dragon-path-mp3/ and https://aniwilliams.com/product/medicine-song-ii-mp3/

11 Taylor, p. 72.

12 Ibid., p. 107.

13 Henry Smith Williams, *The Historians' History of the World: Volume 10, Spain and Portugal,* Hooper & Jackson Ltd., London and New York, 1909, p.11.

14 Ibid.

15 Ibid.

16 Carlos Martin la Moneda, in private correspondence with the author, April 25, 2023: http://martinlamoneda.com.

17 Fulcanelli, p. 169.

18 Ibid., p. 149.

19 Taylor, p. 127.

Chapter 26

1 Feugère, Saint-Maxent, Koker, 'Taurus,' translated by Marcus Williamson and Corella Hughes, "Notes Le Serpent Rouge," http://www.connectotel.com/rennes/serpnote/serpf.html, January 17, 1999.

2 See appendix A list of 64 Magdalena churches.

3 https://socratic.org/questions/how-can-there-be-64-codon-combinations-but-only-20-possible-amino-acids

4 According to the late Knight Templar (OCMTH Order of Paris) Joseph Andreas (Tobi) Dobler of the Commandery of Marie Madeleine of Rennes-le-Château and honorary Commander of Jerusalem, in conversation with the author.

5 G.R.S. Mead, *Fragments of a Faith Forgotten,* Theosophical Publishing House, London, 1900, pp. 453–4.

6 *Pistis Sophia: A Gnostic Gospel,* translation G.R.S. Mead, Mockingbird Press, 2016, p. 40.

7 Williamson and Hughes.

8 Manly P. Hall, *The Secret Teachings of all Ages,* quoted in Williamson and Hughes.

9 Adrian Seville, "The geographical *Jeux de l'Oie* of Europe," *Belgeo,* 3–4, 2008, https://doi.org/10.4000/belgeo.11907

10 Tasos Kokkinidis, "Archaeologist Claims Solved Mystery of the Phaistos Disc in Greece," 'Greek Reporter website July 21, 2022: https://greekreporter.com/2022/07/21/phaistos-disk-mystery-solved/#:~:text

11 Moneda.

12 Michael P. Closs, Anthony F. Aveni, and Bruce Crowley, "The Planet Venus and Temple 22 at Copán" *Indiana-Anthropological Studies on Latin America and the Caribbean*, vol. 9, 1984, p. 223: https://doi.org/10.18441/ind.v9i0.221–247. Ani Williams, "Return of Venus," *Magdalene's Gift* CD, 2004, https://aniwilliams.com/product/magdalenes-gift-mp3/

13 V.G.Gurzadyan, "The Venus Tablet and Refraction University of Rome," 'La Sapienza', Italy and Yerevan Physics Institute, Armenia (Published in Akkadica, v. 124 (2003), pp. 13–17.) Note: Venus takes 8 years to complete one synodic cycle, and 8 of these cycles equals 64 years.

14 Rabbi Chaleb, *The Sixth and Seventh Books of Moses: Formulas of the Magical Kabala,* Empire Publishing, New York, NY, 1938, p. 22.

15 The Northern Cross is an alternate name for Cygnus; the Summer Triangle is comprised of the bright stars Deneb in Cygnus constellation, Vega in Lyra, and Altair in Aguila.

16 Ani Williams, "The Swan," *Guardians of the Dragon Path* and *Luna Trece: Thirteen Moons* albums, Songaia Sound Productions, 2023, and White Wing Productions, Loma Linda, California, 1996: https://aniwilliams.com/product/guardians-of-the-dragon-path-mp3/ and https://aniwilliams.com/product/luna-trece-mp3/

17 Callimachus, "Hymn 4: To Delos," The Poems of Callimachus, translated by Frank Nisetich, Oxford University Press Oxford, 2001, p. 47.

In Conclusion

1 Chaleb, p. 6.

Illustration Credits

22 map illustrations designed by Tudor Sebastian Vlaicu, with the exception of Illustration #14, the Cassini map from the Paris Observatory 1700s, with added sites by the author.

Back cover photo "Bugarach," by Dani Valdés: www.danivaldes.com.

All photographs without credits were either photographed by the author or from Wikipedia and used under the public domain international usage agreement.

The wheel symbol between quotes is from a Greek drachma coin from the city of Rhodes, Catalonia. The wheel and ouroboros is a design using a Saint Benedict medallion, by Tudor Sebastian Vlaicu.

Image introducing Parts I-VI is the Iberian Lady of Offerings, Gran Dama Oferente, 3rd-2nd century BCE, found at Cerro de los Santos, currently in National Mus. of Archeology, Madrid. Wiki Commons.

About the Author

Ani Williams is a harpist, singer, composer, sound therapist, and author, world-renowned for her dozens of albums of cross-cultural sacred music, as well as decades of pioneering work in Bio-Acoustic Medicine. Currently living in southern France, she was born in Los Angeles of a lineage of respected poets and authors, a legacy that is evident in her writing style. Williams' long-awaited book, *Guardians of the Dragon Path,* is the result of a life of world travel, eighteen years of walking the lands surrounding the Pyrenees, extensive scholarly research, and a series of uncanny dreams that guided her quest of discovery—a shining example that "truth is indeed stranger than fiction." This is the first in a trilogy.

Photo by Dani Valdés.

Guardians of the Dragon Path Music Album, Lyric Book, and Path of Songs Videos

Guardians of the Dragon Path double album is a "Camino de Canciones," a path of songs journey to Catalonia's temples of Artemis, Isis, and Hygeia—the mountain hermitages of the Black Madonna of Montserrat and Maria Magdalena, the legendary Celtic Princess Pyrene and much more.

A compilation of twenty songs, including two brand new releases: "Guardianes—Seal of Magdalena," and "Tears of Isis," music to accompany the reader's journey to sanctuaries on the Camino de Santiago and beyond. The 33-page lyric book with images and stories is included, as well as a specially created Path of Songs map with music videos of sites on the quest, all designed to provide a multi-media experience of the extraordinary Pyrenean legacy.

The album package is an extra cost of $22. It includes 1 hour, 40 minutes of music, a lyric book, and an interactive music video map with films shot on location at sites in the book. Visit www.aniwilliams.com or use the QR code below.

Printed in Great Britain
by Amazon